Never Too Late

Never Too Late

The Adult Student's Guide to College

Rebecca Klein-Collins

with the *Washington Monthly*

THE
NEW
PRESS

NEW YORK
LONDON

Requests for permission to reproduce selections from this book should be mailed to: Permissions Department, The New Press, 120 Wall Street, 31st floor, New York, NY 10005.

"Highest-Paying Mid-Skill Occupations." Copyright © Emsi. All rights reserved. Used by permission of Emsi.

"College Grads Get Jobs in Recovery," "Earnings for Majors," "Earnings of Middle Skill Jobs," and "Understanding Credentials." Copyright © Georgetown University Center on Education and the Workforce. All rights reserved. Used by permission of Georgetown University Center on Education and the Workforce.

Published in the United States by The New Press, New York, 2018
Distributed by Two Rivers Distribution

ISBN 978-1-62097-321-9 (pb)
ISBN 978-1-62097-322-6 (ebook)
CIP data is available

The New Press publishes books that promote and enrich public discussion and understanding of the issues vital to our democracy and to a more equitable world. These books are made possible by the enthusiasm of our readers; the support of a committed group of donors, large and small; the collaboration of our many partners in the independent media and the not-for-profit sector; booksellers, who often hand-sell New Press books; librarians; and above all by our authors.

www.thenewpress.com

Book design and composition by Lovedog Studio
This book was set in Fairfield Light

Printed in the United States of America

Contents

CHAPTER 1

Going Back to College: The Decision, Now the Questions   1

CHAPTER 2

You. An Adult. In College. Is This Really Happening?   8

CHAPTER 3

Why Do *You* Want to Go Back to School?   19

CHAPTER 4

Tips for Exploring New Career Options   25

CHAPTER 5

Making Sense of the College Landscape   46

CHAPTER 6

Comparing Colleges and Programs   68

CHAPTER 7

Smart Ways to Pay: Tuition as an Investment
in Your Future   80

CHAPTER 8

It's About Time!: Finding the Program That
Fits Your Schedule and Timeline   102

CHAPTER 9

Face-to-Face or Cyberspace: Deciding What
Works for You   116

CHAPTER 10

Why Learn It Twice?   129

CHAPTER 11

Apply Yourself: Navigating the Admissions Process   148

CHAPTER 12

From Service to School: Resources for Veterans
and Their Dependents   159

CHAPTER 13

Getting College Support to Succeed   183

CHAPTER 14

What If My Skills Are Rusty?   197

CHAPTER 15

Lean on Them . . . Your Personal Support System   206

Acknowledgments   219

APPENDIX A: *College Rankings for the Adult Learner*   222

APPENDIX B: *Glossary*   346

APPENDIX C: *Tips as You Start Your Studies*   360

APPENDIX D: *Adult Learners Interviewed
for This Book*   367

References   372

About the Authors   374

Never Too Late

CHAPTER 1

Going Back to College: The Decision, Now the Questions

So, you're thinking about taking the plunge and going back to school—that's great news!

Why is that great? Because there are so many ways you will benefit from getting more education and earning that college degree or other credential. You are probably well aware of the fact that people with college degrees tend to make more money—but there are even more reasons to want that diploma. People with college degrees are more likely to stay employed—or find new employment—even when the economy tanks. They also tend to be in jobs with better healthcare and retirement benefits, and they are more likely to have healthy lifestyles and longer life expectancies. And—a real bonus—they are more likely to be happy (Trostel October 14, 2015).

To sum it up, going back to school for your degree is a very good decision!

But clearly you have questions—that's why you are reading this book. You are probably wondering:

+ What am I going to study?
+ What college should I choose?
+ How do I know if that college is worth the price?

+ Can I make this work with my schedule?
+ How do I make sure that it won't take forever for me to finish?

Those are really important questions because, let's face it, going back to school as an adult can be a big undertaking. You already have a very full life. You may be working, raising and supporting a family, taking care of aging relatives, volunteering for a worthy cause, or serving in the military. You might even be doing all of the above. You don't want getting a degree to take you forever, and you don't want to waste your time or money. You have to make college work *for you, the person you are at this moment in time.*

How This Book Will Help

Going back to college as an adult is not easy, but it doesn't need to be impossible. It's important for you to know that **some colleges are better than others at making sure that adults like you have the best chance to succeed.** Colleges that tend to serve adults better

+ find ways to create schedules for people who work full-time or irregular hours;
+ provide support services to help adult learners like you succeed in their courses;
+ do a better job of making sure that you will keep going and earn a degree;
+ offer options to help you go faster and finish your degree more quickly—and at a lower cost;
+ offer degree programs that have a good reputation with employers so that your new degree can open the door to better-paying jobs—or a different career path entirely!

But how do you figure out which college will be best for you? The typical college guide is aimed at high school students who have very different life circumstances and priorities in terms of what they are looking for in a college. Also, many eighteen-year-olds have more freedom to go to school far from home and live in a dorm. That's not the case for the typical adult wanting to go back to school. Adults in their thirties, forties, fifties, or sixties often have established commitments that make them rooted to a much smaller geographic area. You may not have the luxury to consider a college three hundred miles away! But you do need to find a college that offers what you need in terms of academic programs, flexibility, and support.

This book is designed to help you find a college that will be right for you, for your schedule, for your budget, and for your educational and life goals. But it will also help guide you to colleges that will help you finish your degree, and do so quickly, no matter where you live. It won't do you much good to start college and not finish—getting that degree is what is most important.

A lot of adults make the decision to go back to school but don't spend much time thinking about which college is the best one for them. They may take the advice of their uncle Joe to enroll in that college down the road, or they may sign up with the online university with the slickest billboard or TV ads. Some of these colleges will make it **really easy** for students to enroll—and, of course, to pay tuition, whether through loans or through the students' own sav-

Adult students want to—

+ complete their degrees;

+ do it around their schedules;

+ do it affordably;

+ finish on time— or *sooner.*

I was born in Cuba and moved to Miami when I was nine. I'm currently fifty-eight years old. Right after high school I enrolled in college to study criminology. But during my first year in college, I fell in love and got married. I got married and quit school. I dedicated a lot of years to being a wife and mom to three kids. A few years ago, I got divorced after thirty-four years. Necessity pushed me into considering going back to school. Financially, I needed a job that would give me more money.

My three children are college graduates. My oldest son is an editor in Hollywood. They have succeeded in their careers. Mom is following in their footsteps instead of the other way around! When I complete it, they will be so proud.

—*Mary, adult student, age 58, Miami Dade College*

ings. That could be a really expensive mistake—and one that won't get you to your goal. It is important to avoid colleges that promise a lot, put you in debt, and don't help you succeed.

You owe it to yourself to find the best possible option for a high-quality college degree that works with your current life circumstances but will also help you finish. Set aside your cousin's recommendations for now, and don't get sucked in by a pop-up internet ad. Get in the driver's seat and take the wheel. Taking just a little extra time to learn about your options and define your goals can help you make the best decisions about going back to college, and this book will guide you in that process.

Think about the best way to select and buy a car. Sure you want it to look nice, but a smart consumer also looks at the details. Is it the right size for what I need? Will it get me where I need to go? What are the features that will make the driving experience fun? What is the sticker price? Is it possible to get a discounted price? What are the hidden costs? How will I pay for it and how much debt can I afford to take on?

You should ask just as many—if not more—questions about the college or university you are considering. It is a critical purchase for you, and you owe it to yourself to get the best value you can for your money.

This book is designed to help you choose a college based on several important considerations:

1. What you decide to study
2. Affordability
3. Flexibility
4. Ensuring your success

In **Chapter 2: You. An Adult. In College. Is This Really Happening?** we face head on some of the anxiety you may have about this decision to go to college, and why it is that you should put those fears aside. Adults may not fit the stereotypical image of a college student, but adults are now the "new normal" in higher education. You should not feel alone or different, and you need to know that you are probably more prepared than ever before in your life to take this step.

Chapter 3: Why Do You Want to Go Back to School? will help you think through why it is you want to go back to school (*spoiler alert*: it may

> After high school, I didn't go to college right away. Growing up, I was a computer nerd, and technology had a huge impact on me. But because I had those skills, when I was nineteen, I worked at a temp agency for a major bank. It turned out that I was a fast typist, so I was hired at the bank full time. And that job just grew. For the past ten to twelve years, I've been working in the city, in finance and investment. I recently went back to school because I didn't have a degree, but I wanted to change my career in the future and I knew I needed the degree.
>
> *—Alex, adult student, age 30, Moraine Valley Community College and DePaul University School for New Learning*

not only be to advance in your career or make more money). Having a clear goal at the start will be helpful not only in choosing a college, but also in motivating you when you are putting in long hours of study down the road. **Chapter 4: Tips for Exploring New Career Options** provides you with some resources to help you figure out where you want to go in your career. What kind of job and career do you want to have? And which jobs have promising outlooks given the changes in today's labor market? **Chapter 5: Making Sense of the College Landscape** offers a crash course on the rapidly changing world of higher education. If you went to college five, seven, or ten-plus years ago, you will find out that a lot has changed. The best part is that today there are more options than ever before for working adults. But caution! The flip side is that there are some colleges or universities in this new landscape that may look like they are a good choice, but are actually more focused on making a profit off of their students than meeting their educational needs. These colleges don't really put much effort into helping students finish what they started, or they award degrees that employers do not value when making hiring or promotion decisions.

That's why, in **Chapter 6: Comparing Colleges and Programs**, we'll walk you through a ranking of colleges that takes into account what is important for you as an adult—things like a good track record in helping students succeed, options to meet the scheduling constraints of working adults, programs to help adults finish more quickly, and what students who attend those colleges earn ten years after they enter.

Chapter 7: Smart Ways to Pay: Tuition as an Investment in Your Future is about the money question. College can be an expensive undertaking, so this chapter will help you anticipate what those costs will be and what options you might have to help you pay for it.

The next three chapters all have to do with finding flexibility in a college program. You're not an eighteen-year-old, fresh out of high school, with the ability to dedicate four years to full-time study. You've most likely got a job, a family, and probably other responsibilities to boot. Your time is probably the most valuable thing to you at this stage in your life.

> **"You want to finish quickly because time is one of the *most valuable* things to you."**

You need to take that into consideration in your choice of college. **Chapter 8: It's About Time!: Finding the Program That Fits Your Schedule and Timeline** highlights the various ways that colleges can offer flexibility and work around your busy schedule, or help you accelerate and finish your degree more quickly. This is the twenty-first century, so we of course have technology-based solutions to the time problem. Online learning can be ideal for working adults, especially those with crazy or irregular schedules, so **Chapter 9: Face-to-Face or Cyberspace: Deciding What Works for You**, will help you think through whether online learning is an option that could work for you. Finally, you could shave a lot of time off the process if you already have a lot of learning under your belt. **Chapter 10: Why Learn It Twice?** discusses how some colleges have great policies about accepting credit from other colleges you may have attended previously (transfer credit) or awarding college credit for things you may have learned outside of the classroom. This could mean not having to repeat or take some courses in order to earn your degree—and that will save you both time and money.

Chapter 11: Apply Yourself: Navigating the Admissions Process walks you through the various steps you'll take to apply to a college—things like understanding deadlines for submitting paperwork and applications, ordering transcripts, asking for a review of other prior learning you may have, and filling out the application.

Have you served in the military? If you are a veteran, or if you are a dependent of a veteran, you have some unique opportunities for financial

> Just go back. Try doing one year at a community college. Just do it. You're still going to be older anyway. What's the worst thing that could happen?
>
> —*Andy, adult student, age 30,*
> *DePaul University School for New Learning*

help, but you also may have some unique challenges when you go (back) to college. **Chapter 12: From Service to School: Resources for Veterans and Their Dependents** discusses the particular challenges of transitioning from military to civilian life in the context of going to college. It also shares information specific to veterans on earning credit for your military training, on maximizing the use of GI Bill education benefits to cover school-related costs, and on services specifically for veterans that many colleges offer.

And then, once you've got a handle on the guidance provided in these pages, you'll be ready to craft your own plan to apply and attend the right educational program for you!

The final section of the book is about ensuring your success. **Chapter 13: Getting College Support to Succeed** identifies all sorts of help that a college or university may offer, including tutors, writing labs, peer groups, and so on. You may worry about whether you are up to the academic challenge of your classes—that's understandable, particularly if you haven't been in a classroom in a while. As you'll learn in chapter 2, you probably will be a better college student than you think. But there may be some basic skills that you might need help brushing up on. **Chapter 14: What if My Skills Are Rusty?** will explain how colleges can help you with that, and how you can work on your own to improve your skills as you get ready to hit the books. **Chapter 15: Lean on Them ... Your Personal Support System** helps you think through what kind of support you have already—and what you will need—from your family and friends. It also provides tips on how you can manage your time and find balance between work, family, and school.

CHAPTER 2

You. An Adult. In College. Is This Really Happening?

You know it's the right thing to go back to school, but take a moment to think about how you are feeling about it.

If you are both excited *and* terrified, well, that just means you're a normal human being.

Going back to school is a big undertaking. It's a commitment of time and energy—not to mention money. But even if it's absolutely the right thing to be doing, and the right time to be doing it, and you find a way to make it affordable, and you've spent the right effort to make the best decisions possible, most people who go back to school still find the whole idea to be frightening.

Fear of Being Too Old

Let's cut to the chase: what keeps many adults from following through on their back-to-college plan is about more than money or finding the right program. Instead, one of the biggest barriers is simply fear about being an adult student.

**"All the other students are going to be so young —
I will feel so out of place!"**

You need to know that you will not be alone. Sure, it's possible you might be the oldest person in some of your classes, but there will likely be a lot of people just like you—with families, jobs, and busy lives. In fact, 38 percent of all college students today are older than 25 and, for three-quarters of all college students, school is not their only activity (Lumina Foundation 2015). They are trying to balance school with parenting and work responsibilities.

Your instructors and professors will not look at you funny or wonder what you are doing there. They will treat you with respect, and they will welcome you as they do any other student. In fact, it's more likely than you think that they have taught other students in your age group.

> Thirty-eight percent of all undergraduates today are 25 or older.

Fear of Being Too Busy

Another fear that many adults have is that they simply don't have time to fit school into their busy lives.

**"Will I be able to handle school with all of
my work and family responsibilities?"**

Working full time and taking care of family and other responsibilities— sometimes that alone can be overwhelming. How can you squeeze even more into your days?

Without a doubt, it is hard to add one more thing to your schedule, but colleges today are making it much easier for you to go back to school. Many colleges offer flexible schedules for courses as well as online options. You will find that there are evening and weekend courses, accelerated courses, self-paced programs, and so on. Some big colleges and universities have satellite campuses scattered around a region so that there are convenient locations for the busy working adult.

Fear About Not Being a Good Student

There are a lot of people out there who are nervous about college because they weren't good students in high school, or they had a bad experience when they first went to college, or maybe they are the first person in their family to go to college. It's not uncommon for people to think that they are simply not "college material."

**"Last time I was in school, I wasn't the best student—
what makes me think I can do better now?"**

It is a source of pride to get into college, but it also can be a source of confusion and self-doubt. Can I do it? What if I'm not cut out for college? Will my family and friends think I'm being ridiculous to try to get a college degree?

You should keep in mind that, as someone with life and work experience, you are coming to school with some pretty big advantages. Think of them as perks in this new job of being a student.

PERK #1: EXPERIENCE IN THE SCHOOL OF LIFE

18, 19, or 20. Those are the ages most people think of when they picture college students. If you know of anyone that age, or can think back to those times in your own life, you know that people that age do not have a lot of life experience, generally speaking, compared to people who are 10 or 20 years older, or even just 5 years older. With years come experience and that experience brings a lot of learning. That learning can make a big difference when adults return to college.

A Word from the Experts

The experience that adults bring to their own education makes them unique. Not only can they help themselves with that, they can help others in the classroom. Experiences can vary so much that adult learners are able to help others that may not have their unique knowledge.

—*Stephanie Luetgers, FlexPath coach, Capella University*

Had I gone to college when I was just out of high school, at eighteen, I would not have put this much effort into it. I would have been a C student. Me having life experience for six to eight years, having a full-time job, and going back . . . now I understand so much more. More than anything, I have a desire to learn. I wouldn't have had that before when I was younger.

—Alex, adult student, age 30, Moraine Valley Community College and DePaul University School for New Learning

Chapter 8 of this book explores how some people may be able to earn college credit for what they have learned from previous experiences, but that's not the only benefit of life experience. Adults can draw on what they've learned at work, in the military, in their personal life, and in volunteer experiences to make deeper connections to what they learn in college. Adults bring their wisdom to the classroom, and they use their experiences to better understand their college coursework.

Those deeper connections that someone like you can make between classroom learning and real life will help you as you learn new things in college. This is not a guarantee, of course, but with all of your experience in the School of Real Life, you may now be in a better position to do well in school than you were when you were younger. And it's not just about deeper connections to coursework. Often adults have acquired important skills through years of work and experiences—like the ability to organize, focus, or problem-solve—that they didn't have when they were younger. These skills can be invaluable when it comes to getting a degree.

> Adults have MORE skills than children and teenagers. They may have forgotten some things. But they have learned a lot of other things that will help them be *better* students now.

Just for fun, try out the School-Transferable Skills quiz located at the end of this chapter. It may help you see that you already have a lot of important skills that will help you succeed when you start your new college program.

PERK #2: GREATER CAPACITY FOR SELF-DISCIPLINE AND MAKING CONNECTIONS

Research has found that the prefrontal cortex of the brain is not fully developed until someone reaches their mid-twenties. Why does that matter? Because that's the part of the brain that helps you, as a human, understand consequences, form judgments, and control impulses and emotions (Edmonds 2008). Younger college students right out of high school do not have fully developed brains, and you do! Sure, you may see that your adult brain may not learn things as quickly as your teenage one, but it has a big advantage over your younger brain when it comes to things like rational decision making, problem solving, and self-control.

PERK #3: PERSPECTIVE ON WHAT IS IMPORTANT

When you think about all that you know now about life, what advice would you give to yourself at age nineteen or twenty-one?

How would you answer that question today? Maybe your advice to your teenage self would be to try new things, dare to be different, or not be afraid to ask for help. Maybe your advice would be to appreciate the guidance and experience of older relatives. Maybe your advice would be to better understand the value of money. ("Compound interest is your friend!")

In fact, even though you *still* may not practice this advice as consistently as you would like, you do have a lot of wisdom that you have gained from your life experience that your younger self could not have had. As an adult, you bring this wisdom to college with you. For example:

- ✢ You know the value of your money. The years you have spent managing your own finances give you a different perspective than the average nineteen-year-old possesses. You know what it takes to pay down something like a student loan debt, and you have a clear sense of your own stake in your education.
- ✢ You probably won't care as much about what the "cool kids," or anyone for that matter, think of you. Perhaps that means you will be less likely to be too proud or self-conscious to ask your instructor questions when you don't understand a new concept or lesson.
- ✢ You know that what you are learning in class has value in the real world, so you want to do well. Perhaps that will motivate you to seek out tutoring resources if you need some help.

> What really helps is maturity. If you're paying for a class, you're going to go to class. You're not there to mess around. I have more discipline now as an adult. I am a better student because of it.
>
> —"Kirk," adult student, age 26, Miami Dade College

All of which is to say that **you are probably not the same person today that you were back then.** Personalities and temperaments change, and so do learning and studying habits. Embrace that change. The new you may very well be "college material," but you won't find out until you try.

A Word from the Experts

Many adults think of themselves as the older version of themselves when they were first in college, as the nineteen-year-old that was last there. Now they have a job and kids and experiences and they're still thinking of themselves as that person. It's important to change that mentality.

—Scott Gabbert, academic advisor,
DePaul University School for New Learning

> I do wish I was more focused earlier. I feel like I wasted a lot of time in my life. I would have gone back earlier. Now I'm more clear on what I want to do. I'm more mature—I wish I would have been more mature earlier. This time, I want to finish and accomplish other goals I've set for myself. I've set up different habits, study habits, etc. That's what comes to mind.
>
> —"Natalie," adult student, age 45,
> SUNY Empire State College

Think of these advantages as outweighing some of the challenges and fears you may have about going back to college. Yes, it's going to be new and possibly a little scary at first. But you are bringing valuable experience that will deepen your learning. You also have significant behavioral advantages over a 19-year-old with a not-yet-fully-developed brain, and you know far more than they do—and maybe more than you once did—about how important education is for your future.

School-Transferable Skills Quiz

Many adults are afraid to go back to school because they are afraid they will not do well. They think:

+ "I used to be a bad student."
+ "I've forgotten so much."
+ "Now that I have been out of school for so long, I will be even *worse!*"

But those adults are wrong. They are not the same person they were 10 or 15 years ago. Even those who might feel stuck or like they've hit a dead end have accomplished a lot in their lives and learned valuable skills along the way.

You, too, have developed a lot of practical skills just from having to balance your responsibilities and get things done in your life. Take a moment to check off the skills you have—you'll very likely see that you already have what it takes to succeed in college.

This exercise will help you name skills you have gained on the job and in life that also will also help you in school.

 The point of this exercise is to show you that you already have many of the skills you need to do well in school. It may help you find skills you need to improve, too. Many schools have programs to help you gain those skills.

Read each of the four sentences below.

 A. I am **very good** at this.
 B. I do this **well enough**.
 C. I need **some help** with this.
 D. I am **not good** at this at all.

Now read over the "school-transferable skills" listed in the chart. **For each skill, circle A, B, C, or D.**

What Are My School-Transferable Skills?

	I am very good at this	I do this well enough	I need some help with this	I am not good at this at all
Classroom Skills: Listening				
Listen carefully and understand what someone is saying	A	B	C	D
Explain what they said to someone else	A	B	C	D
Understand what is important in what they are saying	A	B	C	D
Take notes on what someone is telling me	A	B	C	D
Classroom Skills: Speaking				
Let people know I have something to say	A	B	C	D
Disagree with others in a nice way	A	B	C	D
Say what I mean	A	B	C	D
Describe events and objects	A	B	C	D
Use information to defend what I believe	A	B	C	D
Present ideas effectively in speeches	A	B	C	D

What Are My School-Transferable Skills?

	I am very good at this	I do this well enough	I need some help with this	I am not good at this at all
Persuade/influence others to a certain point of view	A	B	C	D
Participate in group discussions and teams	A	B	C	D

Reading Skills

	I am very good at this	I do this well enough	I need some help with this	I am not good at this at all
Read carefully and understand what I am reading	A	B	C	D
Know when I agree with something I am reading	A	B	C	D
Explain what I have read	A	B	C	D

Writing Skills

	I am very good at this	I do this well enough	I need some help with this	I am not good at this at all
Write clearly	A	B	C	D
Write with proper grammar	A	B	C	D
Spell correctly	A	B	C	D
Express ideas in writing	A	B	C	D
Describe something in writing	A	B	C	D
Write clear and polite letters	A	B	C	D

Language Skills

	I am very good at this	I do this well enough	I need some help with this	I am not good at this at all
Speak more than one language	A	B	C	D
Read more than one language	A	B	C	D

Problem-Solving Skills

	I am very good at this	I do this well enough	I need some help with this	I am not good at this at all
Figure out what to do in a new situation	A	B	C	D
Think through a problem and decide what to do	A	B	C	D
Decide how best to use my time	A	B	C	D
Learn from my mistakes	A	B	C	D
Keep working on something, even when it gets challenging	A	B	C	D
Ask for help when I need it	A	B	C	D

What Are My School-Transferable Skills?

	I am very good at this	I do this well enough	I need some help with this	I am not good at this at all
Math Skills				
Keep track of how much money I have	A	B	C	D
Do my own tax return	A	B	C	D
Add and subtract	A	B	C	D
Multiply and divide	A	B	C	D
Use fractions	A	B	C	D
Research Skills				
Find out whether something is true	A	B	C	D
Know the right question to ask when I am trying to solve a problem	A	B	C	D
Combine ideas and information from different places	A	B	C	D
Understand what is important when I am making a decision	A	B	C	D
Identify appropriate information sources	A	B	C	D
Search written, oral, and technological information	A	B	C	D
Compile numerical and statistical data	A	B	C	D
Classify and sort information into categories	A	B	C	D
Patiently search for hard-to-find information	A	B	C	D
Utilize electronic search methods	A	B	C	D
Study Skills				
Remember facts	A	B	C	D
Remember ideas	A	B	C	D
Keep my work materials neat	A	B	C	D
Keep track of where I put things	A	B	C	D
Get my work finished on time	A	B	C	D
Organize what I am supposed to do	A	B	C	D

What Are My School-Transferable Skills?

	I am very good at this	I do this well enough	I need some help with this	I am not good at this at all
Planning and Organizational Skills				
Identify and organize tasks or information	A	B	C	D
Coordinate people, activities, and details	A	B	C	D
Develop a plan and set objectives	A	B	C	D
Set up and keep time schedules	A	B	C	D
Anticipate problems and respond with solutions	A	B	C	D
Develop realistic goals and actions to attain them	A	B	C	D
Arrange correct sequence of information and actions	A	B	C	D
Create guidelines for implementing an action	A	B	C	D
Create efficient systems	A	B	C	D
Follow through, ensure completion of a task	A	B	C	D

Now take a look at the skills where you circled A or B. Those are the skills you already have that may help you succeed in college. Write them down and refer back to them as you start to explore your college options. You can do this. You have what it takes!

I already have good skills in these areas:

_____

_____

_____

_____

I may need to develop more skills in:

_____

_____

_____

_____

CHAPTER 3

Why Do *You* Want to Go Back to School?

There are lots of reasons why a college degree is a good thing—and there are probably a lot of reasons why you personally might have decided to go back to school for that degree. As you are starting this process of exploring where you want to go to school and what you want to study, it is crucial to spend a moment thinking about the "why." *Why do you want to go to school? Why do you want a college degree?* It is important to uncover the "why" because that is what your motivation will be once you get started.

Putting in the work of attending classes, doing assignments, studying, reading, writing, and so on is going to be a big undertaking. If you know very clearly why you are doing it, and what is motivating you to do it, that can help you reenergize and refocus during the times when you might feel discouraged or tired.

In this chapter, we lay out some of the main reasons people like you want to go back to school.

There's No Right Answer!

There are so many reasons why people decide to go to college as adults. The reasons may be work or career related, since some of the best jobs out there require some kind of postsecondary credential. The reasons may be more personal, having to do with improving yourself or finishing something you started a few years ago, or many years ago.

These are all good reasons, but have you taken the time to figure out which are the reasons that are the most powerful in pushing *you* forward? Do you know which ones are *so powerful for you* that they will keep you going after you get started?

Take a look at the reasons in this chart and think about each one. Is it a reason why you want to go back to school? And, if so, how important is that reason in your decision to go back to school? Indicate whether each reason is important to you, and, if so, how important. You may have some reasons that are not listed—if so, add them to the chart!

Chances are that many of these reasons apply to you in some way. But which are the most important? Take a look at which of the reasons you checked as "very much a key reason" or "the most important reason for me." Those are the ones that will really keep you going.

What's the one exception? If you are going back to school because someone in your life—whether a boss or a friend or a partner—wants you to, that's okay. But make sure it's what *you* want, too. If you aren't passionate about this decision for your own reasons, you may find it hard to reach the finish line. And finishing is the whole point!

	Not a reason for me	Some-what a reason for me	Very much a key reason for me	The most import-ant reason for me
To qualify for promotions at my current workplace	O	O	O	O
To change careers to something with better long-term employment and advancement prospects	O	O	O	O
To change careers so that I can do something I love	O	O	O	O
To improve myself	O	O	O	O
To make more money	O	O	O	O
To have more job security	O	O	O	O
To be more knowledgeable	O	O	O	O
To learn a new skill	O	O	O	O
To set an example for my kids	O	O	O	O
To help my kids with their homework	O	O	O	O
To learn how to start my own business	O	O	O	O
To be able to provide more for my kids	O	O	O	O
To finish what I started	O	O	O	O
To say that I have a college degree	O	O	O	O
Because my boss/friend/partner wants me to	O	O	O	O

A Word from the Experts

Motivation is a critical factor. You need to know what your goals are. I tell students that often it's more of a marathon than a sprint, and you need that motivation to keep you moving during those times.

—Jillian Stubbs, 49er Finish program coordinator and academic advisor, University of North Carolina–Charlotte

EXERCISE: FIND YOUR PERSONAL SLOGAN!

Here's another exercise: take your top two or three reasons and craft a sentence or two about why you are going back to school. For example,

"I am going to get my degree because I am someone who finishes what they start, and I want to be a role model for my kids."

Or

"This degree is going to put me in a career that will give me opportunities for years to come."

I was out of school for fifteen years taking care of five children, and after the recession hit, I realized that I needed to start supplementing my husband's income. But with children, I couldn't work at 7-Eleven and support them the way I needed to. I said to myself, "If I don't get an education, I won't be able to support my kids." That was my motivation and it got me through. It is so easy to let go and give up. You might register and buy your supplies and be ready to go, and then you realize that you have to spend three hours a day studying. Without the motivation, at that point, it won't be hard for you to give up. You have to have the mind-set of "I'm here for a reason and I can't mess around with this."

—Geraldine Fitiseman, online success coach, School of Applied Technology, Salt Lake Community College—and former adult student

Or

"I'm getting this degree now, not later, because I deserve to have a job that I love and that pays me well."

Or

"Everyone else at work has a degree. I don't want to continue being the only one without one."

This will be your mantra, your slogan, so make it powerful enough that it will motivate you as you pursue this degree. Make it speak to what is driving you, personally, through this process.

Your Slogan Here:

_____

_____

_____

_____

Write this on a Post-it and stick it to your computer or your bathroom mirror. Remind yourself every day why you are doing this—your reasons are very important!

> I would say—decide first and foremost why you're doing this. It seems simple, but I don't think it's said enough. What do you want out of this? What do you want it for? What do I want to be doing? Not what degree do I want—but what would I use it for? Once you find out the job you want, look for other people who have that life, and find out what degrees they have and work backward. Don't get a degree without thinking about what you will do with it.
>
> —"Jean," adult student, age 35,
> SUNY Empire State College

For the past sixteen years I've been working at ABC news. It's an exciting job in some ways. I like what I do, but I've been doing it for so long and I'm ready to move into a more senior position. That's one of the reasons I'm going back to school.

—*"Natalie," adult student, age 45, SUNY Empire State College*

———

I'm forty-seven and have been in IT since I was eighteen, just out of high school. I started in computer sales in the '80s, then got into the IT world through the years. The position I hold today, I wouldn't be allowed to apply for, because I don't have a degree. Now a degree is required. Recently, I decided that I want to move to a different position in a different organization, and I realized I need a degree.

—*Keith, adult student, age 47, Capella University*

CHAPTER 4

Tips for Exploring New Career Options

When a Better Job Is Your Motivation

All of the reasons for going back to school are important ones, but chances are that if you are like most adults, a big part of your motivation for getting a degree is to improve your employment prospects. Economic data show that this is a really smart reason!

The U.S. Bureau of Labor Statistics publishes a chart every year showing how different levels of education result in higher earnings and lower unemployment. Here is the chart for 2016.

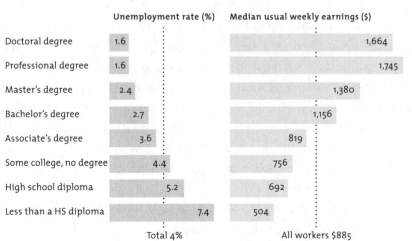

Unemployment Rates and Earnings by Educational Attainment, 2016

	Unemployment rate (%)	Median usual weekly earnings ($)
Doctoral degree	1.6	1,664
Professional degree	1.6	1,745
Master's degree	2.4	1,380
Bachelor's degree	2.7	1,156
Associate's degree	3.6	819
Some college, no degree	4.4	756
High school diploma	5.2	692
Less than a HS diploma	7.4	504
	Total 4%	All workers $885

Note: Data are for persons age 25 and over. Earnings are for full-time wage and salary workers.
Source: U.S. Bureau of Labor Statistics, Current Population Survey

The right side of the chart on the previous page shows the average earnings for each level of education. Someone with a bachelor's degree earns, on average, $1,137 per week, compared to only $678 for the person with only a high school diploma. That 68 percent more per week, on average, for the person with a degree really adds up to a big difference over a lifetime. Lifetime earnings for someone with only a high school diploma? $973,000. For someone with a bachelor's degree? $2.3 million! (Georgetown University Center on Education and the Workforce 2011)

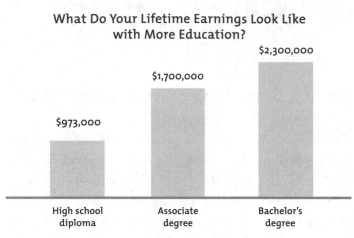

What Do Your Lifetime Earnings Look Like with More Education?

$2,300,000

$1,700,000

$973,000

High school diploma

Associate degree

Bachelor's degree

:Source: Georgetown University Center on Education and the Workforce, 2011

Now go back to the chart on the previous page and look at the left side. Someone with a bachelor's degree is also far less likely to be unemployed, on average.

That unemployment part is really important. Remember the economic downturn we had in 2008? During the Great Recession, the United States had several years when the economy was really struggling and a lot of people were out of work. But as the economy started to improve, and as companies started to hire again, it turns out that most of the new jobs—a whopping 99 percent—went to people with at least some college education. People with bachelor's degrees benefited most of all: 8.4 million of the 11.6 million new jobs went to people with bachelor's degrees, and those jobs are the ones that also paid the best (Georgetown University Center on Education and the Workforce 2016). New jobs created in our economy are those that are more likely to require some kind of college credential—that's important to keep in mind as you think about your own career and your own financial future.

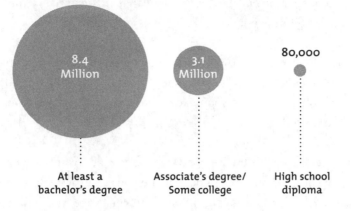

College Grads Get Most of the Jobs in Recovery

8.4 Million

3.1 Million

80,000

At least a
bachelor's degree

Associate's degree/
Some college

High school
diploma

Source: Georgetown University Center on Education and the Workforce, America's Divided Recovery:
College Haves and Have-Nots, 2016

What Does "a Better Job" Mean to You?

The data are clear—a college degree can be a big help in getting you a job or advancing your career.

But do you know what kind of job it is that you want? Do you know what a good career path for you might be? Consider whether you are a Career Advancer, a Career Changer, or a Career Explorer.

Career advancers. Maybe you've been told you need a degree to get a promotion in your current field. If that's the reason you want to get a college degree, then you are a Career Advancer. You probably have a pretty good idea of the kind of degree you need to position yourself for that kind of opportunity. If you don't, you should ask your boss or someone in the human resources department or maybe a co-worker you trust to give you some advice about the type of degree you should be pursuing. Ask questions like:

✛ What kind of degree will help me advance at this company? Or, what kind of degree will help me qualify for the specific job that I want?

✛ What degree level should be my goal? Bachelor's? Master's? Industry certification?

✛ Will getting an associate degree help me advance while I continue to work on my bachelor's?

+ Is there a specific area of study that I should major in?
+ Are there specific colleges in the area that this company would recommend for its employees?

By asking people who are in the know at your place of work, you should be able to find out what direction you should take. That can help lead you to the kind of college program you need in order to succeed—and maybe even to a specific college.

Career changers. Maybe you are changing careers and you have a really good idea of what it is you want to do. Maybe you've always wanted to be a nurse or a teacher or work in the IT field. In that case, you have some clarity about the direction you want to go—and that is a good place to find yourself. But keep in mind that all professions are not equal. Some jobs are ones that are going to do well in our economy—both now and in the future—while other jobs may not have as rosy an outlook. It's important that you do a little research to make sure you understand more about the specific job you are interested in. You want to be sure it is both a good fit for you and that it is a job that offers you long-term employability.

Career explorers. If you know you want a degree in order to have a better employment situation, but you don't know exactly what career you want to

A Word from the Experts

Adults should explore how their degree will fit into their career plans—or how it will get them to a job that will increase the happiness factor in their lives. To help them determine these things, I ask them about where they see themselves in two years. If they're uncertain, I tell them to take just one class and see how they do. If they do well, it continues from there and we talk about more long-term and short-term goals. I've also started pointing them to online learning styles and skill assessments. I ask them, "What are the positions that you want that you can't get now without a degree?"

—*Baxter Gamble, advisor,*
Complete the Degree Chicago

> I've always been technology literate. I was a tech specialist in the army. I decided to study cyber security because there's a need and there's a specific duty—i.e., I can protect people at Target, or I can protect homeland security, or government information for outside bodies. I'm interested and there's a growing need.
>
> *—Clifton, adult student, age 33,*
> *University of Maryland University College*

pursue, do not worry. You are not alone! Not everyone knows exactly what they want to study when they make the decision to go back to school.

There are a lot of different paths for you to explore, and you should spend a little bit of time thinking through possible options. You will want to think about what you are interested in and what kind of work appeals to you. But you also need to think very practically about your career. Learn about what kinds of jobs are "growth jobs," meaning that they are in demand right now and expected to be even more in demand in the years to come. Learn about what is involved in the day-to-day work of specific jobs. Learn about the starting salaries and mid-career salaries for people already in those jobs. There are a lot of resources listed in this chapter to help you with this exploration.

Keep in mind that you can always start school even if you aren't sure yet about what it is you are going to major in. Both associate degrees (sometimes called two-year degrees) and bachelor's degrees (sometimes called four-year degrees) usually have some general education requirements—those are required courses in, for example, math, communications, and social sciences. You can work on taking those classes and earning those credits while you continue to figure out your long-term game plan.

Important Considerations for Your Career Exploration

When you are researching possible jobs and career paths, consider things like:

✛ Is this a job that I will like doing?
✛ Is this a job that is in demand?

+ What is the salary for this job?
+ What kind of credentials do I need?

Is This a Job That I Will Like Doing?

Part of your career exploration needs to include taking a good look at yourself to understand what your interests are, what you are already good at, and what kind of work you would enjoy doing. This is to set some general parameters for career options that would be good fits for you—and maybe even rule out some options. For example, someone who likes working with numbers might want to explore accounting or jobs that require data analysis skills, while someone who is really good at building relationships with people might consider sales or counseling careers. The flip side of that coin is that if you are someone who doesn't have a lot of patience with younger children, you might want to rule out elementary education!

There are several online tools that can help you identify what those work preferences and job interests might be. Check out the end of this chapter for some places to get started.

Is This a Job That Is in Demand?

Do a little bit of homework to make sure that the career you have your eye on is in demand. When you graduate and get that degree, you want to

A Word from the Experts

It's difficult for many to decide what their goal is going to be for college. If you're going to school as an adult, because it's expensive and you're probably balancing other elements of life, it is very important to have a sense of where you're going. But there is a fine line to walk of knowing what you want and staying open to new opportunities. Use your general education requirements to expose you to new ways of thinking and stay open to the spark that might happen in college that directs you somewhere away from what you originally intended.

—*Kathy Weinkle, career and education advisor,*
CAEL Advising Services

be able to get hired for that new job. You also want to make sure that it's expected to be a job that will be in demand by employers for years down the road.

> **DO** trust federal government websites like O*NET, the U.S. Department of Labor, reports from local economic development agencies, or guidance from a local One-Stop Center.

> **DON'T** rely solely on the brochures or ads from a training program or college. The information found there and on their websites might make a lot of assurances about future pay and employment that may not always be accurate.

The economy is constantly changing, and sometimes big changes can result in certain jobs not having much of a shelf life. Some jobs become obsolete because of automation or the rise of other new kinds of technologies. Take a look at these jobs, for example:

Jobs in Decline

Job	% Decline Expected Between 2014 and 2024
Telephone operator	−42%
Postal service mail sorter	−34%
Watch repairer	−26%

Source: Bureau of Labor Statistics, Office of Occupational Statistics and Employment Projections

They are on the list of the fastest-declining jobs today. When you think about it, these declines are kind of easy to understand. With the rise of the cell phone, there isn't as much need for telephone operators. With the rise of electronic documents and delivery systems, there is less need for "snail mail" postal delivery systems and support. And did you notice that fewer people wear watches today? When you are tethered to your smartphone, the watch starts to feel like more of a fashion accessory rather than an important tool to get you through your day. So, fewer watches, less need for watch repair.

A Word from the Experts

Students also need to ask about what the school has to offer. Everyone comes into our college wanting to work for Tesla Motors, but once I show them everything we have on campus, Tesla is the last thing on their mind after that. Whichever path you take, it's important to know if there will be jobs for you at the end of the education path you choose.

—Patty Aragona, adult learner concierge,
Truckee Meadows Community College

Your best bet is to choose a new career that isn't likely to shrink very much over time. Do some research on what jobs and industries are growing—both across the United States and in your specific part of the country.

The U.S. Bureau of Labor Statistics provides lists of jobs and industries that are expected to have **the most job openings** between 2016 and 2026 (see table on the next page):

If a job category is growing, that generally means it is expected to be in demand. The jobs that are growing *and* that pay well are often those that require some kind of college degree. Employers will be looking to hire more people to fill these kinds of jobs, so it would be a smart move to get the kind of degree or credential that would make you a good candidate for those jobs. Spending time and money to get that degree or credential is probably going to be a smart investment in the long run.

The *Occupational Outlook Handbook* website (see tools and resources at the end of the chapter) is a great place to explore different careers and see whether they will be growing or shrinking. (It will also tell you about the expected salary, the education needed, what people in this job do all day, what the work environment is like, and so on.)

Why college degrees are needed today more than ever. Today the jobs that are growing are usually the jobs that require interaction with other people or that involve work that is not routine. They require higher-level thinking that employers tend to think can be found in people who have college degrees.

Most New Jobs, Projected, 2016–2026

Most new jobs: 20 occupations with the highest projected numeric change in employment

Occupation	Number of New Jobs (Projected), 2016–2026	Median Pay 2016
Personal care aides	777,600	$21,920/yr
Combined food preparation and serving workers, inc. fast food	579,900	$19,440/yr
Registered nurses	438,100	$68,540/yr
Home health aides	431,200	$22,600/yr
Software developers, applications	255,400	$100,080/yr
Janitors and cleaners, except maids and housekeeping cleaners	236,500	$24,190/yr
General and operations managers	205,200	$99,310/yr
Laborers and freight, stock, and material movers, hand	199,700	$25,980/yr
Medical assistants	183,900	$31,540/yr
Waiters and waitresses	182,500	$19,990/yr
Nursing assistants	173,400	$26,590/yr
Construction laborers	150,400	$33,430/yr
Cooks, restaurant	145,300	$24,140/yr
Accountants and auditors	139,900	$68,150/yr
Market research analysts and marketing specialists	138,399	$62,560/yr
Customer service representatives	136,300	$32,300/yr
Landscaping and groundskeeping workers	135,200	$26,320/yr
Medical secretaries	129,000	$33,730/yr
Management analysts	115,200	$81,330/yr
Maintainence and repair workers, general	112,500	$36,940/yr

Source: U.S. Bureau of Labor Statistics, Office of Occupational Statistics and Employment Projections

Location matters! Remember that it may not be enough to look at a specific job's outlook at the state level. You might want to go deeper and look at a specific local area, especially if you expect your job search to focus on a relatively small region after you graduate. Take teachers, for example. The research you do on teaching jobs will tell you whether they are in demand or how much they pay, but those factors may vary a lot depending on the school district. Some school districts are desperate for teaching candidates, while others may see a lot of competition for a few openings. Some districts pay relatively well, while others do not.

Keep in mind that there can be a lot of variability—the list of growth jobs can be different in your particular part of the country. For that reason, be sure to take a close look at what the outlook is for different careers in your particular part of the country.

WHAT IS THE SALARY FOR THIS JOB?

It also is a good idea to do some research about salaries for a particular job so that you know what to expect. Find out what the average starting salary is and how that salary typically grows for someone with several years of experience. As noted above, the Bureau of Labor Statistics provides that information through the *Occupational Outlook Handbook* website.

Location, Location, Location . . . The specific salaries for a particular job or college major can be very different in your part of the country compared to the country as a whole. In your geographic area, the pay scale may be higher or lower than average. You can explore different majors and their earnings in different parts of the country through this interactive tool by the Georgetown Center for Education and the Workforce: https://cew.georgetown. edu/cew-reports/valueofcollegemajors.

A Word from the Experts

"Employers we spoke with described their ideal candidate as a hard-working, technically astute individual with strong problem-solving and communication skills who can work effectively as part of a team. Certainly employers need applicants with basic technical training in their field, whether it is molecular biology, welding, or quality engineering. But as one executive said, you can look perfect on paper and have the right credentials, but that alone won't get you the job. Why is that? Because if someone can't also work on a team, communicate verbally and in writing, be a creative problem-solver, and continually work hard and learn new things, they ultimately act as a drag on company productivity and profit, whether they are technically qualified or not" (Jaschik 2016).

—*Matthew T. Hora, assistant professor in adult teaching and learning at the University of Wisconsin–Madison, and Ross J. Benbow, associate researcher with the Wisconsin Center for Education Research at the University of Wisconsin–Madison*

If you are in a position where you are starting college without a clear idea of your eventual career choice, that's okay. In that case, you might at least think through how different areas of study pay off in the long term. Average salaries can be very different for people who choose and complete degrees in different kinds of majors. On average, the highest salaries go to people with majors in STEM fields (science, technology, engineering, and math), healthcare, and business. The majors with the lowest salaries, on average, include early childhood education, human services, visual and performing arts, social work, teacher education, and religious vocations (Georgetown University Center for Education and the Workforce 2015).

Should you be making this decision purely based on future salary potential? Money is not the only thing that matters to some people. Some of the lowest paying jobs—teachers, social workers, religious leaders—may be the right choice for you because they can also be the most fulfilling for reasons other than the pay. And pay increases are relative. A particular job in education may not give you the highest possible paycheck, but that education job might still provide a significant increase in income when compared to your current job. Social workers and teachers, in particular, may be very much in demand in your area. Just make sure to go in with eyes open. Don't have unrealistic expectations about what the job is likely to pay.

A **bachelor's degree in liberal arts** may not have an obvious tie to specific high-demand occupations, but the liberal arts curriculum can help develop broad transferable skills that many employers say are critical—and hard to find. Those degrees can help launch careers in business, sales, management, and other professions.

Researchers have found that the broad, transferable skills that are associated with liberal arts degrees can make a real difference in the workplace—and employers know it.

What Kind of Credentials Do I Need?

If you know what kind of job you want, it's important to understand what specific educational credential is required or preferred to get that job. What are employers asking for in job postings for those kinds of positions? Do you need a four-year bachelor's degree? Do you eventually need a master's degree? Will an associate degree or short-term certificate help you start climbing your way up the ladder?

National occupational information may not always provide the full picture for what is happening in your local employment landscape. Take nursing, for example. Someone wanting to be a nurse might discover that the easiest and quickest route to nursing is to become a licensed practical nurse, or LPN. Yet many hospitals these days hope to fill their open nursing positions with *registered nurses*, or RNs. That requires at least an associate degree in nursing (plus the passing of a national licensing exam called the NCLEX), and many employers these days have an even stronger

What kind of degree? In addition to the information provided through the *Occupational Outlook Handbook*, look at local job listings to see what credentials employers in your area are asking for, and ask a lot of questions about this topic when you start to look into the colleges you might attend.

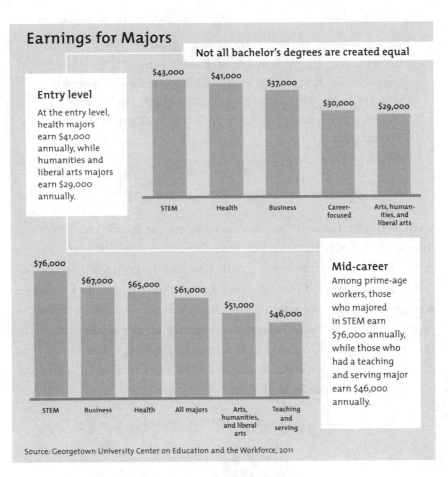

Earnings for Majors

Not all bachelor's degrees are created equal

Entry level

At the entry level, health majors earn $41,000 annually, while humanities and liberal arts majors earn $29,000 annually.

$43,000 — STEM
$41,000 — Health
$37,000 — Business
$30,000 — Career-focused
$29,000 — Arts, humanities, and liberal arts

Mid-career

Among prime-age workers, those who majored in STEM earn $76,000 annually, while those who had a teaching and serving major earn $46,000 annually.

$76,000 — STEM
$67,000 — Business
$65,000 — Health
$61,000 — All majors
$51,000 — Arts, humanities, and liberal arts
$46,000 — Teaching and serving

Source: Georgetown University Center on Education and the Workforce, 2011

preference for RNs with bachelor's degrees. Do a little homework to make sure you are getting the right credential for the career that you want in your local area.

WHY YOU MIGHT WANT TO CONSIDER A SHORT-TERM CERTIFICATE OR TECHNICAL ASSOCIATE DEGREE

Remember how we said that the best jobs today are those that typically require some college education? One thing to note is that "college education" does not necessarily mean a four-year bachelor's degree.

Jobs that require a college degree are sometimes called *high-skill jobs*, but there is a category of *middle-skill jobs* as well—they require some college education, but not as much as a bachelor's degree. That might mean an associate degree in a technical or healthcare field, or possibly even a

> I looked at my skills and strengths, and I looked at jobs available in the private sector that would best leverage those skills. Where could I bring value to the market? Looking at majors—I was torn between engineering or business. These are both challenging degrees that require quantitative skills. I am also thinking about finance as an option.
>
> —"Kirk," adult student, age 26, Miami Dade College

technical certification that you can earn in a relatively short period of time— often much less than two years.

If a four-year degree is more than you can take on right now, consider that many middle-skill jobs pay good wages. More than half of these jobs pay upwards of $35,000 per year, and two out of every five of these jobs pay $50,000 or more (Georgetown University Center on Education and the Workforce 2012).

Earnings of Middle-Skill Jobs

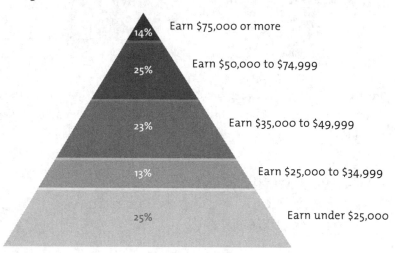

14% Earn $75,000 or more

25% Earn $50,000 to $74,999

23% Earn $35,000 to $49,999

13% Earn $25,000 to $34,999

25% Earn under $25,000

Source: Georgetown University Center on Education and the Workforce, Career and Technical Education: Five Ways That Pay Along the Way to the B.A., 2012

Examples of middle-skill jobs include:

✢ Registered nurses
✢ Dental hygienists

+ Information security analysts
+ Nuclear technicians
+ Paramedics
+ Web developers

Highest paying mid-skill occupations

2012 Wages for Jobs That Typically Require Certificte or 2-Year Degree for Entry

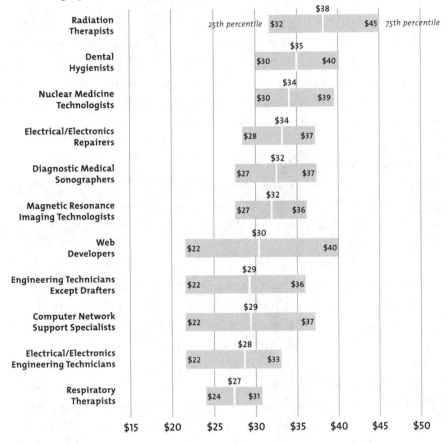

Source: EMSI, "Middle-Skill Spotlight: An Analysis of Four In-Demand Sectors with a Community College Focus, 2014

If you decide to go the middle-skill job route, that does not mean you need to give up a goal of one day getting a bachelor's degree. Doug Shapiro of the National Student Clearinghouse says, "If you can spend one year or eighteen months and get a certificate that has immediate value, you don't have to take that longer-term risk of starting out in a bachelor's degree program that you might not finish and end up in debt" (Shapiro 2016).

You can always get a shorter-term credential, start working in a middle-skill job, and then continue your studies from there. Be sure to ask *before you enroll* about whether the shorter-term credential can eventually count toward a bachelor's degree program.

Tools and Resources for Exploring Personal Skills and Interests

There are several resources available online to help you explore your skills and interests. Some of them will cost you some money. You might also consider talking to some of the colleges you are considering to see if they have interest inventories that you could use before making a final decision about enrolling. Enter the resources below into a search engine to check out the guidance they can offer you.

Self-Directed Search (SDS)
Based on the work of psychologist John Holland, the SDS is an interactive tool used by students, professionals, veterans, and others seeking college majors or career options based on activities, skills, and interests. Fees may apply.

CliftonStrengths Assessment (formerly Clifton StrengthsFinder)
Developed by Gallup, CliftonStrengths is a web-based assessment designed to help people uncover their talents and identify ways to develop them further based on thirty-four talent themes. Fees may apply.

Kiersey Temperament Sorter
The Kiersey Temperament Sorter is a seventy-question-based personality instrument that helps people identify their personality type and how they interact with others. Fees may apply.

> When I went back the second time, I wanted to study management. Especially after so many years working [for a child welfare organization and establishing policies for my department]. I wanted to get more education to help me understand more of what I do and put it into practice. The second time around, I was pretty firm in what I wanted to do.
>
> —*Mary, adult student, age 58, Miami Dade College*

DiSC

The DiSC profile involves responding to a series of questions that are used to produce a detailed report about your personality and behavior. Results can be used to reveal how you communicate and interact with others. Fees may apply.

Tools and Resources for Career Exploration

If you want to explore different careers to help you figure out what to study, you can seek out a local American Job Center for assistance, and you can even ask for some guidance from the colleges that you are considering attending. In addition, there are a lot of resources available to you online, and a few of them are listed below. Do some exploring and open your eyes to some possibilities you may not have considered before!

American Job Centers (also known as One-Stop Centers)

The U.S. Department of Labor supports a system of job centers across the country. These centers, which might also be called Career Centers or One-Stop Centers, are designed to provide a full range of assistance to job seekers, including career counseling. The website will have information on the job center near you.

My Next Move

My Next Move is a website that was developed by the U.S. Department of Labor to help people figure out what they want to do for a living. It provides ways to investigate careers through a simple search by job title or industry. In addition, it provides some help for people who aren't sure what they are interested in. You start by completing a short interest inventory that gives you scores on different types of work that can guide your career interests. (See sidebar on the following pages for the different categories of work and examples of careers in each category.)

From there, the website asks you to think about what kind of preparation (such as formal education and credentials) you are willing to take on. Once you select the level of preparation, the site gives you a list of careers that are related to your interest profile and the amount of education you specified. You can then investigate the details of each career option in the list.

How Your Interests Can Point to a Career

We all have different inclinations and our own ways of viewing and interacting with the world and people around us. The My Next Move website—an offering of the U.S. Department of Labor—describes how different interests can lead to different types of occupations and careers.

REALISTIC

People with **realistic** interests like work that includes practical, hands-on problems and answers. Often people with realistic interests do not like careers that involve paperwork or working closely with others.

They like:
- Working with plants and animals
- Real-world materials like wood, tools, and machinery
- Outside work

INVESTIGATIVE

People with **investigative** interests like work that has to do with ideas and thinking rather than physical activity or leading people.

They like:
- Searching for facts
- Figuring out problems

ARTISTIC

People with **artistic** interests like work that deals with the artistic side of things, such as acting, music, art, and design.

They like:
- Creativity in their work
- Work that can be done without following a set of rules

How Your Interests Can Point to a Career (*Continued*)

SOCIAL

People with **social** interests like working with others to help them learn and grow. They like working with people more than working with objects, machines, or information.

They like:
- Teaching
- Giving advice
- Helping and being of service to people

ENTERPRISING

People with **enterprising** interests like work that has to do with starting up and carrying out business projects. These people like taking action rather than thinking about things.

They like:
- Persuading and leading people
- Making decisions
- Taking risks for profits

CONVENTIONAL

People with **conventional** interests like work that follows set procedures and routines. They prefer working with information and paying attention to details rather than working with ideas.

They like:
- Working with clear rules
- Following a strong leader

Source: U.S. Department of Labor, My Next Move, www.mynextmove. org.

> I always knew that I wanted to go back and finish. What really prompted me this last time—I was trying to figure out one of the things I wanted to do. I was researching the area of counterterrorism. I found a school that had an advanced certificate program in counterterrorism, but I needed my BA degree.
>
> —"Natalie," adult student, age 45, SUNY Empire State College

The site tells you about each career in terms of:

+ Required knowledge, skills, and abilities
+ Personality that is well suited to the job
+ The kind of technology that is used in that job
+ Educational credentials needed
+ Outlook in terms of salary—with the option of looking nationally, at the state level, and even locally
+ Links to even more information

Career One-Stop Skills Profiler

Another option for self-assessment is through the Career One-Stop Skills Profiler, which is also developed by the U.S. Department of Labor. On this website, the assessment asks you to rate individual skills that you have in the following areas:

+ Basic skills
+ Social skills
+ Technical skills
+ Complex problem-solving skills
+ System skills
+ Resource management skills
+ Desktop computer skills

The website then provides you with a list of job types and occupations and a score for how well your existing skills match those job types and occupations. Then you can explore those job types and occupations according to the state that you live in. The Career One-Stop website also has other tools to help you think through your interests and work values, and to help you do research on different careers.

My Skills My Future

The U.S. Department of Labor and the Career One-Stop website also provide My Skills My Future as another avenue for exploring new careers. You can enter the name of any career and get detailed information on that career, including:

+ A general description of the career and job duties
+ Current employment and projected openings
+ Typical wages and salaries, with links to job listings
+ Typical training needed, with links to training programs that can then be filtered by location

If you do not have a clear career direction, you can enter a current or past job you have held to find other jobs or careers that are similar or that you might aim for with additional educational credentials or training.

Occupational Outlook Handbook

Below is a description that appeared on the website:

The *Occupational Outlook Handbook (OOH)* provides information on what workers do; the work environment; education, training, and other qualifications; pay; the job outlook; information on state and area data; similar occupations; and sources of additional information, for 329 occupational profiles covering about 83 percent of the jobs in the economy.

CHAPTER 5

Making Sense of the College Landscape

When you send your kids to school, the options are usually pretty straightforward. You go to elementary school, then middle school (if that is separate from elementary in your city), then high school. From kindergarten up through high school, you go for free to the local public school, or you pay tuition to go to a private school, or you opt for home schooling. But when you get to educational options after high school, the picture changes dramatically.

After high school, the next step in education can be to pursue a degree from a college or university. That kind of education is what is sometimes called *higher education*. But it's important to understand that your educational options are not limited to colleges and universities. There are a lot of different educational choices for the high school graduate outside of colleges and universities, and altogether these options can be lumped into what is called *postsecondary education*. That term generally means any kind of learning that happens after ("post") high school ("secondary education").

A lot of these new learning options didn't exist five or ten years ago, so if it's been a few years since your last college experience, you may be surprised at what you find in today's postsecondary educational landscape.

Why So Many Changes?
Why So Many Options?

Some of the changes in postsecondary education are the result of—you guessed it—the rise of the internet. Online learning is a big deal these days, and not just at the for-profit colleges that do a lot of the advertising you may have seen on TV. Several public and nonprofit colleges also offer online programs these days. In addition, there are various types of online learning programs now, leading to different types of course delivery and program design. This is really transforming what postsecondary education looks like.

There are also different types of *credentials* you can obtain, which means not just the standard associate degree (two-year) or bachelor's degree (four-year). There are many options for these kinds of credentials in healthcare (some examples include pharmacy technician, physical therapy aid, medical billing and coding, EKG technician), IT (web designer), and the skilled trades. The four-year bachelor's degree is still the gold standard but, as you learned in chapter 4, there are a lot of good jobs these days that may require only a shorter-term credential.

Finally, there are many programs today that offer flexibility in how to take classes because colleges are discovering that a lot of their students are just like you—working adults who don't want to spend a lot of time or money but who want a high-quality degree as well as educational programs that fit their busy lives.

A Different Language

This chapter will lay out all of the different postsecondary options out there for you to consider as you think about the next steps in your educational journey. There are a lot of terms used in the world of postsecondary and higher education that you'll probably never encounter anywhere else. Just knowing what they mean can help you understand the landscape.

There are additional terms defined in other chapters of this book as well. The complete set of definitions can be found in the glossary at the end of the book.

Public? Private? Nonprofit? For-Profit? What's the Difference?

All four-year colleges award bachelor's degrees. Depending on your income, and how much need-based financial aid you receive, the net price for you (what you actually need to pay) could be as little as $1,000 a year or as much as $65,000 a year. To understand the huge range of prices, it's useful to understand where the colleges' funding is coming from.

Public colleges get some of their financing from tuition, but they also get some of it from state or local taxes. That's why state colleges have lower tuition for in-state students, because state residents are already supporting the college with their tax dollars. For students coming from out of state, tuition at a state school could be as high as (or higher than) a private, non-profit college. On the other hand, states in some regions have reciprocal agreements to offer reduced tuition to students from other states in that region, benefiting students from the region by increasing their choices and reducing tuition. For example, the Southern Regional Education Board's Academic Common Market provides tuition discounts for more than 1,900 academic programs in—and for residents of—Alabama, Arkansas, Delaware, Florida, Georgia, Kentucky, Louisiana, Maryland, Mississippi, Oklahoma, South Carolina, Tennessee, Texas, Virginia, and West Virginia. Similarly, residents of Illinois, Indiana, Kansas, Michigan, Minnesota, Missouri, Nebraska, North Dakota, and Wisconsin may be able to receive tuition discounts in other states in the Midwest Student Exchange. Many public colleges also offer reduced rates or in-state tuition rates to military veterans.

Public colleges vary widely in size, cost, quality, and the kind of degrees they award. Most community colleges are public, for example, and so are the big state flagships, which are often the oldest and most well known universities in the state. Flagships are public, supported in part by taxpayer dollars. Not all colleges with a state or city in their name are either public or flagships, however. University of Washington, Indiana University at Bloomington, University of Texas at Austin, and University of Maine are examples of state flagships. The Massachusetts Institute of Technology (MIT) and Southern New Hampshire University, on the other hand, are both private institutions. It is not always obvious from the name!

Vocational and Technical Schools

Vocational schools, also called career schools, offer training for a variety of jobs, so they can be a good choice if they are reputable and if the training they offer is your end goal. Some technical schools are also colleges that offer associate degrees, and some vocational schools partner with colleges to provide opportunities to earn college credit while learning a skill. But never assume that credit from a vocational school (or, for that matter, many private, for-profit colleges) will transfer to a public or nonprofit college or university. The Federal Trade Commission is pretty straightforward, warning, "Not all these schools are reputable. Research any school you hope to attend, its training program, its record of job placement for graduates, and its fees before you commit. . . . Look into alternatives, like community colleges. The tuition may be less than at private schools," even for the same or a similar course of study. (Federal Trade Commission n.d.)

Private nonprofit colleges don't get tax dollars in most states, which is why the sticker price is usually higher. This does not always mean that the cost to an individual student is higher. Private funding sometimes means there's more financial aid (either need-based or merit-based) available for students. Private nonprofit colleges also vary widely in size, cost, and quality. Almost all the Ivy League schools that you probably know by name—Harvard, Yale, Princeton, Dartmouth, the University of Pennsylvania—are in this category, but these are schools that generally do not focus on the adult learner, except at the graduate levels, where adult students are looking to earn master's degrees, PhDs, law degrees, medical degrees, etc. There are many excellent private nonprofit schools that may be in your area, that may be affordable to you, and that have a range of program offerings specifically for the working adult.

For-profit colleges are privately run companies offering a range of degrees. There are high-quality for-profit colleges, but be aware that there are also many for-profit colleges with high student dropout rates that turn out to be a waste of time and money. Some for-profits have also earned a reputation for loading up students with a lot of debt in the process. There's nothing worse than having to pay off a student loan for a degree that you never actually earn! The National Association for College Admission Counseling points out that they're called for-profit because they're in business to earn money for their owners. (National Association for College Admission Counseling n.d.). Educating students may not always be their main mission.

In addition to researching the reputations of for-profit options carefully, one question an informed consumer should ask a representative of a for-profit college is, will the credits I earn at your college transfer to a public university or a private nonprofit college? Knowing the answer to that question in advance will help you understand your options for transferring, or for earning a master's or professional degree later.

Public two-year colleges vary in their mission, but all of them offer associate degrees and certificates of completion that meet requirements for some occupations (such as culinary or hospitality management, allied health, fire technology, real estate appraisal, or tax preparation). Many degree paths at community colleges include *general education requirements*, and while the specific curriculum is unique to the campus, general education courses are usually designed to prepare students to transfer to four-year colleges. In general, most community colleges have an open-access, open-door philosophy: almost anyone, regardless of their grades or career goals, is welcome. Public two-year colleges may have names that include *community college*, *technical college*, or *junior college*.

Program or Degree	Schools Where Offered	Typical Time to Graduation (for Full-Time Student)
Career, technical, trade, or vocational courses	Career, technical, vocational, and trade schools. Community and junior colleges	1–2 years
Associate degree	Community, technical, and junior colleges	2 years
Bachelor's degree	Four-year colleges and universities. *Some community colleges also have started to offer select bachelor's degrees.*	4 years

Should You Go to a Two-Year College, and *Then* Transfer?

Great question! Some people say yes, because two-year colleges (or community colleges) are a much cheaper option. Other people say no because many students who go to a community college intending to transfer never actually do.

In truth, it depends on your educational goals, finances, and logistics.

If your long-term goal is to end up with an associate degree in a technical field or a vocational certificate, or to prepare for a specific licensing exam, then the answer is yes, go to a community college. But if your main goal is a bachelor's degree, then starting at a four-year college may be a smarter bet. Transferring from a community college to a four-year college is not always a smooth process. It requires a clear plan from day one as well as sorting through a lot of additional rules and information.

Still, community college can be a great way to get started because of its lower cost—and because community colleges may offer the kind of schedule and programming that you need to balance all of your commitments at this stage in your life. **Recommendation: Just make sure the community college credits will transfer to your final destination college.**

Minority-Serving Colleges and Universities

Education in the United States has often been called the great equalizer, seen as open and accessible to any American regardless of race, creed, or gender. To be sure, that has not always been the case. Some colleges and universities were *originally created* with the intent to serve students from traditionally marginalized populations, and there are often special programs in place at colleges that over time have come to serve large populations of students who have been underserved by other public and private educational institutions. Today, more colleges than ever emphasize diversity and inclusion in their admissions and campus culture, yet many students continue to find special and specific benefits from attending minority-serving institutions (MSIs).

Whether you are a member of a traditionally underserved group, or are simply interested in a college experience that emphasizes a perspective, history, and culture different from your own, you may want to explore what these colleges have to offer. We will describe in more detail two of these types of institutions—historically black colleges and universities and Hispanic-serving institutions—but there are other types you may consider: tribal colleges (serving Native American students), Jewish universities, and Asian American and Pacific Islander serving institutions. These colleges can provide a high-quality education, while offering a strong sense of community and networking for your career post-graduation.

Historically Black Colleges and Universities (HBCUs)

Many colleges were founded following the Civil War specifically to educate black students (particularly freed slaves) in the climate of postwar segregation (Provasnik, Shafer and Snyder 2004). The Higher Education Act of 1965 officially recognized these colleges, "established prior to 1964, whose principal mission was, and is, the education of black Americans," as historically black colleges and universities (HBCUs). As of 2015, 102 HBCUs exist in nineteen states, as well as Washington, DC, and the Virgin Islands, with most located in the South (Alabama hosts the most of any state, with fifteen).

In addition to the unique scholarship and internship opportunities that are often available to students at historically black colleges and universities through public and private sources, research shows there are a number of other potential benefits to attending an HBCU, particularly for black students. One study found that HBCUs are particularly successful in awarding bachelor's degrees in STEM fields to African American students, while another found that these colleges also confer a disproportionate percentage of all business and management degrees earned by African American students (Leichter 2016). According to a Gallup–Purdue University study, black graduates of HBCUs are more likely to have felt supported while in college, and to be thriving afterward, than their black peers at predominantly white institutions (Seymour and Ray 2015). Although the evidence suggests that HBCUs are uniquely prepared to support the needs of black students, other students may also benefit from attending an HBCU. Gallup found that HBCU students reported more opportunities for experiential learning (e.g., applied internships, long-term projects, and extracurricular activities) than average. There may also be great benefits for future professional networking that can come from attending an HBCU. For a full list of HBCUs, check the website of HBCU Connect.

TOP HBCUS IN THE BEST COLLEGES FOR ADULTS RANKINGS

St. Philip's College (TX, two-year): #149

Florida Agricultural and Mechanical University (FL, four-year): #296

Jackson State University (MS, four-year): #335

Winston-Salem State University (NC, four-year): #379

Hispanic-Serving Institutions (HSIs)

Unlike HBCUs, which were historically designated to serve black students, Hispanic-serving institutions (HSIs) are defined by the U.S. Department of Education as any accredited institution of higher education with an enrollment of full-time undergraduate students that is at least 25 percent Hispanic/Latino. Colleges and universities that meet these criteria can apply to receive additional grant money to develop programs, scholarships, and other services that support Hispanic/Latino students. According to the Hispanic Association of Colleges and Universities (HACU), the 435 institutions eligible to be HSIs in the 2014–15 school year were located in eighteen states as well as Puerto Rico—most are in Western states. California alone is home to over 150! The number of HSI-eligible institutions is also increasing steadily every year, having more than doubled in the twenty years between 1994 and 2004.

HSIs are mostly colleges and universities that evolved over time to serve growing numbers of Hispanic/Latino students. Colleges that receive HSI funding from the federal government are likely to have special programs and services in place to support the particular needs of Hispanic/Latino students, and the approaches vary widely from college to college. A 2016 study by *Excelencia* in Education has also found an initial connection between HSIs and increased college access and completion among Latino students (Santiago, Taylor and Calderón Galdeano May 2016).

For a list of HSI-eligible institutions, check out the HACU website.

HBCUs and HSIs: Making the Decision

Ultimately, it is up to you to decide whether attending an HBCU or HSI is right for you. While many will offer African American and Latino students a number of benefits, particularly in terms of support and resources, you should count this as just one more factor among the many others we have identified in choosing a college. Many colleges and universities—from flagships to private schools to community colleges—will have a number of services and supports for students from particular cultural, ethnic, or language backgrounds. These can include cultural student organizations, diversity centers, and ethnic studies departments. If having a vibrant and robust African American or Latino community at college is important to you, be sure to research whether the colleges you are interested in can offer that experience.

Top HSIs in the Best Colleges for Adults Rankings

Capital Community College (CT, two-year): #8

California State University–Dominquez Hills (CA, four-year): #11

Naugatuck Valley Community College (CT, two-year): #23

California State University–Hayward (CA, four-year): #23

Gateway Community College (AZ, two-year): #26

College of the Canyons (CA, two-year): #31

Mesa Community College (AZ, two-year): #32

University of New Mexico–Main Campus (NM, four-year): #33

The Credit Hour

What's a Credit Hour?

You'll hear a lot about credit hours in college—you need this many credit hours to graduate, or a course is worth that many credit hours, and so on. But what is a credit hour? It's a little confusing because it sounds like it's some kind of measure of time, but it's meant to be much more than that. According to the U.S. Department of Education, a credit hour is "a unit of measure that gives value to the level of instruction, academic rigor, and time requirements for a course taken at an educational institution." (U.S. Department of Education Office of Postsecondary Education 2011). The credit hour is basically a way for colleges to indicate how much work students and faculty are expected to put into a course so that specific learning outcomes are achieved.

The credit hour is by no means a perfect measure of student learning, but it is one way to compare one course with another in terms of how much work you'll do. There is an aspect of time involved. Most college courses are 3-4 credit hours, and federal regulations suggest that each credit hour be worth an hour of instruction and two hours of work outside of class each week. That means that a 3-credit course will usually consist of 3 hours of class time and 6 hours of non–class time work each week— for each week in a term. If your term is 15 weeks, your 3-credit class will have 45 hours of class-time instruction (3 x 15 = 45) and about 90 hours of work outside the class time (6 x 15 = 90).

WHAT'S THE DIFFERENCE BETWEEN SEMESTER CREDITS AND QUARTER CREDITS?

Colleges typically offer courses according to a term schedule. Most colleges have terms that are *semesters*, and there are two semesters in a school year: fall and spring. Each semester is usually 15 weeks long. The credits that you earn for a course in those schools are *semester credits*. There are some colleges that operate using terms that are *quarters*. Each quarter is 10-11 weeks long in fall, winter, and spring. Those colleges award *quarter credits*.

Since semesters are longer than quarters, semester credits are worth more than quarter credits. That means that if you transfer from a college with semesters to a college with quarters, or vice versa, the number of credits that you previously earned will need to be converted. Here are some typical conversion formulas that might be used:

Total quarter credits x 2/3 = Total semester credits
Total semester credits x 1.5 = Total quarter credits

Types of Credentials: The Traditional Degree and Beyond

Associate and bachelor's degrees are what colleges have traditionally offered to their graduates. Associate degrees are sometimes called two-

> I returned to the same college I originally attended—so I had all those credits, more than I thought. So when I went back, I completed my associate degree last semester and that helped me get promoted. That was a first step. I was able to show to my supervisors that I was serious. I am ready to move forward.
>
> —*Mary, adult student, age 58, Miami Dade College*

year degrees because they are designed to be completed after two years of full-time study, and bachelor's degrees are sometimes called four-year degrees because they are designed to be completed after four years of full-time study. You generally need around 60 semester credit hours for an associate degree, and 120 semester credit hours for a bachelor's degree—but some degree programs may require more so check the fine print!

You do not need to earn an associate degree before you can get a bachelor's degree! If your main goal is a bachelor's degree, it may be best to enroll in a bachelor's degree program from the start.

There are three main types of associate degrees: associate of arts (AA), associate of science (AS), and associate of applied science (AAS). The AA and AS degrees are designed for students who may eventually transfer to a bachelor's degree program, with the AA degree focused on liberal arts and the AS degree focused on sciences. The AAS degree is typically focused on preparing students for the workplace, often in more technical fields—examples include culinary arts, aviation, manufacturing technology, power plant technology, construction management, and paramedic. While some of the credits in an AAS degree may transfer to a bachelor's degree, many may not.

There are also different types of bachelor's degrees. Bachelor of arts, or BA, degrees allow a student to take a wide range of liberal arts subjects, with some requirements for the chosen major course of study. A bachelor of science, or BS, degree typically has a stronger focus on a particular major (often in more technical or scientific areas like computer science, nursing, or biochemistry) with fewer options for study outside of that subject.

Bachelor's degrees have their own requirements that may not perfectly

Articulation agreements. Some colleges have what are called articulation agreements with each other. This means that they have established a simplified process for transferring credits from one institution to another. Many two-year colleges (community colleges) have articulation agreements with one or more four-year institutions that are designed to make it easier for students to transfer to bachelor's degree programs.

align with your associate degree—and it also could be the case that not all of your associate degree credits will be accepted if you transfer to a bachelor's program. So, if you know that you want to earn a bachelor's degree, do your research on those programs to learn what the degree requirements are and what the policies are about transferring credit from an associate degree program. You might be better off going after the bachelor's degree from the very start.

After completing a bachelor's degree, you can continue to earn other credentials at the graduate level. Many professional graduate degrees are master's degrees (for example, in business, teaching, counseling, etc.) or doctorates.

There are other postsecondary credentials that may be what you need to achieve your particular career goals. Some colleges offer **shorter-term credentials** that will train you in specific skills or for a particular job—for example, there are short-term credential programs for web developer, computer support specialist, administrative support specialist, HVAC technology, and welding. These programs usually take less than a year to complete but can range from six months to two years of full-time study. They may or may not help you get a better-paying job, and they may not necessarily award college credit that will count toward an associate or bachelor's degree. You might change your mind someday and want to finally get that degree after all, or you may want to get a short-term certificate on the way to a degree. So it may be important for all of the courses you take now to eventually count toward a degree as well!

Some colleges are recognizing that the students in their shorter-term programs would benefit from having a pathway to an associate or bachelor's degree, so they are creating what are called **stackable credentials.**

These credentials do award college credits, and the college will offer follow-on programs that build on the original credential toward an associate or bachelor's degree. If a shorter-term credential is something that will help you in your career, it may be worth considering. In fact, in some cases, all you may need is one or two courses to upgrade your skills and meet a particular need for your current job. But if you go the credential route, *ask whether college credits are awarded* and if there are pathways to build on that credential to work toward a degree.

Certificates and licenses are special industry-recognized credentials that are generally offered by a government agency or a private organization to people who complete a special training program, pass an exam, and/or have the required work experience. Some college and university degree or certificate programs may include training that prepares students for certification or licensing exams. One example is in nursing, where an associate degree in a nursing program results in a degree, but the graduate cannot work as a nurse without also passing the nursing licensing exam called the NCLEX. After passing that exam, the graduate is then issued a license by the state. Cosmetologists, engineers, and plumbers are other examples of professions that may require a government-issued license in addition to formal education or training. Industry certifications are common for fields like IT, real estate, accounting, investing, personal finance, insurance, and others. You'll need the formal education from the college or university, and then you'll need to apply for a license or certification, which may require additional testing.

College credit? Or noncredit? If you are taking vocational training courses at a community or vocational college, you may or may not be earning college credit. Many classes and programs exist that are designed to help students with specific personal or professional development but that do not offer college credit. Taking these courses will not lead to the earning of a degree or certificate.

If a degree or certificate is your goal, make sure that each course you take—and pay for—will award college credit that will count toward that goal.

Have you heard of digital badges? Badges are one example of a micro-credential that can be awarded to someone who has a specific skill. According to EDUCAUSE, "badges signify accomplishments such as completion of a project, mastery of a skill, or marks of experience" (EDUCAUSE Learning Initiative n.d.). A badge is a digital token that appears as a logo or icon on a web page, and it is a digital storage tool for details about the recipient's skill or accomplishment.

Badges are a relatively new phenomenon, so they are not available everywhere and their potential value in the job market is not yet fully understood. But some colleges are offering them as stand-alone options, or as part of a stackable credential. Some employers are offering them to employees who complete special training programs. Community groups and industry associations can offer them as well. Right now, badges are not as valuable as degrees in the labor market as a whole, but you may run across them as you explore your postsecondary options. **Recommendation: As with any short-term credential, ask how a badge can count toward a longer-term associate or bachelor's degree.**

Earning a Degree You Didn't Expect: The New Phenomenon of Reverse Transfer

There are a lot of students who start out taking courses at a community college and then transfer to a four-year college to pursue a bachelor's degree without first earning an associate degree. That's a perfectly acceptable pathway to a degree (and it's a great way to make sure that you don't end up taking too many classes at the community college that may not end up transferring to the four-year college).

Earlier in this chapter, you learned that you don't need to get an associate degree on your way to a bachelor's. But what if it might be helpful to you to have an associate degree as you continue your studies? Some community colleges are offering something called *reverse transfer*, which is the option of transferring credits from a four-year college *back* to a community college so that students can get a two-year degree that could help them find a better job or qualify for a promotion—or simply to have something that shows their accomplishment. This is not available at every college or for every student. But if it is something that you think would help you, ask about it!

If you are a student who went to college previously and earned 60 or more credits, ask your local community college if reverse transfer is an option for earning an associate degree.

If you are someone who plans to start out taking classes at a four year college, ask if reverse transfer might be an option for earning an associate degree along the way, if that associate degree will help you in your career.

Accreditation

Accreditation is a process in which educational institutions or their individual programs are recognized and endorsed after meeting established standards for quality.

It's important to make sure your school and program of study have the right accreditations from a regional or specialized accrediting body because otherwise you may have trouble transferring to another school if you need to. Plus, future employers may not consider hiring candidates

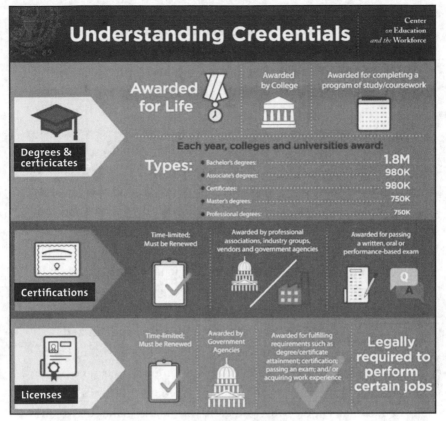

Understanding Credentials   Center *on* Education *and the* Workforce

Degrees & certicicates	Awarded for Life	Awarded by College	Awarded for completing a program of study/coursework

Each year, colleges and universities award:

Types:
- Bachelor's degrees: **1.8M**
- Associate's degrees: **980K**
- Certificates: **980K**
- Master's degrees: **750K**
- Professional degrees: **750K**

Certifications	Time-limited; Must be Renewed	Awarded by professional associations, industry groups, vendors and government agencies	Awarded for passing a written, oral or performance-based exam

Licenses	Time-limited; Must be Renewed	Awarded by Government Agencies	Awarded for fulfilling requirements such as degree/certificate attainment; certification; passing an exam; and/or acquiring work experience	Legally required to perform certain jobs

Source of Infographic: Georgetown University Center on Education and the Workforce

Source of data: Georgetown University Center on Education and the Workforce analysis of data from the U.S. Department of Education, Integrated Postsecondary Education Data System, 2013

with degrees earned from institutions or programs that lack appropriate accreditation.

There are three types of accreditation—regional and national accreditation are focused on the entire institution, and programmatic/specialized accreditation is focused on a specific program.

✛ **Regional:** Regional accreditation means that the institution has been recognized as meeting standards established by the U.S. Department of Education and the Council for Higher Education Accreditation (CHEA). Regional accreditation status is conferred by one of the seven regional accrediting bodies, each based on a specific region of the country (see table). Regional accreditation is important because that means that students going to the college can be eligible to receive federal financial aid.

In addition, it is easier to transfer to another institution from regionally accredited schools. **Regional accreditation is the best kind of accreditation.**

✛ **National:** National accreditation is similar to regional accreditation in that nationally accredited schools can offer federal financial aid to their students. If you have plans to eventually transfer to a regionally accredited institution from an institution that is only nationally accredited, you should find out ahead of time if your credits will transfer. While nationally accredited institutions will usually accept credit from regionally or nationally accredited institutions, regionally accredited schools often do not recognize coursework taken at nationally accredited schools.

✛ **Programmatic or specialized:** If you plan to enroll in a program that prepares students for entry to a specific profession or occupation (like nursing, medicine, business, teacher education, engineering, law, etc.), you should make sure that the program is accredited by the appropriate specialized accreditor.

> **Question:**
> What if the school I want to attend isn't accredited?
>
> **Answer:**
> Don't go there! Your degree might not be worth the money you spend.
>   All of the colleges in our rankings are accredited!

Additional Programs Designed with the Adult in Mind

Thus far this chapter has covered the traditional postsecondary education options. That is, those that have been around for a while. But it's useful to keep your eyes open for other opportunities that may be a good fit for your needs as an adult learner. Here are some examples, many of which are covered in more detail in chapters 8, 9, and 10.

✛ **Accelerated degree programs.** These are programs that are designed to go at a faster pace or that are offered on a compressed schedule. (See chapter 8.)

✛ **Online or distance learning.** There are a lot of opportunities to earn your degree completely online—and not just at national

Regional Accreditors and Their Geographic Areas

Middle States Commission on Higher Education

Institutions of higher education in Delaware, the District of Columbia, Maryland, New Jersey, New York, Pennsylvania, Puerto Rico, and the U.S. Virgin Islands, including distance and correspondence education programs offered at those institutions.

New England Association of Schools and Colleges, Commission on Institutions of Higher Education

Postsecondary degree–granting educational institutions in Alaska, Idaho, Montana, Nevada, Oregon, Utah, and Washington, and the accreditation of programs offered via distance education within these institutions.

North Central Association of Colleges and Schools, the Higher Learning Commission

Degree-granting institutions of higher education in Arizona, Arkansas, Colorado, Illinois, Indiana, Iowa, Kansas, Michigan, Minnesota, Missouri, Nebraska, New Mexico, North Dakota, Ohio, Oklahoma, South Dakota, West Virginia, Wisconsin, and Wyoming, including the tribal institutions and the accreditation of programs offered via distance education and correspondence education within these institutions.

Northwest Commission on Colleges and Universities

Postsecondary degree–granting educational institutions in Alaska, Idaho, Montana, Nevada, Oregon, Utah, and Washington, and the accreditation of programs offered via distance education within these institutions.

Southern Association of Colleges and Schools, Commission on Colleges (SACS COC)

Degree-granting institutions of higher education in Alabama, Florida, Georgia, Kentucky, Louisiana, Mississippi, North Carolina, South Carolina, Tennessee, Texas, and Virginia, including the accreditation of programs offered via distance and correspondence education within these institutions.

Western Association of Schools and Colleges (WASC), Accrediting Commission for Community and Junior Colleges

Community and other colleges with a primarily pre-baccalaureate mission located in California, Hawaii, the U.S. territories of Guam and American Samoa, the Republic of Palau, the Federated States of Micronesia, the Commonwealth of the Northern Mariana Islands, and the Republic of the Marshall Islands, which offer certificates, associate's degrees, and select bachelor's degrees.

Western Association of Schools and Colleges (WASC), Senior Colleges and University Commission

Senior colleges and universities in California, Hawaii, the U.S. territories of Guam and American Samoa, the Republic of Palau, the Federated States of Micronesia, the Commonwealth of the Northern Mariana Islands, and the Republic of the Marshall Islands, including distance education programs offered at those institutions.

For more information, see the U.S. Department of Education, Office of Postsecondary Education, http://ope.ed.gov/accreditation/Agencies.aspx

for-profit colleges. Many public and nonprofit colleges offer online degrees, which can be great options for working adults with unpredictable schedules and busy lives. (See chapters 8 and 9 for details.)

✛ **Competency-based education (CBE).** These are programs focused on student mastery of specific competencies rather than on successful completion of courses. Many CBE programs are fully online and self-paced, meaning that you may be able to finish them more quickly than a traditional degree program. The pricing of these programs can also be lower than more traditional degree programs. (See chapter 8 for more information.)

✛ **Prior learning assessment (PLA).** Some colleges offer options for evaluating what you already know for college credit. This is particularly useful for adults with a lot of learning from their work experience, military experience, hobbies, or self-study. Earning credit through PLA is much cheaper than taking the courses from the college, so this option can save you a lot of time and money. (See chapter 10 for more information.)

✛ **Student-designed degrees.** Colleges may offer special degree options in which students can customize their degrees based on specific interests or as a way to bridge multiple disciplines.

✛ **Adult learner centers.** Some larger institutions have a special department, school, or center for adults. These centers may offer adults options including student-designed degrees, weekend courses, and prior learning assessment. These centers are not the same as continuing studies departments, which tend to offer individual noncredit courses.

- **Degree completion colleges.** Some colleges offer maximum flexibility and transferability of previous college work. Students save time because these colleges require students to take only courses that complete their remaining degree requirements. Completion colleges are ideal for the student who may have previously completed courses at more than one other institution and/or who has significant college level learning from noncollege experiences that could be evaluated through PLA.

New Ways to Learn

There are several new ways that people can learn these days, and it may be useful for you to know that these options exist. You may want to seek these out on your own for independent learning outside of a degree program, or you may discover that some colleges have incorporated them into their degree programs in some way.

- **MOOCs.** Funny name, but serious opportunity for learning! MOOC stands for massive open online course. These are college level courses that are provided online—*and for free*. There are lots of companies that offer MOOCs, but some of the most famous ones are Coursera, edX, and Udemy. The courses are often taught by faculty from some of the most elite institutions in the country. Many will have assignments and assessments so that you will have a good sense of what you are learning. MOOCs can be a great way to acquire a new skill or explore a new subject area with zero risk in terms of cost or academic failure.

  In general, MOOCs are not offered for college credit and the MOOC companies do not offer associate or bachelor's degrees. However, there are several MOOCs that for a relatively small fee will provide students the option of earning credit by taking a final assessment or otherwise demonstrating their learning. There are also some colleges that will offer prior learning assessment options (see chapter 10) for students who take MOOCs. **Just be aware that there is no guarantee the college where you eventually enroll will accept the credit for your MOOC**

> A two-year school was so good for me. Tuition is so expensive. Since I went somewhere where my financial aid covered most of my tuition, I never had that moment where I was like, "What am I doing here?"
>
> *—Andy, adult student, age 30,*
> *DePaul University School for New Learning*

learning. Whether or not you can find a college that will offer credit for these independent learning experiences, MOOCs can be a great way to sample a college course and whet your appetite for officially enrolling at a college or university.

✣ **Open educational resources.** Also known as OER, open educational resources is a broader category of learning resources that you can access for free on the internet. You can find full courses, lectures, homework assignments, lab and classroom activities, and more online. MOOCs are one kind of OER. As with MOOCs, if you learn independently through OER, you can always look for a college that will agree to evaluate what you have learned through prior learning assessment (see chapter 10). Some colleges are making use of OER and incorporating them into their curriculum.

✣ **Boot camps.** No, these programs probably aren't going to make you do push-ups, but like a military boot camp an educational boot camp is designed to get its participants to focus on a particular goal with great intensity for a short period of time. The boot camp concept for civilian job training is very new. As of this writing, the boot camp approach has been used most often to train computer programmers, web developers, and user experience (UX) designers. The programs are short-term—6-12 months—and students are required to be enrolled on a full-time basis. The idea is to train people in a well-defined set of programming skills that allow graduates of the program to be hired as computer programmers relatively quickly. Some of these programs have reported that they have high graduation rates, high job-placement rates, and high salaries for their graduates. However, these are often nonaccredited programs that don't award college credit or financial aid—and the cost can be steep—so proceed with caution. Some colleges are forming partnerships with boot camps, so credit and financial aid could be a possibility for certain programs. As with every educational program you are considering, ask a lot of questions to make sure that the program can deliver on its promises and help you succeed.

There are lots of ways for you to learn—and earn a degree—in the postsecondary landscape. There are the traditional associate and bachelor's degrees from accredited colleges, and today there are many more options such as boot camps, MOOCs, accelerated programs, and competency-based degrees. You are no longer limited to the traditional college program.

CHAPTER 6

Comparing Colleges and Programs

With so many postsecondary education options, how do you choose a college? There are so many options!

For a high school senior looking at college options, there literally are thousands of choices. Those who leave home to attend a residential college can go in state, to the state next door, online, or clear across the country. But adults typically have a narrower set of options. You may have a job that you don't want to leave, a mortgage, kids, a working spouse, or ailing parents—any one of those things are enough of a reason to conclude that you have two realistic choices:

Choice 1: A college close to home

Choice 2: A college that offers online degree programs

Instead of focusing on all the ways you are limited in your back-to-school choices, spend some time figuring out what options *do* exist for you at this stage in your life and evaluate those options. Which of the available options will help you learn what you need to succeed? Which will be affordable? Which will help you finish your degree? Which will give you options for finishing quickly?

Your first step is to create a list of the colleges that are your best options, and then the second step is to do the important research to figure out which college is the ***best choice for you***.

Step 1: Narrow Down the Choices

The first step is to identify the various options you have in terms of *regionally accredited colleges and universities*.

FINDING THE SCHOOLS THAT ARE CLOSE TO HOME

To find out which colleges are in your geographic area, visit the College Navigator, a website hosted by the National Center for Education Statistics. This website can provide you with a lot of information about specific schools, if you have a particular school in mind. But it also can tell you which colleges are close to where you live. Enter your zip code and a mileage range (how many miles you would be willing to commute to class), then the degree type (bachelor's versus associate, or four-year versus two-year) and it will produce a list for you. If there are not many schools on your list, try expanding the mile range to see if that helps.

Check the accreditation status for each college by clicking on the college name and then opening the Accreditation tab. As was described in chapter 5, the best type of accreditation is *regional*, which means accreditation from one of the following agencies:

- ✛ Middle States Commission on Higher Education
- ✛ New England Association of Schools and Colleges, Commission on Institutions of Higher Education
- ✛ North Central Association of Colleges and Schools, the Higher Learning Commission
- ✛ Northwest Commission on Colleges and Universities
- ✛ Southern Association of Colleges and Schools, Commission on Colleges (SACS COC)
- ✛ Western Association of Schools and Colleges (WASC), Accrediting Commission for Community and Junior Colleges
- ✛ Western Association of Schools and Colleges, Senior Colleges and University Commission

Find out which schools offer a degree program you are interested in by clicking on the Programs/Majors tab (or you could indicate the specific program/major you want in one of the search fields).

> **Why do we care about accreditation?** Remember that it's important that your college is regionally accredited. Accreditation is how the higher education world officially approves a college. It's not an automatic sign of high quality, but without accreditation you could have trouble transferring to another college, going to graduate school, or qualifying for financial aid. See more about this topic in chapter 5.

If you are unsure about what you might major in, look through the choices and see if there is a wide selection of majors that includes a range of areas of study, including liberal arts, business, computer science, physical sciences, social sciences, education, and nursing.

FINDING ONLINE OPTIONS

You might also want to consider online programs. In this case, the distance from your zip code won't matter at all! Staying on the College Navigator website, clear out the zip code and distance fields. Then, under More Search Options, check the Distance Learning Only option. The results should provide you with a list of online colleges you might also consider—but be sure to check their accreditation status as well! You can zero in on a shorter list of online options by filtering your search in other ways—for instance, by entering a program/major.

EXPLORING DEGREE COMPLETION COLLEGES

Finally, you might want to consider one of the degree completion colleges that were designed specifically for students who have a lot of learning from other college experiences or from work and life experience. Some of the best-known colleges in this category are:

+ Excelsior College (NY)
+ SUNY Empire State College (NY)
+ Thomas Edison State College (NJ)
+ Granite State College (NH)
+ Charter Oak State College (CT)

+ Governors State University (IL)
+ Colorado State U. Global (CO)

Check out their websites to learn about the kinds of degrees that they offer. If there is a degree program that fits your goals, then you might want to consider learning more about this kind of college.

CREATE A LIST OF COLLEGES TO RESEARCH FURTHER

Create a list of the colleges that may be possibilities for you and your educational goals. This is just the first step in a process that narrows down the thousands of colleges to a group of practical choices for you. Over time, you'll do more research that will help you narrow down your list to a handful of your best options.

Colleges to Consider List

Colleges to Consider	Local or Online?	Degree Programs to Consider	Accreditation?

Step 2: Do Your Own Research Using Our Rankings as a Starting Point

Remember, as you narrow down your choices and select a college, consider these four important things:

1. **What to study.** Choose a college based on academics. Make sure it offers the right area of study and the right degree or other credential for your goals.

2. **Affordability.** Choose a college that you can afford, and do everything you can—applying for grants, scholarships, transfer credits, and other money savers—to minimize your out-of-pocket costs and loans.

3. **Flexibility.** Choose a college that will work for your personal circumstances and your schedule, and look for special options or programs that can help you finish faster.

4. **Ensuring your success.** Choose a college that has a good record of helping students earn degrees and offers services to help you succeed academically. Be sure to take advantage of those support services once you enroll.

What you decide to study is likely based on what your career goals are. Or, alternatively, you could choose a liberal arts or science major for your bachelor's degree to keep your options open or to meet a general degree requirement for promotional opportunities. (See chapter 4 for resources on exploring careers and majors.)

If what you plan to study is specialized, you could start to narrow down your college options on that basis alone. Most adults will still find that they have multiple college options available to them. That is a good position to be in, because then you can evaluate multiple colleges based on affordability, flexibility, and ensuring your success.

So how do you answer questions about those other three factors: affordability, flexibility, and ensuring your success? First, take a look at the **rankings of colleges for adult learners** included in this book. These rankings have been designed around factors that are important for your

> My number one consideration in choosing a college was, first and foremost, adult programming and the ability to take night classes. That's where I started. After that, it became location. I had a choice in Chicago—I looked at school rankings. Degree selection was important. Because I have been taking a lot of classes at a community college, I don't need to go for four years, so price started taking a back seat.
>
> —*Alex, adult student, age 30, Moraine Valley Community College and DePaul University School for New Learning*

The New Rankings of Colleges for Adult Learners

There are a lot of college rankings out there that are supposed to tell prospective students what the best schools are in the country, or in a region of the country, or for specific areas of study. However, most rankings focus primarily on measures that are important to students who just graduated from high school and their families.

The rankings we've included here are different because they have you and your needs in mind. The *Washington Monthly's Best Colleges for Adults* rankings uses eight measures to calculate each school's overall score:

1. **Ease of transfer/enrollment.** This is based on measures of how easy it is for adult students to either initially enroll or transfer in from another college.

2. **Flexibility of programs.** This considers whether colleges are flexible enough to meet the needs of adult students—offering things like prior learning assessments, online degrees, advising services after hours, and weekend and/or evening classes.

3. **Services available for adult students.** This measure reflects whether a college offers services that adult students are most likely to use, such as general services for adult students, financial aid counseling, on-campus day care, counseling services, job placement services, or veterans' services.

4. **The percent of adult students (age 25+ plus) at the college.** The higher the percentage, the greater the adult student presence at the college. Colleges serving large numbers of adults likely see the adult student as an important "customer."

5. **Graduation rate of part-time students.** The U.S. Department of Education released data on part-time students' graduation rates in 2017, and we are the first to use this in college rankings. This is important because adults typically attend college part-time.

The New Rankings of Colleges for Adult Learners

(Continued)

6. **Mean earnings of independent (adult) students ten years after entering college.** If the goal is to improve your earning potential, then this could be an important measure to consider as it reflects the employment success of the college's graduates.

7. **Loan repayment rates of adult students five years after entering repayment.** This measure is a good indication of how well the college does in meeting students' financial needs through federal loans—but not overburdening them with so much debt that they will have trouble repaying it with the kinds of jobs they get after leaving the college.

8. **Tuition and fees for in-district students.** This is the sticker price, and it is seen as a simple measure of affordability. The net price, or the price that the average student actually pays, may be different.

Here we provide you with a snapshot from the rankings of four-year colleges in Nebraska as an example of the sort of information you will find about higher-education options in your state in the appendix.

Nebraska
FOUR YEAR COLLEGES

Rank	Name	Sector	Ease of transfer (5 pts for 4 year, 4 pts for 2 year)	Flexibility of programs (9 pts)	Services for adult students (6 pts)	Percent of students over age 25	Graduation rate of part-time students	Mean earnings of independent students 10 years after college entry	Loan repayment of independent students 5 years after leaving college	In-district tuition and fees (at a 9 month rate for 2 year colleges)	Percent of credentials awarded as bachelor's degrees
2	BELLEVUE UNIVERSITY	Nonprofit	5	8	2	80%	64%	61268	64%	7365	100%
107	CREIGHTON UNIVERSITY	Nonprofit	5	8	6	6%	24%	81117	74%	37606	99%
192	UNIVERSITY OF NEBRASKA AT LINCOLN	Public	4	7	6	6%	50%	48679	68%	8537	100%
206	PERU STATE COLLEGE	Public	5	6	6	25%	40%	38205	58%	6790	100%
247	NEBRASKA WESLEYAN UNIVERSITY	Nonprofit	5	8	4	18%	62%	52110	65%	31394	99%
270	CHADRON STATE COLLEGE	Public	4	8	6	23%	26%	35853	58%	6252	100%
281	UNIVERSITY OF NEBRASKA AT OMAHA	Public	4	6	6	22%	35%	46463	60%	7204	100%
387	COLLEGE OF SAINT MARY	Nonprofit	5	7	6	33%	26%	39451	55%	29954	83%
680	UNIVERSITY OF NEBRASKA AT KEARNEY	Public	4	4	5	9%	30%	40058	59%	6953	100%
724	WAYNE STATE COLLEGE	Public	4	5	4	8%	26%	35318	57%	6427	100%

UNRANKED: Concordia University, Doane College, Doane College-Lincoln Grand Island and Master, Hastings College, Midland Lutheran College, Union College, York College

The far left column shows the overall *national* rank of the institution in serving adult learners, based on combined scores in the eight different categories. For any college you may be considering, even if it didn't rank particularly well, look carefully at information in each of the categories to give you some idea of where that college is strong in serving adult learners. Note that some colleges are "unranked"— that just means that we do not have enough data to include them in the rankings at this time. *"Unranked" does not mean that these colleges should not be considered.*

If the colleges you are considering are not ranked well, don't panic. There are plenty of colleges that may be a great fit for you even if they do not rank well with the data that are currently available. **Metrics and rankings should only be a starting point in your research.** The top-ranked college in the country might not be good for your goals or for your individual circumstances. There is plenty that you can research on your own to make sure you enroll in the right college *for you*.

success as an adult student. They look at each college in terms of how easy it is for students to enter as a transfer student (after all, so many adults have already taken previous college courses), how flexible their programs are for someone who is juggling work and family responsibilities, how invested the college is in programs and services that will help you succeed as an adult student, and how much students who attend those colleges earn ten years after entering.

A short explanation of the rankings is provided here to give you a sense of how they can help you in your college search. The full list of rankings for every state is provided in Appendix A.

Step 3: Be Disciplined in Your Decision Making

The rankings won't answer all of your questions—and there are many colleges that aren't ranked because we don't have complete data for them— but they are a great place to start. You will also want to use chapters 7 to

> I was looking for a school that had an articulation agreement with the state system. If they had that agreement with the state of Florida, that was my number one priority. Number two—rough proximity to my home. After that, flexibility—classes at night. Then cost—community college costs so much less!
>
> —"Kirk," adult student, age 26, Miami Dade College

15 to help you think through what else will be important to you in your college decision and how to find that information about the colleges that you are considering.

The rest of this book will give you lots of information on how you can make college affordable, how college programs can be designed to fit your schedule, and how some colleges might be able to get you to a degree faster while providing you with needed support along the way.

As you work through the remaining chapters, keep in mind that college and university websites should provide you with most of the information you need to make an informed decision. Spending time on the college websites is an important component of your research. If the information you are looking for is not on the website, you may need to submit a question on a contact form or call the admissions office with a specific question.

Keep in mind that while the college website is an important source of information, it is also a marketing tool for the college. The photos that you

Don't forget to check it out in person! If you are looking at schools within your commuting radius, take the time to drive to the campus. (You might even want to call ahead and ask to schedule a tour.) How does it feel to you? Is there adequate parking? Do you sense friendly, dedicated staff and enthusiastic students?

If you're going to attend at night or on the weekends, be sure to check out the campus during what will be your class times. Whether you will be attending on-campus classes or online courses, be sure to thoroughly read through the websites of the schools you are considering.

see have been chosen to present a particular image of that college. Use the website as a source of information about the college's mission and programs but also try to visit in person. A more accurate picture of what the college is like can be gained by meeting and talking with actual students, staff, and faculty.

If there are specific courses you know you want to take, you may be able to locate the syllabus (an outline of what the course will cover that may also list the required reading and assignments) to see if the material is of interest and value to you. You also can try to contact the faculty member who teaches the course, or the department chair, if you have a specific question.

Use the worksheet at the end of this chapter to help you compare up to three colleges or universities, based on criteria presented in this book. In the blank space provided, you can add criteria of your own that are important to you as you make your decision. Or create your own customized list based on criteria you have identified as most important to you.

BUYER BEWARE!

Some colleges and universities use aggressive sales techniques. If your internet search takes you to screens that ask for your phone number before you can research the college, be prepared for a call, sometimes within minutes of your web visit. This does not necessarily mean that you should avoid those websites or those colleges. A wide range of colleges have adopted these kinds of marketing practices. Their websites are used for "lead generation" so that they can follow up and answer your questions—and encourage you to consider their programs. Just be aware that some schools may use this opportunity to put a lot of pressure on you to enroll quickly, before you've had a chance to gather all the information you need and weigh all of your options. If they get you on the phone and offer easy access to loans to pay for expensive programs, tread carefully! Such schools may be more focused on making a profit than on your successful educational experience. Also, check the URL (web address) of the school to be sure it ends in **".edu."** All college and university websites end in .edu. If the website ends in a ".com," these are commercial businesses, which may provide education, skills, and training but are not generally designed around ensuring the student's well-rounded, overall success and financial well-being.

Comparing Colleges Worksheet

My Criteria for Choosing a College or University Place a check mark in the columns if the statements below are true. *Add your own criteria in the space provided at the bottom of the table.*	College A College A name goes here.	College B College B name goes here.	College C College C name goes here.
The college has a good ranking according to this guide. If not, there is evidence the school has high-quality programs that will help me finish my degree quickly.			
The college is regionally accredited.			
The college offers my preferred academic program.			
Tuition and fees are affordable.			
The college is close to my work or home, or offers online courses and programs.			
Course offerings are available that fit my schedule.			
The college has scholarships for adult students.			
The college offers prior learning assessment options so that I can earn credit for what I already know at the college level.			
The college accepts CLEP, DSST, or UExcel exams, which will help me save time and money.			
The college provides career services to students and graduates.			

Comparing Colleges Worksheet *(Continued)*	College A	College B	College C
	College A name goes here.	College B name goes here.	College C name goes here.
The college provides child care.			
The college is adult-student friendly.			
The college has the kind of support I will need (such as tutoring, a learning center, developmental courses, advising and career counseling, etc.).			
The college is well known and respected.			
_____			
_____			
_____			
_____			
_____			
_____			

CHAPTER 7

Smart Ways to Pay: Tuition as an Investment in Your Future

When you look at the sticker price, going to college looks like an expensive proposition. And it is! But if you are someone without a college degree in today's job market, you have probably heard people tell you something like, "You can't afford *not* to get a college degree." The reason is that what you pay to go to college is a short-term expense—but over your lifetime, you can expect to benefit significantly from your degree in the form of higher wages and a more rewarding career.

Think of tuition as an *investment in your future*. And think about your future earnings as a *return on your investment* in your education.

Take, for example, a 30-year-old human resources assistant interested in advancing in his field. A college degree could cost as much as $50,000, but it could take him from making $39,000 a year as an associate to making a median salary of $58,000 per year as a human resources specialist. Continuing to work as an HR assistant could bring some promotion opportunities, but they might not offer very big jumps in pay, and he would likely hit a ceiling without additional education or credentials. But with a college degree, this same HR specialist has clear pathways into management positions with annual salaries of $75,000 and more over time. In the table below, we provide a "back of the envelope" calculation of lifetime earnings for both scenarios. There are a lot of assumptions built into these rough estimates—for instance, a 2.0 to 2.5 percent salary increase each year is not always the experience of the average worker, and it may take longer than three years to be promoted. Also, the total cost of $50,000 out of pocket for tuition is probably on the high end of what you might expect to pay if you stick to public colleges and universities, or if you have help through scholarships, federal grants, or employer tuition assistance.

HR Associate Example

One "Back of the Envelope" Scenario: HR Associate to HR Manager

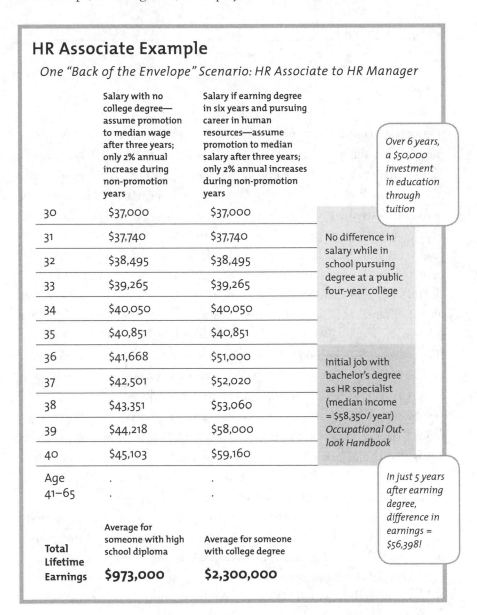

	Salary with no college degree—assume promotion to median wage after three years; only 2% annual increase during non-promotion years	Salary if earning degree in six years and pursuing career in human resources—assume promotion to median salary after three years; only 2% annual increases during non-promotion years	
30	$37,000	$37,000	*Over 6 years, a $50,000 investment in education through tuition*
31	$37,740	$37,740	No difference in salary while in school pursuing degree at a public four-year college
32	$38,495	$38,495	
33	$39,265	$39,265	
34	$40,050	$40,050	
35	$40,851	$40,851	
36	$41,668	$51,000	Initial job with bachelor's degree as HR specialist (median income = $58,350/ year) *Occupational Outlook Handbook*
37	$42,501	$52,020	
38	$43,351	$53,060	
39	$44,218	$58,000	
40	$45,103	$59,160	
Age 41–65	. .	. .	*In just 5 years after earning degree, difference in earnings = $56,398!*
	Average for someone with high school diploma	Average for someone with college degree	
Total Lifetime Earnings	**$973,000**	**$2,300,000**	

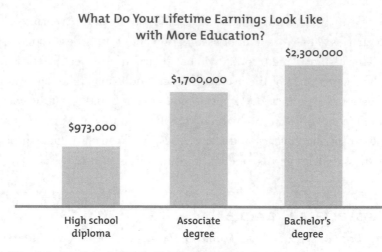

What Do Your Lifetime Earnings Look Like with More Education?

$973,000 — High school diploma
$1,700,000 — Associate degree
$2,300,000 — Bachelor's degree

:Source: Georgetown University Center on Education and the Workforce, 2011

But just take a look at how quickly there might be a return on his investment in that college degree. In the five years after earning a degree, a new HR specialist can make a significantly higher salary—over $9,000 more per year. With this kind of increase in wages, the former HR associate could break even within five years after graduating, earning back the money he paid for college tuition. Every year after that would see even more return on that original investment, particularly if he receives promotions to management positions that pay $75,000 per year or more. Over a lifetime, the difference in earnings can be really significant. Researchers looking at lots of different kind of occupations have found that, on average, *lifetime earnings* for someone with only a high school diploma is $973,000, but that grows to $1.7 million for the average person with an associate degree, and $2.3 million for the average person with a bachelor's degree (Georgetown University Center on Education and the Workforce 2011).

This is not to say that every job that requires a bachelor's degree pays more than every job that requires only a high school degree. But if you know that the degree you are seeking is going to lead to higher pay, then the cost of going to college is going to be worth it, even if it means you might have to take on some loans to do it.

The danger comes when someone pays a lot of money for college—or takes on a lot of debt through student loans—*and then does not finish college at all.* You don't want to end up with $10,000 or $20,000 of student loan debt without the degree or career (and income) that will help you pay down that debt. That's like having to continue to pay the note on an uninsured car that was totaled! Without finishing a degree—one that matters in today's labor market—you can't earn more money to pay back those loans. You're in the hole—twice.

That is why it is really important to choose your college wisely. *Make sure that the college offers everything you need to help you succeed and finish that degree!*

The Importance of Planning

Besides picking the best college you can, and one that will make sure you have what you need to finish your degree quickly, the most important thing you can do is establish a clear plan for the financial part of going back to school.

The first step is to figure out what it's going to cost. Then the next step is to figure out how to pay for it.

Best scenario:
New degree and higher paying job. Use extra salary to pay down any student loans.

Worst scenario:
Lots of loans and no degree to show for it.

What's It Going to Cost

The total costs of going to college can get complicated for adults. For all students, there are tuition and fees, as well as books and supplies. But dig into the details a bit to figure out what the actual costs are going to be *for you* if you are balancing school with the other things in your life.

✛ **Tuition and fees.** Is your plan to take a few classes at a time? Or are you planning to take a full course load? The answers to those questions will make a difference in how much you can expect to pay each year, and if you decide to take just a few classes per semester it also will mean that it will take you longer to finish—and you'll have more years of the added costs of going to college.

Colleges typically have information on tuition and fees on their websites. Sometimes this sticker price is not the price that students end up paying, especially when it comes to private colleges. But that's a good place to start for estimating your costs.

There are good online sources of information on college costs for traditional-aged students—one is the College Scorecard and another is College Abacus. You can also visit the Net Price Calculator Center, which will connect you to the net-price calculator on a specific college's website. (Keep in mind that these websites are designed primarily for students going to college right after high school. The cost estimates on these sites assume that you are going to be attending college full-time, and they also include the cost of living expenses. The net price for adults may be different if the adult student is planning on part-time study while living at home and working full-time.)

✛ **Books and supplies.** The college website (or the net-price calculator on its website) may also provide you with an estimate for the cost of books and supplies. If not, call the college's financial aid office and ask if they can give you an estimate. Some colleges are moving to using lower-priced ebooks, and some are starting to use more "Open Educational Resources" (which are free), while others still stick to the traditional textbooks. According to the College Board, a good estimate for books and supplies at a four-year public college is about $1,298 each year for a full-time student.

✛ **Technology costs.** You might need a new computer and access to broadband internet—regardless of whether you are taking classes online or not. A lot of your assignments will require access to information or resources that may be available only online.

✛ **Change in living expenses—especially meals.** Chances are if you are continuing to live in your current home while you go to college, your housing expenses are not going to change too much. But other living expenses might change. For example, you might need to increase your food budget to allow for eating more meals out while you are going to school. You might be eating on the run—or you might not have as much time to cook.

✛ **Change in childcare expenses.** You might need to enlist more babysitting or childcare services to cover times when you are in class or studying. (Note that our college rankings include this as part of the metric called "services for adult students.")

- ✛ **Change in transportation expenses.** Unless you are taking all of your classes online, you will need to figure out if there will be extra costs in terms of driving (gas and parking) or public transit to get you to and from classes.
- ✛ **Foregone wages.** You might be in a job where you have the option of working occasional overtime hours for additional pay. When you are going back to college, you may be less inclined to work those extra hours, or you may even choose to negotiate a part-time or reduced schedule with your employer in order to make it all work. If you think that those choices will help you succeed in your studies, then absolutely choose them! Just keep in mind that this may affect your income, so consider foregone wages to be a very real cost of going to school.

As you start to look at individual colleges and what they cost, consider all of these costs and how they may differ for each college. The costs will depend on how easy the college is to get to, whether you would be taking classes online, whether they offer cheaper textbook options, etc. Here is a worksheet to help you think through these costs and compare them. *This worksheet is designed for someone who is planning to continue to work at their current job and remain in their current living situation.*

CUTTING COSTS

As you consider what it will cost to go to college, think about ways that you can adjust some of the numbers in your cost comparison worksheet:

- ✛ **Can you reduce the number of courses you need to take to complete a degree?** If you ever earned credit from another college, some of those credits may transfer. If you have a lot of learning from your work or other experiences, could that be evaluated for prior learning assessment credit? If the colleges you are considering offer those options, then you might be able to reduce the tuition and fees in your cost estimate. (See chapter 10 for more information about these options.)
- ✛ **Can you opt for taking some classes at a community college?** Check with the colleges you are considering to see if credits from a community college will transfer and count toward a

College Cost Comparison Worksheet

	College 1	College 2	College 3

Tuition costs

How many courses will you take? Multiply cost per credit hour x number of credits you plan to take. The number of courses you need to take may depend on whether you have transfer credits or prior learning that can count toward your degree.

Note that the tuition rates may be different for taking individual classes as a part-time student vs. attending as a full-time student.

$ _____ $ _____ $ _____

Fees

Find out what the fees will be for enrolling, including technology fees, library fees, athletic fees (if any), etc. Determine how often those fees are charged and calculate for the number of years you expect to be enrolled.

Note that the fee schedule may be different for taking individual classes as a part-time student vs. attending as a full-time student.

$ _____ $ _____ $ _____

Books and supplies

Check the college's website to see if it provides an estimate. If information is not available, budget $150 per course.

$ _____ $ _____ $ _____

Technology costs

Do you need to purchase a laptop? Do you have broadband internet access at home, or will you need to add that? Determine what that extra cost will be. The laptop would be a onetime cost, but the internet fees will be monthly for as long as you will need them.

$ _____ $ _____ $ _____

Meals and other living expenses

Do you expect to eat more takeout when you take on college courses? Determine what that extra cost will be for the number of years you expect to be enrolled.

$ _____ $ _____ $ _____

College Cost Comparison Worksheet *(Continued)*

	College 1	College 2	College 3
	_____	_____	_____

Childcare

Will you need to pay more in babysitting and childcare costs in order to go to school? Determine what that extra cost will be for the number of years you expect to be enrolled.

$ _____ $ _____ $ _____

Transportation

Will you be driving to class and paying for parking? Will you be taking public transit? Determine what that extra cost will be for the number of years you expect to be enrolled.

$ _____ $ _____ $ _____

Foregone wages

Do you expect to cut back on overtime or work hours? Consider whether you expect to earn less in salary while you are going back to school. This is not a cost you will pay for as you do a grocery bill or tuition bill, but it will decrease the amount of money you will have available to cover all the other costs, so you need to factor it in. Determine what that extra cost will be for the number of years you expect to be enrolled.

$ _____ $ _____ $ _____

Other

What other expenses might you have in order to make it possible to go to college?

_____

$ _____ $ _____ $ _____

TOTAL COST
Total all columns here.
This is the total cost to you of going to school.

$ _____ $ _____ $ _____

Full-Time or Part-Time?

If you continue to work full-time while going to school, most likely you will only go to school part-time. This could be a very practical way to finish your degree since you will continue to earn money and not interrupt your career.

But might it make sense to go full-time? If you go to school full-time, you may be more likely to finish and you will finish sooner than if you go part-time.

There also may be financial benefits to going full-time. By not working, you will reduce your family's income, which might make you eligible for more financial aid—and some of that financial aid may provide funds to cover some living expenses. Talk to a financial aid advisor at a college to explore your options.

degree there. If so, consider whether you might start out at a community college to lower your overall costs. Starting out with a lower-cost option also can be a good way to get your feet wet as you get used to going back to school.

✛ **Can you trim some of your current living expenses?** If you are busy going back to college, you may not have the time to do some of the other things you typically do in your free time. Do you expect to have less time to go to the movies or take vacations? Whatever expenses you cut from your current budget can offset some of the other costs like foregone wages or childcare.

How to Pay for It

Now that you have a good idea of what it is going to cost you to go to college, it's time to figure out how to pay for it. There are lots of options for you to explore—yes, some of those options are loans. But there are other things that you should consider first, including grant aid, help from your employer, help from the college, scholarships, your savings, federal loans—and, only after you've considered all of those sources, perhaps consider loans from private banks.

FEDERAL STUDENT AID

The federal government may be a source of funds to pay for your education, based on information you submit online through the Free Application for Federal Student Aid, or FAFSA. There are three types of aid:

1. Grants, which are funds for tuition for low-income students (and sometimes also for living expenses) that do not have to be paid back
2. Work study, which can provide students with a part-time job while taking classes
3. Loans, which allow students to borrow money that needs to be paid back with interest

Resources to Pay for College

1. Federal or state student aid, including Pell grants and GI Bill benefits
2. Help from your employer's tuition assistance program
3. Price reductions or scholarships from the college
4. Other scholarships
5. Personal savings
6. Federal loans
7. Private bank loans, ONLY if necessary

In this section, we will focus on the grants that are available. For more detailed information, visit http://studentaid.gov.

The Most Common Types of Federal Grants

✢ **The Federal Pell Grant.** This government-funded grant provides financial aid for low-income college students. Applicants must demonstrate the requisite level of financial need to be considered. Grant awards are determined by financial need and the full-time or part-time status of the student. Students are limited to no more than twelve semesters of aid through this program. The maximum award was $5,815 for the 2016–17 school year.

What's a grant? A grant is money for your education—either from a college or from the federal government that you don't have to pay back.

If you have a choice between a grant and a loan, take the grant!

> **Are you a military veteran or on active duty in the military?**
> If so, you might be eligible for grant aid through your veterans administration (VA) or military benefits. The GI Bill is an especially good resource for veterans who qualify. See chapter 12 for more information.

✛ **The Federal Supplemental Educational Opportunity Grant (FSEOG).** The FSEOG is available to students who have qualified for the Pell grant but still have significant financial need.

✛ **The Federal TEACH Grant.** The TEACH Grant is an example of an award-for-service program. The grant provides federal funding to students who agree to take a teaching position in a high-need field, or critical-shortage facility, following graduation. If recipients do not meet their service obligations, the funds received will be converted to a direct unsubsidized loan.

✛ **Iraq and Afghanistan Service Grant.** If a student does not meet the income requirements for the Pell grant, but the student's parent/guardian was a member of the U.S. armed forces and died as a result of military service performed in Iraq or Afghanistan after the events of 9/11, the student may be eligible for funding under this grant.

STATE AID

Don't forget about your state! There are many states that offer resources to people going back to school. Generally, information is available on the website of your state higher education agency. Some states are experimenting with "free college" initiatives that may include options for you as an adult. But more likely you will find special state scholarships or grants, lists of private scholarships, state loan repayment programs, retraining grants for specific occupations, disability grants, and other options (Tanabe 2009, 126).

Here are the names of the higher-education agencies in each state to start exploring:

AK: Alaska Commission on Postsecondary Education

AL: Alabama Commission on Higher Education

AR: Arkansas Department of Higher Education

AZ: Arizona Commission for Postsecondary Education

CA: California Student Aid Commission

CO: Colorado Commission on Higher Education

CT: Connecticut Department of Higher Education

DC: District of Columbia State Education Office

DE: Delaware Higher Education Commission

FL: Florida Department of Education Office of Student Financial Assistance

GA: Georgia Student Finance Commission

HI: Hawaii State Postsecondary Education Commission

IA: Iowa College Student Aid Commission

ID: Idaho State Board of Education

IL: Illinois Student Assistance Commission

IN: State Student Assistance Commission of Indiana

KS: Kansas Board of Regents

KY: Kentucky Higher Education Assistance Authority

LA: Louisiana Office of Student Financial Assistance

MA: Massachusetts Department of Higher Education Office of Student Financial Assistance

MD: Maryland Higher Education Commission

ME: Finance Authority of Maine

MI: Michigan Higher Education Assistance Authority

MN: Minnesota Office of Higher Education

MO: Missouri Department of Higher Education

MS: Mississippi State Office of Financial Aid

MT: Montana Guaranteed Student Loan Program—Commissioner of Higher Education

NC: College Foundation of North Carolina

ND: North Dakota University System

NE: State of Nebraska Coordinating Commission for Postsecondary Education

NH: New Hampshire Postsecondary Education Commission

NJ: New Jersey Higher Education Student Assistance Authority

NM: New Mexico Higher Education Department

NV: Nevada Commission on Postsecondary Education

NY: New York State Higher Education Services Corporation

OH: Ohio Board of Regents

OK: Oklahoma State Regents for Higher Education

OR: Oregon Student Assistance Commission

PA: Pennsylvania Higher Education Assistance Agency

RI: Rhode Island Higher Education Assistance Authority

SC: South Carolina Commission on Higher Education

SD: South Dakota Board of Regents

TN: Tennessee Higher Education Commission

TX: Texas Higher Education Coordinating Board

UT: Utah Higher Education Assistance Authority

VA: State Council of Higher Education for Virginia

VT: Vermont Student Assistance Corporation

WA: Washington Higher Education Coordinating Board

WI: Wisconsin Higher Educational Aids Board

WV: West Virginia Higher Education Policy Commission—Financial Aid and Outreach Services

WY: Wyoming Student Loan Corporation

Federal Loans

When grants, scholarships, and employer assistance are not enough, your next option is a federal student loan. You may have heard scary stories about people with hundreds of thousands in student loan debt. You will not be that person if you choose your college wisely. The reality is that most student loan debt never gets that high. There is nothing wrong with taking on a little debt if the result is going to improve your career prospects and your earnings. But, as student loan expert Sandy Baum writes in her book *Student Debt*, "No one should borrow money to go to a postsecondary institution with an abysmal graduation rate or poor job outcomes for those who do graduate. . . . But that doesn't mean that all borrowing for college is bad. It just has to be cautious and well informed" (Baum 2016).

The process for federal loans is the same as for grants—you need to fill out the FAFSA! Here are some things to consider when it comes to loans:

- ✣ **Federal loans are usually better than private loans.** Federal loans typically have lower interest rates and more flexible repayment plans. You would be wise to avoid private loans because they typically do not offer the same benefits as the federal loans do in terms of low interest rates and good repayment options. Private loans often have variable rates rather than fixed, they may require that you begin repayment immediately rather than after graduation, and they may not have the consumer protections that you will have with a federal loan.

- ✣ **Borrow only what you need.** You may be approved for an amount much larger than you actually need. Try to limit the amount you borrow so that you are keeping your debt as low as possible. If you are only taking classes half time so that you can work, you may be eligible to take loans to cover living expenses as well. Don't take that money unless you need it! You could end up owing more than someone who is going to school full-time because you will be taking longer to finish.

- ✣ **Consider your salary after graduation.** Calculate what your student loan payments will be if you borrow a certain amount. Will the starting salary you expect post-graduation allow you to improve your financial situation and pay back your loans? If not, figure out how you can pursue your degree at a lower cost. Instead of a private school, look for a public four-year college or a community college. You don't want to have the career of your dreams but then be saddled by a debt you struggle to repay.

How to Get Federal Grants and Loans: the FAFSA!

FAFSA Basics

To access any federal funds from the U.S. Department of Education, you will need to fill out the FAFSA, or Free Application for Federal Student Aid, which can be found at www.FAFSA.gov. Most of the grants through the federal government are based on financial need, and the FAFSA is the form that communicates the basics of your financial situation.

To fill out the FAFSA you will need to provide things like your social security number and driver's license number, as well as details on the number of dependents you have and whether anyone else in your family is currently in college. You will also need to provide detailed financial information including:

+ Information on your recent federal tax returns
+ Untaxed income including child support, interest income, and veteran benefits
+ Other financial information like your savings and checking account balances, investments, and other assets

The government will use all of this information to calculate your Expected Family Contribution (EFC) to your education. Different formulas

Should I put tuition on my credit card? Fast answer: no! It's not a good idea to use your credit card for tuition unless you plan to pay that credit card bill off immediately. Credit cards have much higher interest rates than loans, and federal loans will have the option of income-based schedules for repayment.

If you need help paying for college, take the time to fill out the FAFSA and get the loans that were designed for college studies.

are used for traditional-aged students (dependent students) than for adults (independent students).

If you are eligible for a grant, the college you apply to will subtract your EFC from the cost of attendance at that school to determine how much aid you may be able to receive.

Special FAFSA Tips

+ **Remember that the FAFSA is *free*.** There is no charge to apply.
+ **Don't miss the deadline.** You can submit the FAFSA as early as October 1 for the following school year. But check with the college to find out if it has specific "priority deadlines" for submitting your FAFSA application for the term that you plan to enroll in. Meeting this deadline will ensure that you are considered for the maximum amount of aid available from a limited pool of funds.
+ **Submit it, even if you don't think you'll qualify for federal grants.** Most colleges will base their own grant and scholarships on the FAFSA. You also will need it to apply for any federal loans.
+ **Consider the tradeoffs of working less.** If you are thinking about whether or not to reduce your work schedule or quit your job in order to go to school full-time, consider whether that decision might have an impact on your eligibility for federal aid. Contact the financial aid office at the school to get specific information about whether a change in your employment would make a difference in the financial aid you would receive.

Complete the FAFSA at http://FAFSA.gov.

HELP FROM YOUR EMPLOYER'S TUITION ASSISTANCE PROGRAM

Many employers offer tuition assistance as a benefit for their employees. It may be called a tuition assistance program, an education benefit, or something else.

These programs vary widely from employer to employer, but if you have this as an option, you should absolutely take advantage of it. In most cases, it is like getting free money to pay for your education.

> Even though I filled out a FAFSA, I still didn't know about student loans—I didn't understand. I didn't know what a Pell grant was. I had to manually apply. I was so worried about how I'd pay for the credits. One morning—I went in and I talked to a financial advisor, and he showed me a Pell grant chart—and showed me that the Pell grant would pay for my whole tuition. I wish I would have had a better understanding before. I didn't know what all that was.
>
> —Andy, adult student, age 30,
> DePaul University School for New Learning

Ask your human resources department if this is a benefit where you work, and if so, find out the details of the program. There may be limits on the amount of money that is available per year (typically, employers will not cover benefits exceeding $5,250 per year because of tax implications). You may be required to pay the tuition with your own money and then be reimbursed later. Or, you may be limited to certain degree programs that your employer values more than others.

Here are some specific questions to ask:

+ Is there a tuition benefit or educational assistance benefit?
+ Are there restrictions on which kind of degree or certificate programs will be covered?
+ What specific expenses are covered by the program? In addition to tuition, does it cover all fees? Books and supplies? Transportation?
+ Are there specific colleges that are "preferred providers" of this company/organization? If so, do they offer tuition breaks or special programs for employees of this company/organization?
+ What is the process for applying for these tuition benefits? Does my program of study need to be approved in advance of enrollment? Are there specific deadlines for submitting required forms?
+ How much is the benefit per year?
+ Will the program pay my tuition bill directly (prepay)? Or will I need to pay the tuition bill and submit for a reimbursement? If

it is a reimbursement, does that take place after I pay the bill or after I successfully complete the course(s)?

✛ Are there conditions attached to this benefit? For example, am I obligated to stay at this employer for a certain number of years after using the benefit? Or do I need to earn a minimum grade in order to qualify for reimbursement?

Once you find out how to access these resources, make sure you get all of your paperwork in on time to take advantage of these benefits.

GRANTS, SCHOLARSHIPS, AND PAYMENT PLANS FROM THE COLLEGE

The college you attend might offer grants and scholarships as well. As you are applying to a particular college, ask the financial aid office about these options and get detailed information on the application process.

Colleges often offer payment plans that might be helpful to you, but be careful to understand all of the terms of the plan. You might not be able to register for the next semester if you have not paid the prior term in full.

OTHER SCHOLARSHIPS

Don't leave money on the table! You might be able to find other kinds of scholarships to help you pay for college. Scholarships are usually "free money," but check the fine print in case you are required to meet certain conditions. There are a lot of different entities that offer scholarships, including corporations, community groups, individuals, foundations, clubs,

A Word from the Experts

The academic road and financial road are very different paths so it's important to be thinking about both early. Consider how you'll pay for college, not just this term, but in the terms after that until you graduate.

—*Scott Gabbert, academic advisor,*
DePaul University School for New Learning

and churches. You will need to do some research to find a scholarship that you are eligible for, and you will need to spend time preparing the application materials. If you do find something that seems like it's targeted to you, give it a shot—and treat it as seriously as you would a job application. Here are some places to start looking online:

- ✛ Adult Learner's Guide to Finding Scholarships and Grants by St. Leo University. This downloadable publication is a guidebook for adults on scholarships and grants. It provides links to searchable scholarship databases and a list of select scholarships for adults.
- ✛ Big Future by the College Board. The College Board has a site that allows you to search for scholarships based on over two dozen criteria, including "returning adult student."
- ✛ Peterson's. Peterson's offers a useful searchable database on scholarships.
- ✛ FastWeb. This website has a searchable database with many options for students over age twenty-five.

SAVINGS

Grants, scholarships, and employer tuition assistance should be where you look first when it comes to thinking about how to pay. If you have exhausted those options, the next stop is your own money. You don't want to spend all of your savings—you would be wise to keep some of it on hand just in case unexpected expenses come up while you are in school. But if you have additional savings, you might consider using some of that for college rather than taking out a loan.

If you have a lot of time before you expect to be paying tuition, consider starting a college savings program. There are special savings accounts designed to save for college like the Coverdell Education Savings Account, 529 plans, or state prepaid tuition plan. These may have some tax benefits that you can take advantage of.

Some people opt to take funds out of their retirement accounts to pay for college. While that may be permissible under the tax laws, it may not be in your best interest down the road when you need that money for retirement. Federal loans are usually a better choice.

ONE OTHER THING TO CONSIDER: INCOME TAX BENEFITS

If you have to use your own money to pay for college, it may not be a total loss because those expenditures may help you qualify for some breaks at tax time. There are two tax credit programs that you may qualify for. If not, you have the option of using the education tax deduction.

The **American Opportunity Tax Credit** allows you to claim a credit of up to $2,500 for qualified education expenses for each student who qualifies. You can take the credit for only four years for the same student, and the student must be enrolled at least half time for at least one academic period during the tax year.

What's the difference between a tax credit and a tax deduction? A tax credit reduces the amount of money you owe to the federal government by the amount of the credit. So if you qualify for a $4,000 tax credit and your overall tax liability to the IRS is $11,000, then your tax liability is reduced to $7,000.

A **tax deduction** reduces the amount of your taxable income. So you will probably owe fewer taxes, but it won't be dollar-for-dollar.

If you have a choice, go for the tax credit!

> What do I wish I had known earlier? I regret not knowing how all these schools have their own scholarships on their websites. Had I known about that, I would have saved thousands of dollars.
>
> —*Alex, adult student, age 30, Moraine Valley Community College and DePaul University School for New Learning*

The **Lifetime Learning Credit** allows you to claim a credit of up to $2,000 for qualified expenses per student. There is no limit on the number of times you can use this credit.

If you do not qualify for these credits, you may be able to take the **Tuition and Fees Deduction** for $2,000 to $4,000.

There are income limits for both the credits and the deductions.

Keep in mind that you cannot combine these credits and deductions in any way, so choose the best one for which you qualify. The credits will give you more tax savings than the deduction so, if you can, claim the credit.

Read more about these options at the IRS website, Tax Benefits for Education Information Center.

Putting It All Together: The Financial Aid Shopping Sheet

The colleges you are considering will likely give you a lot of information on your financial aid options as part of the admissions process. Some colleges have started to use the federal government's financial aid shopping sheet, shown on the following page. You can use this to compare aid packages offered by the different colleges you are considering.

University of the United States (UUS)
Student Name, Identifier

⬇ Download

Costs in the 2014-15 year

Estimated Cost of Attendance   **$X,XXX** / yr

Tuition and fees	$ X,XXX
Housing and meals	X,XXX
Books and supplies	X,XXX
Transportation	X,XXX
Other education costs	X,XXX

Grants and scholarships to pay for college

Total Grants and Scholarships ("Gift" Aid; no repayment needed)   **$X,XXX** / yr

Grants and scholarships from your school	$ X,XXX
Federal Pell Grant	X,XXX
Grants from your state	X,XXX
Other scholarships you can use	X,XXX

What will you pay for college

Net Costs   **$X,XXX** / yr
(Cost of attendance minus total grants and scholarships)

Options to pay net costs

Work options

Work-Study (Federal, state, or institutional)	$ X,XXX

Loan Options*

Federal Perkins Loan	$ X,XXX
Federal Direct Subsidized Loan	X,XXX
Federal Direct Unsubsidized Loan	X,XXX

*Recommended amounts shown here. You may be eligible for a different amount. Contact your financial aid office.

Other options

Family Contribution   **$X,XXX** / yr
(As calculated by the institution using information reported on the FAFSA or to your institution.)

- Payment plan offered by the institution
- Parent or Graduate PLUS Loans
- Military and/or National Service benefits
- Non-Federal private education loan

Graduation Rate
Percentage of full-time students who graduate within 6 years

XX.X%

Low	Medium	High

Loan Default Rate
Percentage of borrowers entering repayment and defaulting on their loan

X.X%   X.X%

This institution   National

Median Borrowing
Students who borrow at UUS typically take out $X,XXX in Federal loans for their undergraduate study. The Federal loan payment over 10 years for this amount is approximately $X,XXX per month. Your borrowing may be different.

$

Repaying your loans
To learn about loan repayment choices and work out your Federal Loan monthly payment, go to:
http://studentaid.ed.gov/repay-loans/understand/plans

For more information and next steps:
University of the United States (UUS)
Financial Aid Office

123 Main Street
Anytown, ST 12345
Telephone: (123) 456-7890
E-mail: financialaid@uus.edu

> I was unaware of how academia worked. It never occurred to me to do anything other than pull out my credit card and pay for it. I paid for it all in my undergraduate program. When it came time to get my master's—I was at this point really aware that I needed to find financial resources.
>
> —*Cristy, adult student, age 63, SUNY Empire State College*

RESOURCES

U.S. Department of Education. A great source of information on financial aid is the federal agency that awards the money. Check out the resources and guides that are available at the Federal Student Aid website at http://student aid.ed.gov.

Video Guides to Federal Financial Aid. If you would like additional help in understanding more about federal aid and how to complete the FAFSA, there are some online videos that have been produced by Bank of America and the Khan Academy that might be helpful to you. One in particular— "How to Finance a Return to College"—is designed specifically for the adult learner. You can find these videos at the Better Money Habits website.

Mapping Your Financial Journey: Helping Adults Plan for College. National College Transition Network and National Endowment for Financial Education (NEFE) collaborated to create this publication, which is geared toward financial planning for adult students intending to go to college.

CHAPTER 8

It's About Time!: Finding the Program That Fits Your Schedule and Timeline

	SUNDAY	MONDAY	TUESDAY	WEDNESDAY	THURSDAY	FRIDAY	SATURI
8AM					Laundry!		
9AM	Hike w. kids	Office	8.30— Mom's DR appt.	Work from home	Office	8.30 Meeting re: potholes & traffic	Devon's soccer game
10AM			Office (Bring Lunch!)			Office (Bring Lunch!)	
11AM							
12PM	Picnic Lunch	Post Off Bank. Lunch		Groceries & Lunch	Library		
1PM	Reading for class	Office		Work from home	Office		

Finding time for your education can be a challenge in and of itself. How many times have you said, "I'd love to get my degree, but I just don't have time right now"? Well, now is the time to find the time and make sure it's blocked out on your calendar. College classes have never been as flexible as they are today. And, with some creative thinking and your strong desire to make it happen, you will find the time!

It all starts with your calendar. Take a look at your typical week. When do you have availability for taking classes and studying? How does your personal body clock align with your calendar and existing responsibilities? Can you study in the early mornings, or maybe after the kids have gone to bed? How do your weekends look?

Take a highlighter and mark the days and times you think you could study and attend classes (either online or in person). You'll see a pattern emerge. Now think about when you're most productive—is it in the morn-

Your Calendar

	SUNDAY	MONDAY	TUESDAY	WEDNESDAY	THURSDAY	FRIDAY	SATURDAY
6AM							
7AM							
8AM							
9AM							
10AM							
11AM							
12PM							
1PM							
2PM							
3PM							
4PM							
5PM							
6PM							
7PM							
8PM							
9PM							

A Word from the Experts

When I work with adult students, one of the first things I start with is a calendar of the week and we go through, realistically, which hours are open and which are busy in their schedule. It is usually a moment of revelation for students. They think, no wonder I'm having so much trouble with this, I only have five hours free in my week to get everything done for school!

—Debbie Smith, associate director of academic advising and academic advisor, University of North Carolina–Charlotte

ings or are you a night person? Include this in your thinking. Consider when your work is at its busiest and when your workload eases up a bit. All of these considerations will help you find the time for your actual classes as well as the studying and work required to succeed in them.

Your time availability is as important to your ultimate success as hard work and studying! It's a valuable resource that will help you not only start college, but persist to the finish line.

Yes, you can find a college program that fits your schedule. The choices available to you today to help you save time (and money) are plentiful. In order to make a good decision, be sure to do your research before committing to a college or university program. Time is a key factor in this decision in three ways: scheduling, pace, and duration. You may end up being more successful—and finishing more quickly—with a program that is **schedule sensitive**, **a time saver**, or **differently paced**. You might also find a college that offers all three!

Schedule Sensitive

First, it's a matter of being able to *find the time* in your schedule for your education. Pick the college that offers you the kind of programming that fits your busy lifestyle and your particular life and work circumstances. This choice is just as important as choosing the academic or career program that aligns with your career goals. The reason is simple. You want the best chance to complete your studies and the greatest opportunity

It's a Matter of Time

Schedule Sensitive: Does the college offer programs that work with your schedule?

Time Saver: Does the college offer ways for you to finish your degree in a shorter period of time?

Differently Paced: Can you handle a program that moves more quickly through lessons and courses? If so, that can save you a lot of time.

to succeed. If the schedule is a mismatch from the start, it's going to be harder for you to stick with it and reach your goals.

Here are some of the different options you may have at the colleges you are considering:

+ **Traditional daytime classes.** This might be an option for you, particularly if you are a stay-at-home parent or if you work a swing or night shift. Day classes are usually offered two or three days a week: either on Tuesday and Thursday or on Monday, Wednesday, and Friday. With good planning and assistance from an academic advisor or admissions counselor, you might be able to schedule all of your classes for the same days of the week. You may be able to schedule them in the early mornings, or maybe midday works best for you. Traditional daytime classes usually are a semester (fifteen to sixteen weeks) long. If you're a parent, the academic calendar aligns fairly closely with your children's school calendar.

+ **Evening and weekend classes.** Colleges that serve the adult learner usually offer evening courses, and some even offer courses on the weekends. Evening classes run in semesters or trimesters. If evenings seem to be when you can find the time to attend courses, there is bound to be a great community college close by or other colleges in your area may offer evening classes.

A benefit of attending classes at night or on the weekend is that you'll find fellow students who are juggling work and life responsibilities as well. This extra support and encouragement

> **A word of caution.** When you add evening classes onto a full day's schedule, it can be exhausting. Be sure to consider your commute time and when you might be able to grab a bite to eat if you'll be coming straight from work or other obligations. You might want to start out slowly by taking one evening course before attempting to take more. Attending night school is more of a marathon than a sprint. You don't want to burn yourself out quickly.

from folks who are dealing with many of the same challenges can be helpful.

+ **Online programs.** Online options are more common than ever—in 2014, 5.8 million students took online courses. That's one in every four students! (WCET 2016)

Online programs generally allow you to participate in a class whenever it is convenient for you. Most online courses are asynchronous, meaning you do not have to be in a class at a certain time. Rather, you complete your studies and assignments independently, submitting them by deadlines and due dates. Online courses enable you to be online working in the middle of the night, on your lunch hour, or any time that suits your schedule and body clock. This is helpful for people whose schedules are different every week or otherwise unpredictable. See also chapter 9 to help you think through whether online courses might be a good choice for you.

Time Savers

Many college programs are also designed to save you time. Accelerated programs are structured to accelerate degree completion through a required sequence of course modules or they may condense courses from 15 weeks to 7–8-week terms. Other options include completion colleges (which will accept a lot of your previously earned credits through transfer), summer terms, and getting credit for what you already know (also known as prior learning assessment).

ACCELERATED PROGRAMS

Many colleges and universities offer accelerated programs, established especially to serve the busy, working adult student. These programs aren't for everyone, but if you are highly motivated and the academic major is interesting to you, an accelerated program could save you a lot of time and help you reach your goal more quickly.

One form of acceleration uses a cohort model—meaning you will work through the courses with a group of students that remains the same throughout the program. These programs may require that you have some college credits already under your belt before you can start—for example, an accelerated bachelor's program may require that you have already earned sixty credit hours. With an accelerated program, you will work through a series of courses or modules meeting once a week over a 12- to 18-month period, essentially completing your major. Majors for these programs are usually management/leadership oriented, with popular majors in business or healthcare. If you are interested in this model, you should seek advising assistance at the college to ensure you take the right courses to qualify for the program when you're ready.

Another form of acceleration is often referred to as *condensed courses*. These courses pack the content of a traditional semester-long course (16 weeks) into a 7- or 8-week period. The workload is heavier, but you're able to progress through the program more quickly, and that is particularly helpful if you are attending part-time.

College Programs by Time Factor

Schedule Sensitive:

- ✦ Daytime programs
- ✦ Evening/weekend programs
- ✦ Online programs

Time Saver:

- ✦ Accelerated programs
- ✦ Completion colleges
- ✦ Summer terms
- ✦ Testing for credit/prior learning assessment

Differently Paced:

- ✦ Self-paced online courses (free or low-cost options are available)
- ✦ Competency-based programs

COMPLETION COLLEGES

The missions of some colleges and universities are devoted to serving adult students. These colleges offer maximum flexibility and transferability of previous college work. Students choose these colleges to *finish their degrees*. Students save time because these colleges require students only to take courses that complete their remaining degree requirements.

Completion colleges are ideal for the student who may have taken and passed a few courses at one college, a few at another college, a few at a third college, etc. Not all colleges will give you transfer credit for all of those courses but completion colleges generally do, and they find a way to make them all count toward your degree.

Institutions such as Excelsior College, Thomas Edison State University, and Charter Oak State College are among the largest completion colleges serving students throughout the United States and internationally (see box for other examples). Their offerings include online courses, exams that allow you to test for credit, flexible degree programs, recognition of your previous college coursework with modest to no residency requirements—that means they may not insist that you earn at least a significant number of your credits from them ("in residence").

If you have already accumulated college credits from the last time you attended college, be sure to check out one of these completion colleges and the colleges and universities near you that might have a degree completion program designed especially for busy adult students.

SUMMER TERMS

Is summer school for you? For some people, summer sessions are a great time to make good progress toward your educational goals. Summer terms are generally shorter in duration, which could make the workload a bit more intense since it's compressed into a shorter time period. However, summer terms can work particularly well with some busy people's lives. Some adult students find it easier to make time for classes while their children are in summer camps and activities, which might be a less strenuous time than the regular school year. Others take vacation days to allow enough time for the workload. But for other people, summer is the most difficult time to go to college. Whatever your schedule is, be sure to consider the momentum that can be created by taking a summer course or two.

TESTING FOR CREDIT/PRIOR LEARNING ASSESSMENT

As you can see, there are lots of choices for you to make when it comes to choosing a program that is right for you. An often overlooked consid-

> It's important to know the time commitment—not just the in-class commitment but the homework and class time. Fellow students want to meet at weird times—it works fine for people who are nineteen years old, but not for me.
>
> —*Clifton, adult student, age 33, University of Maryland University College*

> Being exhausted—working full-time—driving to school, it can be tough. But you have to stay committed. . . . Being thirty, it's more difficult for me . . . I have no social life right now. I'm accepting that tradeoff because it's worth it.
>
> —*Alex, adult student, age 30, Moraine Valley Community College and DePaul University School for New Learning*

eration is taking tests for credit and other forms of prior learning assessment (PLA). There are three major testing programs: CLEP (College-Level Examination Program), DSST exams (formerly DANTES Subject Standardized Tests), and UExcel Credit by Exam. **Always check with your college advisor to make sure these tests will count toward your degree or certificate requirements.** For more information on CLEP tests, go https://clep.collegeboard.org. For more information on DSST exams, go to www.getcollegecredit.com. And for more information on UExcel Credit by Exam, go to www.excelsior.edu/exams.

Do you speak fluent Spanish?
The CLEP Spanish exams are their most popular tests. If you speak Spanish, taking a test for credit can save you lots of time and money.

These tests, offered in a scheduled and proctored testing session, provide an excellent means for earning credits by testing, saving you time and money. Tests typically cost around $100 each; some cost a bit more and some cost less. Study guides are available for most tests and sometimes you can even take a practice test to get a better sense of what the questions are like. You can take tests to earn credits in history, literature, foreign languages, and many other subjects that may fulfill your general education, electives, and (depending upon your college's policies) major requirements. Passing one test for about $100 can yield three credit hours. *Now that's a bargain!*

If you aren't a big fan of tests, keep in mind that there are other ways to earn college credits for what you know. To learn more about all forms of prior learning assessment as a means of earning college credit for what you already may know—and at a much lower cost than taking a course—see chapter 10.

Differently Paced

Still other kinds of college programs allow you to progress through the curriculum at your own pace. You can progress quickly through subjects or topics you are familiar with and spend more time learning more challenging material.

FREE ONLINE COURSES

There are a number of ways you can independently pursue education through web providers such as Saylor Academy and massive open online courses from Coursera, EdX, and Udacity. These organizations are dedicated to making high-quality college courses available for *free*.

Also, because these courses are offered by private companies, the courses are not on the traditional

Important time-saving reminder. Make sure your previous college credits will count toward your degree requirements. When your credits count, you will save time and money—not to mention frustration! Ask about transfer credit policies.

15-week college-course schedule. You can complete the Saylor courses at your own pace; as quickly or as leisurely as you'd like. The Coursera and Udacity courses vary in duration. However, the downside is that most of the courses are not offered for college credit. So, if you strategically take one, check with the college where you expect to enroll to find out if they have ways to award credit for these courses through some form of prior learning assessment. Proving what you have learned from these cours-

You have to make it a priority. Check your schedules. You have to make time for school. You have this time every day at the end of the day for your family. Recreation takes a third or fourth place in your life. I don't have children that I have to cook for and come home to, so I have an advantage. I know how my workers, my classmates— some have small children. It's hard.

—*Mary, adult student, age 58, Miami Dade College*

> I liked the flexibility. You can meet with professors one-on-one, or [do] online work, or classroom small-group study sessions. I work unusual hours. I leave at 3 a.m. for work. I thought the flexibility would work best.
>
> —"Natalie," adult student, age 45, SUNY Empire State College

es can be done by taking exams (such as CLEP, DSST, and UExcel) or documenting your learning in a formal academic portfolio and submitting it for assessment by faculty, as described in the section called "Testing for credit/prior learning assessment" above. But be aware that not every college offers these options, so be sure to ask before you sign up! To learn more about prior learning assessment as a means of earning college credit, see chapter 10.

Low-cost self-paced online courses

Another option that helps you save time and money can be found at www.StraighterLine.com. StraighterLine's affordable courses are "guaranteed to transfer" to any of its one hundred accredited college and university partners. If your college accepts StraighterLine courses, you may be able to earn your general education credits for less money (and faster, too!). The pricing is based on a subscription model, in which you pay $99 per month for a membership and then only $59 per course; so if you take six courses over ten months, that will cost $1,284 as of fall 2016. You can take StraighterLine courses while enrolled in your college or prior to enrolling. These courses complement your institution's program requirements when you choose a "guaranteed transfer" partner college or university. Just make sure your college is among StraighterLine's "guaranteed transfer" partners or check with your institution before registering for StraighterLine courses.

New self-paced programs (aka competency-based education)

New self-paced, competency-based degree programs are emerging on college campuses and online throughout the United States. These programs

> I work full-time, have kids at home, and I need to work at my own pace. I have a tight schedule, deadlines. I can't be tied down to a situation where I have to go to a classroom at a specific time. I need to be able to take the class when I have time, which varies every day. I might have had an hour in the morning, the next day, I have an hour in the afternoon to concentrate.... Find the program that you can manage with your schedule. One that is flexible. I wouldn't have been able to complete a program that had a rigid schedule. No way. Finding the right program that can meet your timeline requirements was essential.
>
> —*Keith, adult student, age 47, Capella University*

have a faculty-determined list of academic (and sometimes workplace) competencies that are required in order to earn the degree or certificate. These competencies are reflective of what a student needs to know and be able to do. Students progress through the program by demonstrating competencies through projects, assignments, and assessments (or tests).

In some of the programs, you have the option of going through the material at your own pace—faster when you understand the material quickly, and slower if you need more time to learn difficult concepts. If you already know the competency, you can go straight to demonstrating that competency through a special assessment. If you pass the assessment, you move on to the next set of competencies. This feature also allows you to control the pace of your studies and go more quickly if you come to the program with a lot of prior learning. Many of these programs set up tuition based upon a subscription model—meaning you pay a flat fee for tuition per term rather than paying per credit hour. For students with a lot of prior learning or who can learn new materials quickly, the flat rate allows for an "all you can eat" kind of approach. Pay one price and learn as many competencies as you can during a defined period of time. This model gives some students the opportunity to save money and time.

These programs may be referred to by the colleges as competency-based education or CBE. It is recommended that you make a full commitment to complete the CBE program, because transferring the competencies down the road to a new college may be difficult.

Summary of Types of Programs

TYPE OF COLLEGE PROGRAM	BEST FOR:
Schedule Sensitive	
Daytime program	*Adult who works nights or swing shifts. Stay-at-home parents.*
Evening/weekend program	*Adult who works during the day and has a babysitter available in the evenings.*
Online program	*Adult who is computer literate and highly motivated. Perfect for adults who travel frequently or whose schedules may be irregular or unpredictable from week to week.*
Time Saver	
Accelerated programs	*Adult who can devote more time to studying as required to progress more quickly through the curriculum. In some cases, the work is condensed into a shorter period of time.*
Completion colleges	*Adult with credits from one or more colleges in the past, or adults with considerable learning from work or life experiences.*
Summer terms	*Adult who can take vacation time or is generally more available during the summer months.*
Prior learning assessment	*Adult who has already acquired college-level knowledge in a particular subject or discipline.*
Differently Paced	
Self-paced online courses	*Adult who wants to progress at his or her own pace or who wants to try out college courses at a low cost.*
Competency-based programs	*Adult who wants to progress at his or her own pace and is self-motivated. Adult who is familiar with the content of the program through related work experience.*

Competency-Based Education Program Examples (All Available Online)

Western Governors University

University of Wisconsin Flexible Option

University of Northern Arizona's Personalized Learning Program

Brandman University

Texas Affordable Baccalaureate Program

Capella University FlexPath

. . . and many more!

CHAPTER 9

Face-to-Face or Cyberspace: Deciding What Works for You

When it comes to deciding on the right academic program to fit your career aspirations, life goals, and your schedule, how your program is delivered is a major consideration. Finding what works for your schedule and your learning preferences is important. For instance, as we discussed in chapter 6, if your program is offered only on campus and you find yourself needing to be on campus right after work, the dreaded commute could eventually discourage you, especially in bad weather. On the other hand, if you prefer opportunities to meet new people and being present for the professor's lecture, an online program may not be right for you. Sounds simple, right?

There are a lot of different kinds of considerations when deciding whether or not to take online courses. In this chapter we will help you think through the various pros and cons of both on-campus and online options.

Thinking Through "Bricks and Mortar" versus Online

As you consider your college choices, you can opt for the classroom experience—in a physical, "bricks and mortar" classroom on a college campus—or you can expand your options by considering taking some or all of your classes online.

THE VALUE OF A "BRICKS AND MORTAR" EXPERIENCE

Picture college and you likely think of a large expanse of green grass with young students studying and chatting. Even in this world of online learning, a "bricks and mortar" classroom experience is still an option, and a very popular one! Whether a school is made up of plain-looking average buildings or fancy ones with impressive architecture, there are many benefits to being on campus for your classes. Colleges that are interested in serving adult learners like you will offer evening or weekend courses in-person, and many accelerated online programs may have face-to-face aspects (see chapter 8 for more information about how different programs are scheduled and paced and otherwise help you save time).

Choosing a college close to home or close to work presents an opportunity for you to truly **go** to college! What does *going to college*, in a real college classroom, mean? You will . . .

1. **Experience the college environment.** If you are taking daytime courses, you'll be able to see the campus at its best—bustling with faculty, students, and staff! All of the offices will be open, so if you need to check with the registrar to see if all of your transcripts have been sent, or stop by the financial aid office to ask a question—the offices are available to you. You'll be able to tap into any college service during daytime hours. However, if you're attending at night or on the weekend, many offices will likely be closed.

2. **Meet your instructor and fellow students in person.** There is something special about being back in a classroom with an interesting instructor and motivated students. The class interaction helps keep you attentive while the instructor teaches. If you have questions, you can usually ask them, right there, on the spot. Sometimes, camaraderie develops among students that becomes a positive force in helping you to stick with your studies.

3. **Participate in face-to-face learning.** Some students simply prefer being in a classroom for their learning experiences. Know-

ing that you will be in the same room as the instructor and other students can motivate you to come prepared for class (having read your textbook and done your assignments). If you fall behind, the face-to-face interaction will quickly pressure you to catch up and be better prepared for the next class. Being in the college environment will help you remain motivated, particularly since you have waited so long to experience it again or for the first time.

The bricks and mortar experience can fit your schedule, whether daytime, evening, weekend, or summer classes. Just be sure to factor in your commuting time, babysitting costs, and other tasks that must be set aside because you are going to college! It also demands that you be there on time and in the right place, so if the commitment is a stretch for you, perhaps you should consider an online or blended course. The good news is you have lots of options. And it will all be worth it—especially if you hang in there and reach your educational goal.

THE VALUE OF AN ONLINE LEARNING EXPERIENCE

Oftentimes, students choose an online learning experience over a face-to-face experience because of scheduling conflicts with bricks and mortar

A Word from the Experts

I usually recommend that students take one online class to test the waters before they jump in with a fully online course load. If you start out with all online classes, you might find that it's not the right option for you and that will set you back. Students have to realize that there are still deadlines to meet so to be well suited for online learning, you need to have time-management skills and self-motivation. I also think that students should like to read and write, because that's going to be the primary way that you get your instruction, to a much greater extent than in a traditional class.

—*Carey Kilmer, assistant director of continuing and distance education, South Dakota State University*

classes. Online learning is the most flexible delivery mechanism, in terms of being able to work around a student's other life and work responsibilities because they are usually *asynchronous*, meaning that you don't have to participate in the course during a specific time of day or week. You can work on the course whenever you can fit it into your schedule. This makes it great for students whose schedules are unpredictable or just don't fit within the routine schedule of bricks and mortar classes.

It is important to note, though, that online courses are not easier than courses offered in the traditional face-to-face mode. In fact, they present some unique challenges for students. The online student needs to be independent, organized, and highly motivated. Being confident in your reading and writing skills also goes a long way in successfully completing courses online.

Do You Think Online Learning Might Be a Good Choice for You?

Step one: Take a quiz to help figure out if it might be a good fit. See the quiz provided on the following page as a start. If you are still not sure, lots of online programs offer other free quizzes on their websites to help you think this through. Some states do, too. For example, the state of Washington's State Board for Community and Technical Colleges offers a quiz called "Is Online Learning for Me?"

Step two: Make sure that you have an up-to-date computer setup with a speedy, secure connection to the internet.

Step three: Before you commit yourself to a full program, take an online course tutorial or simulation as a trial run. Do you like the format? Are you able to navigate around and find what you need? Take a free test drive. Here are some examples:

✛ **Columbia College:** Explore the college's online Student Practice Course beginning with the announcements. It lays out all the components of the online courses that the college offers. You can click through the pages and see examples of student tech support and a menu where students can set preferences for the course site.

✢ **Oregon State University:** This college's website has a course demo with five demonstration modules. The modules walk you through an online classroom with sample assignments and multimedia activities from three courses.

Step four: Now you're ready to take your first online course. Are you able to stick to the schedule of lessons, discussion, and feedback? If you enjoy the experience, you will feel much more confident about signing up for future online courses and programs.

Is Online Learning Right for Me?

Will online courses fit your circumstances and lifestyle? This short questionnaire will help you determine if online learning is right for you. Answer each question and score yourself as directed at the end.

1. *My need to take this course now is:*
   A. High—I need it immediately for a specific goal.
   B. Moderate—I could take it on campus later or substitute another course.
   C. Low—it could be postponed.

2. *Feeling that I am part of a class is:*
   A. Not particularly necessary to me.
   B. Somewhat important to me.
   C. Very important to me.

3. *I would classify myself as someone who:*
   A. Often gets things done ahead of time.
   B. Needs reminding to get things done on time.
   C. Puts things off until the last minute or doesn't complete them.

4. *Classroom discussion is:*
   A. Rarely helpful to me.
   B. Sometimes helpful to me.
   C. Almost always helpful to me.

5. When an instructor hands out directions for an assignment, I prefer:
   A. Figuring out the instructions myself.
   B. Trying to follow the directions on my own, then asking for help as needed.
   C. Having the instructions explained to me.

6. I need faculty comments on my assignments:
   A. Within a few weeks, so I can review what I did.
   B. Within a few days, or I forget what I did.
   C. Right away, or I get very frustrated.

7. Considering my professional and personal schedule, the amount of time I have to work on an online course is:
   A. More than enough for an on-campus course.
   B. The same as for a class on campus.
   C. Less than for a class on campus.

8. Coming to campus on a regular schedule is:
   A. Extremely difficult for me—I have commitments during times when classes are offered.
   B. A little difficult, but I can rearrange my priorities to allow for regular attendance on campus.
   C. Easy for me.

9. As a reader, I would classify myself as:
   A. Good—I usually understand the text without help.
   B. Average—I sometimes need help to understand the text.
   C. Slower than average.

10. When I need help understanding the subject:
    A. I am comfortable approaching an instructor to ask for clarification.
    B. I am uncomfortable approaching an instructor but I can do it anyway.
    C. I never approach an instructor to admit I don't understand something.

Add 3 points for each "A" that you circled, 2 for each "B" and 1 for each "C."

If you scored 20 or more, a distance learning or online course is a real possibility for you.

If you scored between 11 and 20, distance learning or online courses may work for you, but you may need to make a few adjustments in your schedule and study habits to succeed.

If you scored 10 or fewer, distance learning or learning online may not currently be the best alternative for you; talk to an advisor about this further before you enroll.

Anatomy of an Online Course

Learning online is very convenient. You can access your online course at any time from any place that has Wi-Fi. In fact, when you look at your

Summary of Important Considerations

Bricks and Mortar versus Online Programs

	BRICKS AND MORTAR	ONLINE
Class discussions	You will benefit from hearing other students' ideas and opinions. You may or may not be expected to speak. Sometimes the discussion can run off course, but the instructor will redirect.	You will need to post to a discussion board. This means you will need to thoughtfully consider how you will add value to the online discussion. Every student is usually required to post to the discussion board, so every student's voice is heard.
Instructor interaction	Variable, depending upon the instructor's style. For extra help, you will need to make an appointment to meet with your instructor during her/his office hours.	Variable; however, you will likely be able to email your instructor directly with questions regarding assignments or topics.
Attendance	Set days/nights and times. Some courses require attendance (as part of the course grade), while others depend only upon the exams or papers due for the grade.	Generally, online courses are asynchronous, although some instructors may ask you to be online on a certain day/time—it's usually a matter of staying on track with the curriculum, working day or night, and turning in your assignments or taking quizzes on time.
Assignments	Due on particular days.	Due on particular days.
Course length	15 weeks Some condensed or accelerated courses could run 7 or 8 weeks.	Varies
Grades	Based upon assignments and exams.	Based upon assignments and exams.
Exams	Generally administered in the classroom.	Exams may be given online and completed within a certain amount of time. Other exams may require you to find a proctor (usually at a college library or testing center) to take the exam.

It was crucial to switch to online. I work my life around that. I can work my schooling around my life. I wasn't happy with bricks and mortar at all.

—Clifton, adult student, age 33,
University of Maryland University College

calendar, you can likely squeeze in online studying day or night, weekends and holidays. But, you may be wondering, what does an online course look like? And how will I know what to do?

The good news is that online learning has been around for a very long time now—long enough to make it more intuitive than ever before. In other words, online courses are set up to make it easy to find your way around the course! Online courses at any given college will probably be structured in the same way from course to course, so once you take one online course, you will know what to expect in terms of how future courses will be organized, look, and feel.

A lot of the work is done by students on their own, but many courses require participating students to post to the discussion boards on a regular basis. This is where you will engage with and get to know other students in the class. While online courses give you the freedom to work on your course at any time, there are deadlines for the assignments. Also, you can't just put off all the work until the last minute—most courses require you to do some work every week. Online learning requires you to stick with it, week to week, just like you would have to show up for class day to day in campus-based courses. You are essentially managing yourself and your time.

My daughter started kindergarten—my son was not in school yet, day care, doing it alone, it was crazy. I found Empire. One of my friends got her degree from Empire and she urged me to give it a try. I realized I could get an entire degree online! I did it, I applied, got in, and got my degree online.

—"Jean," adult student, age 35, SUNY Empire State College

Weighing the Pros and Cons

Bricks and Mortar versus Online Programs:
Summary of Important Considerations

ONLINE LEARNING

Pros	Cons
Convenience: Accommodates your schedule.	Limited cheerleading. Depending on the program, there may not be anyone monitoring your progress and cheering you on, except you!
Thoughtful Interaction—your posts to the discussion board need to add value to the discussion and must be well thought out and written.	You may miss the moment-to-moment excitement of face-to-face discussions. Discussion boards can be dry reading and aren't a perfect substitute for live conversation.
Well-designed online courses expose you to lots of voices, are designed for students with different learning styles, and can engage students in unique ways.	Poorly designed online courses are heavily text-based and can be tough to wade through.
Flexibility: If you travel for work, or have multiple commitments with family obligations, online enables you to study anytime and make progress.	It can feel like an isolated experience since so much of the motivation to persist needs to come from within.
No commute time.	Technology can sometimes be frustrating.

FACE-TO-FACE

Pros	Cons
A true college campus experience can inspire and motivate you.	You need to be there rain or shine, on time and ready to focus. Parking may be a challenge.
Being able to see and hear your professor in person.	Lectures and note taking can become tedious, especially after a long day at work or taking care of children.
Discussions enable you to hear varying perspectives along with the enthusiasm or emotions behind the ideas being shared.	Sometimes discussions can be dominated by a few people and some students find it intimidating to speak up on a topic.
Meeting fellow students face-to-face helps to form new friendships and a support network to keep learning.	The commute time.
You can usually ask your professor a question directly in class or as the class is wrapping up.	Typically, you'll move through the material at the same pace as everyone else in the course.

Helpful hints for online learners. Manage your time by blocking out hours each week to read, study, and do your online assignments. Plan for at least fifteen hours of study time for each three-credit-hour course. Do not procrastinate. Stay on track by checking in with your course frequently. Stay motivated, even if it's as simple as envisioning yourself walking across the stage at graduation!

How Do You Choose the Right Online Program?

There are many online program options—from regional and national providers to your local college right down the street. In fact, even if you choose a bricks and mortar experience, you may still need to take an on-line course or two due to the availability of the courses you will need to complete your degree requirements. That said, tuition and fees for online courses vary widely. Community college online courses tend to be the most affordable, with public four-year colleges and universities being more moderately priced, and private colleges and universities being the most expensive. There are many trade-offs to consider.

For instance, you may have heard of a particular online university or seen its advertising, but is its tuition affordable and are its programs re-spected? Just as you should do for any other school, be sure to check the college's accreditation. If it has a regional accreditation, then you can feel good about how your education will be perceived by your current and future employers.

Always check out the institution's website. If its site is easy to under-stand, provides real information, and has the tone and tenor of a college

The FlexPath program at Capella is totally online: access to teach-ers, writing center, staff. You can work on group projects but you don't have to. You're encouraged to connect with other students—you can email each other—you can talk to each other, post on the blog, etc., questions, responses, but you don't have to.

—*Keith, adult student, age 47, Capella University*

Another choice—blended courses. A blended course (also called a hybrid course) is a combination of face-to-face meetings and online work. These courses allow you to enjoy the benefits of both online and bricks and mortar courses. You won't be required to come to campus as often, but you will need to work online between face-to-face classes. Blended courses are growing in popularity and may be available to you at a college you are considering.

you might like, be sure to research it further. If the website is just a pop-up box asking for your name and contact information, be very cautious. You can be sure that this school will aggressively market to you, and this can be a red flag signaling that the educational offerings may not be the quality or caliber you are seeking.

Be prepared to ask a lot of questions before you take the leap. Consider this list of questions to ask the college before enrolling:

- How long have you been offering online courses?
- Do your alumni go on to graduate school?
- What do employers say about your programs?
- How much is the tuition per credit hour?
- What are the fees that I will be required to pay?
- How long are the courses—16 weeks, 8 weeks, 7 weeks, less?
- What is the average class size?
- Who teaches the online courses?
- If I have a question for my instructor, is there a requirement that s/he needs to get back to me within a specific time frame?
- What resources are available to me if I need help?
- How interactive are the courses? Do they use multimedia or are they primarily text based?
- What happens if I have to go out of town or am deployed?
- How will I be required to take tests? Online or in a proctored setting?
- How many students drop out of your online courses?

[
Regional accreditation means your institution has been evaluated by its peers as offering high-quality educational programs. It's sometimes called "the gold standard" in accreditations because it is often viewed as the most rigorous.
]

IF YOU WANT TO READ MORE

The Guide: A Resource for Going to College as an Adult. WICHE Cooperative for Educational Technologies, December 2012.

CHAPTER 10

Why Learn
It Twice?

One of the benefits of going to college as an adult is that you bring so much from your life and work experiences to your studies. You have been learning a lot in the years since high school, and that learning has real value to you. Your knowledge and experience can of course give you better insights into topics covered in your college classes, but there's much more. You may already have learning that can earn you college credits *before you even enroll in a single class.*

How is that possible?

Maybe you are like so many other people who have taken college classes before. Those classes may count as **transfer credits** in your new degree program. Or you may have learned a lot in the military, on the job, through volunteer work, or in many other kinds of life experiences—in some cases, that learning can count as credit through **prior learning assessment**.

Not Your First Rodeo? Make Sure Your Credits Transfer

This may not be the first time you have gone to college. Perhaps you went to college right after high school, took a few classes (or even a few semesters), and then stopped. This can happen for any number of reasons—money is tight, family responsibilities take over, a good job comes along, or life just gets in the way.

Ways to Earn Credit for What You Already Know
Transfer credit
Prior learning assessment

Perhaps over the years since high school you enrolled in college to give it a try. Or took a few community college courses that you needed to have for work reasons. Or opted to start at a community college as a cheaper alternative, with the intention to eventually transfer to a four-year school.

Many adults who are enrolling in college already have some college experiences under their belts. If you have taken college classes before and earned credit for those courses, *don't forget about those credits as you choose what college to attend now!*

Many colleges have **transfer policies** that will allow you to have your old credits count for something in your new degree program. That is important because if you can get those credits to count, that means there are fewer courses you need to take to earn your degree.

If a college will accept your old credits in transfer, that will save you a lot of time and a lot of money!

Do Your Research

Even though a lot of colleges will accept your transfer credits, you can't just assume that the college of your choice will give you credit for all of the courses you have taken before.

+ **Different colleges have different policies on transfer credits.** They may accept credits from some colleges but not others. Or they may have limits on the number of credits that they will accept in transfer.

+ **What you plan to study matters.** If your previous credits were from taking business courses, but now you want to study nursing, your business credits may not count toward your nursing degree. Also, even if the college itself allows for transfer credits, specific degree programs at that college may have stricter policies.

+ **General education course credits are a safe bet for transferring in.** Most undergraduate degree programs have general education course requirements. If your previous coursework is in general education (for example, math, English/composition, natural sciences, social sciences, humanities), those credits might be able to satisfy general education requirements in your new program.

To do an initial exploration, try using the online resource called **Transferology** (www.transferology.com). You can enter information about the courses you have already taken and learn about colleges in the Transferology network that may accept those credits.

But your best bet is to ask the colleges where you are thinking of applying and follow these steps:

+ **Find out about the college's transfer credit policy.** The website should provide some general information about how the college handles transfer students and transfer credits. Some colleges may have what are called *articulation agreements* with certain schools. This means that there is a simplified process for transferring credits from those institutions.
+ **Get a copy of your official transcripts.** A *transcript* is the official academic record of a student at a particular institution. The transcript usually lists the courses taken, grades and credits earned, and grade point average or GPA.

Are you planning to save money by starting at a community college? That's a smart option! But if your plans are to transfer to a four-year college down the road, find out whether the courses you take at the community college will count toward that next degree. You might need to talk to an admissions advisor at the four-year institution to make absolutely sure.

If you are not sure where you will go next, stick to general education courses that have a better chance of transferring.

You don't want to waste time and money taking classes that won't transfer!

- ✛ **You will need one transcript from each college where you took courses and earned credits.** There should be a way to order transcripts through each college's website. There will likely be a small cost to get the transcripts, but this is an expense you should definitely pay. If you end up getting transfer credits accepted, you'll more than make up the cost by not having to take those courses again! (And you will need copies of those transcripts later anyway, when you fill out the college application.)
- ✛ **Talk to an admissions advisor.** Before you make your final decision about where to enroll, make an appointment with someone in the admissions office to learn about whether your specific courses and credits will transfer to your new degree program.
- ✛ **Factor in transfer credit awards as you make your decision about where to go to college.** Having your previous college learning count toward your degree matters because those credits can save you a lot of time and money. You may ultimately decide to enroll in a program that does not accept many transfer credits, and that's okay. Sometimes the program that is best for you is worth it anyway.

SPECIAL CASES IN TRANSFERRING CREDITS

Are you—or have you ever been—in the military? If so, you have a special kind of transcript called the Joint Services Transcript. Colleges typically have special policies about how they award credit for the training you received in the military that is listed on that transcript. (See chapter 12 for more details.)

Have you taken courses at a university in a foreign country? If you have course credit—or even credentials or degrees—earned from a foreign country, it may be possible to have that count toward your degree at a college in the United States. This may require you to have your academic history formally reviewed and evaluated. Ask the admissions advisor at your college if this may be an option and what process you need to follow.

Do you have a lot of college credits that you earned previously—but no degree or credential yet? Some four-year colleges may offer something called a *reverse transfer* credential. This means that if you are enroll-

> **A degree completion institution** is a college or university that is designed to serve students with a lot of previously earned credits, even if those credits were earned at multiple institutions. Degree completion colleges count most transfer credits toward a degree, with few limits on the number of credits that can come from other institutions. These colleges also have robust offerings for earning credit for prior learning—learning that was acquired on the job, in the military, or through other life experiences. See more information in chapter 8.

ing in a four-year institution with 60 credits or more, the college can offer you the option of applying those credits toward an associate degree. That means you may already have a college degree! You can use that associate degree to apply for higher-level jobs while you continue to work towards a bachelor's degree. This is not available at every college. (See further discussion on this in chapter 5.)

Do you have 60–90 credits—or more—that you earned previously? Students with a lot of previously earned college credit might want to consider enrolling in a degree completion institution. These colleges offer maximum flexibility and transferability of previous college work. Completion colleges are also ideal for the student who may have taken and passed a few courses at one college, a few at another college, a few at a third college, etc. (See more on this in chapter 8.) Not all colleges will give you transfer credit for all of those courses, but completion colleges generally do, and they find a way to make them all count toward your degree.

Prior Learning Assessment (PLA)

You've probably noticed at this point in this book that there are a lot of unfamiliar terms in higher education. One term you should become more familiar with is *prior learning assessment*. It may be known at some schools as *credit for prior learning* or *assessment of prior learning* or even *credit by exam*. But whatever term is used, just know this: prior learning assessment can help you save a lot of time and money in earning your degree.

What Is PLA?

Not all college-level learning takes place in the classroom. You may have learning from work, training programs, volunteering, or other experiences.

Prior learning assessment, or PLA, is the term used for various methods of assessing the learning that a student has acquired from outside of a traditional college setting. A college can use PLA to evaluate that learning and then award college credit when the learning is equivalent to what is normally learned in the classroom.

People can gain college level learning in so many ways and from many sources, such as:

- Formal training classes provided by an employer
- Work experience and learning while doing
- Training received in the military
- Volunteer experiences and responsibilities
- Learning a foreign language from family or from living in a different country
- Free online courses
- Licenses, certifications, and other credentials
- Continuing professional education, including some continuing education units (CEUs)
- Seminars and in-service training programs
- Hobbies and recreational activities
- Independent reading and research
- Study at postsecondary/proprietary schools that may be licensed but not accredited

. . . and the list goes on!

What Assessment Methods Are Used?

Prior learning assessment is just one method or tool. There are lots of methods that colleges may choose to use to evaluate a student's prior learning, including exams, individual assessments, portfolio assessments, and formal evaluation of training programs.

Exams

Standardized exams. Some colleges award credit to students who have good scores on standardized tests—these are tests offered by various organizations on specific topics that are comparable to college courses. The most popular examples of PLA exams are:

+ **College Level Examination Program (CLEP) Exams.** Tests of college material offered by the College Board. There are thirty-three exams in five subject areas: history and social sciences, composition and literature, science and mathematics, business, and world languages.

+ **DSST Exams.** Formerly known as the DANTES Program, now owned and administered by Prometric, this tests knowledge of both lower-level and upper-level college material. There are more than thirty exams in subjects such as social sciences, math, applied technology, business, physical sciences, and humanities.

+ **UExcel Credit by Exam.** Developed and offered by Excelsior College, these are standardized exams in business and technology, education, humanities, natural science and mathematics, nursing, and social sciences/history.

+ **Thomas Edison Credit-by-Exam Program (TECEP).** Offered through Thomas Edison State University, these exams are for English composition, humanities, social sciences, natural sciences and mathematics, business and management, computer science technology, and applied science and technology.

A Word from the Experts

Adults have had life experience and they've had jobs—they can almost earn their credentials with what they have learned. Now they just need the paper to show it. It's not that we're saying we don't want them to take the class, but if you can take a test and earn the credit that way, why not?

—Patty Aragona, adult learner concierge,
Truckee Meadows Community College

✛ **Advanced Placement (AP) Exams.** If you took AP courses in high school, you might be able to earn credit for a good score on an AP exam as well.

CLEP, DSST, and UExcel exams can be taken at various testing sites across the country, typically located at colleges and universities. TECEP exams are taken online through ProctorU, or a pen and paper version can also be arranged.

✛ **Challenge exams.** Some colleges also offer a different kind of test that the faculty at that institution develops themselves. These can be called **challenge exams** or **departmental exams**. (In California, a version of this is called **Credit by Exam**.) Sometimes these are offered on a case-by-case basis—that is determined by the specific department—rather than as a formal college offering.

Individualized Assessment

Some colleges offer more individualized assessments so that students can earn credit for learning that may not be covered by available standardized exams. For example, students with strong technical skills may be asked to demonstrate those skills in a performance-based or project-based assessment. In other cases, an individual's skills and knowledge might be evaluated through an interview (in person or via Skype).

Portfolio Assessment

A portfolio is a document that a student develops in order to make the case for the student's college-level learning that can then be formally evaluated by a faculty assessor. Typically, portfolios are written narratives with supporting documentation that provides additional evidence of the student's learning. Developing a portfolio can require a significant time commitment from the student, but many students find the process to be rewarding because they are not merely presenting their learning but also reflecting on what they learned and its relevance to a particular course's learning outcomes and the student's degree goals.

Formal Evaluation of Training Programs

Do you have a special professional license or certification? Or have you completed special training through your workplace? Did you receive any

> I have occasional frustrations, having to take courses that would seem to be a waste of time. That's not a great value. But—if there's something that you already know, you can test out of it. Miami Dade has CLEP exams.
>
> —"Kirk," adult student, age 26, Miami Dade College

formal training as part of military service? If so, you may be eligible for a different kind of PLA in which the training program itself is formally evaluated for college credit.

Evaluated noncollege programs. The National College Credit Recommendation Service (NCCRS) and the American Council on Education (ACE) conduct evaluations, for a fee, of training that is offered by employers or other nonaccredited providers. Some colleges provide this service for local employers and nonaccredited providers as well. The result of these evaluations is credit recommendations for anyone successfully completing that training. This category also includes ACE credit recommendations for military training and occupations as part of a contract with the U.S. Department of Defense.

Colleges that offer credit through this method will need to see some evidence that you successfully completed the training. Then they can refer to the ACE and NCCRS websites to see if there is recommended credit for that training. It is then ultimately the college's decision whether or not the recommended credit will be awarded to you as part of your degree program.

On the following page are some examples of the kind of training programs that are evaluated by the **ACE College Credit Recommendation Service**. As you can see from just this short list of examples, there is a wide range of training that has already been evaluated for credit. So think back to what kind of training you may have had over the years—perhaps you have had some training that can count toward your degree!

Real-Life Examples of Students Earning Credit through Prior Learning Assessment

Here are some examples of students who have earned credit through PLA:

✛ "Ted" originally learned drafting in high school and decided to take some time off before college to earn some money for tuition. He started work with a local manufacturer and, in the course of the job, he taught himself 3D modeling. When he decided to go

Training Programs Evaluated by ACE

TRAINING PROVIDER	COURSE	ACE CREDIT RECOMMENDATION
Dale Carnegie Training®	How to Win Friends and Influence Business People	1 semester hour in organizational behavior or organizational effectiveness
Jiffy Lube International	Service Center Management Training	3 semester hours in supervision or business administration, and 3 in business management or management
Project Management Leadership Group, Inc.	Advanced Project Management	1 semester hour in project management
Microsoft Corporation	Managing Office 365 Identities and Requirements	2 semester hours in information technology, computer information systems, and information systems
Virginia State Police Academy	Intermediate Forensics Course	3 semester hours in forensic science or crime scene investigation

Are you active in the military or a veteran? If so, all of the training you received from the military is on your Joint Services Transcript. Your college can refer to ACE's Military Guide for credit recommendations for the training you received. See chapter 12 for more information about PLA for veterans and active military.

back to school in his mid-fifties to get a degree in industrial engineering, he looked at the various course descriptions and saw his own experience in the course descriptions. He used the PLA portfolio assessment form to earn credit in parametric modeling that helped him earn an associate degree from Ivy Tech, and then a few years later a bachelor's degree from Indiana Institute of Technology. Ted is now an instructor at a two-year college.

✢ "Gabriel" is originally from Honduras but grew up in Indiana. After high school, he joined the U.S. Air Force and ended up being stationed in Texas. After being discharged, Gabriel worked for seven years at an IT company as a systems administrator and then for the state department of transportation as a business systems analyst. He took community college courses for a while and then eventually enrolled at St. Edwards University to pursue a degree in organizational communication. From everything he had learned on the job—through both experience and training—he was able to use portfolio assessment to earn credits in several courses, including interpersonal communication, conflict resolution, computer-mediated communication, and English tech and business writing.

✢ "Angela" grew up in Brooklyn, New York, and moved to Connecticut when she was twelve. After high school, Angela took college courses at two different institutions but never finished a degree. She started her own marketing business and was able to work from home while raising a family. While away from formal education, Angela continued to learn through free online courses she found at Coursera. She loved how many different courses were offered as well as the freedom to learn without commitment. This inspired her to go back to school, so she enrolled at Charter Oak State College—a degree completion college—to finish her business degree when she was in her mid-forties. At that point, Angela needed only ten more courses to complete her degree. She was able to transfer in all of her earlier college credit and earned additional CLEP credits in introduction to management, managerial accounting, abnormal psychology, and management information systems. That left only five courses to complete for her degree.

✛ "Ron" shipped out to marine boot camp on August 28, 2001, just a few months after his high school graduation and two weeks before the September 11 attacks reshaped the role of the American military. After basic training, Ron deployed to northern Africa. Ron loved the opportunity to learn about a part of the world very different from the small town in northern Kentucky where he had grown up. When he returned to the United States at age twenty, Ron joined the elite Marine Security Guard, which is tasked with defending American embassies around the world. After serving in Austria and Canada, Ron separated from the marines and moved back to northern Kentucky, where he planned to start a family. Frustrated with the work opportunities available to him, Ron wanted to use his GI Bill benefits to pursue a degree. He enrolled at Northern Kentucky University (NKU), where the university's faculty and staff encouraged him to figure out how he could turn what he learned from his military experience into academic credit. NKU reviewed Ron's military transcript using American Council on Education (ACE) credit recommendations and accepted thirty credits toward graduation. He subsequently earned three credits in business writing through portfolio assessment, using documentation of his learning through examples of reports and other materials that he had written in previous military and civilian jobs. The process of developing his portfolio took Ron about ten to twelve hours over the course of two months. He says that he could have finished it even more quickly had he not been working full-time and enrolled in several other classes while working on his portfolio. After graduation, Ron put his degree in organizational leadership to work at the small pharmaceutical company where he worked while attending classes.

COMMON QUESTIONS ABOUT PRIOR LEARNING ASSESSMENT

Question: Do I need to be enrolled in a college to get PLA credit?

Answer: To get the best benefit from PLA, is it highly advised that you first be enrolled in a program. Using assessment methods without having an educational plan is risky because not every college accepts PLA credit and, even within colleges, degree programs' requirements and policies can vary significantly. Be sure to ask about PLA as you shop for colleges—one college's programs may offer more PLA options than another, and that is an important consideration since PLA can save you time and money.

Question: How much credit can I earn?

Answer: That depends on several things such as how much college-level learning you have completed, whether there are limits on PLA credits at

Prior Learning Assessment Can Save You Time and Money

Credits you earn through PLA—and that then count toward your degree—are worth both time and money.

PLA credits in your degree plan mean there are fewer credits you need to earn to get your degree. That's fewer courses you need to take and to pay for!

Look at an example of a student who earned nine credits through three different PLA assessments. If that student paid $125 per assessment, she paid $375 total. If courses at the student's college are worth three credits each and cost $600 per course, the student can cut three courses from her schedule and also cut $1,800 from her total tuition bill. That's a net savings of $1,425!

Am I a Good Candidate for PLA?

Do you have several years of work experience?	YES	NO
Do you have proof or evidence that shows what you learned?	YES	NO
Have you completed any formal training programs or apprenticeships?	YES	NO
Have you done significant learning on a specific topic on your own through books or online resources?	YES	NO
Are you now—or were you previously—in the military?	YES	NO
Have you had volunteer experiences that have required you to learn a new skill or subject?	YES	NO

If you answered YES to any of these questions, PLA may be a good option for you. If so, keep this in mind when you are considering where to go to college. The college that offers you PLA as part of the degree plan can save you a lot of time and money.

The LearningCounts website has a College Credit Predictor tool to help you explore this question further. Go to www.learningcounts.org, click on "Resources" at the bottom of the page, then click on "Credit Predictor."

your college, and whether the degree program you choose has requirements that align with the subjects for which you are earning PLA credit. Some students earn just 3 credits from PLA, while others with significant prior learning can earn 20 credits or more. CAEL research found that the average number of PLA credits earned by adults at colleges that had relatively strong PLA offerings is 17, which is equivalent to more than a semester, or 4-6 months of school, for a full-time student (Klein-Collins 2011).

Question: How much does PLA cost?

Answer: Colleges set their own prices for PLA services and there is a lot of variation. But PLA typically will cost a lot less than taking the course:

+ *Standardized exams* typically cost between $80 and $120 for the

exam, and there might be an additional administrative fee of
$25–$30.

+ *Challenge exams* usually cost less than $250, with a median
   price of $100.
+ *Portfolio assessment* can involve two different charges—one
   charge to take a portfolio development course (often a credit-
   based course or a shorter workshop option) and the assessment
   itself. The course is usually priced like a regular course at the
   institution. The median fee for portfolio assessment is $175.
+ *Review of noncollege training*, including military transcripts,
   usually involves no charge to the student (Klein-Collins, 2015).

WHAT ARE THE BENEFITS OF PLA?

The big benefits to PLA are the **savings of time and money**. If PLA
credits can count toward your degree, those are credits that you don't need
to earn. That means fewer courses to take and fewer courses to pay for.

But in addition to saving time and money, the credit-earning boost from
PLA may ultimately help you get to the finish line. Studies have
found that students who earn PLA credit have higher graduation rates
than their peers who do not earn PLA credit. For example, a 2010 Council
for Adult and Experiential Learning (CAEL) study of more than 60,000
students at forty-eight institutions found that adult students with PLA
were two and a half times more likely to earn a college degree than adult
students without PLA (Klein-Collins 2010).

A Word from the Experts

I think that students are surprised to see—particularly those who
come as dropout students—that their knowledge actually does
translate into that mythical college-level credit. They see themselves
in their degrees in a way that people usually don't in a traditional
environment.

—Michele Forte, assistant professor and faculty mentor,
Center for Distance Learning, SUNY Empire State College

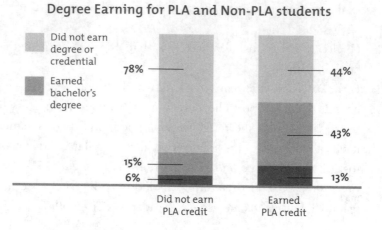

Degree Earning for PLA and Non-PLA students

Did not earn degree or credential

Earned bachelor's degree

78%

44%

43%

15%

6%

13%

Did not earn PLA credit

Earned PLA credit

Earning PLA credit does not guarantee that you will finish your degree, but it certainly gets you closer to the finish line. And when the finish line feels within reach, you might be even more motivated to keep going!

WHAT ARE THE LIMITATIONS OF PLA?

As good as PLA can be for many students, it's important to know about some of its limitations.

+ **PLA is not available at every college.** Not every college offers PLA. Or a college may offer credit for AP or CLEP exams but nothing else. If you do not see information about PLA on the website, ask an academic advisor if PLA is an option for your degree program. If you anticipate spending a few years at a community college and then transferring to a four-year institution, keep in mind that PLA credit earned at one institution may not be accepted by the next institution.

+ **There are usually limits to the number of PLA-awarded credits that can count toward your degree.** You may have completed a lot of college-level learning, but PLA may be an option only for a limited number of credits in your particular degree plan. It's important to know what those limits are before you pay for any PLA assessments.

+ **Your financial aid may not cover the cost of PLA.** Federal grants (like Pell) and loan programs cannot include PLA as part

> **Does your employer offer tuition assistance? It may pay for preferred learning assessment.** Some employer tuition assistance programs may cover the cost of PLA. If yours does not currently cover that cost, ask the benefits managers if they will consider it. Make sure they see how it will save them money compared to paying for full tuition!

of your overall cost of attendance. In other words, assessment is not an eligible expense. One exception may be a portfolio development course that is offered for credit since that can be treated like any other course under financial aid. *GI Bill rules are different as those benefits can pay for "national tests" that include CLEP, DSST, and a few other options.*

How Do I Find Colleges That Offer PLA?

If PLA is a possible option for you, your next step is to find a college that offers it. Here are some suggestions for finding those colleges:

If you have narrowed down your college choices . . .

+ Go to the college's website and use the search function to locate "Prior Learning Assessment" or "credit for prior learning." You can also try searching for "adult learners" as information about PLA may be listed as a specific offering for students like you.

+ Call the admissions office and ask about PLA.

+ Use the "Contact Us" feature on the college's website to ask about PLA options.

Consider colleges listed in the Top 100 Best Colleges for Adult Learners. Those who score high in "flexibility of programs" are often those that offer PLA options. See the appendix for the full set of rankings for colleges in your state.

Questions to Ask a College About Prior Learning Assessment

+ Is prior learning assessment (PLA) available?

+ Is PLA limited to certain degrees or programs?

+ What are the costs associated with PLA?

+ Is there a way for me to test out of courses if I think I already know the content?

+ Is there a way for me to create and submit a portfolio to demonstrate what I have learned in other areas of my life?

Consider degree completion institutions. Those are the colleges that are designed to help adults with learning from lots of different sources complete their degrees quickly. Students with a lot of prior learning can complete most of their degree through PLA at these institutions. See chapter 8 for more information on these colleges.

Consider colleges on PLA vendor lists:
To identify colleges that offer CLEP and DSST testing sites, visit:

+ CLEP at http://clep.collegeboard.com
+ DSST at http://getcollegecredit.com

To identify colleges that recognize formal evaluations of training programs, visit:

+ ACE at http://www2.acenet.edu/CREDITCollegeNetwork/
+ NCCRS at http://www.nationalccrs.org/colleges-universities

RESOURCES

Janet Colvin and the Council for Adult and Experiential Learning, *Earn College Credit for What You Know*, fifth ed. (Kendall Hunt Publishing, 2012).

ACE College Credit Recommendation Service at www.acenet.edu/high-er-education/topics/Pages/Credit-Evaluations.aspx.

NCCRS (National College Credit Recommendation Service) at www.nation-alccrs.org.

CHAPTER 11

Apply Yourself: Navigating the Admissions Process

Now that you have had a chance to think about options for continuing your education, revisit the "Comparing Colleges Worksheet" in chapter 6. Explore how the colleges you are considering stack up against each other in terms of academics, affordability, flexibility, and support services. Think through all of the things that each college offers and **choose the one that offers you what you need academically and that will help you finish your degree quickly**.

When you have made your choice, then it's time to start the admissions process!

Getting Ready for the Admissions Process

MAKE THE CONNECTION TO THE ADMISSIONS OFFICE

After you have done your research and you have narrowed your choices to one or two, the first step in the admissions process is for you to connect with your prospective college or university so that you can get answers to very specific questions you may still have.

You can do this by calling the college and asking for the admissions office or by emailing admissions (contact information is available on the college's website).

A college admissions office is responsible for recruiting and enrolling new students. The admissions staff will answer your questions about the college, help you determine if it offers the program you are interested in, and if you meet the entrance qualifications.

Admissions processes vary from college to college. Each college will have its own set of admissions requirements—find out exactly what those requirements are and if there are deadlines for submitting your application and other documents.

+ **Open admissions.** One type of admissions is called open admissions, which means the college has a mission of access where nearly everyone who applies is accepted and admitted to the college. Many adult-friendly college and university programs—including and especially community colleges—have open admissions. The application process is usually not very difficult for these schools.

+ **Selective admissions.** Admissions processes at more traditional colleges and universities will be more selective. Selective admissions means you will need to meet certain institutionally determined criteria to be accepted. For these processes, you will need to adhere to a schedule of deadlines in order for you to be considered for admission. You may also need to take a college admission qualification test like the SAT or ACT.

+ **Rolling admissions.** Rolling admissions means you can apply at any time because there are frequent program start dates, not just the traditional beginnings of semesters in August and January.

When you reach out to the admissions office, consider what additional questions you still have about the college if you weren't able to find all the information you needed from the website. Add to that list of questions the specific things you might want to know about applying to the program you are interested in.

Have your questions in order so your outreach can be as efficient as possible. You may want to select questions from the table below:

Questions to Ask the Admissions Representative Before you Enroll

MY CRITERIA	QUESTIONS TO ASK
Academics	✦ Does it offer the academic major or program I need?
	✦ Are there admissions requirements that I must fulfill before I can be accepted?
	✦ Is it regionally accredited?
	✦ Does it provide online courses or programs that will help me complete my degree sooner or more conveniently?
	✦ Do you accept national for-credit exams such as CLEP, DSST, or UExcel exams?
	✦ Will you evaluate my transcripts as part of the admissions process? (This is to make sure that any of your previous college coursework will count toward your degree—remember to try to get a decision on this from the college before you enroll.)
	✦ Will my employer or future employer value this degree?
	✦ How do I apply? (Or, would you please send me the application?)
	✦ What is the deadline for the application?
Finances/Money	✦ How much will it cost? Does it fit my budget? Can the college help me with the financial aid process?
	✦ Does it have a payment plan?
	✦ Does it have scholarships for which I may be eligible?
	✦ If my employer offers prepaid tuition assistance, does the college accept third-party payments?
Flexibility	✦ Will my transfer credits be accepted?
	✦ Will I be able to test for credit or use prior learning assessment methods to earn credit for what I already know?
	✦ Will the course schedule work with my schedule?
	✦ If taking face-to-face courses (not online) is the campus close to work and/or home?

Questions to Ask Admissions *(continued)*

MY CRITERIA	QUESTIONS TO ASK
Ensuring Your Success	✦ Does it provide support services such as tutoring, coaches, or developmental English or math to help me brush up on my skills?
	✦ What kind of career services does it offer?
	✦ Does it offer day care services?
	✦ Does it offer internships?

GATHER YOUR DOCUMENTATION

You will need all of this documentation as part of the admissions process. Begin by requesting student copies of your transcripts from the last school you attended, whether high school or college. These will help you fill out the application for admission because you will need to include dates of attendance for all of your previous educational programs. You also will need to send official transcripts directly to the college(s) you hope to attend.

DOCUMENTATION CHECKLIST

Order your educational transcripts. Transcripts for each school you have attended should be sent to the college you want to attend; it may also be helpful to order a set of transcripts for your personal records. There is usually a modest fee for each transcript requested. Most colleges have set up an online process to request transcripts. You will need to provide your name (the name you used when you attended the college), the year(s) you

A Word from the Experts

Students should always go see an academic advisor in the department of the degree program or college that they choose because that person will be the last word on the procedures and policies there.

—*Baxter Gamble, advisor, Complete the Degree Chicago*

attended, your social security number, date of birth, and the address for the college to which you need the transcripts sent.

Order your high school/GED transcript. If you have not attended a college or university already, you will need your high school transcript. Follow the same process as described above. There generally will be information available on your high school's website for requesting transcripts. You will need to order a transcript only from the high school from which you graduated. If you have a GED or alternative high school credential, you will need to order a transcript from the provider or provide a copy of your diploma.

Order your score reports for any national for-credit exams you have taken (such as CLEP, DSST, or UExcel exams) if the college accepts them. This entails going to the testing agency's website to request a score report or downloading the forms from the site. Use your web browser to find the form you need:

+ CLEP—Search "CLEP Transcript Request."
+ DSST—Search "DSST Transcript Order Form."
+ UExcel—Search "UExcel Examination Transcript Request."

Make copies of any certifications or licenses you have acquired.

If you are a military service member or veteran, **order your JST (Joint Services Transcript) at** https://jst.doded.mil.

If you have taken any formal training programs that have been evaluated by the American Council on Education or the National College Credit Recommendation Service, go to their websites to order transcripts.

> I chose this college because it was a reputable online school. Beyond that, I looked at all the degrees that looked interesting to me and what the course offerings were. I read through course descriptions to see what looked good. I also looked at the bios of the faculty to see where they got their degrees. I wanted to find people who would nurture me and help me get what I wanted out of my own degree. It seemed like the right fit.
>
> —*"Jean," adult student, age 35, SUNY Empire State College*

If the college requires vaccination records, work with your doctor's office to obtain them.

REVIEW THE ACADEMIC CALENDAR

The calendar is usually posted on the college's website, but it also may be found in the college's catalog. A college catalog is essentially the college's or university's contract with you, the student. It includes everything you need to know about its academic policies. When you review the academic calendar, note college breaks (between semesters, holidays, and summertime) and class times, registration dates, and payment deadlines. Be sure to check out when finals week is each semester or quarter. This will help you plan your schedule accordingly. Whether you go full-time or part-time, understanding start dates for course offerings, as well as when the semester (or term) ends, will make you more confident in your planning. When you compare the academic calendar to your own calendar, you can block out the time you will need for studying and attending class.

Apply!

You are now ready to fill out the application for admission. Depending upon your decision-making process, you may wish to apply to more than one college. Applications are fairly easy to complete. The hardest part is actually detailing where you have previously attended college and where you graduated from high school. You will have already ordered your student copies of transcripts—these will help you to easily complete this sec-

> We are in an era now [when] much more emphasis is placed on academic credential or level. There's no way around it. There's no bad side to it. Just go for an informational meeting. Go online to the campus website. See what campus you want to attend—attend a free session.
>
> —*Cristy, adult student, age 63, SUNY Empire State College*

tion. While you can apply to more than one college at a time, you may want to limit it to only the colleges you are seriously considering since colleges typically require you to pay a fee with your application. Application fees generally run from $25 to as high as $75.

Some applications may ask you to include a personal essay. Here are some tips for you as an adult writing this essay:

+ Write about your personal experiences and why you have decided to continue your education.
+ Be honest and authentic.
+ Explain why going to college is so important to you and what you hope to do with your degree. You don't have to say that you expect to be a CEO in ten years! It's okay to say that you just want to finish what you started, or that you want a degree to show that you can accomplish something.
+ Provide examples from your work or home life of times when you have demonstrated determination or when you have followed through on other goals.

The essay also provides an opportunity to address your past academic history—good or bad. A bad academic history may not be the big deal you think it is: *Admissions directors know that adults have moved past adolescent issues that may have resulted in poor grades.*

Here are two examples of the beginnings of essays that may help you think about your own essay:

My path toward the degree has not always been an easy one. I have encountered many challenges along the way, as evidenced by my old transcripts. I lacked some maturity when I first went to college right out of high school, and I ended up wanting to get a job and get away from school for a while. I gradually worked my way up to a position as a marketing manager for a local nonprofit agency. My work experiences have improved my communication skills and helped me to develop a new confidence in myself from setting and achieving goals. My career is focused now and now I really want a degree so that I can open up new doors for myself professionally. I know I have the maturity and confidence to study, work hard, and earn my degree . . .

My life has not been a straight line to a degree. I took college classes off and on while starting a family and raising my kids. It's been a slow process, and now that my kids are all in school full-time, I want to finally finish what I started. While I had always expected to have finished college by now, I think that taking my time has been good for me because some of my life experiences have helped me understand the direction I want to take now with my degree . . .

Remember, though, that your essay **must be in your own words**, and not copied from something you find in a book or on the internet. That would be seen as *plagiarism*, which is when you copy another person's writing or ideas and fail to disclose the source. It is academic dishonesty and is not tolerated at any college or university, whether it's for your college application or for your term papers in class. So use the examples above to inspire you to come up with *your own personal statement*. Use *your* words to express *your own* story.

Enroll in College!

Once you've been accepted, it's time to take action and commit to furthering your education. Your next step is to enroll in the college you have selected. Be sure to seek the advice of an admissions representative or academic advisor—do not try to pick out your courses on your own. Whether you will be attending full-time or part-time, during your first term as a student you will want to be sure to take the *right* courses.

Once you register for your courses, you are officially enrolled! Tuition may be due prior to registration, when you register, or within the

The Admissions Process Overview

Step 1: Decide where you would like to go and the academic programs or majors you are interested in pursuing.

Complete the FAFSA (for financial aid). You can fill out the electronic form at https://fafsa.ed.gov.

You may go through the admissions process with more than one school. However, it is important that you plan ahead if you are applying to selective admissions schools. Start at least six months prior to when you actually want to start taking classes.

You will receive a Student Aid Report (SAR) once the FAFSA has been processed. This is your documentation to use to reach out to your chosen college's financial aid department. The department will provide information to you about how to proceed.

Be sure to include all of your questions. Ask specifically if they will do an evaluation of your previous college credits when you apply.

This can be found online at the college or university website, or the admissions office will email it to you.

Step 3: Complete the application for admission.

Include all of your previous academic history.

Have transcripts for your high school and all of the colleges you have attended sent to the college's registrar or records office. Information on how to order transcripts will be found on the college website.

Step 5: Ask for an evaluation of your transfer credits and any prior learning assessment credits you may have earned from national for-credit exams or military service.

The evaluation (which is considered "unofficial" until all of your official transcripts have been received) is usually completed by an admissions office representative.

The Admissions Process Overview (continued)

Step 6: Wait for the admissions decision.	The time frame for finding out if you've been accepted varies depending upon your college and the time of year. For instance, open and rolling admissions colleges are always very busy in August and September. Selective colleges will provide a date when you can expect to hear the admissions decision.
Step 7: You've been accepted!	Congratulations! If you've selected an adult-friendly institution, you will most likely be accepted fairly quickly. For competitive programs, such as nursing, the process will take longer, but you will be provided with the dates and more specific information.
You've been provisionally accepted.	Sometimes the decision may be provisionally accepted, which means you may need to successfully take a few courses before you can be fully admitted to the institution.
You've been denied admission.	This simply means you didn't get accepted . . . and you should select a different college. It does happen, but don't worry, you will find the college that is right for you. You now need a Plan B, which could mean applying to another college or looking into your local community college. They are generally open to anyone who has completed high school or a GED. And they are affordable!
Step 8: Check on the status of your financial aid, if you applied for aid. The financial aid office will explain to you how to proceed with registering for your courses. Enroll and register for courses.	It is important to work with an advisor to determine which courses are best for you. Academic advisors will help you get off on the right foot, taking the right balance of courses. Sometimes courses fill up quickly, especially the ones that are required before you can take more advanced courses. An academic advisor will help you navigate course registration.

> I did research online and went and walked in to talk to someone. At my age, I find that it's easier to communicate face-to-face. I made appointments and met with counselors.
>
> —*Mary, adult student, age 58, Miami Dade College*

first month. In most cases there also are additional fees that may include lab fees, technology fees, campus service fees, among others. If you have made arrangements for a payment plan, or prepaid tuition assistance from your employer, or if you are a financial aid student, you will need to check with the financial aid office to ensure your aid has arrived.

CHAPTER 12

From Service to School: Resources for Veterans and Their Dependents[*]

If you have served in the military, you will be going to college with a very different life experience than other adults. The military experience you had helped to shape you as a person, and it taught you valuable skills that you put to use in your service. Many of those skills will serve you well as you go to college, too!

This chapter provides some information that is specific to the veteran's student experience. It describes the challenges that some veterans experience during the transition to college. But more importantly, it describes the many ways that your military background can be an *asset* to you. It may be demonstrated in the kind of work you do in the classroom, and it also can help you complete your degree in a shorter period of time and at a lower out-of-pocket cost. You probably are well aware of the great financial benefits for education that are available through the GI Bill, but your military experience can offer you even more than that!

[*] Sections of this chapter are adapted from *Valuing Military Learning: A Guide to Prior Learning Assessment and More*, a resource guide prepared by the Council for Adult and Experiential Learning for the Multi-state Collaborative on Military Credit, 2016.

As you start to explore where to go to college, you also should keep an eye out for different colleges that reach out to veterans like you and what kind of support they offer for veterans who enroll. Some do much more than others. For instance, some may do more to help you get credit for the learning you have gained from your military service, or connect student veterans to each other for support, or provide good information and assistance in accessing—and making the most of—GI Bill benefits. Others may provide high-quality advising and career services designed especially for veterans.

The Military to College Transition

If you have only recently separated from the military, you may be discovering that you are experiencing a bit of culture shock during your transition. You were trained by the military to be part of a very structured and hierarchical organization, where there is a clear chain of command and mission. While there are, of course, rules and laws in civilian life, as well as some expectation of what counts as good conduct, civilian life isn't nearly as well ordered and organized as the military is. In civilian life, there is more of an emphasis on individuality and personal freedom. In the military, individuality isn't what's important—instead, there is a focus on unit cohesion centered around the carrying out of a well-defined mission (Coll and Sherman 2012).

Civilian Culture	Military Culture
Emphasis on individuality	Emphasis on unit cohesion
Individual achievement	Emphasis on the mission
Personal freedom	Loyalty to duty
Fluid social relationships	Chain of command

Source: J. Coll and A. Sherman, "Promoting Mental and Emotional Health for Veteran Students: A Non-Clinician's Overview" presentation, 2012

For some people, moving between these worlds—in either direction—can be a shock to the system!

It's not like entering civilian life is visiting another planet. But do keep those cultural differences in mind because they can present challenges for some veterans as they try to figure out the college landscape.

For example, in the military, most of your day-to-day activities were decided by your superiors. In college, you are largely on your own for making decisions, both large (where to go to school, what degree to pursue) and small (which classes to take, when to study). It also may not be entirely clear when to do what—Do I talk to admissions first or financial aid? Do I take algebra before economics or can I do that at the same time? Do I talk to my professor first if I'm having trouble or do I go straight to the writing lab? I have three hours to study, but what should I tackle first and how long should I spend on each task? There may not be a single right answer to any of these questions, and that can be hard when you have become used to the way things work in the military, where there is a much more clearly defined way of operating.

In addition, some veterans may find that it can be difficult to relate to classmates who have had a very different life experience. To be sure, many adult learners may find it a challenge to relate as a peer to the average 19-year-old who came to college straight from high school. But for veterans who may have been away from home for years—perhaps even in challenging or dangerous environments—making those kinds of connections may feel even more challenging.

Each veteran is different, of course. But if you are feeling disconnected or overwhelmed by the college environment, keep in mind that these are common feelings for veterans.

✦ **If you need clearer instructions . . .** Ask if there is a single point of contact to serve student veterans. If there is not, seek out someone at the college who can advise you on your enrollment questions, academic choices, and time-management strategies. Ask them to be as specific as possible with their guidance and instructions, if that is what will help you feel comfortable navigating that environment. Reaching out to a student veteran group (if one exists) may also help point you in the right direction.

✦ **If you are finding it hard to relate to your classmates . . .** Ask if there are veterans support groups or social groups affiliated with the college. There may be an informal veterans group, or

Student Veterans Groups

Some veterans find it valuable to connect with other veterans at their college. Other veterans may have a better understanding of your past experiences or share your perspective on making the transition to civilian life.

If you think this might be important to you, ask prospective colleges about whether they have an active student veterans group on campus.

Student Veterans of America (SVA) is a national organization that supports veterans who are going back to school. There may be an official SVA chapter at the college you attend. Learn more at www. studentveterans.org.

there may be an official chapter of Student Veterans of America that is active at that college.

✛ **If you are experiencing significant feelings of stress or depression . . .** Do not ignore those feelings. Tell your advisor right away. They may be able to connect you with someone who can help you. Your state's veterans services website might offer a list of resources. Or contact the Veterans Crisis Line by phone (call 1-800-273-8255 and press #1), by sending a text message to 838255, or through a web chat service at www.veteranscrisisline. net.

The Value of the Vet in the Classroom

Earlier in this book, we talked about how adult students bring a lot to the classroom from their experiences in life and work. Veterans have had a particular life experience and training that also can be valuable in the classroom. Some veterans may have experienced different countries and cultures during their service. In addition, veterans are often particularly good at working as part of a team, taking the initiative, finding solutions to problems, adhering to official policies, and self-advocating in a respectful manner (Woll 2010). These are skills that translate well to the classroom.

The Value of Veterans in the Classroom

Emphasis on unit cohesion	✦ Team players ✦ Willing to lend a hand
Emphasis on the mission	✦ Motivated students ✦ Prepared to take initiative ✦ Focused on identifying solutions to problems
Loyalty to duty	✦ Prepared to take responsibility ✦ Punctual
Chain of command	✦ Seek to meet or exceed expectations ✦ Respect for policies ✦ Advocacy in a respectful manner

Adapted from P. Woll, "Teaching America's Best: Preparing Your Classrooms to Welcome Returning Veterans and Service Members", Bethesda, MD: Give an Hour and National Organization on Disability, 2010

What Colleges Do for Students Who Are Veterans

As more and more veterans are heading to college, more and more colleges are offering special programs and services to help them. You may find such services to be helpful to you, so you may want to investigate whether colleges you are considering offer these kind of benefits to their student veterans.

- **Single point of contact for veterans.** In some states, public universities and colleges are required by law to have a designated central point of contact for all veterans, service members, and dependents. Additionally, all colleges participating in the national Principles of Excellence program for the U.S. Department of Veterans Affairs must "designate a point of contact to provide academic and financial advice." Ask of the colleges you are considering if they have a central point of contact for veterans. This person can provide you with information about eligibility for education benefits, benefit application processes, academic counseling, financial aid counseling, and student support services. If

A note on academic accommodations for disabilities.
If you have a service-connected disability or any other need for an accommodation, meet with the designated office for students with disabilities at the college where you enroll. You may qualify for academic accommodations, such as additional time for testing and/or use of adaptive equipment. Make sure you know what documentation is required and how long it may take to get that information. Explore accommodation options for a disability—they are intended to even the playing field, not to give you an unfair advantage.

the college is participating in the Principles of Excellence program, the college will provide you with a personalized form detailing your total costs. You should feel free to make contact with this person *before applying to the college* to get a better sense of student veteran services.

✦ **Resource centers and lounges for student veterans.** Some colleges offer a veterans resource center that provides a single location where veterans can access information about on- and off-campus resources. Another offering may be a veterans lounge where student veterans can connect with each other in an informal setting. A lounge like this is also often used for meetings of student veterans clubs.

✦ **Assistance with veterans' educational benefits.** The rules governing veterans' benefits through the GI Bill and other programs are complex and not always easy to understand. Some colleges provide advisors who are knowledgeable in the many rules and regulations regarding veterans benefits and how they interact with other sources of financial aid. You might also contact the state agency that oversees financial aid (see chapter 7 for a list of these agencies).

✦ **Special veterans orientation sessions or workshops for veterans returning from service.** A veterans-specific orientation is an important way to inform student veterans about where and how to obtain academic and social veterans-specific resources. Such sessions may also aim to alleviate concerns about your transition to higher education after years in the military.

+ **Peer services and support groups.** Peer services and support groups for veterans can alleviate stress and the sense of isolation experienced by some student veterans. Some of these groups are local chapters of Student Veterans of America.

+ **Support groups for women veterans.** For many women veterans, the transition to civilian life has been particularly complicated and difficult. Some colleges help facilitate special support groups for women veterans to connect with and support each other.

+ **Social clubs and activities for veterans.** Colleges may have special options for veterans to connect socially. There may be parties, study breaks during finals, sports, outings, and veteran-led national holiday events.

+ **Services for families of veterans.** Recognizing that military and veteran students often have family responsibilities, some schools choose to provide special services to address those needs, including childcare.

+ **Housing options (if relevant).** Some veterans commute to college from their existing homes, while others may need to find new housing to attend the college of their choice. Some colleges offer special on-campus housing for married students or student veterans, and some can provide help with off-campus housing needs as well.

A Word from the Experts

Many veterans feel uneasy as they make the transition to college—the environment, culture, and requirements are vastly different than the military. I always advise veterans to pick an institution that offers the degree that they want—the one they feel that they can have a meaningful career in. After they select the degree, then pick the school that fits your learning style and lifestyle. Lastly, pick a college that truly supports the veteran with the transition and programs to succeed while in school. Student veterans are strategic assets and are the future leaders of the United States of America.

—*Roman Ortega Jr., director of veterans affairs and recruitment, Lewis University*

Principles of Excellence Colleges

Colleges participating in the Principles of Excellence program have agreed to:

✦ Provide students with a personalized form covering the total cost of an education program.

✦ Provide educational plans for all military and veteran education beneficiaries.

✦ End fraudulent and aggressive recruiting techniques and misrepresentations.

✦ Accommodate service members and reservists absent due to service requirements.

✦ Designate a point of contact to provide academic and financial advice.

✦ Ensure accreditation of all new programs prior to enrolling students.

✦ Align institutional refund policies with those under Title IV, which governs the administration of federal student financial aid programs.

To see if your college participates in this program, check out the website for the GI Bill Cost Comparison Tool.

If you think this might be important to you, ask prospective colleges about whether they have an active student veterans group on campus.

Student Veterans of America (SVA) is a national organization that supports veterans who are going back to school. There may be an official SVA chapter at the college you attend. Learn more at www.studentveterans.org.

✦ **Special policies for veterans on tuition and fees.** Some colleges offer tuition discounts for veterans so it pays to ask. In addition, because GI Bill payments sometimes do not arrive in time to meet tuition payment deadlines, some college have policies to allow veterans to register for classes anyway, waive the late fees, or otherwise not penalize veterans for the delay.

- **Special policies for veterans regarding service deployment.** Some veterans also may be members of the National Guard or reserve forces and may have service requirements that interfere with their educational activities. National Guard members or active military may be deployed unexpectedly, or they may have annual training or a longer military-duty weekend. Some colleges have policies in place so that students can meet those service requirements without financial or academic penalties.

- **Academic advisement for veterans.** Some veterans may not have a clear idea about what kind of degree they want to pursue so they choose a program based on what they did in the military or on a friend's suggestion. Some colleges will work with veterans before they enroll to help them make good decisions using interest inventories and other tools.

- **Career advising and job placement services for veterans.** Many veterans are not sure how their military training and experiences may be related to skills that are in demand among civilian employers. Career and education advisors who are well trained in understanding the strengths, skills, and competencies of veterans can help student veterans make these transitions with greater ease and help to "translate" military skills and experiences as veterans prepare résumés, work on their networking skills, and apply for jobs after graduation.

- **Policies to recognize transfer credits, credit for military training, and prior learning assessment.** As mentioned throughout this book, not every college offers prior learning assessment as an option. If you have significant training from the military, investigate what colleges provide in terms of options for earning college credit for that training. It can save you significant time and money in earning your degree. At a minimum, colleges should be evaluating Joint Services Transcripts to award appropriate credit based on transcript recommendations, and they should treat credits from Community College of the Air Force transcripts as they would credits from any other accredited institution. In general, it may be really helpful to you to at-

Jeffrey "Chip" Dodson served as a law enforcement specialist and a professional military education instructor in the air force. When he decided to pursue his bachelor's degree, Azusa Pacific University accepted credit for his military training and Community College of the Air Force credits, which saved him one year of college. His advisors then suggested that he look into portfolio assessment. After taking a PLA portfolio course and submitting his portfolio, Chip was ultimately able to earn six credits, three for English composition and three for a social science course. Chip recommends that other veterans utilize portfolio assessment because "it saves you time and money. Simple as that."

tend a college that has good policies on transferring credits and articulation of credits from other accredited colleges.

✢ **Health and counseling services.** Some colleges have stress management and health resources available on and off campus.

Funding Your Education

If you are a recently discharged veteran, there are several ways to help fund your education. Before you start applying, it's a good idea to get the 10,000-foot view of available benefits. This section provides a step-by-step guide to help you better determine your eligibility and figure out which benefits best meet your educational needs right now.

STEP 1: UNDERSTAND YOUR ELIGIBILITY

Your eligibility for military educational benefits may depend on the following things: the character of your discharge or service, whether you were active duty or reserve, when you began service, how long you served, and if you made contributions to an education plan.

Commonly used educational benefits include:

✢ **Post-9/11 GI Bill (chapter 33).** According to the VA, this benefit is for military members who have at least 90 days of aggregate active duty service after September 10, 2001. It provides up to

Best colleges for vets lists. There are several organizations that have ranked colleges on how well they serve veterans, including US News & World Report, Military Times, and College Factual. By all means take a look at these lists and learn how the colleges earned their rankings. But don't assume that the colleges on that list will necessarily meet your specific needs. Put in the time to evaluate each college choice on its own merits—the degree programs offered, location, flexibility it provides to adult learners, acceleration options like PLA, and affordability. Make sure it is a regionally accredited institution. Make your decision using the best and most complete information you can find!

36 months of educational benefits. Benefits for tuition are paid directly to the school, while monthly housing allowances are paid directly to the veteran. Most veterans in recent years have taken advantage of their eligibility for this program. Under this program, you may have the option to transfer any unused benefits to a spouse or dependent, provided you have at least ten years of service or have completed six years of a ten-year service commitment. A transfer of benefits must be formally approved by the U.S. Department of Defense.

GI Bill® is a registered trademark of the U.S. Department of Veterans Affairs (VA). More information about education benefits offered by VA is available at the official U.S. government website at http://benefits.va.gov/gibill.

+ **Montgomery GI Bill Active Duty (chapter 30).** According to the VA, this benefit is for service members who have at least two years of active duty. It provides up to 36 months of educational benefits to eligible veterans. Monthly benefits are paid directly to the veteran. This program is the predecessor to the Post-9/11 GI Bill.

+ **Montgomery GI Bill Selected Reserve (chapter 1606).** This is a benefit for those who are currently in the selected reserve.

✛ **Vocational Rehabilitation and Employment (chapter 31).** If you have a service-connected disability, consider applying for chapter 31 Vocational Rehabilitation and Employment (VR&E) services. This VA program creates an individualized plan to help you prepare for, find, and maintain suitable jobs. This includes educational training, tutorial assistance, and résumé preparation.

Special Notes:

✛ **Dependents Educational Assistance Program (chapter 35).** If you are the spouse or dependent of someone with a permanent and total service-connected disability, or someone who died as the result of such a disability, or who is missing in action, or who is currently detained by a foreign government in the line of duty, you may be eligible for a special educational assistance program through the VA. Check out the VA website for more information about the Dependents Educational Assistance Program. If

Michelle Mondia has worked as a medic in the air force national guard for the past eighteen years. Although she received advanced-level medic training in the military, it didn't equate to a civilian degree. Michelle found a new program at Joliet Junior College. The first of a larger statewide initiative, JJC's program allows veterans who have completed the Medical Education and Training Campus (METC) Basic Medical Technician Corpsman Program within the last five years to earn certificates as licensed practical nurses (LPNs)—and to do so in as little as eight weeks. Upon successful completion of the certificate, Michelle and the other veterans in her classes will be prepared to sit for the NCLEXPN examination to become an LPN.

you are a veteran with a permanent and total service-connected disability, your spouse and dependents may be able to receive educational assistance through this program.

+ **Reserve Educational Assistance Program (chapter 1607).** This is a benefit for reservists who have been called to active duty in response to a war or national emergency and is known as REAP. This program is no longer active, as it has largely been replaced by the post-9/11 GI Bill. REAP beneficiaries who were attending an educational institution on November 24, 2015, or during the last semester, quarter, or term ending prior to that date, are eligible to continue to receive REAP benefits until November 25, 2019.

+ **Monthly Housing Allowance (MHA).** The post-9/11 GI Bill also offers a monthly housing allowance that is based on the zip code for the main campus of your college. The allowance is also dependent on your eligibility percentage, whether you take online or hybrid courses, and your rate of pursuit (you need to be attending at least half-time).

STEP 2: COMPARE BENEFITS

Once you know which benefits you're eligible for, explore how each benefit fits in with your needs. A good resource is the U.S. Department of Veterans Affairs (VA) Comparison Tool. The tool lets you compare how various benefit programs will cover educational costs and related living expenses at a specific institution. Enter your military status, the specific GI Bill benefit you want to use, your months of service, the names of all of the colleges you are considering, and whether or not you will be taking all of your courses online. You will be able to access detailed information about your total expected GI Bill benefits, including housing allowance.

Another useful nonofficial source of information on different veterans benefits is EarnUp, found at Earnup.org/veterans-benefits.

STEP 3: KNOW THE TOTAL COST OF ATTENDING SCHOOL

The VA Comparison Tool is a terrific place to start. But it doesn't necessarily compare *all* costs of education. You can estimate additional costs by using a school's net-price calculator. This tool calculates the estimated cost of attendance—including tuition, fees, books and supplies, room and board (meals), and other related expenses. You can find net-price calculators on the websites of many colleges and universities, or you can search for your school's calculator at the U.S. Department of Education's online Net Price Calculator Center. *As noted in chapter 7, students who plan to attend college part-time should be careful not to rely too heavily on net-price calculators, as the calculated price assumes that you will be attending college full-time.*

STEP 4: KNOW WHAT BENEFITS YOUR SCHOOL ACCEPTS

Contact your school's designated veterans and military personnel office to learn what types of military educational benefits the school is approved for by the VA. Private and public institutions must follow specific financial regulations. Each school should be able to explain what type of military educational benefits they process and can accept on your behalf. If you are enrolling at a public college or university, you may have access to state funding for veterans in addition to benefits offered through the VA.

STEP 5: APPLY FOR VETERANS EDUCATIONAL BENEFITS

Once you have determined which benefits best meet your needs, it's time to apply! You can submit a paper application (available for download at the VA's eBenefits website) to your local VA Regional Processing Office or apply online using the Veterans Online Application (VONAPP) system. To learn more, visit the eBenefits VONAPP web page.

Most applications require confirmation of your service. Submitting a copy of your DD214 (service member's copy #4) is not required, but doing so might help reduce the time you will need to wait for a response from the VA. Also, although filling out the application does not obligate you to use the benefit, you will still need to supply your bank routing information to complete the application.

The VA website states that the application process generally takes one month for first-time claims and about one week for reenrollment. Keep in mind that wait times are longer in the fall when the volume of claims is higher. In case there is an unexpected delay, allow 8-12 weeks for the process to be completed.

STEP 6: CONFIRM APPROVAL

You will confirm the approval of benefits by taking your certificate of eligibility to your school's certifying official (the Department of Veterans Affairs will send this to you via regular mail, not electronically). Create and log into your e-benefits account to verify your benefits status at the VA's eBenefits web page.

STEP 7: EXPLORE ALTERNATIVE BENEFITS AND FINANCIAL ASSISTANCE

The GI Bill may not be your only option to pay for college. There are other educational benefits and types of aid you may be able to use in addition to or instead of your earned military educational benefits. It pays to do a little investigation.

ADDITIONAL FEDERAL VETERANS EDUCATION BENEFITS

✢ **VA Work-Study Program.** If you are attending education or training on a full-time or three-quarter-time basis, you may be eligible for a VA work-study allowance. Participants in this program earn an hourly wage equal to the federal minimum wage or state minimum wage, whichever is greater. The college may pay you the difference, if any, between the amount the VA pays and the amount the school normally pays other work-study students. VA work-study jobs are focused on providing services that are related to VA work. Visit the VA website to access the application and additional information about this program.

✢ **The Veterans Access, Choice and Accountability Act of 2014.** This new law enables recently released veterans using Post–9/11 or Montgomery GI Bill–Active Duty benefits to pay in-state tuition at public universities and community colleges. This means that you no longer have to wait to establish residency in order to pay lower tuition in your new home state. This in-state status will also be granted to veterans' spouses and children. See the VA's GI Bill resident rate requirements web page (www.benefits. va.gov).

✢ **The Yellow Ribbon Education Program.** This is another source of financial support for student veterans attending college. Schools that participate provide additional funding support toward tuition costs. Verify your eligibility and check if your school is a participant by visiting the VA's Yellow Ribbon Program web page. Note: Funds for the Yellow Ribbon Program are limited by the participating school and thus may not be available for all eligible veterans.

ADDITIONAL NONMILITARY FEDERAL STUDENT AID

There also are many types of nonmilitary federal student aid available, as explained in chapter 7 of this book. To apply for these programs, you will need to complete a different set of paperwork through the Free Application for Federal Student Aid (FAFSA).

ADDITIONAL STATE AID FOR VETERANS

Several states have additional sources of support that may cover your tuition costs and can sometimes be used in combination with some federal military educational benefits. These may be limited to attendance at public colleges and universities. You can inquire about the existence of such programs with your state VA department.

ADDITIONAL PRIVATE AID FOR VETERANS

Other organizations offer educational assistance to military personnel, veterans, and their dependents. The following is a sample listing of such organizations:

✢ Military Officers Association of America (MOAA): www.moaa. org
✢ Army Emergency Relief: www.aerhq.org
✢ Air Force Aid Society: www.afas.org

+ Marine Corps Scholarship Foundation: www.mcsf.org
+ Navy Marine Corps Relief Society: www.nmcrs.org
+ Coast Guard Mutual Assistance: www.cgmahq.org
+ National Association for Uniformed Services (NAUS): www.naus.org
+ Student Veterans of America: studentveterans.org
+ American Legion: www.legion.org
+ Veterans of Foreign Wars: www.vfw.org

When you are exploring other funding options, keep in mind that if it sounds too good to be true, it probably is! Guard your private information while online and use only trusted sources—if they charge you a fee to process your application, it may not be a viable organization. If your school has a veterans' resource center or veterans' services office, the staff there can direct you to a veterans financial aid specialist who can help you navigate your options.

EMPLOYER TUITION OPTIONS

If you are currently employed, note that some employers offer tuition assistance to employees who are seeking to improve their skills in areas related to their jobs. It's always worth discussing these options with your employer's human resources office.

Credit for What You Learned in the Military

Any adult going back to school should be aware that they may have college-level learning that they have acquired from their life and work experiences, or from noncredit instruction. Adults with a lot of this kind of learning can save themselves considerable time and money in earning a degree if they attend a college that awards college credit for learning that is formally evaluated. This kind of opportunity is often referred to as prior learning assessment (PLA) or credit for prior learning (CPL). These options are covered in detail in chapter 10 of this book.

As a veteran, you may find PLA really important because you may have considerable options for earning credit for your military training and expe-

Jason Wolfe joined the U.S. Navy right out of high school at age eighteen. He worked as an Aviation Boatswain Mate (ABE), launching aircraft on ship flight decks. After his military discharge, Jason began working on his college degree. He learned from his advisor at Indiana Tech that he could use CAEL's prior learning assessment service, LearningCounts.org, to get credit toward both an AA and a BA in industrial and manufacturing engineering. Jason earned twenty-four credits, the equivalent of eight college-level courses, through portfolio assessment. For each class for which he earned credit, he wrote a five- to ten-page paper and attached additional evidence such as supporting documentation, certificates he had earned, and reference letters from peers. Each paper demonstrated his command of the subject matter, its theoretical principles, and how he applied those principles to resolving real-life engineering issues. As soon as the credits were awarded, he received his associate degree, and two months later he earned his bachelor's.

rience. The military provided you with top-notch training and unequaled learning experiences, and that knowledge can translate into college credit.

As we explained in chapter 10, PLA isn't just one method or tool. To help familiarize you with how PLA works, we'll walk you through the following types of PLA that are particularly useful for veterans:

- ✛ Formal Evaluation of Training Programs
  - ✦ For active military or veterans, using transfer guides for military training and transcripts
  - ✦ For nonmilitary training programs
- ✛ Portfolio Assessments
- ✛ Exams

FORMAL EVALUATION OF TRAINING PROGRAMS FOR ACTIVE MILITARY AND VETERANS

Many schools have transfer guides that detail how your military training will transfer to their institutions. To determine transfer eligibility, the first thing you'll need to do is provide the school with an official transcript of your formal military training, called the Joint Services Transcript (JST) for the army, navy, marines, and coast guard or—for air force members—the Community College of the Air Force (CCAF) transcript.

Because CCAF is an accredited institution, CCAF transcripts are generally treated just like academic transcripts from other institutions. For training in other military branches, many schools rely on recommendations developed by the American Council on Education (ACE) to determine which military training/occupations have learning outcomes equivalent to college-level courses and can transfer to their institution for credit. The ACE Military Guide is a terrific resource for finding out (1) which military occupations and training courses are recommended to equate to postsecondary credit and (2) how many credits should be awarded for each. You can find ACE recommendations on your JST, or you can manually search the recommendations on the ACE website.

Important: When your institution transcribes your JST, it is important that they award credits that will count only toward your program requirements. Due to the financial aid eligibility requirement called **Satisfactory Academic Progress (SAP)**, the transcription of too many unused credits can lead to financial aid ineligibility for the student in question. Many—but not all—schools have policies in place to prevent this outcome; if you have an extensive military training history, you are advised to confirm with your school that excess credits will not be automatically posted to your transcript.

ACTION STEPS:

✛ If you have a JST, read your transcript or search the ACE Military Guide online to see ACE's credit recommendations for your military occupation and training courses.

✛ Contact the veteran coordinator or veteran representative in the office of admissions at the college you are considering. Ask if they will conduct an unofficial evaluation of your college transcripts, including military transcripts, so that you can get a sense of whether your previous learning will count toward a degree at that institution. Once you decide to attend a college, they will need to do a more formal evaluation based on official transcripts (see the following action steps).

✛ Order your military transcripts. If you served in the army, navy,

Transferology.com is a useful website that may help you determine how your military learning experiences will be treated at a specific institution if that institution has joined the Transferology system. Simply create an account and search for the type of training you received in the "Military Credits" section of the "Will My Courses Transfer" page of the website. You can then select "Search for Matches" to see which colleges and universities offer credit for your training, as well as the specific courses for which credit is granted.

marines, or coast guard, your transcript is provided through the Joint Services Transcript and may be obtained at https://jst.doded.mil/official.html. If you served in the air force you may order your CCAF transcript at www.airuniversity.af.mil/Barnes/CCAF.

✛ Identify and reach out to the school's point of contact for a formal determination of credit articulation and transfer.

FORMAL EVALUATION OF TRAINING PROGRAMS FOR NONMILITARY TRAINING PROGRAMS

If you already have professional licenses or industry certifications, or if you have completed noncollegiate instructional programs that are occupation specific, you can request an evaluation of the associated coursework and career activities for academic credit. Even if you are pursuing education in a different field, those experiences and credentials could possibly count toward your education and be very important to your future career.

EXAMS

Some schools offer customized exams to verify college-level learning achievement. These may be final exams for current courses or *challenge exams*. Challenge exams are designed by school faculty to assess whether an incoming student with prior learning can meet the learning objectives of a specific course.

Standardized testing is also available. Many of these tests are approved national tests under the GI Bill and certain testing fees can be reimbursed (see box). You will need to check with your school to find out which tests it accepts. Some examples of the more widely accepted standardized exams are:

+ College-Level Examination Program (CLEP) Exams
+ UExcel Credit by Exam (Excelsior College Exams)
+ DSST Exams (formerly DANTES Subject Standardized Tests)

You may be able to take some of these exams at the college—or, if you are on active duty, you may be able to take them at the education center on base.

PORTFOLIO ASSESSMENTS

A portfolio is a written document you prepare that describes the knowledge and skills gained from experiences you want assessed for college credit. Portfolios can be useful to veterans and service members when there are no credit recommendations or standardized tests available. Generally speaking, GI Bill benefits do not cover the cost of portfolio assessment itself but may cover it if the assessment is offered as part of a course.

New Developments for Veterans: Accelerated and Bridge Programs

Veterans who received specialized training in the military are often frustrated to discover that in order to perform the same job in the civilian sector, they must obtain additional licensure or certification, or even a college degree. This disconnect is why program evaluations are so important for veterans. Many states have realized that their occupational requirements are out of sync with military training. Some have begun reviewing occupations that require licensure or certification in the civilian world with an eye toward how those requirements correspond to military training and experience. Ask if your school has an accelerated or bridge program based on these evaluations. Such programs can reduce the amount of time necessary to obtain a credential by recognizing and providing credit for military training and experience.

Here is a quick PLA checklist to help you become a better-informed consumer:

+ Ask at your school's registrar's office or assessment and testing office what types of PLA methods are available and obtain a list of the school's required action steps to receive credit and a summary of its policies on PLA.
+ Order your records to be delivered to your new school.
+ Schedule an appointment and meet with your academic advisor. Bring copies of all of your prior learning records, including your Joint Services Transcript or CCAF transcript, so your advisor can help you determine the degree or program of study and course schedule that corresponds with your intended career path.
+ Take ownership of your academic path. Remember to review the school's degree plan and course descriptions as well as your previous learning records. Request that the institution help you get academic credit for your previous learning.

CAREER GUIDANCE RESOURCES FOR VETERANS

If you know you want to go back to school but are not sure about the right direction for your civilian career, there are a lot of resources out there to help you. In addition to the resources outlined in chapter 4 of this book, check out these other resources specifically designed for veterans like you.

Career OneStop Veterans Reemployment
www.careeronestop.org/ReEmployment/veterans/default.aspx
This website offers education and employment tools specifically crafted for veterans.

DANTES Career and Transition System
http://dantes.kuder.com
This interactive site was designed specifically to help service members transition into the civilian workforce; it includes tools such as assessments of interests, skills, and work values. Individuals receive their own unique log-in so they can save their information and begin the process of finding a career and the postsecondary education path that will get them there.

A Note About Prior Learning Assessment Credits

All schools do not determine prior learning assessment credits using the same methods or standards. Even if your top choices in schools offer the same types of PLA, their policies and procedures for awarding college credit for prior learning may be vastly different. Each school also has its own regulations and restrictions. For example, they may limit the amount of institutional credit you can get from PLA, PLA options may be limited to specific degree programs, or credit may be restricted to use toward program electives only. Some schools will review transcripts for credit only after you have enrolled, or even after you have successfully completed one full term of study.

You should take time to understand the policies in place at your school of choice and how they will affect your educational path. The more you know and understand about PLA and your school's policies on PLA, the better equipped you will be to maximize the benefits from your military training and skills. See more details about prior learning assessment in chapter 10 of this book.

O*Net Military Crosswalk
www.onetonline.org/crosswalk/MOC

This online resource provides a tool to search jobs by military occupational classification (MOC) and translate them to civilian occupation titles.

My Next Move for Veterans
www.mynextmove.org/vets

My Next Move allows veterans and service members to research various career fields they may be interested in. It gives the breakdown of the knowledge, skills, abilities, and education required for the different occupational fields as well as the average salary.

OTHER RESOURCES

Veterans Upward Bound
www2.ed.gov/programs/triovub/index.html

This is a free Department of Education program designed to help low-income, first-generation college students who are veterans enter and succeed in their postsecondary education. The resources offered by the program are designed to help identify learning needs and help veterans succeed in school. If you are a veteran, are low income, and your parents do not have a college degree, you may find this program to be helpful to you. To find out whether there is a program near you, search online for "Veterans Upward Bound" and your state name.

Student Veterans of America
http://studentveterans.org/index.php

Student Veterans of America (SVA) is a nonprofit organization that provides services and support to veterans pursuing degrees. Individual chapters of SVA can be found on many college campuses. They provide peer-to-peer support to veterans in college.

CHAPTER 13

Getting College Support to Succeed

Imagine: you've found a college, enrolled in classes, and are happily on your way to the degree you've always dreamed of. But now you've hit a bump in the road. Maybe it is figuring out how to solve that one seemingly *impossible* math problem, or not knowing where to even begin researching an essay about how texting has affected teen literacy (you know it has but you need sources!), or what to do when you spill coffee on your keyboard during a late-night study session.

All of us struggle at various points in our college careers. Luckily, your college likely provides a whole host of services and resources to carry you over the bumps, large and small, and on to success.

The purpose of this chapter is to let you know what kinds of services colleges may offer—and to encourage you to use them if you need them!

Locating Your School's Resources

For any new college student (young or old), one of the most overwhelming first steps is figuring out where everything is, regardless of whether you are on campus or online—and where do you even begin looking for help?

Careful!

Not all colleges will offer all of the services mentioned in this chapter and, even if they do, some may be better than others. For example, some career centers may offer more up-to-date career advice than others, some colleges will have stronger relationships with employers for access to employment opportunities than others, and some career centers may be better at helping students in some industries rather than others.

If you think that a particular service will be important for your college success, be sure to research whether the schools you are applying to offer it and how it compares to what other schools offer.

You can use the exercise at the end of this chapter to help identify what services are important to you and track whether schools you are interested in offer them.

Many schools provide orientations for new or transfer students—some even have orientations tailored specifically for adult students. Whether it is a whole day in person or an interactive online tour, this is your first chance to discover what your school has to offer. Take advantage of that orientation session if you possibly can.

However, if your school doesn't provide orientation, or if you can't attend, there are a number of other ways to figure out what is available and where:

1. **Student handbook.** Colleges will often provide a book (or a digital copy if you are online) with all of the information you need to know (or might have forgotten) about the school and its policies, including the various student services that are available.
2. **Website.** Most departments on campus typically have a web page—you can either look for the "Student Services" section on the colleges' main website, or do a page search for the specific department you need.
3. **Academic advisors.** In addition to helping you register for classes or manage your schedule, these staff members will often know a lot about the school and what it offers, and can point you in the right direction for getting help with things other than academics.

4. **Other students**. Two heads are better than one! If you are comfortable reaching out, you can always ask your classmates and fellow students if they know where to get writing help or who can help you log in to your email; chances are they've had similar questions and may have some tips to share.

What if you have a problem but don't know which department to even look for? Following are some typical services that colleges and universities offer to students and what they can offer you as an adult learner: academic assistance, technology troubleshooting, as well as personal and social support.

ACADEMIC SUPPORT

Colleges and universities want you to succeed. They also recognize that you may need extra support in meeting the academic standards they expect of their graduates, which is why many offer a number of common academic services to students, including tutoring, writing help, and accommodations for students with learning or other disabilities.

First Stop . . . Your Instructor

If you are struggling in a class—maybe you don't understand the material, or you are working hard but still not getting the grade you want—your first

I Don't Need Help! Next Chapter . . .

Are you sure? Sometimes we don't know we need help until it's too late—until, say, we failed that last midterm, or we can't get online to participate in an important class discussion. That's why it's important to know what support services your institution offers, even if you don't need them right now. If you know what is available, you'll know where to go when you need it!

And, while it's never too late to ask for help, knowing when to ask is important, too. Meeting regularly with your academic advisor or utilizing a professor's office hours can help you identify when you are struggling. Let them know how you are doing in your classes and if you are finding anything to be especially difficult. They might know when it's the right time for you to seek out some extra help.

> What helped was engaging with professors outside of class. Like this one professor—she and I spent so much time together talking about class, and she gave me a lot of perspective about life. She made me feel so much better about chasing down the passion instead of the profession.
>
> —Andy, adult student, age 30,
> DePaul University School for New Learning

step in your search for help should be to talk to your instructor. Professors have regular office hours when they are available to talk with students who have questions (often these times will be outlined in the course syllabus). Even if you aren't available at those times, many professors are willing to meet outside of office hours if you ask. Remember, your instructors want you to succeed—and their job is to help you do just that. Take advantage of their availability and, if they have suggestions for you, take their advice. Your instructor also can refer you to other academic resources the college offers if you need additional help.

Tutoring

Now is the time to set aside any negative stereotypes you might have of tutoring—that it means you aren't smart enough, or that it is available only for a price. Smart college students take advantage of all the help they can get, and with many colleges offering tutoring for free (or at a very affordable rate), you can't afford *not* to use it, especially if you're having trouble in a subject or class. While colleges can vary as far as who fills the role—knowledgeable undergraduates, experienced graduate students, or adjunct instructors—tutors are there to help support your studies in almost any subject.

A variety of formats will likely be available, so consider what would best suit your needs.

Drop-in: If you just need some quick help working through a problem, many tutoring centers will offer drop-in times where you can sit down with a tutor in a particular subject area for a short period of time.

One-on-one: If you feel you need more in-depth help with a class or a subject area, you may also be able to schedule longer, or recurring, one-on-

one appointments with individual tutors who can track your progress over time and help you grow.

Guided study groups or supplemental instruction (SI): Many tutoring centers also offer peer-led study sessions oriented around a particularly difficult class. Students who have mastered the material and been trained in group facilitation will lead students in informal study sessions where they can review course material by sharing notes, discussing readings, practicing problems, or studying for upcoming exams.

Online: Some colleges offer virtual access to tutoring for online students, either through their online learning platform, by phone, or by Skype. If your college doesn't offer remote tutoring, there are a host of online tutoring services (such as Tutor.com) that you can try. However, these are typically much more expensive than the services your college provides (particularly if those are free!), so you should definitely check with your college's tutoring center first to see if they can meet your needs.

WRITING CENTER OR LAB

Writing college-level essays and papers is something many people struggle with when returning to school, especially if your job doesn't require you to write on a regular basis. Recognizing this, many schools have centers devoted specifically to helping students improve their writing.

As with tutoring, you can access your school's writing center in a number of ways, such as **drop-in advising** for quick suggestions and feedback, or a **scheduled consultation** where a staff member can read and

A Word from the Experts

As academic advisors, we generally talk to students about [their performance] in terms of their grades. So if their grades are slipping, we check first if they've had a conversation with their instructor. Because in many cases, the instructor is willing to work with them. They're not all going to do that, but the first step is to ask.

—*Debbie Smith, associate director of academic advising and academic advisor, University of North Carolina–Charlotte*

Preparing for a Tutoring Session

Plan ahead. To get the most out of the services, make tutoring and/ or supplemental instruction (SI) sessions a part of your regular study routine at the beginning of the semester.

Be prepared. Attempt all of your assignments or problems before attending a session and write down questions to ask your tutor or SI leader.

Budget your time. By preparing ahead, you should be better prepared to prioritize the questions and problems you would like to review.

Be patient. Tutors and SI leaders are there to help you review material and provide feedback. **They will not know everything** but can help you find the answers!

Don't give up! Tutoring and SI sessions may feel uncomfortable, but it is important that you don't give up after your first session. Feel free to set tutoring sessions with different tutors, or plan to visit a couple of the scheduled SI sessions in order to figure out what works best.

Adapted from materials obtained from Saint Louis University.

review a specific piece of your writing before you meet in order to provide more in-depth feedback. In either case, make sure you are well prepared for the appointment by writing down your goals for the session as well as specific questions. Colleges with lots of online classes may offer the ability to submit a paper online and meet with a staff member via **Skype for an online chat**.

As with tutoring, it pays to take the initiative and seek out this help early if you think that writing may be a challenge for you. If you know that writing is not your strong suit, go ahead and schedule an appointment! Even if you haven't had a paper assigned yet, bring in another piece of writing you have done and ask for feedback on that.

A Word from the Experts

If I'm going to an institution, I would like to know, "Are you giving me everything I need to be successful in my journey so that I can achieve my goal?" Ask the institution to answer that question.

—Tom Porch, retention planning and initiatives manager at the Department of Student Advising and Retention, University of Maryland University College

DISABILITY/ACCESSIBILITY SERVICES

If you have been identified as having a learning, physical, psychological, or emotional disability that may affect your ability to learn, your college is required to provide appropriate academic adjustments and other accommodations. These can vary according to your particular circumstances, so it is recommended that you consult the disability services center at your college.

As always, the earlier you identify and reach out to your college's disability services staff, the better. They can walk you through the process of applying for and receiving accommodations, as well as describing what is available to you.

For more information around preparing for college as a student requiring accommodations, please see this resource from the U.S. Department of Education: *Students with Disabilities Preparing for Postsecondary Education: Know Your Rights and Responsibilities*.

THE LIBRARY

If you're already on campus and have tried locating any of the services mentioned so far, you may have found them in the library. Gone are the days when libraries were just silent rows of books: at most colleges they are now vibrant centers of activity, learning, and engagement, housing a seemingly bottomless well of resources to help you through your college career.

Of course the main role of the library is still to offer students access to books, articles, and any other academic resources you might need. But what if you have a specific question you need to answer for a paper or a test—you're pretty sure you have to look it up in a book or online, but where do you start?

In these cases, the **reference librarian** is your best friend. These wise souls are trained to help you find the right book, article, photo, or website, no matter how obscure. You can find them either behind the reference desk or online—many university libraries now offer reference and research consultation via online chat or by email. Some universities also offer services to send you books and other materials if you are an online or distance student.

Online and Tech Support

Today's university is increasingly going digital. Even if you aren't taking classes online, your college's technology support center will likely be a vital lifeline while you are in classes. Whether it's logging in to your email/student account, connecting to the Wi-Fi, or uploading a paper for class, these wizards are your go-to resource for navigating the often mystifying landscape of technology in the classroom (physical or digital). Find out what services different colleges offer to their students and factor that into your decision making.

Career Services

Maybe you already have your dream job, and going back to school is either for your own pleasure and growth or so you can make a little more money doing what you love.

However, if you are going to college because you want a different kind of job or career, many colleges have some kind of career service center to help you prepare for a job search or think through career options.

You may have done some research yourself about possible careers—perhaps through the resources outlined in chapter 4. Career services can help you continue that exploration. They may have additional interest assessments or insights into local labor markets and employer needs that can help narrow your choices.

Later, once you are ready to start looking for a job, career services can help with that, too. In addition to employing counselors who have looked at hundreds (maybe thousands!) of résumés, cover letters, and mock interviews—and who would be more than happy to review yours—many

Common Library Services

Research guides and workshops. Information and resource lists specific to individual subjects, disciplines, and research skills

Study rooms. Quiet places for your study group to meet

Free access to computers and labs. On-campus access to computers loaded with useful software plus printers and scanners

Software licenses/subscriptions. Access (sometimes online) to expensive software like Adobe Creative Suite, MATLAB, GIS, etc.

Equipment rental and use. Projectors, video cameras, and possibly even 3D printers for student use

centers offer a wealth of additional networking and support services useful for professionals at any stage of their career.

Many local employers will list open positions on the school's **job board**, as well as attend **annual career fairs** and **networking events**. If you find a position that looks interesting, you may be able to use the center's **subscription services**, like Glassdoor or JibberJobber, to find out a little more about the employer, or **assessment tools** like Myers-Briggs or the Strong Interest Inventory to find out if you're a good fit. Keep in mind that career services centers can be very different from college to college. But you should take advantage of what your school's has to offer and ask for the specific help you need.

PERSONAL SUPPORT

As we described in the previous chapter, determining what sorts of personal support you'll need to go back to school is essential. Colleges also provide a number of personal and social support systems and services you should factor in to that equation.

+ **Childcare:** Some universities and colleges house their own early childhood education center or day care, which often offer discounted childcare rates to current students. However, the hours and ages that care is available can vary by college, so it is best to check to see what your college offers.

+ **Family housing:** Colleges may also specifically designate some on-campus or near-campus housing for families with children who may need it (if they are new to the area, for example). This housing usually provides greater amenities than a typical dorm room, and is usually set apart from the noise and chaos of traditional student housing.

+ **Transportation:** If you are attending a college in a larger city or metropolitan area, your school may offer free or discounted access to public transit.

+ **Health services and counseling:** Most colleges have student health service centers or clinics on campus, and also offer health insurance plans to those without coverage. In addition to routine health and wellness visits, these centers also may offer personalized counseling and mental health support at a reduced rate.

STUDENT GROUPS

For many adults, the priority when returning to school is to learn: to go to classes, absorb as much as they can, and get that degree (or certificate). The idea of joining a student organization may seem like a frivolous distraction if your eye is dead set on making it to graduation. But don't

> The college offered free peer mentoring and tutoring. I didn't think I'd need those, but it was nice to know it was there. And I have used those services. If I'm having any trouble, I just need to contact student services and they will set me up. The writing center is great—they will help edit papers. My partner goes to a different state school and they do not help like that. At my college, if you have a question, they will forward your email to the right person. They never say "I can't help you"—that is important.
>
> *—"Jean," adult student, age 35, SUNY Empire State College*

underestimate the benefit of establishing connections with other students outside of class! In addition to building a community of other students who know what you are working on and going through on a daily basis, student groups can provide additional support (both academic and emotional), resources, as well as opportunities for learning, growth, and exploration outside of class.

ALPHA SIGMA LAMBDA

Even if you are attending classes online, there are still opportunities to get involved in student organizations. One example is **Alpha Sigma Lambda**, a national honor society specifically for full- and part-time nontraditional adult students.

A Word from the Experts

Be open to using what is available on a college campus. Get involved with clubs and student organizations. Make the most of support services. Connect with your advisor. Use the career center to explore. Make connections with fellow students. Ask questions of your professors.

Understand that you're not alone, even if you feel like you are.

—Kathy Weinkle, career and education advisor,
CAEL Advising Services

Colleges for Adult Learners with Alpha Sigma Lambda Chapters

Following are just a few of the colleges from our Top 100 list that have their own Alpha Sigma Lambda chapter:

+ University of Utah, UT

+ Granite State College, NH

+ Southern New Hampshire University, NH

+ Regis University, CO

+ Stony Brook University, NY

+ Park University, MO

+ Hawaii Pacific University, HI

+ George Fox University, OR

In addition to providing an academic and social community of other adult students at your college (and at others around the country), Alpha Sigma Lambda awards a number of scholarships to adult students every year. While the number and dollar amount of these scholarships can vary from year to year, as long as you attend a school with an Alpha Sigma Lambda chapter and meet its eligibility criteria, you can apply for a scholarship—you don't even need to be a member of your college's chapter, although it is recommended.

While the criteria for joining vary according to each college chapter, the organization's aim is to "recognize the special achievements of adults who accomplish academic excellence while facing competing interests of home and work."

Visit the website to see if the college you are considering has a chapter: www.alphasigmalambda.org.

Exercise: Where's My Backup?

Tech support/help desk. Think through what kind of services you think you might find helpful to you as you start your studies. How important do you think they will be? Either by looking at their website, or asking an admissions representative, is it clear whether the colleges you are considering offer these services? Here is a chart that will help you think through and compare services offered by the top colleges you are considering.

	Importance (Not at all – Somewhat – Very	School A		School B		School C	
		Yes	No	Yes	No	Yes	No
Adult student orientation							
Writing center/lab							
Tutoring							
Peer mentorships							
Tech support/ help desk							
Career center							
Childcare							
Family housing							
Health insurance							
Health/counseling center							
Alpha Sigma Lambda							

Knowing What's Available Before You Apply

Much of this chapter has discussed identifying and locating services once you have already enrolled in a college or university and started classes. It also would be useful, however, to consider their availability when you are applying to schools—whether a school offers childcare or full-service tutoring may be the deciding factor between a great college and *your* college.

CHAPTER 14

What If My Skills Are Rusty?

For many of us, just saying the word "algebra" sends shivers up the spine! It has likely been many years since you needed to solve for "x" or thought about what a trapezoid is. College math is one of the most intimidating aspects of going back to school for adults. It can conjure up all kinds of images and insecurities from high school. Don't let math scare you. Thousands of students arrive at college every year with rusty skills in math as well as other subjects. You are not alone. Over half of adults considering college say they are "very likely" or "somewhat likely" to expect to take a remedial class in college. Remedial or developmental courses are intended to help students bring their math and English skills up to speed (or the college level) to provide a solid foundation to succeed in the rest of the coursework you'll take for your degree.

Placement Tests

Many colleges and universities require students to take placement tests in English and math (if you haven't already taken a college course in these subjects)—especially if you have been away from school for a while. The placement tests can use paper and a pencil or be computer delivered. These tests essentially determine if your skills are at the college level, or if they need to be brushed up a bit before taking courses. You may not like exams—and that's okay—but these tests can help you get a better picture of your skills as you start your studies.

Some colleges use placement tests developed by their own faculty. However, many colleges and universities use computer-delivered standardized exams. These exams may be *adaptive*, meaning that the exam adapts its questions to determine your level of skills as you take the test. If you answer a question correctly, it delivers a harder question. If you get an answer wrong, the test will drop back a notch and give you a little easier question. This method can reduce frustration levels for test takers while efficiently determining at what level they are performing academically for math, reading, and writing.

One example of an adaptive placement test that is commonly used by colleges is ***Accuplacer***. To learn more about Accuplacer, and see sample questions, go to the College Board's website and follow the link to its Accuplacer resources. They provide free test-preparation services, along with a free app and skills lab.

Preparing for the Placement Tests

There are a couple of ways you can approach placement tests. One way is to just take them and see what happens. The other way is to prepare for the tests by brushing up on your skills independently before taking the tests.

If you can make time, **studying and practicing in advance for these tests is a really good idea** because it might help you score better and keep you out of remedial courses altogether. This may enable you to place into a higher math or English course, saving you time and money. Also, many students get placed in developmental-level courses and then lose their motivation to keep going. The sooner you get into the courses you *want* to take in college, the more you will enjoy the experience. So study for these tests if you can!

It's not a crazy idea that you could study on your own for a test. It is important to remind yourself that you have gained a lot of knowledge and experience since you were last in school. You are not the same person. As an adult with lots of responsibilities and a budget, you will take your classes much more seriously than you might have in high school, or even if you attended college years ago. You also may find that learning on your own is not impossible. Studying and practicing for the tests will help you familiarize yourself (or refamiliarize yourself) with test taking. Brushing up on your skills is essential and very doable!

> **Avoid remedial courses if you can!** Study for placement tests—it can be worth your while!

How to Practice, Brush Up, and Catch Up with Free Resources

There are lots of resources available online to help you prepare on your own for placement tests. There are also resources to help you improve your time-management skills. Staying organized and managing your time is half of the battle when it comes to juggling college, work, and family

> **When English is not your first language.** If English is your second language, depending upon your reading and writing levels, you may need to improve your English skills. Colleges may ask that you take the TOEFL test that assesses your ability to use English at the college level. If you need to improve your language skills, English as a Second Language (ESL) and English Language Learner (ELL) classes are offered in your community. Adult education centers, community colleges, and churches often provide ESL or ELL classes.

Resources to Help You Brush Up on Your Skills

English (reading and writing)

Check out these helpful websites:

Online Writing Lab (OWL) at Excelsior College
This website offers a wide variety of interactive multimedia activities, quizzes, videos, interactive PDFs, and games—all designed to help writers understand important concepts about writing. There are sections on grammar, citations, and plagiarism —as well as a section that takes you step by step through the various stages of writing a paper.
owl.excelsior.edu

The Online Writing Lab (OWL) at Purdue University
The OWL serves thousands of students worldwide. Its tutors answer writing-related questions submitted online. As you move around the site, you'll find hundreds of how-to documents. It has also produced 30 instructional videos, located on its YouTube channel.
owl.english.purdue.edu/owl

St. Cloud State University Literacy Education Online (LEO)
You can click on phrases that describe your particular problem with writing, such as "my writing doesn't flow" or "it sounds choppy," and it will provide recommendations for how to improve your writing. There are lots of resources here that are easy to find and use.
leo.stcloudstate.edu

TV411 Reading
This site includes lots of videos that address various challenges you may face in studying, reading, and even test taking. The videos are short and direct.
www.tv411.org/reading

For English as a second language (ESL) students	**Lewis and Clark's ESL Independent Study Lab** You'll find over 250 internet resources for listening, pronunciation, vocabulary, reading, grammar, writing, and more on this site. It's all nicely organized allowing you to click on whatever topic interests you. **www.lclark.edu/~krauss/toppicks/toppicks.html** **Purdue University's Online Writing Lab (OWL)** Check out the English as a Second Language section. **owl.english.purdue.edu/owl** *You might also check out local basic and continuing education classes for adults offered at your nearby community center or public schools. Your college may also offer ESL classes, either on campus or at a community center.*
Math	**Free-ed.net Mathematics** Click on your topic of interest and then narrow your choices down to the problems that you would like to learn about. **www.free-ed.net/free-ed/Math** **www.math.com** This site has everything you need to brush up on your math skills, whether it's by type of math problem or by grade level. **www.khanacademy.com** A great site for online math lessons.
Study skills and time management	**Study Guides and Strategies Website** This site hosts every study topic you can think of, such as learning to learn, memorizing and test taking, study skills information, and time management suggestions. **http://www.studygs.net** **University of Minnesota Duluth's Study Strategies Homepage** This site includes a self assessment, time audit, study skills checklist, and many more resources including "Note-Taking Tips and Test-Taking Strategies." **http://www.d.umn.edu/kmc/student/loon/acad/strat/index.html**

Integrated-developmental ed? A possible option to explore. Some colleges and universities have begun to offer developmental content within a college-level course that you are required to take. The benefit is that you can get the extra support you need while taking a course that will count toward your requirements. This approach helps you continue to make progress on your degree while improving your English and writing skills. Make sure you ask your admissions advisor about these options.

obligations. There are easy tips available that can make a world of difference for you.

At many institutions, the admissions advisor and the testing services staff can provide specific insights about the tests you will take and provide resources to help you prepare. In addition to these services and support, check out the resources listed here.

WHAT HAPPENS IF I DON'T SCORE WELL?

If your scores on the placement tests are on the low side, your college will probably sign you up for developmental courses. You might want to negotiate this if you can, particularly if your scores are close to the cutoff. Ask if you can retake the test—and then study ahead of time. Or ask if you can enroll in one or two college-level courses on a trial basis—and then take advantage of faculty office hours, peer study groups, and campus-provided tutoring to help you through any rough spots.

Developmental courses *are* the right choice for some students. If you need to take a developmental course, then make sure to take the course seriously and look at it as an opportunity to build or improve skills that you will need throughout the rest of your program.

Typically, the course numbers for the classes that first-year college students take are 100-level courses, such as Accounting 101, Composition 101, etc. The course numbers for developmental courses are usually 099—in other words, less than a 100-level course. This simply means that you will not get college credit for the 099 course because it is preparing you for college-level work.

The idea behind placement testing and developmental coursework is that they support students in getting to where they want to go—into college programs and ultimately graduating! Stay focused on getting to your program courses as soon as possible, while gaining the knowledge that will serve you throughout your plan of study.

Some students become discouraged when they take only developmental courses because they feel as if they are not making progress toward completing a certificate or degree. If at all possible, try to take a 100-level course that is of interest to you at the same time that you are taking your developmental classes. This will help you stay interested and motivated. Talk to your academic advisor to make sure you do not end up stuck in developmental courses for too long. If you are not making progress, seek help! You do not want to use up too many of your tuition dollars on courses that will not ultimately count toward your degree.

A Word from the Experts

I worked with one adult learner, "John," who decided to return to school in his mid-thirties. He was told he had been out of school so long he needed to take placement exams. He took the exams right away (without studying) and learned that he was placed in a college-level math class, but his scores suggested that he might need to take developmental reading and writing classes. He worked with his admissions advisor and was able to schedule a retest that would be writing an essay on a surprise topic.

John studied and prepared by looking at various websites on writing good essays and techniques on how to organize your thoughts before writing (use an outline!). He entered his retest feeling anxious but also confident. When he received the surprise topic, the topic was, "Is happiness a choice? Why or why not?" John was able to outline his thoughts on happiness and include several examples about choosing to go back to school and tackling the associated challenges.

He later learned that his retest placed him directly into college-level work! John tells me now that the experience created a confidence that stayed with him throughout his studies.

— *Jen Groh, associate vice president, Higher Education, CAEL*

When I went back to school, I didn't think I would be able to retain the information. I was scared. You have these young kids in school, and I didn't think I was up for it. My first semester was nerve wracking. Once you get the hang of it, there are some challenges, but rewards [too]. You dedicate your time and you can very well pass the test, and feel accomplished, and learn something new. Don't be afraid to take that first step.

—*Mary, adult student, age 58, Miami Dade College*

WHAT IF THERE'S NO PLACEMENT TEST?

Some colleges do not require placement exams. In this case, you could easily go directly into college-level English and math courses. But will you succeed? If you are at all concerned about your skills, it is wise to go ahead and brush up on them by taking advantage of the resources listed in this book or by hiring a tutor.

Fifty-eight percent of adults who are considering going back to school think they are likely to take a remedial class in college (Public Agenda 2013).

MATH PHOBIAS

Most general education requirements include college algebra, and you may need to take statistics as well for the degree program that you want to enroll in. Don't let the math requirements scare you. Remember, you are not the same person you were in high school. You've moved on and are much more likely to find math more relevant and useful—and even more doable! Overcoming the challenge of it will help you develop more confidence in your studies.

While there really is such a thing as a math phobia, your fear of math is most likely rooted in fear caused by remembering (or not being able to remember!) math from grade school and high school. Making sure you are in the right level of math class, thanks to placement testing, will help you to develop your math skills and your understanding of basic math concepts.

If you are absolutely positive that something like a college algebra requirement is just not possible for you, talk with your admissions counselor about possible academic programs that do not require college algebra or that allow you to take a different kind of math requirement. Some colleges will have more pragmatic alternatives to college algebra, such as business or applied mathematics. You will probably not be able to avoid math altogether, but you will learn some useful math skills that you will need to function in your profession. Once in your courses, you can always seek help from the college's learning center where tutors may be available to help you.

CHAPTER 15

Lean on Them . . . Your Personal Support System

Going back to college can be challenging, not just for you but also for the people around you—your colleagues, your friends, and, most of all, your family. As with all major life changes, it is going to take some getting used to.

That is why identifying a network of people who will support you—who understand why your education is important and who can offer reassurance, support, and loving care—is a vital step in preparing for college as an adult.

Instead of offering a how-to, this chapter poses questions—for you to ask yourself and the people closest to you. While we will provide some suggestions, ultimately it is up to you and those closest to you to determine **what** *kind of support you will need while in college,* **who** *can help,* and **how/when** *to ask for help.*

Let's start by thinking about three spheres of your life (although there may be others you can think of) that will likely play an important role in your success as a student: your **family**, your **community** (including your friends, neighbors, or religious networks), and your **work**. (If you aren't currently employed, the third may not seem as relevant, but it is still worth considering if you are actively looking for work while in school.)

Weaving together resources and relationships from all three areas of your life can help you knit a strong web of support that will hold you up and keep you steady throughout your time in college.

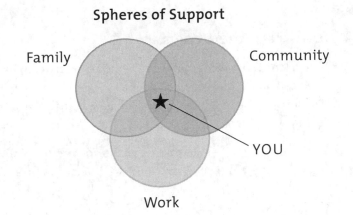

Spheres of Support

Family   Community

YOU

Work

FAMILY SUPPORT

Let's start by thinking about your family. Whether you are married, have children, take care of aging or infirm relatives, or are close to your extended family, family members are the individuals who are most involved in your everyday life and routine. Family can be an important source of support to you as a student—but it's also important to recognize how their lives might be affected by your studies. In addition to thinking through how your family might support your college success, it is also important to think through how your life will change and then consider how these changes will affect your family.

Questions to Ask Yourself and Your Family

Start by writing down all of the questions you think you'll need to answer about how going to college will affect your family (both immediate and extended). Then take a stab at answering them! For example:

✛ **Do your family members support your decision to pursue a college education?** If they recognize and support your decision, figuring out answers to the other questions will be a lot easier.

✛ **Is your family scared or nervous about you going back to school?** If so, why? Are they nervous they won't see you as much, or that you'll change? What could you do to help them feel better about this decision?

✛ **What's in it for them?** Do they understand why you want to go to school? Have you clearly communicated how your journey

A Word from the Experts

It's been a long time since adults have been beginners. They have to get used to being in college but so does everyone else in their life. They're not going to be available in the same way that they used to while they're in school.

—*Gwen Weaver, assistant director of advising,*
DePaul University School for New Learning

back to school could help the entire family (whether through increased income or your greater happiness and fulfillment)?

✛ **Are you the primary caretaker in your household?** If so, college is likely to take up some of the time you devote to taking care of your family—getting the kids to school or making dinner, for example. Are there other family members who can take over some your responsibilities while you are in school? Can you afford childcare, if necessary?

  ✦ If you aren't the primary caretaker, how might your added responsibilities affect whoever is?

✛ **What proportion of your family's income do you provide?** If you are the primary breadwinner in the family, will you be able to continue working while in school?

  ✦ Even if you think you will be able to, what happens if that changes once you are in classes—do you have a backup plan or an alternative source of income you can rely on?

✛ **Are there members of your family who have special needs (specialized healthcare, for example) that you are responsible for?** What arrangements need to be made to provide for them? Is another family member able to take on any of your responsibilities for care, or do you need to hire additional help?

✛ **What are ways that your extended family members would be able to help you through college?** Perhaps your aunt or cousin can watch the kids on occasion, or your brother can help with taking care of dad when he needs a little extra assistance.

✛ **What other practical problems will you face?** Once you're in classes, you won't have as much time or energy as you used to—how else is this likely to affect your family and your home life?

Conversations to Have with Your Family

Okay. So now you have a whole list of questions and possibly a few answers. What next?

A good first step may be to simply start having conversations with family members—call a family meeting or take time to talk about this new journey over dinner. Ask them the questions you've written down and see what their thoughts are. Here are a few suggestions for things to address:

✢ **Take the time to deal with any fears or concerns.** Be patient—you may be excited, but it's okay for others in your family to be nervous. Change is scary! Reassure them that everything will be fine (even if it doesn't always feel like it).

✢ **Get everyone involved in your plans.** Think together about how things will work when you are in school. Hold a family meeting to organize family and household responsibilities—ask your family what they want to help with. Try to rotate the jobs among family members as time goes on.

✢ **Try to find time for fun.** When schedules become hectic and everyone's working hard, it can be easy to put off things that don't feel urgent. Try to build in some deliberate downtime with your family amid your studies, even if it's something simple like eating breakfast together or spending an hour at the park.

✢ **Involve your family in your studies.** Talk about what you're studying and any problems you may be having. Explaining your assignments or learning in a way that is simple enough for children or a nonexpert to understand also can help you build your own understanding of the material.

Most importantly, acknowledge all the help you get. You wouldn't be able to do this without your family's support, so make sure they know it!

SOCIAL AND COMMUNITY SUPPORT

Of course, many of us have lives and activities outside of our families. We are involved in religious communities, community organizations, charities, PTA, home owners' associations, or even local government. Even if you don't participate in any of these, you probably have friends you go to for advice or help when things are difficult. How can these people—your community—support your educational journey?

Questions to Ask Yourself About Your Friends and Community

As before, start by writing down a list of questions that can help you determine where your support may lie among your friends and community. Here are a few examples to get you started:

- ✛ **Are you significantly involved in any community organizations or groups?** Is your time commitment to these organizations sporadic or regular? Do you hold a leadership position?
  - ✦ If so, how many hours a week do you spend committed to the group? Can you still fit it in with school and your other commitments or (more likely) will you need to step back?
  - ✦ Are any of these activities related to your college major or area of study? If so, it may be worthwhile to stay involved and think of ways this involvement can inform your studies.
- ✛ **Who are your closest friends?** How often do you see them in a week or month? What do you usually do? Do they give you energy and encouragement when things are difficult?

✧ **What are your regular social engagements?** Which ones can you not live without (again, which ones give you energy and strength)?

✧ **How often do you use social media?** What do you use it for? Sometimes social media can be beneficial, whether for staying in touch with friends (new and old), communicating with classmates regarding assignments, or soliciting help and encouragement from friends. However, if you find that you use social media primarily to procrastinate, you should try to cut back or stop using it entirely for designated chunks of time.

Conversations to Have with Your Friends and Community

As you were reflecting on the questions above, did you find yourself thinking of one particular friend who always has your back or who is always there with a quick word of encouragement? Or maybe you have a regular social gathering that you know gives you energy—a weekly card game or a monthly book club?

These are all people and communities you should remember to draw on for support when you are in school. You can start, even before classes begin, by approaching that close friend or group, letting them know that you are starting school, and asking if they'll help support you. When you ask, however, be sure to tell them what you are trying to accomplish and why: make sure they know what this experience means to you and why it is important that you succeed.

Identifying Your Community/Social Support Team

As you are thinking about the questions above, what people (or groups) stand out in your mind as potential supporters during your time in college?

Team Member's Name	Best Way to Reach Them *(Phone or Email)*	How They Can Help You

PLANNING WITH YOUR EMPLOYER

Whether or not your decision to go to college is to advance in your work, you'll likely need to figure out how to balance your new commitments with your work obligations. Beyond this, however, your colleagues and employer also can provide important assistance that can make your education easier.

Questions to Ask Yourself about Your Job

✛ **Do you travel regularly?** How might this affect the amount of time you are able to devote to studying? If you travel extensively, perhaps an online or distance learning program would be a better fit for you than a traditional, in-class program (see chapter 9 for different kinds of programs that exist and how to decide which one is right for you).

✛ **Is your work seasonal so that it occupies more of your time during one part of the year than another?** Again, if fall is usually very busy at work, perhaps finding an accelerated program that can be scheduled around that busy time will be best (see chapter 8).

✛ **What is your work schedule like?** If you regularly work long days, night shifts, or irregular hours, you might benefit from degree programs with built-in flexibility.

I have a very close single mom friend, we went through our bachelor's together—we graduated together. She has since applied and is starting her MA in policy at Empire. Sometimes we just carve out two hours to have coffee and just get it all out. It's a saving grace. Someone to slack off with you for a while. Someone who can say— let's get back on the horse now.

—"Jean," adult student, age 35, SUNY Empire State College

✛ **What educational support benefits does your employer offer?** Does your employer offer any of the following: tuition assistance or continuing education funds, flexible work schedules, or the ability to work from home?

✛ **Do your supervisor and co-workers support your college education?** Whether or not you pursue a college degree should not be based on their opinions, but their support and encouragement can make things a lot easier for you.

Conversations to Have with Your Supervisor and Co-Workers

Whether your supervisor or co-workers support your studies should also inform the conversations you have with them around balancing work and

A Word from the Experts

In most cases, adults have a plate full of life. It's not like the nineteen-year-old whose only job is to go school. Adults often don't take the time to consider how they will balance everything, and what specifically they will need to cut when they're completely lacking time. They should also consider what they are going to do when a hurdle comes up because it always will. You can't plan for specific hurdles, but you can understand that something is going to come up and that you're going to have to accommodate it.

—Scott Gabbert, academic advisor, DePaul University School for New Learning

Family members support me—there's a lot that can help, even just talking to my father, just to hear his feedback. He's proud of me. They never finished their degree and I'll be the first to get a degree. He will say, "Stick with it, what you're doing isn't in vain."

—Clifton, adult student, age 33,
University of Maryland University College

school. Unless your college journey is a result of professional requirements or encouragement from a supervisor (in which case they are presumably already supportive), you should raise the idea with your supervisor as early as possible.

Of course once you have a sense that they support you, some of the first things you will want to discuss with your employer and colleagues will be logistical questions of how to balance your work responsibilities and schedule with the demands of being a student. Some options you might discuss with your supervisor are:

✛ **Flexible hours.** Is it possible to alter your work schedule while you are in school to better align with your learning needs? For example, if you traditionally work Monday to Friday from 9 a.m. to 5 p.m., but you have a class you'd like to take on Thursdays at 3 p.m., is it possible to leave early on those days and put in a couple hours of work on weekends instead?

✛ **Remote or flexible workplaces.** A new class schedule may also make it difficult for you to commute to the office regularly: would your employer allow you to work from home or off-site?

✛ **Reduced workload.** If it becomes clear that you can't maintain your current workload and go to school at the same time, perhaps your employer will be willing to temporarily reduce your required tasks (or travel, if that is a significant element of your work) while you are in school.

Many employers offer **tuition assistance** or **continuing education benefits**. What these may look like and how to go about using them is discussed in more detail in chapter 7. Not only do these types of plans offer much-needed financial support, they also ensure that your employer is invested in your education and its success.

Above all, and as with your family and friends, make sure to communicate to your employer in all of these conversations the reasons you are going to college as well as the potential value a degree holds for you personally and professionally. Outline the ways in which a college education will make you a better, more effective employee, even if you need a few accommodations or assistance in the short term.

BOTTOM LINE: TAKE CARE OF YOU!

The most important member of your personal support system, however, is **YOU**. Ultimately you are the one person who is responsible for caring

Dealing with the Doubters

No matter how strong your support network is, there inevitably may be a few people who, for whatever reason, may not accept your decision to go to college. Having a friend, family member, or colleague who isn't supportive of your decision is discouraging!

So how do you handle these wet blankets?

First, recognize that feeling guilty or discouraged isn't going to help you succeed. Instead of letting this person get you down, set aside more time to be with family or friends who are supportive and can push back against that negativity. You also may simply try not to talk about your plans around the doubters. If they keep bringing it up, you may want to avoid them while you are in school, if possible.

Above all, try to maintain a positive attitude toward your studies. No matter how determined you are, this kind of criticism can affect your confidence or motivation. You don't need it! Remember, going to college is your choice and your responsibility—no matter what the naysayers think, if you've done the research and work hard, you can be successful and make college work for you!

for your health and well-being while in school. Maintaining good self-care habits—*especially* when you feel stressed, busy, or overwhelmed—is critical to succeeding in college.

Family, friends, and colleagues can help you succeed but only if you are willing to let them. You'll also need to provide guidance around what they can help with. Following are a few of the self-care areas in which your support network can play a vital role:

✛ **Physical health.** College can involve a lot of sitting—sitting in class, sitting to study, and even sitting to get to school. Even if you think you are too busy to go to the gym or play your favorite sport, you can keep your movement up in small ways. Take the stairs instead of the elevator, park at the back of the parking lot, or read a book for class while you're on the treadmill.

Friends and family can help support you by keeping you accountable for maintaining your physical activity. Make plans with a friend to go to the gym once or twice a week. Or, if you have a pedometer or fitness monitor, set up a competition with work colleagues to see who can take the most steps in a week.

✛ **Mental and emotional health.** College, like any important part of life, can sometimes be stressful or overwhelming. Sometimes our first response to stress is to buckle down and work harder, which can often increase the stress and anxiety we feel. Taking time to decompress mentally is also important while in school, not just for our overall well-being, but because the work we do while stressed can often be lower in quality and take more time than if we had just taken a break and come back to it later.

No matter how busy you are, be sure to schedule regular time for entertainment or your favorite hobby—as long as the activity gives you energy, gets your mind off school, and is healthy, go for it!

As with your physical health, your support network can play an important role in keeping you accountable to make time for yourself mentally and emotionally. Whether it is going out for coffee or to a movie with a friend, or simply reading in silence with a family member, ask others to help you take a step back from school every once in a while.

Your college may have resources to help support you as well— not just with balancing life, work, and school and on managing stress, but also other services to help you succeed.

Building Your Personal Support Team

By now you have thought carefully about the three spheres of personal support in your life. Ideally, you also have had conversations with your family, friends, and colleagues about what college will mean for your relationships and the ways in which they might support you on your journey.

Now take all of this information and lay out what this web of support will look like. Document who these people are and how they will support you by filling out your network of support below:

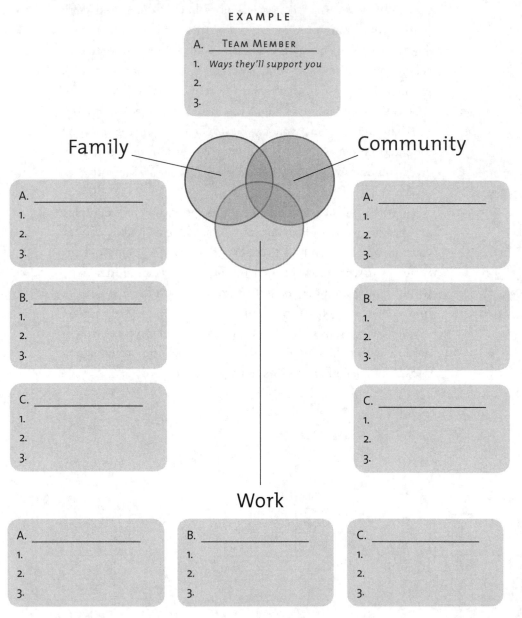

EXAMPLE

A. ___TEAM MEMBER___
1. *Ways they'll support you*
2.
3.

Family

A. _____
1.
2.
3.

B. _____
1.
2.
3.

C. _____
1.
2.
3.

Community

A. _____
1.
2.
3.

B. _____
1.
2.
3.

C. _____
1.
2.
3.

Work

A. _____
1.
2.
3.

B. _____
1.
2.
3.

C. _____
1.
2.
3.

Acknowledgments

The authors put the words on the page, but they rely on so many others to make a book like this happen. We are especially grateful to Bill Moses and others at the Kresge Foundation who recognized the need for a new kind of college ranking, along with companion publications like this one, to help students as they make important decisions about their postsecondary learning. Paul Glastris and his team at the *Washington Monthly* deserve special recognition for helping to flesh out the idea for this book and working closely with CAEL every step of the way to make sure that the book addresses the full range of questions that an adult learner should consider. As a top-notch journalist and committed advocate for students struggling to make sense of the postsecondary landscape, Paul's editorial guidance was indispensable.

We also are grateful to Tara Grove at The New Press for her editorial guidance and critical insights on the kinds of information adults need as they consider what to study and where to enroll. Seton Hall's Robert Kelchen is the mastermind behind the college rankings that are published every year by the *Washington Monthly*—his professional work is committed to measuring what matters for higher education accountability, and the field benefits every day from his immersion in and analysis of available data. We also recognize the great work of Jane Sweetland, author of *The Other College Guide: A Roadmap to the Right School for You*, which is the companion guide to the *Washington Monthly*'s Best Bang for Your Buck college rankings. Jane provided guidance to CAEL at the onset of this project and granted us permission to use her writing—which we did. Some of her descriptions of college types made it into our chapter titled "Making Sense of the College Landscape." They were just too good not to borrow for this book!

This book also benefited greatly from the stories of the adult learners we interviewed, who are profiled in Appendix D. Their experiences and ambitions and dreams are what motivate all of us at CAEL every day.

We valued the words of wisdom of the many professionals who work closely with adult learners at colleges and universities across the country, and we are grateful for the time they gave to share their insights. They are:

+ Patty Aragona, adult learner concierge, Truckee Meadows Community College
+ Geraldine Fitiseman, online success coach, School of Applied Technology, Salt Lake Community College
+ Michele Forte, assistant professor and faculty mentor, Center for Distance Learning, SUNY Empire State College
+ Scott Gabbert, academic advisor, DePaul University School for New Learning
+ Baxter Gamble, advisor, Complete the Degree Chicago
+ Carey Kilmer, assistant director of continuing and distance education, South Dakota State University
+ Scott Kizzire, assistant vice president of enrollment management, Bellevue University
+ Stephanie Luetgers, FlexPath coach, Capella University
+ Tom Porch, retention planning and initiatives manager, Department of Student Advising and Retention, University of Maryland University College
+ Debbie Smith, associate director of academic advising and academic advisor, University of North Carolina–Charlotte
+ Jillian Stubbs, 49er Finish program coordinator and academic advisor, University of North Carolina–Charlotte
+ Gwen Weaver, assistant director of advising, DePaul University School for New Learning
+ Kathy Weinkle, career and education advisor, CAEL Advising Services

We are further grateful to the other experts that we consulted during the project, including Sandy Baum of the Urban Institute and Lauren Walizer of the Center for Law and Social Policy.

CAEL has spent more than forty years working on behalf of the adult learner, and so this book drew heavily on our own staff's expertise. Staff who were notably helpful in sharing their expertise in advising adult students included Donna Younger, Laura Winters, Enosa Avery, and Elizabeth Hibner. Donna shared with us a booklet that she had written in 2013 for Pearson with Amy Baldwin and Brian Tietje called *The College Experience for Adult Learners*, which provided us with helpful directions for some of the later chapters in this book. In addition, many of CAEL's best ideas for advising adults on college were captured in a short booklet created several years ago called *A Consumer's Guide to Going to School*, developed in large part by CAEL's Susan Kannel. That consumer's guide gave a lot of initial direction for this book as well as definitions that became the starting point for our glossary. CAEL's Tucker Plumlee and Sean Hudson provided invaluable research and editorial assistance—Sean was especially helpful in summarizing our student stories and organizing the *Washington Monthly* rankings by state. Additional researchers for the book included Kathleen Glancy and Meaghan Green, and additional editorial assistance came from CAEL staff Amy Sherman, Gabi Zolla, Jennifer Groh, Mary-Celeste Schlusser, and Shawn Hulsizer. Friends of CAEL who reviewed select chapters included Baxter Gamble of Complete the Degree Chicago; Kathie Reilly of CAEL Advising Services; Rhonda Contreras of CAEL's Learning Counts; Jesus Fernandez, Ed. D; Yvonne Campbell of the Great Lakes Higher Education Guaranty Corporation; Roman Ortega Jr. of Lewis University; and Jaqueline Moreno of the Illinois Student Assistance Commission.

A big thanks also goes to CAEL's Leaders Council for supporting our research and policy efforts on behalf of adults pursuing postsecondary credentials.

Above all, we are grateful to the inspirational leadership of CAEL's president and CEO Pamela Tate. She has done more than anyone we know to advocate for the adult learner. She deserves outsized credit for the information and guidance provided in this book.

Appendix A.
College Rankings
for the Adult Learner

There are a lot of college rankings out there that are supposed to tell prospective students what the best schools are in the country, or in a region of the country, or for specific areas of study. If you search online, you'll find rankings from U.S. *News and World Report, Forbes, Money, Barron's Fiske, Princeton Review, Kiplinger's Personal Finance,* and the list goes on. . . .

So why not use those to find the school of your dreams? There's a good reason. Those rankings focus mostly on measures that are important to students who just graduated from high school and their families. The top-ranked schools might provide a great education, but they might not be located nearby, and they might not offer what *you* need as an adult with respect to scheduling or programs that will help you finish a degree and do so quickly. *Most high-profile college rankings were not developed with the adult learner in mind.*

Why is that important? Throughout this book, you'll learn about what some colleges do for adults that is different from how colleges serve the eighteen- to twenty-two-year-old student. Adult-friendly colleges design their programs for people with full-time jobs, or with unpredictable schedules. Adult-friendly colleges find ways to recognize the learning that you may have acquired outside of the classroom—and ways to have that learning count toward your degree. Adult-friendly colleges know that you are on a budget, and so they find new and innovative ways to cut costs. And adult-friendly colleges know that you are probably there because you want to advance in your career or because you have some solid experience informing your decision to launch a new career. And they care just as much as you do that you find good job and career options after you graduate.

The rankings we've included here have you and your needs in mind. The *Washington Monthly's Best Colleges for Adults* list was compiled for the first time in 2016. These rankings offer a robust list of the top four-year colleges and two-year colleges in our specially tailored rankings for adults.

For each state, there is a list of four-year colleges and another list of two-year colleges (or community colleges). The schools are listed in order of how they are ranked—the lower the number, the better the school scored nationally. Eight measures were factored into each school's overall score:

1. **Ease of transfer/enrollment.** This is based on measures of how easy it is for adult students to either initially enroll or transfer in from another college. (These topics are discussed in chapter 10 of this book.)

2. **Flexibility of programs.** This considers whether colleges are flexible enough to meet the needs of adult students—offering things like prior learning assessments, online degrees, advising services after hours, and weekend and/or evening classes. (These topics are discussed in chapters 8, 9, 10, and 15 of this book.)

3. **Services available for adult students.** This measure reflects whether a college offers services that adult students are most likely to use, such as general services for adult students, financial aid counseling, on-campus day care, counseling services, job placement services, or veterans' services. (These topics are discussed in chapters 13 and 14 of this book.)

4. **The percent of adult students (age 25-plus) at the college.** The higher the percentage, the greater the adult student presence at the college. Colleges serving large numbers of adults likely see the adult student as an important "customer."

5. **Graduation rate of part-time students.** The U.S. Department of Education released data on part-time students' graduation rates in 2017, and we are the first to use this in college rankings. This is important because adults typically attend college part-time.

6. **Mean earnings of independent (adult) students ten years after entering college.** If the goal is to improve your earnings potential, then this could be an important measure to consider as it reflects the employment success of the college's graduates.

7. **Loan repayment rates of adult students five years after entering repayment.** This measure is a good indication of how well the college does in meeting students' financial needs through federal loans—but not overburdening them with too much debt that they will have trouble repaying with the kind of jobs they get after leaving the college.

8. **Tuition and fees for in-district students.** This is the sticker price and it is seen as a simple measure of affordability. The net price, or the price that the average student actually pays, may be different.

Take a look at the rankings for your state and find the entries for the local colleges you are considering. If the college scored in the top 100–150, then it scored well in most or all of the seven key categories. For any college you may be considering, even if it didn't rank particularly well, look carefully at how each college was scored in the different categories to give you some idea of where that college is strong in serving adult learners.

If the colleges you are considering are not ranked well, don't panic. There are plenty of colleges that may be a great fit for you even if they do not rank well according to the data that are currently available. **Metrics and rankings should be only a starting point in your research.** The top-ranked college in the country might not be good for your goals or for your individual circumstances. There is plenty of material you can research on your own to make sure you enroll in the right college *for you*.

What Does "Unranked" Mean?

You'll see that there are a lot of colleges that are **unranked** in our list. That's not a warning sign about quality—it just means that we do not have enough data to include them in the rankings.

There are three main reasons why a college may be unranked:

1. The government lacks data on the earnings of that college's graduates.
2. There are no data on student loan repayment (this is common for community colleges, since some community colleges discourage students from taking out loans because the tuition rates are relatively low).
3. The college did not complete the College Board's annual survey of programs and services.

What Does It Mean if the College I Am Considering Is Not on the List?

All of the schools in our rankings list are eligible for federal financial aid and they are accredited institutions. If your college isn't on the list, it may be that it is not accredited. That means it hasn't gone through a formal review process for quality as colleges and universities are expected to do. **We don't recommend attending unaccredited schools.** (For more on accreditation, see chapter 5.)

What If I Don't See a College That Looks Like It's Right for Me in My State?

These rankings have been presented by state because a lot of adults like to attend a college that is located near their home. You may not live in a place where the local colleges have what you need in terms of academic programs or services to help you succeed. If that is the case, don't forget to look into online programs at some of the top-ranked schools or at degree completion colleges described in chapter 5.

Now get ready to explore your college options!

The *Washington Monthly's Best Colleges for Adults* rankings are calculated by Robert Kelchen, assistant professor in the Department of Education Leadership, Management, and Policy at Seton Hall University.

Ranking of Best Colleges for Adults

Alabama

Four Year Colleges

Rank	Name	Sector	Ease of transfer (5 pts for 4 year, 4 pts for 2 year)	Flexibility of programs (9 pts)
60	UNIVERSITY OF ALABAMA	Public	5	9
155	SOUTHERN CHRISTIAN UNIVERSITY	Nonprofit	5	7
344	TROY STATE UNIVERSITY–MAIN CAMPUS	Public	5	7
359	UNIVERSITY OF SOUTH ALABAMA	Public	5	7
394	JACKSONVILLE STATE UNIVERSITY	Public	5	7
397	AUBURN UNIVERSITY MAIN CAMPUS	Public	4	5
531	FAULKNER UNIVERSITY	Nonprofit	3	7
705	AUBURN UNIVERSITY–MONTGOMERY	Public	3	6
716	HUNTINGDON COLLEGE	Nonprofit	3	5
732	UNIVERSITY OF MONTEVALLO	Public	3	5
737	SPRING HILL COLLEGE	Nonprofit	5	8
757	ALABAMA STATE UNIVERSITY	Public	4	6
802	OAKWOOD COLLEGE	Nonprofit	2	3

UNRANKED: Alabama A&M University, Athens State University, Birmingham Southern College, Columbia Southern University, Judson College, Miles College, Samford University, South College, Stillman College, Talladega College, Tuskegee University, University of Alabama at Birmingham, University of Alabama at Huntsville, University of Mobile, University of North Alabama, University of West Alabama

Two Year Colleges

Rank	Name	Sector	Ease of transfer	Flexibility of programs
331	NORTHEAST ALABAMA COMMUNITY COLLEGE	Public	4	5
424	ENTERPRISE STATE JUNIOR COLLEGE	Public	3	7
453	JEFFERSON STATE COMMUNITY COLLEGE	Public	3	8
541	GADSDEN STATE COMMUNITY COLLEGE	Public	4	6
579	CENTRAL ALABAMA COMMUNITY COLLEGE	Public	4	7
585	GEORGE C WALLACE STATE COMMUNITY COLLEGE–HANCEVILLE	Public	3	6
600	JOHN C CALHOUN STATE COMMUNITY COLLEGE	Public	3	5
604	LAWSON STATE COMMUNITY COLLEGE	Public	3	7
615	VIRGINIA COLLEGE–BIRMINGHAM	For-Profit	3	6
616	NORTHWEST SHOALS COMMUNITY COLLEGE–MUSCLE SHOALS	Public	4	6
627	SOUTHERN UNION STATE COMMUNITY COLLEGE	Public	3	6
632	GEORGE C WALLACE STATE COMMUNITY COLLEGE–DOTHAN	Public	3	6

Services for adult students (6 pts)	Percent of students over age 25	Graduation rate of part-time students	Mean earnings of independent students 10 years after college entry	Loan repayment of independent students 5 years after leaving college	In-district tuition and fees (at a 9 month rate for 2 year colleges)	Percent of credentials awarded as bachelor's degrees
6	8%	51%	48,823	51%	10,470	100%
3	85%	43%	44,381	37%	10,180	91%
5	43%	21%	40,973	38%	8,260	87%
5	19%	28%	48,918	43%	7,548	96%
5	18%	41%	39,018	43%	9,300	100%
5	4%	51%	56,422	69%	10,696	100%
5	43%	55%	46,067	36%	20,130	98%
5	24%	27%	38,681	42%	9,640	99%
4	21%	62%	41,000	54%	24,427	100%
5	11%	33%	35,376	54%	12,040	100%
5	3%	15%	40,755	30%	35,798	99%
5	10%	15%	33,914	26%	9,220	100%
6	14%	0%	36,488	33%	16,720	99%
4	24%	51%	30,506	45%	4,380	0%
5	26%	14%	32,971	45%	4,380	0%
4	31%	12%	32,892	44%	4,440	0%
5	32%	32%	29,632	0%	4,080	0%
3	24%	14%	31,722	31%	4,380	0%
3	28%	32%	31,200	40%	4,380	0%
4	35%	15%	32,052	39%	4,460	0%
6	34%	18%	27,909	0%	4,380	0%
3	76%	24%	29,468	18%	14,632	11%
3	24%	16%	28,891	36%	4,351	0%
3	23%	24%	32,389	38%	4,080	0%
5	34%	22%	31,790	0%	4,320	0%

Rank	Name	Sector	Ease of transfer (5 pts for 4 year, 4 pts for 2 year)	Flexibility of programs (9 pts)
678	JAMES H FAULKNER STATE COMMUNITY COLLEGE	Public	3	4
695	JEFFERSON DAVIS COMMUNITY COLLEGE	Public	4	2
698	LURLEEN B WALLACE JUNIOR COLLEGE	Public	3	6
703	BISHOP STATE COMMUNITY COLLEGE	Public	3	4
707	GEORGE C WALLACE STATE COMMUNITY COLLEGE–SELMA	Public	3	6
734	SHELTON STATE COMMUNITY COLLEGE	Public	3	6
751	ALABAMA SOUTHERN COMMUNITY COLLEGE	Public	3	2
755	BEVILL STATE COMMUNITY COLLEGE	Public	3	4
762	CHATTAHOOCHEE VALLEY COMMUNITY COLLEGE	Public	1	4
767	VIRGINIA COLLEGE AT MOBILE	For-Profit	0	4
775	VIRGINIA COLLEGE–HUNTSVILLE	For-Profit	0	3
777	VIRGINIA COLLEGE–MONTGOMERY	For-Profit	0	2

UNRANKED: Capps College, Fortis College, Herzing College, J F Drake State Technical College, J F Ingram State Technical College, Marion Military Institute, Reid State Technical College, Snead State Community College, Southeast College of Technology, Trenholm State Technical College, Tri-State Institute

Alaska

FOUR YEAR COLLEGES

Rank	Name	Sector	Ease of transfer	Flexibility of programs
147	UNIVERSITY OF ALASKA–ANCHORAGE	Public	5	7
181	UNIVERSITY OF ALASKA–SOUTHEAST	Public	4	8
584	UNIVERSITY OF ALASKA–FAIRBANKS	Public	4	7

UNRANKED: Alaska Pacific University

TWO YEAR COLLEGES

UNRANKED: Alaska Vocational Technical Center, Career Academy, Charter College

Arkansas

FOUR YEAR COLLEGES

Rank	Name	Sector	Ease of transfer	Flexibility of programs
280	UNIVERSITY OF ARKANSAS MAIN CAMPUS	Public	3	8
314	ARKANSAS TECH UNIVERSITY	Public	5	8
396	ARKANSAS STATE UNIVERSITY–MAIN CAMPUS	Public	5	6
499	WESTARK COLLEGE	Public	4	8
738	UNIVERSITY OF CENTRAL ARKANSAS	Public	3	6
788	UNIVERSITY OF ARKANSAS AT PINE BLUFF	Public	3	2

Services for adult students (6 pts)	Percent of students over age 25	Graduation rate of part-time students	Mean earnings of independent students 10 years after college entry	Loan repayment of independent students 5 years after leaving college	In-district tuition and fees (at a 9 month rate for 2 year colleges)	Percent of credentials awarded as bachelor's degrees
4	26%	4%	31,177	41%	4,380	0%
5	39%	8%	31,384	0%	4,088	0%
4	20%	31%	29,866	0%	4,380	0%
5	36%	21%	27,877	0%	4,380	0%
4	29%	16%	29,831	0%	4,080	0%
4	22%	9%	28,452	0%	4,107	0%
5	15%	27%	26,481	0%	4,380	0%
2	25%	30%	28,958	0%	4,410	0%
2	35%	15%	30,979	34%	4,254	0%
1	55%	49%	29,468	18%	14,632	0%
1	67%	34%	29,468	18%	14,632	2%
1	60%	49%	29,468	18%	14,632	0%

Services for adult students (6 pts)	Percent of students over age 25	Graduation rate of part-time students	Mean earnings of independent students 10 years after college entry	Loan repayment of independent students 5 years after leaving college	In-district tuition and fees (at a 9 month rate for 2 year colleges)	Percent of credentials awarded as bachelor's degrees
5	43%	21%	47,395	59%	7,112	53%
5	57%	25%	40,643	54%	7,504	34%
3	46%	21%	41,915	52%	7,346	45%

Services for adult students (6 pts)	Percent of students over age 25	Graduation rate of part-time students	Mean earnings of independent students 10 years after college entry	Loan repayment of independent students 5 years after leaving college	In-district tuition and fees (at a 9 month rate for 2 year colleges)	Percent of credentials awarded as bachelor's degrees
6	10%	48%	47,631	59%	8,820	100%
5	20%	36%	34,782	46%	6,624	54%
6	20%	32%	34,105	48%	8,200	77%
5	24%	27%	33,458	48%	5,390	61%
4	10%	27%	37,748	53%	8,224	97%
6	14%	24%	31,983	35%	6,676	94%

Rank	Name	Sector	Ease of transfer (5 pts for 4 year, 4 pts for 2 year)	Flexibility of programs (9 pts)
800	HENDERSON STATE UNIVERSITY	Public	3	2
808	PHILANDER SMITH COLLEGE	Nonprofit	2	6

UNRANKED: Central Baptist College, Harding University, Hendrix College, John Brown University, Lyon College, Ouachita Baptist University, Southern Arkansas University Main Campus, University of Arkansas at Little Rock, University of Arkansas at Monticello, University of the Ozarks, Williams Baptist College

Two Year Colleges

Rank	Name	Sector	Ease of transfer	Flexibility of programs
15	SOUTHERN ARKANSAS UNIVERSITY TECH	Public	4	7
74	ARKANSAS STATE UNIVERSITY–MOUNTAIN HOME	Public	4	6
153	MISSISSIPPI COUNTY COMMUNITY COLLEGE	Public	4	5
214	OUACHITA TECHNICAL COLLEGE	Public	4	7
312	NORTHWEST ARKANSAS COMMUNITY COLLEGE	Public	3	7
360	PULASKI TECHNICAL COLLEGE	Public	3	5
420	ARKANSAS STATE UNIVERSITY–BEEBE BRANCH	Public	3	8
427	PETIT JEAN COLLEGE	Public	3	7
463	SOUTH ARKANSAS COMMUNITY COLLEGE	Public	2	6
524	NORTH ARKANSAS COLLEGE	Public	3	6
647	PHILLIPS COMMUNITY COLLEGE OF THE UNIVERSITY OF AR	Public	3	5
679	RICH MOUNTAIN COMMUNITY COLLEGE	Public	4	2
728	ARKANSAS STATE UNIVERSITY–NEWPORT	Public	2	6

UNRANKED: Arkansas Baptist College, Black River Technical College, Cossatot Technical College, Crowley's Ridge College, East Arkansas Community College, Garland County Community College, Mid-South Community College, Ozarka College, Shorter College, Southeast Arkansas College, University of Arkansas Community College–Batesville, University of Arkansas Community College–Hope

Arizona

Four Year Colleges

Rank	Name	Sector	Ease of transfer	Flexibility of programs
189	UNIVERSITY OF ARIZONA	Public	5	7
250	ARIZONA STATE UNIVERSITY–MAIN CAMPUS	Public	4	8
428	NORTHERN ARIZONA UNIVERSITY	Public	5	6
792	EMBRY RIDDLE AERONAUTICAL UNIVERSITY–PRESCOTT	Nonprofit	3	2

UNRANKED: Argosy University–Phoenix Online Division, Arizona Institute of Business and Technology, Arizona State University at the Downtown Phoenix Campus, Arizona State University East, Arizona State University West, Grand Canyon University, Northcentral University, Ottawa University–Phoenix, Prescott College, Southwestern Conservative Baptist Bible College

Services for adult students (6 pts)	Percent of students over age 25	Graduation rate of part-time students	Mean earnings of independent students 10 years after college entry	Loan repayment of independent students 5 years after leaving college	In-district tuition and fees (at a 9 month rate for 2 year colleges)	Percent of credentials awarded as bachelor's degrees
3	13%	18%	38,574	52%	8,086	99%
2	15%	0%	30,855	44%	12,564	100%
6	33%	68%	30,720	41%	4,677	0%
4	46%	44%	34,105	48%	2,784	0%
6	37%	39%	28,277	41%	2,206	0%
5	29%	34%	28,985	43%	3,620	0%
5	29%	21%	36,324	41%	3,208	0%
6	51%	20%	31,512	33%	5,011	0%
4	24%	23%	30,700	46%	2,712	0%
5	33%	16%	28,582	46%	3,740	0%
5	37%	31%	30,393	45%	2,508	0%
4	32%	32%	27,707	37%	2,088	0%
5	17%	35%	24,341	27%	2,720	0%
4	39%	43%	24,745	0%	2,568	0%
3	25%	25%	34,437	0%	2,664	0%
5	8%	49%	53,465	62%	11,171	99%
5	12%	47%	52,850	56%	10,370	92%
4	21%	49%	44,074	50%	9,482	91%
3	11%	40%	67,898	63%	33,826	100%

Rank	Name	Sector	Ease of transfer (5 pts for 4 year, 4 pts for 2 year)	Flexibility of programs (9 pts)

Two Year Colleges

Rank	Name	Sector	Ease of transfer	Flexibility of programs
26	GATEWAY COMMUNITY COLLEGE	Public	4	7
32	MESA COMMUNITY COLLEGE	Public	4	8
86	PHOENIX COLLEGE	Public	4	6
97	CHANDLER/GILBERT COMMUNITY COLLEGE	Public	4	7
100	ARIZONA WESTERN COLLEGE	Public	4	8
116	RIO SALADO COMMUNITY COLLEGE	Public	4	8
143	PARADISE VALLEY COMMUNITY COLLEGE	Public	3	8
227	ESTRELLA MOUNTAIN COMMUNITY COLLEGE	Public	4	7
257	EASTERN ARIZONA COLLEGE	Public	4	7
314	GLENDALE COMMUNITY COLLEGE	Public	3	7
340	COCHISE COLLEGE	Public	3	6
397	PIMA COMMUNITY COLLEGE	Public	3	9
484	COCONINO COUNTY COMMUNITY COLLEGE	Public	4	4
525	SCOTTSDALE COMMUNITY COLLEGE	Public	3	4
563	CENTRAL ARIZONA COLLEGE	Public	4	6
654	NORTHLAND PIONEER COLLEGE	Public	4	5
670	SOUTH MOUNTAIN COMMUNITY COLLEGE	Public	3	4

UNRANKED: Apollo College, Apollo College–Phoenix Inc, Apollo College–Tri City Inc, Apollo College–Westside, Arizona College of Allied Health, Arizona Institute of Business and Technology, Brown Mackie College–Phoenix, Chaparral Career College, Fortis College, Mohave Community College, Pima Medical Institute, Refrigeration School Inc., Southwest Institute of Healing Arts, Universal Technical Institute Inc., Yavapai College

California

Four Year Colleges

Rank	Name	Sector	Ease of transfer	Flexibility of programs
11	CALIFORNIA STATE UNIVERSITY–DOMINGUEZ HILLS	Public	5	9
23	CALIFORNIA STATE UNIVERSITY–HAYWARD	Public	5	6
35	CALIFORNIA STATE UNIVERSITY–LONG BEACH	Public	4	6
45	UNIVERSITY OF REDLANDS	Nonprofit	5	8
57	FRESNO PACIFIC UNIVERSITY	Nonprofit	5	9
71	NATIONAL UNIVERSITY	Nonprofit	4	8
73	CALIFORNIA STATE UNIVERSITY–MONTEREY BAY	Public	4	8
74	CALIFORNIA STATE UNIVERSITY–STANISLAUS	Public	5	5
76	CALIFORNIA STATE UNIVERSITY–FULLERTON	Public	5	4
77	ANTIOCH UNIVERSITY–LOS ANGELES BRANCH	Nonprofit	4	8
98	UNIVERSITY OF CALIFORNIA–BERKELEY	Public	4	4
99	CALIFORNIA STATE UNIVERSITY–SACRAMENTO	Public	4	6

Services for adult students (6 pts)	Percent of students over age 25	Graduation rate of part-time students	Mean earnings of independent students 10 years after college entry	Loan repayment of independent students 5 years after leaving college	In-district tuition and fees (at a 9 month rate for 2 year colleges)	Percent of credentials awarded as bachelor's degrees
6	53%	21%	36,088	40%	2,094	0%
6	37%	10%	41,383	40%	2,094	0%
6	44%	19%	36,061	37%	2,094	0%
5	20%	10%	47,810	43%	2,094	0%
6	29%	30%	30,366	36%	1,920	0%
5	42%	6%	40,598	30%	2,094	0%
6	34%	14%	37,870	37%	2,094	0%
5	29%	15%	34,231	40%	2,094	0%
5	54%	26%	34,300	0%	2,400	0%
5	31%	12%	37,167	42%	2,094	0%
4	45%	19%	36,000	42%	1,896	0%
3	40%	12%	34,374	38%	2,046	0%
5	28%	17%	32,470	38%	3,060	0%
3	34%	15%	41,780	46%	2,094	0%
3	39%	13%	28,512	32%	2,520	0%
4	34%	15%	30,229	0%	1,760	0%
4	34%	10%	29,852	29%	2,094	0%
5	38%	53%	49,560	55%	6,423	100%
6	33%	50%	56,190	64%	6,564	100%
6	18%	74%	53,059	71%	6,460	100%
5	23%	81%	66,974	68%	46,570	87%
5	49%	52%	45,881	56%	29,370	100%
4	82%	17%	57,124	59%	13,016	90%
6	18%	40%	48,304	71%	6,379	100%
6	21%	59%	47,401	66%	6,728	100%
6	19%	63%	51,445	70%	6,560	100%
4	86%	48%	43,370	55%	20,670	100%
6	6%	75%	77,297	66%	13,509	100%
6	24%	54%	52,348	66%	6,900	100%

Rank	Name	Sector	Ease of transfer (5 pts for 4 year, 4 pts for 2 year)	Flexibility of programs (9 pts)
103	UNIVERSITY OF LA VERNE	Nonprofit	5	8
151	SAN FRANCISCO STATE UNIVERSITY	Public	3	7
196	UNIVERSITY OF CALIFORNIA–LOS ANGELES	Public	2	6
200	SONOMA STATE UNIVERSITY	Public	4	6
214	CHRISTIAN HERITAGE COLLEGE	Nonprofit	5	8
224	SIMPSON COLLEGE	Nonprofit	5	6
227	CALIFORNIA STATE UNIVERSITY–CHICO	Public	4	5
231	CALIFORNIA STATE UNIVERSITY–SAN MARCOS	Public	3	6
240	COLLEGE OF NOTRE DAME	Nonprofit	5	6
242	CALIFORNIA LUTHERAN UNIVERSITY	Nonprofit	4	8
255	PACIFIC UNION COLLEGE	Nonprofit	4	7
271	UNIVERSITY OF CALIFORNIA-IRVINE	Public	3	4
277	JOHN F KENNEDY UNIVERSITY	Nonprofit	3	8
289	DOMINICAN UNIVERSITY OF CALIFORNIA	Nonprofit	5	9
295	SAN DIEGO STATE UNIVERSITY	Public	4	5
326	HUMBOLDT STATE UNIVERSITY	Public	4	6
346	SAN JOSE STATE UNIVERSITY	Public	2	4
348	CALIFORNIA STATE UNIVERSITY–NORTHRIDGE	Public	3	4
355	CALIFORNIA MARITIME ACADEMY	Public	4	4
358	CALIFORNIA POLYTECHNIC STATE UNIVERSITY–SAN LUIS OBISPO	Public	4	3
377	LOYOLA MARYMOUNT UNIVERSITY	Nonprofit	3	7
381	CALIFORNIA BAPTIST UNIVERSITY	Nonprofit	5	6
383	CALIFORNIA STATE UNIVERSITY–BAKERSFIELD	Public	4	4
399	CALIFORNIA STATE UNIVERSITY–FRESNO	Public	3	5
433	WOODBURY UNIVERSITY	Nonprofit	5	7
438	UNIVERSITY OF CALIFORNIA–SANTA CRUZ	Public	3	6
451	UNIVERSITY OF CALIFORNIA–SAN DIEGO	Public	2	4
454	CALIFORNIA STATE POLYTECHNIC UNIVERSITY–POMONA	Public	3	2
468	CALIFORNIA STATE UNIVERSITY–SAN BERNARDINO	Public	3	5
469	UNIVERSITY OF CALIFORNIA–SANTA BARBARA	Public	3	5
482	ANTIOCH UNIVERSITY–SANTA BARBARA BRANCH	Nonprofit	4	3
496	PEPPERDINE UNIVERSITY	Nonprofit	3	6
533	POINT LOMA NAZARENE UNIVERSITY	Nonprofit	4	6
544	UNIVERSITY OF SOUTHERN CALIFORNIA	Nonprofit	2	6
556	UNIVERSITY OF CALIFORNIA–DAVIS	Public	0	4
591	CALIFORNIA STATE UNIVERSITY–LOS ANGELES	Public	3	5
593	CONCORDIA UNIVERSITY	Nonprofit	5	9
594	UNIVERSITY OF SAN DIEGO	Nonprofit	4	4
610	UNIVERSITY OF CALIFORNIA–RIVERSIDE	Public	3	5
629	AZUSA PACIFIC UNIVERSITY	Nonprofit	3	6
648	HOLY NAMES COLLEGE	Nonprofit	5	9

Services for adult students (6 pts)	Percent of students over age 25	Graduation rate of part-time students	Mean earnings of independent students 10 years after college entry	Loan repayment of independent students 5 years after leaving college	In-district tuition and fees (at a 9 month rate for 2 year colleges)	Percent of credentials awarded as bachelor's degrees
5	45%	61%	56,237	55%	39,900	99%
6	20%	57%	54,704	62%	6,484	100%
5	5%	83%	83,408	68%	12,920	100%
6	11%	58%	49,253	63%	7,388	100%
5	36%	31%	44,714	58%	21,650	85%
5	29%	75%	41,404	58%	25,950	100%
6	14%	55%	49,988	66%	7,040	100%
6	18%	58%	51,606	65%	7,383	100%
4	30%	58%	62,671	68%	33,268	100%
5	11%	62%	68,952	66%	39,793	100%
5	15%	60%	63,581	64%	28,629	66%
6	4%	76%	65,189	69%	13,360	100%
2	82%	67%	51,584	52%	23,400	66%
4	19%	52%	59,655	62%	43,400	100%
5	15%	58%	53,599	63%	7,084	100%
6	18%	44%	39,931	59%	7,209	100%
6	20%	61%	62,146	73%	7,418	100%
6	21%	63%	50,835	63%	6,587	100%
4	14%	13%	91,100	75%	6,808	100%
5	3%	63%	61,465	77%	9,075	100%
6	3%	50%	91,104	60%	44,230	100%
5	25%	61%	48,316	52%	31,372	100%
6	20%	50%	49,994	54%	6,857	100%
6	16%	51%	49,556	64%	6,313	100%
3	28%	60%	56,426	63%	37,906	100%
6	5%	60%	49,478	61%	13,539	100%
5	6%	64%	81,811	72%	13,645	100%
6	17%	61%	57,873	70%	7,067	100%
6	20%	52%	49,318	51%	6,610	100%
6	3%	64%	54,118	62%	14,073	100%
4	55%	74%	43,370	55%	18,120	100%
4	7%	84%	94,801	59%	50,022	100%
5	10%	40%	60,059	73%	33,500	100%
5	3%	63%	103,828	69%	52,283	100%
6	6%	70%	81,902	75%	14,046	100%
4	25%	51%	49,656	59%	6,383	100%
4	14%	0%	49,011	69%	32,780	100%
5	5%	50%	81,769	70%	46,140	100%
6	4%	43%	53,858	55%	13,581	100%
4	10%	73%	59,787	66%	36,120	99%
3	22%	7%	61,033	52%	37,074	100%

Rank	Name	Sector	Ease of transfer (5 pts for 4 year, 4 pts for 2 year)	Flexibility of programs (9 pts)
663	SANTA CLARA UNIVERSITY	Nonprofit	2	6
684	CHAPMAN UNIVERSITY	Nonprofit	4	6
722	BIOLA UNIVERSITY	Nonprofit	4	5
773	MILLS COLLEGE	Nonprofit	3	6

UNRANKED: Argosy University–Inland Empire, Argosy University–San Diego, California Institute of Technology, California School of Professional Psych–San Diego, Chapman University–Academic Centers, Claremont McKenna College, Cogswell Polytechnical College, Golden Gate University–San Francisco, Harvey Mudd College, Hope International University, Humphrey's College–Stockton, La Sierra University, Marymount College, Master's College and Seminary, Mount St. Mary's College, Mt. Sierra College, Occidental College, Pitzer College, Pomona College, Saint Mary's College of California, San Jose Christian College, Scripps College, Soka University of America–Calabasas, Stanford University, Thomas Aquinas College, Touro College Los Angeles, TUI University, University of California–Merced, University of San Francisco, University of Sarasota, University of the Pacific, University of the West, Vanguard University of Southern California, Westmont College, Whittier College

Two Year Colleges

Rank	Name	Sector	Ease of transfer	Flexibility of programs
3	FOOTHILL COLLEGE	Public	3	5
13	DIABLO VALLEY COLLEGE	Public	4	7
28	CITY COLLEGE OF SAN FRANCISCO	Public	3	7
31	COLLEGE OF THE CANYONS	Public	4	7
37	SADDLEBACK COLLEGE	Public	3	7
38	EAST LOS ANGELES COLLEGE	Public	4	7
47	ORANGE COAST COLLEGE	Public	3	8
48	OHLONE COLLEGE	Public	4	6
62	NAPA VALLEY COLLEGE	Public	3	6
76	GROSSMONT COLLEGE	Public	4	7
77	SANTA ROSA JUNIOR COLLEGE	Public	3	5
89	SANTA ANA COLLEGE	Public	4	5
94	DE ANZA COLLEGE	Public	3	6
114	COASTLINE COMMUNITY COLLEGE	Public	3	7
120	IRVINE VALLEY COLLEGE	Public	3	8
124	AMERICAN RIVER COLLEGE	Public	3	8
126	MT SAN ANTONIO COLLEGE	Public	4	4
135	RIO HONDO COLLEGE	Public	3	7
148	SANTA MONICA COLLEGE	Public	3	7
155	GOLDEN WEST COLLEGE	Public	3	8
164	LOS ANGELES PIERCE COLLEGE	Public	3	7
180	CABRILLO COLLEGE	Public	3	4
181	EVERGREEN VALLEY COLLEGE	Public	3	8
183	COLLEGE OF SAN MATEO	Public	1	7
188	SAN DIEGO CITY COLLEGE	Public	4	7
197	SAN BERNARDINO VALLEY COLLEGE	Public	4	6

Services for adult students (6 pts)	Percent of students over age 25	Graduation rate of part-time students	Mean earnings of independent students 10 years after college entry	Loan repayment of independent students 5 years after leaving college	In-district tuition and fees (at a 9 month rate for 2 year colleges)	Percent of credentials awarded as bachelor's degrees
4	1%	60%	85,493	79%	47,112	100%
5	3%	53%	54,030	64%	48,710	100%
4	5%	40%	56,213	64%	36,696	100%
4	17%	33%	51,246	58%	45,635	100%
5	42%	13%	64,895	60%	15,51	0%
6	31%	16%	45,356	48%	1,308	0%
6	57%	12%	41,824	47%	1,598	0%
6	32%	11%	44,509	44%	1,154	0%
6	35%	15%	44,365	54%	1,326	0%
6	47%	13%	36,230	44%	1,244	0%
6	29%	17%	40,869	54%	1,184	0%
5	36%	9%	46,783	50%	1,162	0%
6	32%	11%	45,241	58%	1,142	0%
5	33%	14%	38,847	52%	1,386	0%
6	39%	21%	42,891	51%	1,340	0%
5	56%	6%	38,340	50%	1,142	0%
6	30%	13%	47,878	44%	1,549	0%
4	70%	10%	37,158	47%	1,136	0%
6	30%	12%	38,781	46%	1,142	0%
6	52%	14%	34,330	31%	1,104	0%
6	30%	18%	39,690	52%	1,348	0%
6	38%	6%	39,253	48%	1,360	0%
6	28%	12%	37,730	52%	1,142	0%
5	30%	14%	35,923	56%	1,176	0%
6	34%	15%	38,039	40%	1,244	0%
6	40%	12%	43,372	48%	1,456	0%
4	35%	10%	40,185	53%	1,331	0%
6	33%	12%	42,327	71%	1,400	0%
5	43%	12%	33,696	33%	1,139	0%
6	41%	11%	31,948	36%	1,328	0%

Rank	Name	Sector	Ease of transfer (5 pts for 4 year, 4 pts for 2 year)	Flexibility of programs (9 pts)
199	COLLEGE OF THE DESERT	Public	4	4
217	CHAFFEY COMMUNITY COLLEGE	Public	4	6
219	SIERRA COLLEGE	Public	4	5
225	CHABOT COLLEGE	Public	3	7
229	MOORPARK COLLEGE	Public	3	6
239	CUESTA COLLEGE	Public	3	7
242	CYPRESS COLLEGE	Public	4	5
247	SANTA BARBARA CITY COLLEGE	Public	3	6
254	ALLAN HANCOCK COLLEGE	Public	4	6
267	SACRAMENTO CITY COLLEGE	Public	2	8
276	LOS ANGELES HARBOR COLLEGE	Public	3	7
277	SOUTHWESTERN COLLEGE	Public	4	6
279	VISTA COLLEGE	Public	4	7
281	EL CAMINO COLLEGE	Public	4	5
283	BUTTE COLLEGE	Public	4	4
287	CUYAMACA COLLEGE	Public	4	6
288	FRESNO CITY COLLEGE	Public	3	7
295	FULLERTON COLLEGE	Public	3	6
303	LOS ANGELES TRADE TECHNICAL COLLEGE	Public	4	7
305	SAN DIEGO MIRAMAR COLLEGE	Public	3	5
317	BARSTOW COLLEGE	Public	4	8
318	TAFT COLLEGE	Public	4	5
324	GLENDALE COMMUNITY COLLEGE	Public	2	5
350	CERRITOS COLLEGE	Public	3	4
356	LAS POSITAS COLLEGE	Public	3	6
361	VICTOR VALLEY COLLEGE	Public	4	6
366	COLLEGE OF THE SEQUOIAS	Public	3	7
399	WEST LOS ANGELES COLLEGE	Public	1	8
401	PALOMAR COLLEGE	Public	3	5
407	SAN JOAQUIN DELTA COLLEGE	Public	3	6
417	LAKE TAHOE COMMUNITY COLLEGE	Public	3	3
421	EMPIRE COLLEGE SCHOOL OF BUSINESS	For-Profit	3	3
422	LOS ANGELES CITY COLLEGE	Public	3	5
423	COLLEGE OF THE SISKIYOUS	Public	4	5
429	LOS ANGELES VALLEY COLLEGE	Public	3	4
437	LANEY COLLEGE	Public	3	7
443	SHASTA COLLEGE	Public	3	6
458	MENDOCINO COLLEGE	Public	3	6
465	WEST VALLEY COLLEGE	Public	3	5
466	VENTURA COLLEGE	Public	3	4
468	MOUNT SAN JACINTO COLLEGE	Public	4	6

Services for adult students (6 pts)	Percent of students over age 25	Graduation rate of part-time students	Mean earnings of independent students 10 years after college entry	Loan repayment of independent students 5 years after leaving college	In-district tuition and fees (at a 9 month rate for 2 year colleges)	Percent of credentials awarded as bachelor's degrees
6	33%	14%	36,155	49%	1,327	0%
5	31%	16%	34,942	44%	1,169	0%
6	33%	15%	34,500	39%	1,142	0%
5	39%	12%	39,789	36%	1,138	0%
5	22%	16%	42,650	53%	1,388	0%
5	28%	15%	36,557	52%	1,234	0%
5	30%	18%	38,643	39%	1,138	0%
6	30%	13%	39,297	41%	1,466	0%
5	34%	11%	33,699	44%	1,350	0%
6	37%	10%	37,957	37%	1,104	0%
5	34%	12%	36,787	44%	1,244	0%
4	32%	15%	35,957	47%	1,336	0%
4	38%	9%	36,657	34%	1,232	0%
6	28%	13%	35,548	34%	1,142	0%
6	31%	19%	36,298	34%	1,368	0%
6	40%	12%	30,026	29%	1,386	0%
6	38%	13%	32,655	34%	1,304	0%
6	26%	16%	37,241	40%	1,138	0%
6	52%	9%	32,655	0%	1,244	0%
4	47%	12%	41,805	45%	1,142	0%
5	45%	7%	36,565	0%	1,104	0%
6	54%	2%	39,997	0%	1,134	0%
6	38%	18%	33,926	58%	1,175	0%
6	36%	15%	35,821	44%	1,346	0%
5	31%	13%	37,324	42%	1,138	0%
5	34%	13%	33,473	27%	1,126	0%
5	29%	12%	32,588	48%	1,388	0%
6	48%	8%	35,108	37%	1,244	0%
5	35%	13%	38,913	37%	1,338	0%
6	32%	15%	34,771	24%	1,104	0%
6	52%	12%	31,518	39%	1,224	0%
2	48%	100%	33,944	36%	11,790	0%
5	48%	11%	31,373	40%	1,244	0%
5	53%	6%	28,577	26%	1,154	0%
4	42%	13%	36,556	53%	1,244	0%
6	50%	8%	33,564	0%	1,232	0%
5	35%	15%	30,934	39%	1,183	0%
5	44%	6%	27,133	45%	1,423	0%
4	34%	11%	36,088	50%	1,183	0%
5	29%	13%	37,931	45%	1,388	0%
4	35%	15%	31,408	28%	1,386	0%

Rank	Name	Sector	Ease of transfer (5 pts for 4 year, 4 pts for 2 year)	Flexibility of programs (9 pts)
469	MIRACOSTA COLLEGE	Public	3	6
470	SAN JOSE CITY COLLEGE	Public	3	6
472	FEATHER RIVER COMMUNITY COLLEGE DISTRICT	Public	4	4
511	PASADENA CITY COLLEGE	Public	1	6
518	YUBA COLLEGE	Public	3	3
520	REEDLEY COLLEGE	Public	3	5
552	COLLEGE OF THE REDWOODS	Public	3	4
553	SOLANO COUNTY COMMUNITY COLLEGE DISTRICT	Public	1	7
558	CERRO COSO COMMUNITY COLLEGE	Public	3	6
561	GAVILAN COLLEGE	Public	3	4
562	MONTEREY PENINSULA COLLEGE	Public	3	4
575	LOS ANGELES MISSION COLLEGE	Public	1	6
581	IMPERIAL VALLEY COLLEGE	Public	4	5
588	WEST HILLS COMMUNITY COLLEGE	Public	3	4
589	COSUMNES RIVER COLLEGE	Public	3	4
590	CANADA COLLEGE	Public	3	6
591	CONTRA COSTA COLLEGE	Public	2	6
606	MODESTO JUNIOR COLLEGE	Public	3	5
610	CRAFTON HILLS COLLEGE	Public	4	4
626	LONG BEACH CITY COLLEGE	Public	2	7
631	MERRITT COLLEGE	Public	2	4
636	PALO VERDE COLLEGE	Public	3	5
638	BAKERSFIELD COLLEGE	Public	3	3
642	LASSEN COMMUNITY COLLEGE	Public	3	3
652	COLLEGE OF ALAMEDA	Public	2	6
653	COLLEGE OF MARIN	Public	2	3
656	CITRUS COLLEGE	Public	3	4
657	LOS MEDANOS COLLEGE	Public	3	5
677	OXNARD COLLEGE	Public	3	4
691	COLUMBIA COLLEGE	Public	3	3
705	HARTNELL COLLEGE	Public	1	6
716	LOS ANGELES SOUTHWEST COLLEGE	Public	2	6
723	COPPER MOUNTAIN COLLEGE	Public	3	3
724	RIVERSIDE COMMUNITY COLLEGE	Public	0	4
739	PORTERVILLE COLLEGE	Public	3	3
745	MERCED COLLEGE	Public	2	3
756	SAN DIEGO GOLF ACADEMY	For-Profit	0	3

UNRANKED: American Academy of Dramatic Arts–West, American Career College, Andon College, Antelope Valley College, Antelope Valley Medical College, Bryan College of Court Reporting, California College of Technology, California Culinary Academy, California School of Court Reporting–Riverside, California School of Culinary Art, Cambridge Career College, Casa Loma College–Van Nuys, Compton Community College, Computer Education Institute–Riverside, Concorde Career Institute, East San Gabriel Valley Regional

Services for adult students (6 pts)	Percent of students over age 25	Graduation rate of part-time students	Mean earnings of independent students 10 years after college entry	Loan repayment of independent students 5 years after leaving college	In-district tuition and fees (at a 9 month rate for 2 year colleges)	Percent of credentials awarded as bachelor's degrees
4	37%	13%	31,637	47%	1,152	0%
4	50%	11%	33,674	30%	1,331	0%
6	45%	2%	27,372	30%	1,461	0%
5	28%	21%	37,945	54%	1,348	0%
6	36%	11%	32,518	40%	1,144	0%
6	26%	16%	29,116	36%	1,304	0%
5	38%	10%	30,824	39%	1,143	0%
5	37%	13%	39,261	29%	1,140	0%
5	56%	7%	32,483	0%	1,290	0%
5	38%	8%	33,185	34%	1,166	0%
3	45%	5%	40,270	37%	1,174	0%
6	35%	13%	32,416	41%	1,220	0%
6	32%	15%	27,576	0%	1,142	0%
5	31%	14%	31,914	34%	1,380	0%
5	37%	12%	31,383	30%	1,104	0%
4	48%	12%	37,065	0%	1,344	0%
6	38%	15%	37,197	0%	1,308	0%
6	34%	16%	32,791	0%	1,162	0%
4	29%	21%	38,434	0%	1,142	0%
4	33%	12%	31,679	30%	1,182	0%
5	53%	11%	39,724	0%	1,232	0%
3	81%	6%	28,533	0%	1,380	0%
4	32%	12%	35,285	34%	1,326	0%
4	62%	6%	28,642	23%	1,127	0%
5	41%	12%	35,529	0%	1,232	0%
2	51%	12%	42,139	40%	1,488	0%
4	26%	17%	32,453	28%	1,176	0%
4	32%	13%	38,953	0%	1,308	0%
5	35%	14%	31,778	0%	1,388	0%
6	38%	6%	29,453	0%	1,162	0%
5	46%	7%	34,026	0%	1,420	0%
3	51%	9%	31,858	0%	1,244	0%
3	48%	12%	33,087	0%	1,112	0%
4	28%	14%	36,423	49%	1,426	0%
4	29%	13%	30,202	0%	1,322	0%
5	30%	12%	30,670	0%	1,150	0%
1	74%	78%	29,468	18%	17,150	0%

Rank	Name		Sector	Ease of transfer (5 pts for 4 year, 4 pts for 2 year)	Flexibility of programs (9 pts)

Occupational Program, Folsom Lake College, Fresno Institute of Technology, International Professional School of Bodywork, Kaplan College–Chula Vista, Los Angeles County College of Nurses and Allied Health, Los Angeles Film School, Los Angeles ORT Technical Institute, Los Angeles ORT Technical Institute–Sherman Oaks, Maric College, Maric College–Bakersfield, Maric College–Fresno, Maric College–Palm Springs, Mayfield College, Mission College, Moreno Valley College, MTI College of Business and Technology, Norco College, Pima Medical Institute, Platt College, Platt College–Los Angeles INC, Professional Golfers Career College, San Diego Mesa College, San Joaquin Valley College, Santa Barbara Buisness College, Santa Barbara Business College–Santa Maria Branch, Santiago Canyon College, Silicon Valley College, Skyline College, South Coast College, TechSkills of Sacramento, United Education Institute–Los Angeles Campus, West Coast Ultrasound Institute, West Hills College–Lemoore, Western Career College, Western Career College–Citrus Heights, Western Career College–Stockton, Woodland Community College

Colorado

FOUR YEAR COLLEGES

Rank	Name	Sector	Ease of transfer	Flexibility of programs
26	REGIS UNIVERSITY	Nonprofit	5	9
67	UNIVERSITY OF COLORADO AT DENVER	Public	4	6
94	METROPOLITAN STATE COLLEGE OF DENVER	Public	5	7
116	UNIVERSITY OF COLORADO AT COLORADO SPRINGS	Public	4	8
154	COLORADO TECHNICAL UNIVERSITY	For-Profit	4	7
156	COLORADO SCHOOL OF MINES	Public	4	5
268	ADAMS STATE COLLEGE	Public	4	8
361	WESTERN STATE COLLEGE COLORADO	Public	4	6
459	UNIVERSITY OF COLORADO AT BOULDER	Public	4	5
583	UNIVERSITY OF SOUTHERN COLORADO	Public	4	7
618	UNIVERSITY OF NORTHERN COLORADO	Public	3	5
675	FORT LEWIS COLLEGE	Public	3	5
679	MESA STATE COLLEGE	Public	3	6
741	UNIVERSITY OF DENVER	Nonprofit	4	6
782	NAROPA UNIVERSITY	Nonprofit	4	3

UNRANKED: Argosy University–Denver, Aspen University, Colorado Christian University, Colorado College, Colorado State University, National American University–Colorado Springs

TWO YEAR COLLEGES

Rank	Name	Sector	Ease of transfer	Flexibility of programs
68	FRONT RANGE COMMUNITY COLLEGE	Public	3	8
115	PIKES PEAK COMMUNITY COLLEGE	Public	4	6
144	COMMUNITY COLLEGE OF DENVER	Public	4	7
189	RED ROCKS COMMUNITY COLLEGE	Public	3	6
326	COLORADO NORTHWESTERN COMMUNITY COLLEGE	Public	4	6
328	COLORADO MOUNTAIN COLLEGE	Public	3	4
333	PUEBLO COMMUNITY COLLEGE	Public	3	7

Services for adult students (6 pts)	Percent of students over age 25	Graduation rate of part-time students	Mean earnings of independent students 10 years after college entry	Loan repayment of independent students 5 years after leaving college	In-district tuition and fees (at a 9 month rate for 2 year colleges)	Percent of credentials awarded as bachelor's degrees
5	52%	45%	60,503	63%	34,450	93%
5	23%	37%	84,193	66%	9,088	100%
6	43%	28%	42,657	53%	6,930	98%
6	25%	33%	48,042	65%	8,042	100%
4	87%	27%	60,460	34%	11,267	64%
4	7%	57%	88,216	83%	17,842	100%
6	25%	51%	35,281	41%	9,153	67%
5	10%	68%	37,793	64%	9,193	100%
6	6%	32%	54,940	63%	11,531	100%
5	20%	21%	40,803	50%	9,519	100%
5	12%	46%	44,517	64%	8,888	100%
6	14%	30%	39,893	49%	8,104	100%
5	21%	29%	37,668	50%	7,835	56%
5	5%	0%	68,534	59%	46,422	100%
3	35%	44%	28,422	59%	31,170	99%
5	37%	30%	39,124	51%	3,660	0%
6	42%	18%	34,542	42%	3,536	0%
6	35%	17%	33,759	39%	4,233	0%
5	46%	13%	40,461	48%	3,685	0%
4	28%	10%	35,961	54%	3,736	0%
5	39%	25%	33,764	56%	2,212	8%
5	50%	26%	31,341	33%	7,121	0%

COLORADO

Rank	Name	Sector	Ease of transfer (5 pts for 4 year, 4 pts for 2 year)	Flexibility of programs (9 pts)
334	AIMS COMMUNITY COLLEGE	Public	3	7
335	OTERO JUNIOR COLLEGE	Public	4	4
354	NORTHEASTERN JUNIOR COLLEGE	Public	4	8
433	MORGAN COMMUNITY COLLEGE	Public	4	7
485	COMMUNITY COLLEGE OF AURORA	Public	3	7
618	TRINIDAD STATE JUNIOR COLLEGE	Public	3	6
634	ARAPAHOE COMMUNITY COLLEGE	Public	0	9
729	JOHNSON & WALES UNIVERSITY–DENVER	Nonprofit	1	6
737	LAMAR COMMUNITY COLLEGE	Public	3	4

UNRANKED: Bel-Rea Institute of Animal Technology, Blair College, College America–Colorado Springs, Colorado School of Trades, Concorde Career Institute, Denver Automotive and Diesel College, Ecotech Institute, Heritage College of Health Careers, Institute of Business and Medical Careers, Intellitec College–Colorado Springs, Intellitec College–Grand Junction, Intellitec Medical institute, Parks College, Pima Medical Institute

Connecticut

FOUR YEAR COLLEGES

Rank	Name	Sector	Ease of transfer	Flexibility of programs
29	TEIKYO POST UNIVERSITY	For-Profit	5	8
62	ALBERTUS MAGNUS COLLEGE	Nonprofit	4	8
78	CHARTER OAK STATE COLLEGE	Public	4	7
102	UNIVERSITY OF CONNECTICUT	Public	4	7
118	SAINT JOSEPH COLLEGE	Nonprofit	5	9
131	SACRED HEART UNIVERSITY	Nonprofit	5	9
132	FAIRFIELD UNIVERSITY	Nonprofit	3	7
190	EASTERN CONNECTICUT STATE UNIVERSITY	Public	4	7
193	WESTERN CONNECTICUT STATE UNIVERSITY	Public	5	5
310	CENTRAL CONNECTICUT STATE UNIVERSITY	Public	4	5
331	QUINNIPIAC UNIVERSITY	Nonprofit	5	7
354	UNIVERSITY OF BRIDGEPORT	Nonprofit	4	9
430	SOUTHERN CONNECTICUT STATE UNIVERSITY	Public	5	5
642	UNIVERSITY OF HARTFORD	Nonprofit	3	8
752	UNIVERSITY OF NEW HAVEN	Nonprofit	2	8

UNRANKED: Connecticut College, Mitchell College, Trinity College, Wesleyan University, Yale University

TWO YEAR COLLEGES

Rank	Name	Sector	Ease of transfer	Flexibility of programs
8	CAPITAL COMMUNITY COLLEGE	Public	3	8
23	NAUGATUCK VALLEY COMMUNITY COLLEGE	Public	4	6

Services for adult students (6 pts)	Percent of students over age 25	Graduation rate of part-time students	Mean earnings of independent students 10 years after college entry	Loan repayment of independent students 5 years after leaving college	In-district tuition and fees (at a 9 month rate for 2 year colleges)	Percent of credentials awarded as bachelor's degrees
4	32%	36%	33,191	39%	1,835	0%
6	31%	37%	30,742	29%	3,569	0%
3	23%	30%	33,337	43%	4,710	0%
2	26%	39%	32,765	41%	3,494	0%
3	36%	14%	36,898	44%	3,702	0%
3	28%	23%	29,991	40%	3,686	0%
2	42%	12%	40,837	49%	3,493	0%
4	16%	44%	38,952	57%	30,396	53%
2	15%	26%	27,940	35%	3,720	0%
5	75%	38%	49,375	43%	15,258	77%
5	55%	67%	62,150	47%	30,526	87%
2	91%	63%	44,218	61%	7,671	75%
6	3%	55%	62,599	72%	14,066	100%
5	24%	61%	57,222	56%	36,870	99%
5	11%	75%	56,397	58%	38,300	99%
6	5%	82%	87,736	73%	46,000	100%
6	11%	61%	43,827	63%	10,500	100%
6	18%	42%	50,109	64%	10,017	99%
6	19%	48%	49,152	58%	9,741	100%
5	4%	47%	71,469	68%	43,940	100%
5	31%	40%	50,287	51%	31,630	89%
5	14%	42%	46,384	55%	10,054	100%
4	9%	66%	52,682	59%	37,790	84%
4	9%	44%	51,774	56%	37,060	85%
6	54%	24%	39,468	61%	4,236	0%
6	36%	21%	40,135	63%	4,208	0%

Rank	Name	Sector	Ease of transfer (5 pts for 4 year, 4 pts for 2 year)	Flexibility of programs (9 pts)
51	GATEWAY COMMUNITY COLLEGE	Public	3	8
106	ASNUNTUCK COMMUNITY COLLEGE	Public	4	7
175	THREE RIVERS COMMUNITY COLLEGE	Public	3	6
203	NORWALK COMMUNITY COLLEGE	Public	4	5
220	MANCHESTER COMMUNITY COLLEGE	Public	2	8
256	HOUSATONIC COMMUNITY COLLEGE	Public	3	7
413	MIDDLESEX COMMUNITY COLLEGE	Public	2	7
527	TUNXIS COMMUNITY COLLEGE	Public	2	6
572	QUINEBAUG VALLEY COMMUNITY COLLEGE	Public	4	6
746	NORTHWESTERN CONNECTICUT COMMUNITY COLLEGE	Public	3	5

UNRANKED: Briarwood College

Delaware

FOUR YEAR COLLEGES

Rank	Name	Sector	Ease of transfer	Flexibility of programs
598	UNIVERSITY OF DELAWARE	Public	2	7
630	WILMINGTON COLLEGE	Nonprofit	3	7
690	DELAWARE STATE UNIVERSITY	Public	3	7

UNRANKED: Strayer University–Delaware, Wesley College

TWO YEAR COLLEGES

Rank	Name	Sector	Ease of transfer	Flexibility of programs
307	DELAWARE TECHNICAL AND COMMUNITY COLLEGE–TERRY	Public	3	5

UNRANKED: Delaware College of Art and Design

District of Columbia

FOUR YEAR COLLEGES

Rank	Name	Sector	Ease of transfer	Flexibility of programs
172	GEORGE WASHINGTON UNIVERSITY	Nonprofit	4	5
324	GALLAUDET UNIVERSITY	Nonprofit	5	6
448	AMERICAN UNIVERSITY	Nonprofit	4	7
450	UNIVERSITY OF THE DISTRICT OF COLUMBIA	Public	4	6
464	GEORGETOWN UNIVERSITY	Nonprofit	3	4
624	STRAYER UNIVERSITY–WASHINGTON CAMPUS	For-Profit	2	6
662	HOWARD UNIVERSITY	Nonprofit	4	6

Services for adult students (6 pts)	Percent of students over age 25	Graduation rate of part-time students	Mean earnings of independent students 10 years after college entry	Loan repayment of independent students 5 years after leaving college	In-district tuition and fees (at a 9 month rate for 2 year colleges)	Percent of credentials awarded as bachelor's degrees
6	40%	20%	35,717	59%	4,168	0%
5	43%	16%	34,471	51%	4,208	0%
5	43%	19%	37,281	58%	4,208	0%
5	37%	18%	38,048	47%	4,188	0%
5	32%	18%	35,793	69%	4,168	0%
6	41%	13%	33,297	40%	4,168	0%
5	39%	19%	35,602	42%	4,168	0%
4	32%	15%	35,322	60%	4,208	0%
5	40%	17%	28,922	0%	4,198	0%
2	37%	15%	29,946	0%	4,168	0%
5	4%	46%	57,128	65%	12,830	93%
2	61%	40%	46,366	47%	10,670	97%
6	6%	22%	39,627	37%	7,532	100%
6	35%	19%	34,801	47%	3,774	0%
5	10%	57%	11,5463	73%	49,783	93%
5	25%	50%	37,036	60%	16,078	100%
5	3%	65%	72,273	59%	44,853	94%
5	55%	21%	40,340	41%	5,612	61%
4	6%	50%	13,8374	75%	50,547	99%
4	84%	22%	56,974	31%	14,235	73%
5	7%	32%	60,768	43%	24,908	100%

DELAWARE

DIST. COLUMBIA

Rank	Name		Sector	Ease of transfer (5 pts for 4 year, 4 pts for 2 year)	Flexibility of programs (9 pts)

Florida

FOUR YEAR COLLEGES

Rank	Name	Sector	Ease of transfer	Flexibility of programs
14	JACKSONVILLE UNIVERSITY	Nonprofit	5	9
106	UNIVERSITY OF FLORIDA	Public	3	8
187	UNIVERSITY OF NORTH FLORIDA	Public	3	7
244	FLORIDA STATE UNIVERSITY	Public	3	6
265	UNIVERSITY OF MIAMI	Nonprofit	4	7
279	UNIVERSITY OF SOUTH FLORIDA	Public	3	6
296	FLORIDA AGRICULTURAL AND MECHANICAL UNIVERSITY	Public	4	8
299	UNIVERSITY OF CENTRAL FLORIDA	Public	3	5
357	JOHNSON & WALES UNIVERSITY–FLORIDA CAMPUS	Nonprofit	4	7
389	FLORIDA GULF COAST UNIVERSITY	Public	4	5
420	BARRY UNIVERSITY	Nonprofit	4	7
487	LYNN UNIVERSITY	Nonprofit	5	9
541	THE UNIVERSITY OF WEST FLORIDA	Public	3	5
546	STETSON UNIVERSITY	Nonprofit	5	8
568	UNIVERSITY OF TAMPA	Nonprofit	5	6
665	FLORIDA SOUTHERN COLLEGE	Nonprofit	4	8
696	EMBRY RIDDLE AERONAUTICAL UNIVERSITY	Nonprofit	5	4
745	FLORIDA INSTITUTE OF TECHNOLOGY–MELBOURNE	Nonprofit	4	7
766	ECKERD COLLEGE	Nonprofit	3	6
769	SOUTHEASTERN COLLEGE ASSEMBLIES OF GOD	Nonprofit	4	5
794	FLAGLER COLLEGE	Nonprofit	2	5

TWO YEAR COLLEGES

Rank	Name	Sector	Ease of transfer	Flexibility of programs
33	OKALOOSA-WALTON COMMUNITY COLLEGE	Public	4	7
39	FLORIDA COMMUNITY COLLEGE AT JACKSONVILLE	Public	3	8
50	BROWARD COMMUNITY COLLEGE	Public	3	8
79	CENTRAL FLORIDA COMMUNITY COLLEGE	Public	3	8
83	SEMINOLE COMMUNITY COLLEGE	Public	4	7

Services for adult students (6 pts)	Percent of students over age 25	Graduation rate of part-time students	Mean earnings of independent students 10 years after college entry	Loan repayment of independent students 5 years after leaving college	In-district tuition and fees (at a 9 month rate for 2 year colleges)	Percent of credentials awarded as bachelor's degrees
6	40%	52%	63,045	58%	33,930	100%
5	4%	72%	66,515	64%	6,381	96%
6	22%	62%	49,421	57%	5,755	93%
6	6%	73%	51,442	60%	6,507	98%
6	6%	49%	85,005	64%	47,004	100%
6	19%	60%	47,499	58%	6,410	97%
6	10%	39%	47,490	42%	5,785	97%
6	20%	63%	49,425	60%	6,368	96%
5	7%	100%	38,952	57%	30,396	61%
6	12%	45%	46,794	57%	6,118	86%
4	44%	52%	54,038	50%	28,800	100%
4	9%	50%	54,072	48%	36,650	100%
5	31%	51%	41,167	56%	5,776	88%
5	3%	50%	44,795	61%	43,240	100%
5	6%	39%	52,187	54%	27,740	100%
4	10%	45%	43,395	57%	33,150	100%
3	12%	33%	67,898	63%	33,886	94%
4	8%	21%	63,657	39%	40,446	100%
4	13%	49%	50,131	49%	41,538	100%
4	13%	13%	42,086	55%	24,160	95%
5	8%	18%	39,954	50%	17,500	100%
6	39%	31%	33,530	49%	3,123	12%
6	45%	35%	35,484	42%	2,765	9%
6	36%	29%	38,415	45%	2,753	4%
6	36%	42%	33,028	37%	2,570	9%
5	37%	37%	35,154	38%	3,131	4%

Rank	Name	Sector	Ease of transfer (5 pts for 4 year, 4 pts for 2 year)	Flexibility of programs (9 pts)
110	MIAMI-DADE COMMUNITY COLLEGE	Public	3	8
118	PALM BEACH COMMUNITY COLLEGE	Public	3	7
156	BREVARD COMMUNITY COLLEGE–COCOA CAMPUS	Public	3	7
159	GULF COAST COMMUNITY COLLEGE	Public	4	6
182	EDISON COMMUNITY COLLEGE	Public	3	7
201	DAYTONA BEACH COMMUNITY COLLEGE	Public	3	7
216	FLORIDA NATIONAL COLLEGE	For-Profit	4	6
231	HILLSBOROUGH COMMUNITY COLLEGE	Public	3	8
235	POLK COMMUNITY COLLEGE	Public	3	6
240	PASCO-HERNANDO COMMUNITY COLLEGE	Public	3	8
273	VALENCIA COMMUNITY COLLEGE	Public	3	8
294	SANTA FE COMMUNITY COLLEGE	Public	3	5
304	TALLAHASSEE COMMUNITY COLLEGE	Public	3	8
410	LAKE-SUMTER COMMUNITY COLLEGE	Public	4	5
434	LAKE CITY COMMUNITY COLLEGE	Public	3	7
449	CHIPOLA JUNIOR COLLEGE	Public	3	6
477	MANATEE COMMUNITY COLLEGE	Public	3	5
508	FLORIDA KEYS COMMUNITY COLLEGE	Public	3	5
580	WEBSTER COLLEGE	For-Profit	1	7
684	NORTH FLORIDA COMMUNITY COLLEGE	Public	4	4
696	SAINT JOHNS RIVER COMMUNITY COLLEGE	Public	3	3
735	NEW ENGLAND INSTITUTE OF TECHNOLOGY–,, PALM BEACH	For-Profit	0	5
768	MEDICAL CAREER CENTER	For-Profit	0	3
772	GOLF ACADEMY OF THE SOUTH	For-Profit	0	3
778	VIRGINIA COLLEGE–JACKSONVILLE	For-Profit	0	2

UNRANKED: Allied Health Institute, American Motorcycle Institute, Ari Ben Aviator, Brown Mackie College–Miami, Career Institute of Florida, City College, City College Branch Campus, College of Business and Technology–Cutler Bay, College of Business and Technology–Flagler Campus, College of Business and Technology–Hialeah Campus, Concorde Career Institute, Concorde Career Institute–Orlando, Daytona Institute of Massage Therapy, Florida College, Florida College of Natural Health, Florida Computer and Business School Inc., Florida Metropolitan University–Brandon, Florida Metropolitan University–Orange Park, Florida Metropolitan University–Pinellas, Florida Metropolitan University–South Orlando, Florida Metropolitan University–Tampa, Florida Technical College, Fortis Institute, Heritage Institute, Indian River Community College, Institute of Allied Medical Professions, International Academy of Design and Technology–Online, Jones College–Jacksonville, Keiser Career Institute, La Baron Hairdressing Academy, Le Cordon Bleu College of Culinary Arts–Miami, Management Resources Institute, Medvance Institute–Stuart, North Florida Institute, Nurse Assistant Training School Inc., Pensacola Junior College, Professional Health Training Academy, Saber, Saint Petersburg Junior College, South Florida Community College, Southern Technical Institute, Southwest Florida College, Sunstate Academy of Hair Design, The Health Institute–Tampa Bay, Ultimate Medical Academy, Ultrasound Diagnostic School

Services for adult students (6 pts)	Percent of students over age 25	Graduation rate of part-time students	Mean earnings of independent students 10 years after college entry	Loan repayment of independent students 5 years after leaving college	In-district tuition and fees (at a 9 month rate for 2 year colleges)	Percent of credentials awarded as bachelor's degrees
6	32%	31%	33,837	45%	2,834	9%
6	31%	35%	36,290	42%	2,444	4%
6	34%	34%	32,184	40%	2,496	4%
5	40%	25%	31,378	46%	2,370	2%
5	29%	32%	37,434	48%	3,401	10%
6	39%	35%	31,308	33%	3,112	11%
3	65%	71%	24,945	39%	13,250	31%
4	36%	26%	37,304	40%	2,506	0%
5	34%	29%	34,004	56%	3,366	15%
5	29%	32%	32,524	41%	3,155	1%
4	27%	35%	35,893	40%	2,474	1%
6	28%	32%	36,934	37%	2,563	6%
5	22%	31%	34,447	34%	2,026	0%
5	25%	21%	32,118	40%	3,172	4%
3	32%	31%	32,229	48%	3,100	2%
4	22%	40%	32,247	44%	3,120	14%
5	33%	26%	33,195	34%	3,074	12%
4	34%	22%	36,409	37%	3,276	0%
3	78%	25%	32,896	33%	9,360	40%
4	27%	29%	27,430	0%	2,994	0%
2	27%	27%	33,838	38%	2,880	6%
5	44%	32%	32,602	24%	13,770	6%
1	73%	37%	29,468	18%	14,632	0%
1	61%	50%	29,468	18%	17,150	0%
1	69%	35%	29,468	18%	14,632	0%

Georgia

FOUR YEAR COLLEGES

Rank	Name	Sector	Ease of transfer	Flexibility of programs
18	GEORGIA INSTITUTE OF TECHNOLOGY–MAIN CAMPUS	Public	3	8
104	GEORGIA SOUTHERN UNIVERSITY	Public	5	8
239	SHORTER COLLEGE	Nonprofit	4	7
272	GEORGIA STATE UNIVERSITY	Public	5	4
278	UNIVERSITY OF GEORGIA	Public	3	7
291	EMORY UNIVERSITY	Nonprofit	3	7
301	BRENAU UNIVERSITY	Nonprofit	4	5
306	COLUMBUS STATE UNIVERSITY	Public	5	7
327	ARMSTRONG ATLANTIC STATE UNIVERSITY	Public	4	7
402	CLAYTON COLLEGE AND STATE UNIVERSITY	Public	4	6
408	VALDOSTA STATE UNIVERSITY	Public	4	8
410	GEORGIA COLLEGE AND STATE UNIVERSITY	Public	4	7
439	LAGRANGE COLLEGE	Nonprofit	5	8
470	STATE UNIVERSITY OF WEST GEORGIA	Public	5	4
574	ALBANY STATE UNIVERSITY	Public	5	6
661	GEORGIA SOUTHWESTERN STATE UNIVERSITY	Public	4	5
790	SAVANNAH STATE UNIVERSITY	Public	3	6
793	CLARK ATLANTA UNIVERSITY	Nonprofit	4	5
798	FORT VALLEY STATE UNIVERSITY	Public	2	5
806	MOREHOUSE COLLEGE	Nonprofit	3	4

UNRANKED: Agnes Scott College, American Intercontinental University, Atlanta Christian College, Berry College, Brewton–Parker College, Covenant College, Emmanuel College, Georgia Gwinnett College, Georgia School of Professional Psychology, Herzing College, Mercer University, Oglethorpe University, Paine College, Piedmont College, Reinhardt College, Shorter College–Professional Studies, South College, Spelman College, Strayer University–Georgia, Thomas University, Toccoa Falls College, Truett–McConnell College, Wesleyan College, Young Harris College

TWO YEAR COLLEGES

Rank	Name	Sector	Ease of transfer	Flexibility of programs
147	FLOYD COLLEGE	Public	4	7
280	ALBANY TECHNICAL COLLEGE	Public	3	5
313	COASTAL GEORGIA COMMUNITY COLLEGE	Public	4	6
346	GEORGIA PERIMETER COLLEGE	Public	3	8
384	DARTON COLLEGE	Public	3	8
432	DEKALB TECHNICAL COLLEGE	Public	4	6
450	DALTON STATE COLLEGE	Public	4	5
495	AUGUSTA TECHNICAL COLLEGE	Public	4	5
522	BAINBRIDGE COLLEGE	Public	3	7

Services for adult students (6 pts)	Percent of students over age 25	Graduation rate of part-time students	Mean earnings of independent students 10 years after college entry	Loan repayment of independent students 5 years after leaving college	In-district tuition and fees (at a 9 month rate for 2 year colleges)	Percent of credentials awarded as bachelor's degrees
5	4%	74%	83,981	80%	12,212	100%
6	8%	51%	44,239	51%	6,273	100%
4	25%	100%	52,656	43%	21,730	90%
6	20%	53%	49,524	49%	8,974	98%
6	3%	61%	53,058	63%	11,634	92%
4	3%	75%	99,698	74%	47,954	100%
6	53%	42%	48,663	57%	27,160	88%
5	30%	42%	39,369	37%	6,031	84%
5	30%	35%	43,023	54%	5,360	93%
5	42%	35%	43,062	44%	5,340	92%
5	16%	38%	40,806	49%	6,297	98%
5	3%	47%	43,864	65%	9,202	100%
4	11%	67%	44,045	49%	28,490	100%
6	11%	39%	42,449	51%	6,143	100%
5	22%	37%	37,213	27%	5,490	100%
4	27%	37%	37,772	48%	5,262	99%
4	10%	14%	36,864	29%	5,644	98%
4	4%	21%	37,156	40%	22,396	100%
5	16%	15%	31,437	28%	5,594	100%
4	3%	10%	42,800	30%	26,742	86%
5	21%	21%	39,102	47%	3,245	6%
6	56%	55%	25,086	16%	2,662	0%
5	28%	18%	33,123	43%	3,821	42%
4	33%	14%	38,211	38%	3,261	0%
3	43%	24%	35,898	33%	3,398	4%
4	59%	34%	29,090	0%	2,850	0%
5	20%	20%	31,280	43%	3,504	50%
4	50%	45%	28,147	0%	2,704	0%
5	36%	26%	27,036	22%	3,227	0%

Rank	Name	Sector	Ease of transfer (5 pts for 4 year, 4 pts for 2 year)	Flexibility of programs (9 pts)
584	VALDOSTA TECHNICAL COLLEGE	Public	4	5
595	GORDON COLLEGE	Public	3	6
608	ATHENS TECHNICAL COLLEGE	Public	3	5
611	SAVANNAH TECHNICAL COLLEGE	Public	4	5
645	EAST GEORGIA COLLEGE	Public	4	4
676	ATLANTA TECHNICAL COLLEGE	Public	2	6
688	CHATTAHOOCHEE TECHNICAL COLLEGE	Public	3	4
704	SOUTHEASTERN TECHNICAL COLLEGE	Public	3	4
714	COOSA VALLEY TECHNICAL COLLEGE	Public	2	4
717	ABRAHAM BALDWIN AGRICULTURAL COLLEGE	Public	1	5
719	COLUMBUS TECHNICAL COLLEGE	Public	2	3
722	GWINNETT TECHNICAL COLLEGE	Public	0	4
761	NORTH GEORGIA TECHNICAL COLLEGE	Public	2	4
773	GRIFFIN TECHNICAL COLLEGE	Public	0	3

UNRANKED: Andrew College, Asher School of Business Education Corporation, Atlanta Metropolitan College, Computer Learning Centers Inc., Georgia Medical Institute, Gupton Jones College of Funeral Service, Gwinnett College of Business, Interactive College of Technology, Lanier Technical Institute, Le Cordon Bleu College of Culinary Arts—Atlanta, Medix Schools, Miller—Motte Technical College—Columbus, Ogeechee Technical College, Sandersville Regional Technical Institute, South Georgia Technical College, Westcentral Technical College

Hawaii

FOUR YEAR COLLEGES

Rank	Name	Sector	Ease of transfer	Flexibility of programs
51	HAWAII PACIFIC UNIVERSITY	Nonprofit	5	9
180	UNIVERSITY OF HAWAII AT MANOA	Public	4	5
363	BRIGHAM YOUNG UNIVERSITY—HAWAII CAMPUS	Nonprofit	3	6
682	UNIVERSITY OF HAWAII AT HILO	Public	4	5

UNRANKED: American School of Professional Psychology—Hawaii, Chaminade University of Honolulu, University of Hawaii—West Oahu, University of Phoenix—Hawaii

TWO YEAR COLLEGES

Rank	Name	Sector	Ease of transfer	Flexibility of programs
158	HONOLULU COMMUNITY COLLEGE	Public	4	6
195	KAPIOLANI COMMUNITY COLLEGE	Public	2	7
222	WINDWARD COMMUNITY COLLEGE	Public	4	7
258	LEEWARD COMMUNITY COLLEGE	Public	3	6
274	KAUAI COMMUNITY COLLEGE	Public	3	4
406	HAWAII COMMUNITY COLLEGE	Public	3	5
547	MAUI COMMUNITY COLLEGE	Public	3	5

UNRANKED: Education America—Honolulu Campus

Services for adult students (6 pts)	Percent of students over age 25	Graduation rate of part-time students	Mean earnings of independent students 10 years after college entry	Loan repayment of independent students 5 years after leaving college	In-district tuition and fees (at a 9 month rate for 2 year colleges)	Percent of credentials awarded as bachelor's degrees
5	35%	38%	25,151	0%	2,744	0%
3	18%	22%	37,604	39%	3,551	30%
5	37%	36%	30,697	0%	2,794	0%
3	48%	32%	29,663	0%	2,704	0%
5	10%	5%	32,829	31%	3,067	1%
3	67%	27%	26,434	0%	2,756	0%
4	38%	24%	31,883	0%	2,746	0%
4	37%	38%	24,983	0%	2,784	0%
4	35%	49%	27,847	0%	2,764	0%
4	12%	26%	35,290	39%	3,453	30%
4	44%	42%	29,262	0%	2,704	0%
2	48%	31%	37,475	41%	2,796	0%
2	35%	48%	23,161	0%	2,734	0%
4	42%	9%	28,681	0%	2,758	0%
5	40%	28%	55,715	65%	23,440	87%
6	18%	58%	55,286	69%	11,732	99%
4	23%	50%	52,303	77%	5,240	77%
3	27%	45%	36,157	55%	7,650	100%
5	40%	13%	35,040	49%	3,054	0%
5	33%	22%	41,603	59%	3,084	0%
5	38%	10%	34,585	38%	3,064	0%
6	31%	16%	36,729	45%	3,084	0%
6	33%	25%	36,435	53%	3,132	0%
6	37%	23%	31,408	34%	3,084	0%
4	39%	13%	33,667	39%	3,150	3%

HAWAII

Rank	Name	Sector	Ease of transfer (5 pts for 4 year, 4 pts for 2 year)	Flexibility of programs (9 pts)

Idaho

FOUR YEAR COLLEGES

Rank	Name	Sector	Ease of transfer	Flexibility
135	IDAHO STATE UNIVERSITY	Public	5	8
175	LEWIS–CLARK STATE COLLEGE	Public	5	7
269	UNIVERSITY OF IDAHO	Public	4	7
375	NORTHWEST NAZARENE UNIVERSITY	Nonprofit	4	9

UNRANKED: Albertson College of Idaho, Boise State University, Ricks College

TWO YEAR COLLEGES

Rank	Name	Sector	Ease of transfer	Flexibility
112	EASTERN IDAHO TECHNICAL COLLEGE	Public	4	2
337	NORTH IDAHO COLLEGE	Public	3	5
416	COLLEGE OF SOUTHERN IDAHO	Public	3	5

UNRANKED: American Institute of Health Technology Inc., Brown Mackie College–Boise, College of Western Idaho

Illinois

FOUR YEAR COLLEGES

Rank	Name	Sector	Ease of transfer	Flexibility
30	SOUTHERN ILLINOIS UNIVERSITY–CARBONDALE	Public	5	9
41	NORTHEASTERN ILLINOIS UNIVERSITY	Public	5	6
53	WESTERN ILLINOIS UNIVERSITY	Public	5	8
66	LEWIS UNIVERSITY	Nonprofit	5	9
72	GOVERNORS STATE UNIVERSITY	Public	4	8
81	UNIVERSITY OF ILLINOIS AT CHICAGO	Public	4	5
87	AURORA UNIVERSITY	Nonprofit	5	9
130	GREENVILLE COLLEGE	Nonprofit	5	7
137	MCKENDREE COLLEGE	Nonprofit	5	8
162	SOUTHERN ILLINOIS UNIVERSITY–EDWARDSVILLE	Public	5	7
225	SAINT XAVIER UNIVERSITY	Nonprofit	5	8
263	ILLINOIS STATE UNIVERSITY	Public	3	7
275	ROOSEVELT UNIVERSITY	Nonprofit	5	8
317	OLIVET NAZARENE UNIVERSITY	Nonprofit	5	8
320	UNIVERSITY OF ILLINOIS AT SPRINGFIELD	Public	3	6
323	DOMINICAN UNIVERSITY	Nonprofit	5	7
339	UNIVERSITY OF ILLINOIS AT URBANA–CHAMPAIGN	Public	4	6
342	UNIVERSITY OF ST FRANCIS	Nonprofit	4	8

Services for adult students (6 pts)	Percent of students over age 25	Graduation rate of part-time students	Mean earnings of independent students 10 years after college entry	Loan repayment of independent students 5 years after leaving college	In-district tuition and fees (at a 9 month rate for 2 year colleges)	Percent of credentials awarded as bachelor's degrees
6	29%	22%	44,307	50%	6,956	71%
6	33%	28%	36,754	55%	6,120	59%
6	11%	35%	47,941	60%	7,232	98%
4	29%	25%	54,760	70%	28,650	99%
5	57%	48%	29,089	61%	2,434	0%
6	34%	21%	32,619	46%	3,288	0%
6	29%	21%	29,894	47%	3,120	0%
6	19%	47%	54,912	53%	13,073	97%
6	45%	49%	41,907	62%	9,212	100%
6	15%	55%	43,631	61%	12,382	100%
5	21%	58%	56,999	63%	30,050	100%
5	54%	56%	44,313	49%	10,516	100%
6	10%	51%	82,972	68%	14,776	100%
4	20%	76%	46,440	63%	22,830	100%
4	12%	100%	46,515	68%	25,720	100%
5	31%	49%	48,941	65%	28,740	97%
5	14%	46%	52,658	61%	9,796	100%
6	13%	50%	49,895	56%	32,250	100%
6	5%	69%	47,703	64%	12,013	100%
5	28%	41%	49,460	50%	28,119	100%
5	16%	58%	49,130	51%	33,940	99%
5	40%	54%	47,462	61%	11,501	100%
5	12%	73%	43,305	56%	31,570	100%
5	2%	55%	62,003	66%	17,184	100%
4	29%	56%	54,026	61%	30,840	100%

Rank	Name	Sector	Ease of transfer (5 pts for 4 year, 4 pts for 2 year)	Flexibility of programs (9 pts)
378	EASTERN ILLINOIS UNIVERSITY	Public	4	8
437	BENEDICTINE UNIVERSITY	Nonprofit	3	8
485	CONCORDIA UNIVERSITY	Nonprofit	4	7
494	CHICAGO STATE UNIVERSITY	Public	3	8
508	DEPAUL UNIVERSITY	Nonprofit	5	7
525	NORTH CENTRAL COLLEGE	Nonprofit	4	8
548	MILLIKIN UNIVERSITY	Nonprofit	4	9
636	LOYOLA UNIVERSITY CHICAGO	Nonprofit	3	6
655	QUINCY UNIVERSITY	Nonprofit	5	8
747	BRADLEY UNIVERSITY	Nonprofit	5	5
754	ROBERT MORRIS COLLEGE	Nonprofit	4	4
758	COLUMBIA COLLEGE CHICAGO	Nonprofit	5	4

UNRANKED: American Intercontinental University Online, Augustana College, Blackburn College, East–West University, Elmhurst College, Eureka College, Illinois College, Illinois Institute of Technology, Illinois School of Professional Psychology–Chicago, Illinois Wesleyan University, Judson College, Knox College, Lake Forest College, Macmurray College, Monmouth College, National–Louis University, North Park University, Northern Illinois University, Northwestern University, Rockford College, Trinity Christian College, Trinity International University, University of Chicago, Wheaton College

Two Year Colleges

Rank	Name	Sector	Ease of transfer	Flexibility of programs
34	OAKTON COMMUNITY COLLEGE	Public	3	7
40	ILLINOIS EASTERN COMMUNITY COLLEGE– WABASH VALLEY COLLEGE	Public	4	6
46	COLLEGE OF DUPAGE	Public	3	9
73	ILLINOIS EASTERN COMMUNITY COLLEGE–FRONTIER COMMUNITY COLLEGE	Public	4	6
85	KASKASKIA COLLEGE	Public	4	9
107	TRITON COLLEGE	Public	4	6
129	ELGIN COMMUNITY COLLEGE	Public	3	7
132	MCHENRY COUNTY COLLEGE	Public	4	6
136	WILLIAM RAINEY HARPER COLLEGE	Public	2	8
137	COLLEGE OF LAKE COUNTY	Public	3	8
141	SAUK VALLEY COMMUNITY COLLEGE	Public	4	5
150	RICHLAND COMMUNITY COLLEGE	Public	4	6
151	ROCK VALLEY COLLEGE	Public	4	6
196	ILLINOIS EASTERN COMMUNITY COLLEGE–OLNEY CENTRAL COLLEGE	Public	4	6
198	LINCOLN LAND COMMUNITY COLLEGE	Public	4	5
218	MIDSTATE COLLEGE	For–Profit	4	6
224	MORAINE VALLEY COMMUNITY COLLEGE	Public	3	8
230	KISHWAUKEE COLLEGE	Public	3	7
244	DANVILLE AREA COMMUNITY COLLEGE	Public	4	5

Services for adult students (6 pts)	Percent of students over age 25	Graduation rate of part-time students	Mean earnings of independent students 10 years after college entry	Loan repayment of independent students 5 years after leaving college	In-district tuition and fees (at a 9 month rate for 2 year colleges)	Percent of credentials awarded as bachelor's degrees
5	14%	53%	38,282	52%	11,453	100%
4	23%	74%	56,915	58%	31,466	97%
5	16%	71%	47,153	49%	30,640	100%
5	60%	27%	39,722	32%	10,252	100%
5	18%	34%	60,626	49%	37,626	99%
5	5%	45%	48,047	73%	36,654	100%
4	12%	47%	49,711	58%	31,824	96%
6	8%	28%	69,347	69%	41,384	97%
3	10%	42%	37,457	58%	27,128	99%
3	4%	35%	47,276	59%	32,120	100%
5	23%	40%	35,998	37%	25,800	56%
5	10%	26%	35,881	39%	25,334	100%
6	39%	14%	41,422	66%	3,621	0%
5	75%	21%	28,181	55%	3,466	0%
6	34%	24%	39,019	46%	4,050	0%
5	59%	22%	29,283	57%	3,466	0%
6	24%	45%	27,565	35%	4,470	0%
5	42%	21%	36,930	49%	3,870	0%
6	34%	31%	33,352	49%	3,012	0%
6	31%	32%	31,845	44%	3,404	0%
6	34%	23%	39,150	52%	3,360	0%
5	39%	23%	34,911	51%	3,780	0%
5	28%	50%	31,408	51%	3,586	0%
6	39%	32%	30,030	38%	4,230	0%
5	32%	31%	33,969	48%	3,314	0%
5	34%	37%	28,616	47%	3,466	0%
6	35%	31%	31,614	37%	3,024	0%
4	84%	38%	29,600	32%	16,230	45%
6	28%	16%	35,389	42%	4,176	0%
6	25%	31%	34,878	41%	4,290	0%
6	35%	25%	27,506	51%	4,425	0%

Rank	Name	Sector	Ease of transfer (5 pts for 4 year, 4 pts for 2 year)	Flexibility of programs (9 pts)
251	WAUBONSEE COMMUNITY COLLEGE	Public	3	7
272	PARKLAND COLLEGE	Public	4	7
289	LEWIS AND CLARK COMMUNITY COLLEGE	Public	4	5
299	REND LAKE COLLEGE	Public	4	5
315	HEARTLAND COMMUNITY COLLEGE	Public	4	6
323	KANKAKEE COMMUNITY COLLEGE	Public	4	4
325	PRAIRIE STATE COLLEGE	Public	3	7
330	HIGHLAND COMMUNITY COLLEGE	Public	4	6
355	ILLINOIS EASTERN COMMUNITY COLLEGE–LINCOLN TRAIL COLLEGE	Public	4	6
383	SPOON RIVER COLLEGE	Public	4	6
411	MORTON COLLEGE	Public	4	6
425	LINCOLN COLLEGE	Nonprofit	4	7
487	SOUTHWESTERN ILLINOIS COLLEGE	Public	1	8
509	ILLINOIS CENTRAL COLLEGE	Public	2	6
533	BLACK HAWK COLLEGE	Public	3	6
543	JOLIET JUNIOR COLLEGE	Public	3	5
548	LAKE LAND COLLEGE	Public	2	7
556	JOHN WOOD COMMUNITY COLLEGE	Public	3	7
569	ILLINOIS VALLEY COMMUNITY COLLEGE	Public	2	4
602	CARL SANDBURG COLLEGE	Public	2	6
635	NORTHWESTERN BUSINESS COLLEGE	For-Profit	4	5
660	SOUTH SUBURBAN COLLEGE	Public	3	4
663	JOHN A LOGAN COLLEGE	Public	2	3
726	SOUTHEASTERN ILLINOIS COLLEGE	Public	2	7
759	RASMUSSEN COLLEGE–ROCKFORD	For-Profit	0	3

UNRANKED: Americare Institute, City Colleges of Chicago–Harold Washington College, City Colleges of Chicago–Harry S Truman College, City Colleges of Chicago–Kennedy–King College, City Colleges of Chicago–Malcolm X College, City Colleges of Chicago–Olive Harvey College, City Colleges of Chicago–Richard J Daley College, City Colleges of Chicago–Wilbur Wright College, Commonwealth Business College–Moline, Cooking and Hospitality Institute of Chicago, Coyne American Institute Incorporated, Fox College Inc., Lincoln Technical Institute, Maccormac College, Northwestern Business College–Southwestern Campus, Rockford Business College, Saint Augustine College, Shawnee Community College, Taylor Business Institute, Vatterott College

Indiana

FOUR YEAR COLLEGES

22	INDIANA UNIVERSITY–BLOOMINGTON	Public	5	8
197	BALL STATE UNIVERSITY	Public	5	8
216	INDIANA STATE UNIVERSITY	Public	5	7
262	PURDUE UNIVERSITY–CALUMET CAMPUS	Public	5	7

Services for adult students (6 pts)	Percent of students over age 25	Graduation rate of part-time students	Mean earnings of independent students 10 years after college entry	Loan repayment of independent students 5 years after leaving college	In-district tuition and fees (at a 9 month rate for 2 year colleges)	Percent of credentials awarded as bachelor's degrees
5	31%	27%	32,955	50%	3,024	0%
6	28%	18%	31,072	34%	4,710	0%
6	24%	28%	28,071	49%	3,264	0%
6	31%	32%	27,540	39%	3,750	0%
6	28%	16%	29,801	40%	4,320	0%
5	39%	29%	31,471	42%	4,260	0%
5	41%	22%	32,786	35%	3,804	0%
6	32%	15%	29,088	35%	3,663	0%
4	38%	8%	34,713	44%	3,466	0%
4	30%	35%	29,522	41%	4,500	0%
4	34%	21%	36,231	25%	3,892	0%
4	26%	53%	31,202	41%	17,700	36%
6	39%	27%	29,425	36%	3,420	0%
6	29%	22%	32,995	38%	4,200	0%
4	31%	17%	31,448	48%	4,410	0%
5	25%	11%	33,840	45%	3,750	0%
4	30%	33%	28,814	47%	3,789	0%
3	29%	28%	28,444	48%	4,710	0%
5	28%	44%	30,095	43%	3,730	0%
4	29%	23%	29,458	55%	4,390	0%
3	57%	19%	32,423	25%	17,730	0%
5	40%	25%	31,783	0%	4,583	0%
5	40%	16%	29,085	40%	3,510	0%
5	27%	3%	29,788	0%	3,390	0%
1	71%	34%	32,896	33%	9,360	9%
6	2%	76%	53,362	59%	10,388	98%
6	6%	40%	42,758	54%	9,654	98%
6	16%	39%	41,332	52%	8,746	98%
6	35%	22%	41,806	37%	7,029	96%

Rank	Name	Sector	Ease of transfer (5 pts for 4 year, 4 pts for 2 year)	Flexibility of programs (9 pts)
297	INDIANA UNIVERSITY—SOUTHEAST	Public	4	8
313	INDIANA UNIVERSITY—PURDUE UNIVERSITY—INDIANAPOLIS	Public	4	6
442	MARIAN COLLEGE	Nonprofit	5	7
444	GOSHEN COLLEGE	Nonprofit	5	7
472	OAKLAND CITY UNIVERSITY	Nonprofit	5	8
493	INDIANA UNIVERSITY—KOKOMO	Public	4	7
517	PURDUE UNIVERSITY—MAIN CAMPUS	Public	4	5
522	UNIVERSITY OF SOUTHERN INDIANA	Public	4	6
524	INDIANA UNIVERSITY—SOUTH BEND	Public	5	7
596	INDIANA UNIVERSITY—EAST	Public	4	7
628	UNIVERSITY OF INDIANAPOLIS	Nonprofit	4	7
650	INDIANA UNIVERSITY—NORTHWEST	Public	3	8
651	UNIVERSITY OF SAINT FRANCIS	Nonprofit	5	6
692	VALPARAISO UNIVERSITY	Nonprofit	5	7
803	TRI—STATE UNIVERSITY	Nonprofit	3	8
804	UNIVERSITY OF NOTRE DAME	Nonprofit	3	4
807	TAYLOR UNIVERSITY—UPLAND	Nonprofit	3	5

UNRANKED: Anderson University, Bethel College, Butler University, Calumet College of Saint Joseph, Depauw University, Earlham College, Franklin College of Indiana, Grace College and Theological Seminary, Hanover University, Holy Cross College, Huntington College, Indiana University–Purdue University Fort Wayne, Indiana Wesleyan University, Manchester College, Martin University, Purdue University–North Central Campus, Saint Josephs College, Saint Mary-of-the-Woods College, Saint Mary's College, Tri-State University–Fort Wayne Campus, University of Evansville, Wabash College

Two Year Colleges

Rank	Name	Sector	Ease of transfer	Flexibility of programs
338	VINCENNES UNIVERSITY	Public	4	9
662	ANCILLA COLLEGE	Nonprofit	4	5

UNRANKED: Brown Mackie College–Indianapolis, College of Court Reporting Inc., Commonwealth Business College–Main Campus, Fortis College–Indianapolis, Indiana Business College, International Business College–Indianapolis, Ivy Tech State College–Central Indiana, Kaplan College–Indianapolis, Lincoln Technical Institute, Michiana College

Iowa

Four Year Colleges

Rank	Name	Sector	Ease of transfer	Flexibility of programs
3	UNIVERSITY OF IOWA	Public	5	7
49	UNIVERSITY OF NORTHERN IOWA	Public	5	8
115	MOUNT MERCY COLLEGE	Nonprofit	5	7
125	SAINT AMBROSE UNIVERSITY	Nonprofit	5	9
127	SIMPSON COLLEGE	Nonprofit	5	8

Services for adult students (6 pts)	Percent of students over age 25	Graduation rate of part-time students	Mean earnings of independent students 10 years after college entry	Loan repayment of independent students 5 years after leaving college	In-district tuition and fees (at a 9 month rate for 2 year colleges)	Percent of credentials awarded as bachelor's degrees
6	27%	28%	35,578	51%	7,073	91%
6	23%	33%	51,555	53%	9,205	86%
4	28%	57%	48,709	50%	31,500	95%
6	16%	17%	45,933	70%	33,200	100%
5	16%	36%	40,477	49%	23,400	86%
5	21%	34%	39,551	51%	7,073	96%
6	4%	18%	57,214	65%	10,002	94%
6	14%	31%	38,329	53%	7,604	95%
5	21%	18%	36,058	45%	7,073	96%
4	36%	40%	32,923	38%	7,073	94%
5	18%	38%	46,632	47%	27,420	96%
5	23%	25%	39,326	37%	7,073	88%
3	22%	51%	45,055	53%	28,040	73%
4	5%	35%	46,087	54%	37,450	100%
1	1%	33%	37,548	43%	30,960	100%
3	0%	0%	124,876	0%	49,685	100%
3	3%	0%	32,955	56%	31,472	100%
5	13%	14%	32,257	37%	5,575	6%
3	21%	33%	30,563	38%	14,930	0%
6	8%	66%	76,785	62%	8,575	100%
6	9%	59%	44,834	58%	8,303	100%
5	36%	55%	49,120	71%	29,696	100%
6	15%	40%	47,045	68%	29,150	100%
5	15%	73%	49,057	72%	35,876	100%

IOWA

Rank	Name	Sector	Ease of transfer (5 pts for 4 year, 4 pts for 2 year)	Flexibility of programs (9 pts)
195	QUEST COLLEGE	For-Profit	5	9
303	BRIAR CLIFF COLLEGE	Nonprofit	5	9
434	GRACELAND UNIVERSITY–LAMONI	Nonprofit	4	8
460	BUENA VISTA UNIVERSITY	Nonprofit	3	7
571	DRAKE UNIVERSITY	Nonprofit	4	7
767	LORAS COLLEGE	Nonprofit	4	6

UNRANKED: Central College, Clarke College, Coe College, Cornell College, Dordt College, Grand View College, Grinnell College, Iowa State University, Iowa Wesleyan College, Luther College, Maharishi University of Management, Morningside College, Mount St. Clare College, Northwestern College, University of Dubuque, Upper Iowa University, Waldorf College, Wartburg College, William Penn University

TWO YEAR COLLEGES

Rank	Name	Sector	Ease of transfer	Flexibility
105	HAMILTON COLLEGE	For-Profit	4	8
119	HAMILTON COLLEGE–MASON CITY BRANCH	For-Profit	4	7
178	HAMILTON COLLEGE–MAIN CAMPUS	For-Profit	3	8
226	KIRKWOOD COMMUNITY COLLEGE	Public	4	9
241	HAWKEYE COMMUNITY COLLEGE	Public	4	7
250	WESTERN IOWA TECH COMMUNITY COLLEGE	Public	3	8
255	IOWA WESTERN COMMUNITY COLLEGE	Public	4	7
435	DES MOINES COMMUNITY COLLEGE	Public	3	7
440	IOWA CENTRAL COMMUNITY COLLEGE	Public	4	7
452	NORTHEAST IOWA COMMUNITY COLLEGE–CALMAR	Public	4	5
456	SOUTHEASTERN COMMUNITY COLLEGE	Public	4	6
546	IOWA LAKES COMMUNITY COLLEGE	Public	4	6
566	SOUTHWESTERN COMMUNITY COLLEGE	Public	4	5
582	HAMILTON COLLEGE	For-Profit	1	6

UNRANKED: Eastern Iowa Community College District, Ellsworth Community College, Indian Hills Community College, Iowa Valley Community College District, North Iowa Area Community College, Northwest Iowa Community College, Vatterott College

Kansas

FOUR YEAR COLLEGES

Rank	Name	Sector	Ease of transfer	Flexibility
7	FORT HAYS STATE UNIVERSITY	Public	5	7
39	MIDAMERICA NAZARENE UNIVERSITY	Nonprofit	4	9
68	SOUTHWESTERN COLLEGE	Nonprofit	4	7
157	WICHITA STATE UNIVERSITY	Public	5	7
203	BAKER UNIVERSITY COLLEGE OF ARTS AND SCIENCES	Nonprofit	4	9

Services for adult students (6 pts)	Percent of students over age 25	Graduation rate of part-time students	Mean earnings of independent students 10 years after college entry	Loan repayment of independent students 5 years after leaving college	In-district tuition and fees (at a 9 month rate for 2 year colleges)	Percent of credentials awarded as bachelor's degrees
4	83%	20%	41,044	26%	14,325	53%
3	21%	57%	47,744	64%	28,788	100%
5	19%	50%	40,971	61%	27,010	100%
5	40%	68%	37,359	64%	32,210	100%
3	4%	56%	71,293	69%	35,206	100%
3	2%	29%	39,708	72%	31,525	100%
3	77%	35%	41,044	26%	15,352	37%
3	78%	41%	41,044	26%	15,352	58%
3	74%	45%	41,044	26%	15,352	42%
5	22%	20%	32,691	36%	4,670	0%
5	22%	39%	33,501	33%	4,786	0%
5	23%	39%	30,742	47%	4,200	0%
5	22%	26%	34,142	44%	5,472	0%
6	20%	16%	33,369	34%	4,410	0%
5	15%	19%	31,535	37%	5,580	0%
5	17%	29%	31,678	41%	5,012	0%
5	23%	26%	27,368	39%	5,220	0%
5	15%	6%	30,560	43%	5,900	0%
4	16%	25%	30,902	41%	5,460	0%
3	74%	40%	41,044	26%	15,352	41%
6	31%	80%	39,381	59%	4,884	97%
5	31%	73%	58,197	66%	28,150	95%
5	55%	61%	57,733	62%	27,250	88%
6	27%	32%	43,765	53%	7,895	95%
4	33%	53%	57,632	63%	27,955	87%

Rank	Name	Sector	Ease of transfer (5 pts for 4 year, 4 pts for 2 year)	Flexibility of programs (9 pts)
204	SAINT MARY COLLEGE	Nonprofit	5	9
221	FRIENDS UNIVERSITY	Nonprofit	5	7
300	TABOR COLLEGE	Nonprofit	4	9
302	UNIVERSITY OF KANSAS MAIN CAMPUS	Public	4	5
334	EMPORIA STATE UNIVERSITY	Public	5	4
431	KANSAS STATE UNIVERSITY	Public	5	4
466	WASHBURN UNIVERSITY OF TOPEKA	Public	4	8
489	NEWMAN UNIVERSITY	Nonprofit	5	9
532	PITTSBURG STATE UNIVERSITY	Public	5	6
777	KANSAS WESLEYAN UNIVERSITY	Nonprofit	3	6

UNRANKED: Benedictine College, Bethany College, Bethel College, Central Christian College of Kansas, McPherson College, Ottawa University, Ottawa University–Kansas City, Ottawa University–Online, Sterling College

Two Year Colleges

Rank	Name	Sector	Ease of transfer	Flexibility
30	COLBY COMMUNITY COLLEGE	Public	3	7
103	HUTCHINSON COMMUNITY COLLEGE	Public	4	8
125	BARTON COUNTY COMMUNITY COLLEGE	Public	4	6
210	MANHATTAN AREA TECHNICAL COLLEGE	Public	4	5
252	JOHNSON COUNTY COMMUNITY COLLEGE	Public	3	6
300	HESSTON COLLEGE	Nonprofit	4	4
308	LABETTE COMMUNITY COLLEGE	Public	3	4
319	PRATT COMMUNITY COLLEGE	Public	3	6
388	DODGE CITY COMMUNITY COLLEGE	Public	2	7
403	CLOUD COUNTY COMMUNITY COLLEGE	Public	4	6
461	NEOSHO COUNTY COMMUNITY COLLEGE	Public	3	6
480	NORTHWEST KANSAS AREA VOCATIONAL TECHNICAL SCHOOL	Public	4	5
564	WICHITA AREA TECHNICAL COLLEGE	Public	2	6
621	FORT SCOTT COMMUNITY COLLEGE	Public	3	6
731	INDEPENDENCE COMMUNITY COLLEGE	Public	4	3
742	DONNELLY COLLEGE	Nonprofit	3	5

UNRANKED: Allen County Community College, Butler County Community College, Coffeyville Community College, Cowley County Community College, Flint Hills Technical College, Garden City Community College, Heritage College, Highland Community College, Kansas City Kansas Community College, National American University–Wichita, North Central Kansas Technical College, Salina Area Technical School, Seward County Community College, Vatterot College–Wichita, Wichita Technical Institute

Services for adult students (6 pts)	Percent of students over age 25	Graduation rate of part-time students	Mean earnings of independent students 10 years after college entry	Loan repayment of independent students 5 years after leaving college	In-district tuition and fees (at a 9 month rate for 2 year colleges)	Percent of credentials awarded as bachelor's degrees
5	22%	47%	41,117	63%	26,650	99%
5	33%	52%	49,393	55%	26,865	99%
3	17%	83%	52,923	56%	26,590	98%
6	10%	36%	63,340	62%	10,549	100%
6	13%	57%	37,564	55%	6,179	100%
6	10%	33%	47,998	59%	9,874	97%
5	25%	27%	39,689	46%	7,754	71%
4	14%	33%	44,500	57%	27,556	80%
4	13%	39%	39,589	56%	6,910	97%
5	7%	19%	37,776	52%	28,000	100%
5	20%	83%	33,225	57%	3,150	0%
6	27%	20%	32,686	44%	2,976	0%
6	39%	20%	34,142	42%	3,328	0%
3	29%	48%	40,195	52%	5,640	0%
5	31%	19%	39,793	49%	2,790	0%
3	15%	78%	48,657	64%	25,802	0%
5	38%	38%	32,479	53%	2,760	0%
5	25%	21%	32,149	63%	3,232	0%
6	26%	17%	33,738	48%	2,100	0%
5	19%	16%	31,240	45%	2,970	0%
4	27%	21%	35,145	48%	3,520	0%
5	18%	25%	33,278	43%	8,300	0%
3	31%	60%	31,408	40%	7,323	0%
3	16%	38%	28,169	41%	2,820	0%
1	12%	37%	25,276	43%	3,728	0%
4	31%	5%	25,348	15%	7,986	9%

Rank	Name	Sector	Ease of transfer (5 pts for 4 year, 4 pts for 2 year)	Flexibility of programs (9 pts)

Kentucky

FOUR YEAR COLLEGES

Rank	Name	Sector	Ease of transfer	Flexibility of programs
55	UNIVERSITY OF KENTUCKY	Public	5	8
100	NORTHERN KENTUCKY UNIVERSITY	Public	5	9
128	THOMAS MORE COLLEGE	Nonprofit	5	8
167	MURRAY STATE UNIVERSITY	Public	4	9
223	BRESCIA UNIVERSITY	Nonprofit	5	8
379	KENTUCKY STATE UNIVERSITY	Public	5	8
422	SPALDING UNIVERSITY	Nonprofit	5	7
427	BELLARMINE UNIVERSITY	Nonprofit	5	8
492	UNIVERSITY OF LOUISVILLE	Public	4	7
592	MOREHEAD STATE UNIVERSITY	Public	4	8
608	CAMPBELLSVILLE UNIVERSITY	Nonprofit	5	8
706	EASTERN KENTUCKY UNIVERSITY	Public	3	6
768	PIKEVILLE COLLEGE	Nonprofit	3	5

UNRANKED: Alice Lloyd College, Asbury College, Berea College, Centre College of Kentucky, Cumberland College, Georgetown College, Kentucky Christian College, Kentucky Wesleyan College, Lindsey Wilson College, Midway College, Sullivan University, Transylvania University, Union College, Western Kentucky University

TWO YEAR COLLEGES

Rank	Name	Sector	Ease of transfer	Flexibility of programs
99	MADISONVILLE COMMUNITY COLLEGE	Public	4	6
186	HENDERSON COMMUNITY COLLEGE	Public	4	6
193	JEFFERSON COMMUNITY COLLEGE	Public	4	7
389	SOMERSET COMMUNITY COLLEGE	Public	4	6
402	PADUCAH COMMUNITY COLLEGE	Public	3	4
462	OWENSBORO COMMUNITY COLLEGE	Public	3	5
473	ASHLAND COMMUNITY COLLEGE	Public	3	6
510	NORTHERN KENTUCKY TECHNICAL COLLEGE	Public	3	6
517	ELIZABETHTOWN COMMUNITY COLLEGE	Public	3	4
599	HOPKINSVILLE COMMUNITY COLLEGE	Public	2	4
651	SOUTHEAST COMMUNITY COLLEGE	Public	2	5
666	MAYSVILLE COMMUNITY COLLEGE	Public	3	5
668	PRESTONSBURG COMMUNITY COLLEGE	Public	3	5
718	DRAUGHONS JUNIOR COLLEGE	For-Profit	3	4
758	HAZARD COMMUNITY COLLEGE	Public	2	4

UNRANKED: ATA Career Education, Bowling Green Technical College, Central Kentucky Technical College, Daymar College–Online, Galen Health Institutes, Kentucky Career Institute, National Business College, Rets Electronic Institute

Services for adult students (6 pts)	Percent of students over age 25	Graduation rate of part-time students	Mean earnings of independent students 10 years after college entry	Loan repayment of independent students 5 years after leaving college	In-district tuition and fees (at a 9 month rate for 2 year colleges)	Percent of credentials awarded as bachelor's degrees
6	7%	47%	51,731	64%	11484	98%
6	21%	32%	40,154	55%	9,384	97%
5	18%	50%	64,981	60%	29,450	77%
5	18%	62%	37,972	56%	8,400	98%
5	51%	25%	38,567	55%	21,100	88%
6	24%	21%	30,395	39%	7,796	87%
4	34%	47%	44,978	49%	24,338	99%
4	7%	44%	55,180	75%	39,350	100%
4	19%	40%	47,136	60%	11,264	97%
5	14%	38%	30,228	40%	8,496	89%
5	17%	29%	31,633	44%	24,596	87%
4	22%	37%	37,194	53%	8,868	90%
4	7%	50%	36,229	50%	19,600	85%
5	48%	33%	30,029	51%	3936	0%
5	44%	29%	29,650	43%	3,936	0%
6	39%	20%	29,691	33%	4,016	0%
5	39%	24%	27,473	30%	3,936	0%
5	38%	39%	29,334	49%	3,936	0%
5	36%	27%	28,438	47%	3,936	0%
5	41%	25%	28,416	33%	3,936	0%
4	44%	30%	28,341	33%	4,016	0%
5	48%	27%	29,126	34%	3,936	0%
5	47%	16%	31,111	42%	3,936	0%
5	41%	14%	25,653	40%	3,936	0%
3	41%	26%	25,686	27%	3,936	0%
4	31%	14%	26,431	32%	3,936	0%
4	73%	0%	24,476	23%	15,000	2%
0	45%	29%	26,057	34%	3,936	0%

Rank	Name	Sector	Ease of transfer (5 pts for 4 year, 4 pts for 2 year)	Flexibility of programs (9 pts)

Louisiana

FOUR YEAR COLLEGES

Rank	Name	Sector	Ease of transfer	Flexibility of programs
503	LOUISIANA STATE UNIVERSITY AND AGRICULTURAL & MECHANICAL COLLEGE AND PAUL M. HERBERT LAW CENTER	Public	3	5
534	MCNEESE STATE UNIVERSITY	Public	4	7
558	UNIVERSITY OF LOUISIANA AT LAFAYETTE	Public	4	5
572	UNIVERSITY OF NEW ORLEANS	Public	4	6
602	UNIVERSITY OF LOUISIANA AT MONROE	Public	5	4
701	LOUISIANA STATE UNIVERSITY AT ALEXANDRIA	Public	3	5
728	TULANE UNIVERSITY OF LOUISIANA	Nonprofit	3	6
786	LOUISIANA TECH UNIVERSITY	Public	2	4
805	DILLARD UNIVERSITY	Nonprofit	4	2

UNRANKED: Centenary College of Louisiana, Grambling State University, Grantham University, Louisiana College, Louisiana State University–Shreveport, Loyola University New Orleans, Nicholls State University, Northwestern State University of Louisiana, Our Lady of Holy Cross College, Southeastern Louisiana University, Southern University and A & M College, Southern University at New Orleans, Xavier University of Louisiana

TWO YEAR COLLEGES

Rank	Name	Sector	Ease of transfer	Flexibility of programs
109	DELGADO COMMUNITY COLLEGE	Public	3	8
349	LOUISIANA STATE UNIVERSITY–EUNICE	Public	4	6
369	ELAINE P NUNEZ COMMUNITY COLLEGE	Public	3	7
482	BOSSIER PARISH COMMUNITY COLLEGE	Public	4	6
686	SOUTHERN UNIVERSITY AT SHREVEPORT	Public	3	4

UNRANKED: Baton Rouge Community College, Career Technical College–Shreveport, Career Training Specialists, Delta College of Arts and Technology, Delta School of Business and Technology, Education America–Remington College, Herzing College, ITI Technical College, Louisiana Culinary Institute, Louisiana Tech College–Young Memorial Campus, Louisiana Technical College–Alexandria Campus, Louisiana Technical College–Baton Rouge Campus, Louisiana Technical College–Sowela Campus, Louisiana Technical College–Sullivan Campus, Medical Careers Academy, River Parishes Community College, South Louisiana Community College

Maine

FOUR YEAR COLLEGES

Rank	Name	Sector	Ease of transfer	Flexibility of programs
56	UNIVERSITY OF SOUTHERN MAINE	Public	5	8
286	UNIVERSITY OF NEW ENGLAND–UNIVERSITY CAMPUS	Nonprofit	4	8
353	UNIVERSITY OF MAINE	Public	4	7
376	UNIVERSITY OF MAINE AT FARMINGTON	Public	5	7

Services for adult students (6 pts)	Percent of students over age 25	Graduation rate of part-time students	Mean earnings of independent students 10 years after college entry	Loan repayment of independent students 5 years after leaving college	In-district tuition and fees (at a 9 month rate for 2 year colleges)	Percent of credentials awarded as bachelor's degrees
6	5%	40%	61,382	63%	10,814	100%
5	18%	33%	41,486	47%	7,309	91%
6	15%	23%	44,129	59%	9,450	100%
5	28%	20%	44,165	51%	8,484	100%
6	12%	21%	45,082	44%	8,284	95%
6	27%	23%	34,541	39%	6,668	69%
5	14%	26%	79,530	48%	51,010	97%
4	11%	23%	49,094	52%	9,117	96%
3	8%	33%	32,598	31%	17,070	100%
6	51%	22%	33,498	36%	3,911	0%
5	21%	18%	35,116	42%	4,392	0%
4	32%	38%	28,707	49%	4,103	0%
4	42%	3%	33,833	31%	4,079	0%
3	30%	39%	27,839	23%	3,996	0%

Services for adult students (6 pts)	Percent of students over age 25	Graduation rate of part-time students	Mean earnings of independent students 10 years after college entry	Loan repayment of independent students 5 years after leaving college	In-district tuition and fees (at a 9 month rate for 2 year colleges)	Percent of credentials awarded as bachelor's degrees
5	31%	40%	43,864	67%	7,796	97%
5	24%	43%	63,334	64%	35,630	100%
6	8%	34%	43,263	63%	10,628	100%
6	6%	30%	33,340	58%	9,217	100%

Rank	Name	Sector	Ease of transfer (5 pts for 4 year, 4 pts for 2 year)	Flexibility of programs (9 pts)
545	UNIVERSITY OF MAINE AT FORT KENT	Public	4	6
581	UNIVERSITY OF MAINE AT AUGUSTA	Public	4	5
704	UNIVERSITY OF MAINE AT MACHIAS	Public	4	5

UNRANKED: Bates College, Bowdoin College, Colby College, College of the Atlantic, Maine Maritime Academy, Saint Josephs College, Thomas College, Unity College, University of Maine at Presque Isle

Two Year Colleges

Rank	Name	Sector	Ease of transfer	Flexibility of programs
45	ANDOVER COLLEGE	For-Profit	4	7
101	SOUTHERN MAINE TECHNICAL COLLEGE	Public	4	6
152	EASTERN MAINE TECHNICAL COLLEGE	Public	3	6
268	YORK COUNTY TECHNICAL COLLEGE	Public	4	6
348	CENTRAL MAINE TECHNICAL COLLEGE	Public	3	6
392	KENNEBEC VALLEY TECHNICAL COLLEGE	Public	3	4
408	NORTHERN MAINE TECHNICAL COLLEGE	Public	3	5
538	WASHINGTON COUNTY TECHNICAL COLLEGE	Public	3	5

UNRANKED: Beal College, Central Maine Medical Center School of Nursing, College of the Marshall Islands

Maryland

Four Year Colleges

Rank	Name	Sector	Ease of transfer	Flexibility of programs
12	UNIVERSITY OF BALTIMORE	Public	5	9
34	COLLEGE OF NOTRE DAME OF MARYLAND	Nonprofit	4	9
91	UNIVERSITY OF MARYLAND–COLLEGE PARK	Public	5	5
146	UNIVERSITY OF MARYLAND–BALTIMORE COUNTY	Public	4	7
209	TOWSON UNIVERSITY	Public	5	5
229	UNIVERSITY OF MARYLAND–UNIVERSITY COLLEGE	Public	3	8
350	COLUMBIA UNION COLLEGE	Nonprofit	4	8
458	GOUCHER COLLEGE	Nonprofit	3	6
502	HOOD COLLEGE	Nonprofit	5	6
735	FROSTBURG STATE UNIVERSITY	Public	3	3

UNRANKED: Bowie State University, Coppin State College, Johns Hopkins University, Loyola College, Morgan State University, Mount Saint Mary's College, St John's College, St. Mary's College of Maryland, University of Maryland–Eastern Shore, Villa Julie College, Washington College, Western Maryland College

Two Year Colleges

Rank	Name	Sector	Ease of transfer	Flexibility of programs
60	PRINCE GEORGES COMMUNITY COLLEGE	Public	3	7

Services for adult students (6 pts)	Percent of students over age 25	Graduation rate of part-time students	Mean earnings of independent students 10 years after college entry	Loan repayment of independent students 5 years after leaving college	In-district tuition and fees (at a 9 month rate for 2 year colleges)	Percent of credentials awarded as bachelor's degrees
5	29%	33%	34,042	54%	7,575	85%
5	64%	22%	29,490	40%	7,448	62%
5	32%	25%	23,519	44%	7,530	83%
4	82%	33%	41,044	26%	11,601	44%
5	37%	22%	38,351	51%	3,760	0%
6	32%	33%	34,577	52%	3,676	0%
5	36%	12%	33,698	45%	3,540	0%
4	34%	33%	33,906	49%	3,540	0%
4	39%	42%	33,193	50%	3,790	0%
5	29%	40%	32,024	40%	3,464	0%
6	35%	14%	24,655	42%	3,719	0%
4	50%	50%	61,984	49%	8,596	100%
6	49%	61%	56,873	56%	35,019	100%
6	2%	54%	63,687	70%	10,181	100%
6	15%	43%	57,159	64%	11,264	100%
6	12%	48%	52,583	59%	9,408	100%
4	76%	22%	55,591	46%	7,176	79%
5	31%	33%	59,992	45%	23,400	95%
5	2%	100%	76,006	53%	43,416	100%
5	11%	55%	43,979	68%	36,540	100%
4	15%	48%	42,143	58%	8,702	100%
6	41%	12%	46,830	42%	3,650	0%

Rank	Name	Sector	Ease of transfer (5 pts for 4 year, 4 pts for 2 year)	Flexibility of programs (9 pts)
67	COLLEGE OF SOUTHERN MARYLAND	Public	3	8
202	ANNE ARUNDEL COMMUNITY COLLEGE	Public	2	7
208	ALLEGANY COLLEGE OF MARYLAND	Public	4	6
442	HAGERSTOWN BUSINESS COLLEGE	For-Profit	2	5
601	WOR–WIC COMMUNITY COLLEGE	Public	2	4

UNRANKED: Baltimore City Community College, Carroll Community College, Chesapeake College, Community College of Baltimore County, Frederick Community College, Garrett Community College, Hagerstown Community College, Harford Community College, Howard Community College, Lincoln Technical Institute, Medix South, Montgomery College, Rets Technical Training Center, TESST Technology Institute

Massachusetts
FOUR YEAR COLLEGES

Rank	Name	Sector	Ease of transfer	Flexibility of programs
16	UNIVERSITY OF MASSACHUSETTS–AMHERST	Public	5	9
84	BAY PATH COLLEGE	Nonprofit	5	9
89	SALEM STATE COLLEGE	Public	5	7
188	FRAMINGHAM STATE COLLEGE	Public	4	7
207	WORCESTER STATE COLLEGE	Public	5	6
237	UNIVERSITY OF MASSACHUSETTS–LOWELL	Public	5	7
273	SIMMONS COLLEGE	Nonprofit	4	8
292	SUFFOLK UNIVERSITY	Nonprofit	5	6
318	HARVARD UNIVERSITY	Nonprofit	1	8
407	MASSACHUSETTS COLLEGE OF LIBERAL ARTS	Public	4	8
446	COLLEGE OF OUR LADY OF THE ELMS	Nonprofit	3	7
476	UNIVERSITY OF MASSACHUSETTS–BOSTON	Public	3	6
543	LESLEY UNIVERSITY	Nonprofit	4	9
551	BRIDGEWATER STATE COLLEGE	Public	3	6
580	BECKER COLLEGE	Nonprofit	4	7
599	SMITH COLLEGE	Nonprofit	4	6
658	FITCHBURG STATE COLLEGE	Public	4	5
695	EMMANUEL COLLEGE	Nonprofit	2	8
711	UNIVERSITY OF MASSACHUSETTS–DARTMOUTH	Public	4	4
776	NEWBURY COLLEGE–BROOKLINE	Nonprofit	5	7
785	EMERSON COLLEGE	Nonprofit	2	5

UNRANKED: American International College, Amherst College, Anna Maria College, Assumption College, Bentley College, Boston College, Boston University, Brandeis University, Cambridge College, Clark University, College of the Holy Cross, Curry College, Eastern Nazarene College, Endicott College, Gordon College, Hampshire College, Lasell College, Massachusetts Institute of Technology, Massachusetts Maritime Academy, Merrimack College, Mount Holyoke College, Northeastern University, Pine Manor College, Simons Rock College of Bard, Springfield College, Tufts University, Wellesley College, Wentworth Institute of Technology, Westfield State College, Wheaton College, Wheelock College, Williams College, Worcester Polytechnic Institute

Services for adult students (6 pts)	Percent of students over age 25	Graduation rate of part-time students	Mean earnings of independent students 10 years after college entry	Loan repayment of independent students 5 years after leaving college	In-district tuition and fees (at a 9 month rate for 2 year colleges)	Percent of credentials awarded as bachelor's degrees
6	29%	17%	42,088	50%	3,631	0%
6	36%	19%	42,797	45%	4,564	0%
5	24%	27%	34,413	51%	3,750	0%
3	76%	50%	41,044	26%	14,325	38%
5	37%	18%	31,479	47%	2,952	0%
6	8%	64%	51432	65%	14,971	95%
4	60%	57%	47,014	54%	32,739	94%
6	21%	48%	45,509	58%	9,736	100%
5	17%	51%	54,240	68%	9,340	99%
5	23%	48%	47,535	61%	9,202	100%
4	26%	39%	56,512	60%	14,307	94%
4	13%	74%	57,648	77%	38,590	100%
5	6%	45%	79,575	60%	35,578	99%
4	20%	67%	151,484	55%	47,074	100%
5	14%	47%	35,780	54%	9,875	100%
4	35%	86%	47,680	61%	33,412	95%
5	31%	45%	50,994	58%	13,435	99%
4	22%	48%	39,390	52%	25,875	100%
6	16%	41%	41,543	56%	9,603	99%
4	27%	44%	56,424	60%	37,272	74%
5	4%	100%	41,413	59%	47,904	100%
3	16%	53%	43,133	62%	10,135	100%
4	4%	55%	62,501	63%	37,540	100%
4	14%	46%	44,667	47%	13,188	97%
3	10%	9%	36,741	50%	33,510	88%
4	2%	60%	56,498	58%	41,852	100%

Rank	Name	Sector	Ease of transfer (5 pts for 4 year, 4 pts for 2 year)	Flexibility of programs (9 pts)

Two Year Colleges

Rank	Name	Sector	Ease of transfer	Flexibility
12	MOUNT WACHUSETT COMMUNITY COLLEGE	Public	4	8
19	MASSACHUSETTS BAY COMMUNITY COLLEGE	Public	4	5
24	MIDDLESEX COMMUNITY COLLEGE	Public	4	8
42	CAPE COD COMMUNITY COLLEGE	Public	4	7
61	QUINSIGAMOND COMMUNITY COLLEGE	Public	3	8
65	BRISTOL COMMUNITY COLLEGE	Public	3	9
69	BERKSHIRE COMMUNITY COLLEGE	Public	4	6
80	SPRINGFIELD TECHNICAL COMMUNITY COLLEGE	Public	4	5
90	MASSASOIT COMMUNITY COLLEGE	Public	2	8
179	HOLYOKE COMMUNITY COLLEGE	Public	3	7
191	NORTHERN ESSEX COMMUNITY COLLEGE	Public	4	6
209	GREENFIELD COMMUNITY COLLEGE	Public	4	6
529	ROXBURY COMMUNITY COLLEGE	Public	3	6

UNRANKED: Bay State College, Bunker Hill Community College, Dean College, Fisher College, Lawrence Memorial Hospital School of Nursing, Le Cordon Bleu College of Culinary Arts, North Shore Community College, Quincy College, Salter School, Urban College of Boston

Michigan

Four Year Colleges

Rank	Name	Sector	Ease of transfer	Flexibility
31	MICHIGAN STATE UNIVERSITY	Public	4	8
38	UNIVERSITY OF MICHIGAN–ANN ARBOR	Public	3	8
80	EASTERN MICHIGAN UNIVERSITY	Public	5	9
85	SIENA HEIGHTS UNIVERSITY	Nonprofit	5	7
92	FERRIS STATE UNIVERSITY	Public	4	8
148	WESTERN MICHIGAN UNIVERSITY	Public	5	7
232	SPRING ARBOR UNIVERSITY	Nonprofit	5	7
233	LAKE SUPERIOR STATE UNIVERSITY	Public	5	8
235	OAKLAND UNIVERSITY	Public	4	7
261	WAYNE STATE UNIVERSITY	Public	4	8
276	UNIVERSITY OF MICHIGAN–FLINT	Public	5	7
374	GRAND VALLEY STATE UNIVERSITY	Public	5	6
578	UNIVERSITY OF DETROIT MERCY	Nonprofit	5	7
600	CORNERSTONE UNIVERSITY	Nonprofit	4	7
607	UNIVERSITY OF MICHIGAN–DEARBORN	Public	3	5
627	CENTRAL MICHIGAN UNIVERSITY	Public	4	7
656	NORTHERN MICHIGAN UNIVERSITY	Public	3	9
666	AQUINAS COLLEGE	Nonprofit	5	6

Services for adult students (6 pts)	Percent of students over age 25	Graduation rate of part-time students	Mean earnings of independent students 10 years after college entry	Loan repayment of independent students 5 years after leaving college	In-district tuition and fees (at a 9 month rate for 2 year colleges)	Percent of credentials awarded as bachelor's degrees
6	41%	25%	34,664	61%	5188	0%
5	40%	21%	47,066	67%	4,808	0%
5	33%	22%	38,073	66%	4,730	0%
6	43%	19%	35,775	50%	4,320	0%
5	40%	26%	38,074	60%	5,394	0%
6	37%	23%	31,544	57%	4,464	0%
6	42%	32%	33,285	45%	4,866	0%
6	41%	26%	34,001	59%	5,736	0%
6	36%	33%	35,648	61%	4,680	0%
6	33%	24%	31,911	55%	4,502	0%
5	35%	22%	33,559	51%	4,776	0%
4	44%	21%	34,904	51%	5,330	0%
4	63%	13%	38,202	0%	4,414	0%
6	3%	56%	77,482	65%	14880	99%
6	2%	79%	74,484	66%	15,310	100%
6	23%	40%	42,314	49%	11,209	100%
5	47%	68%	46,786	52%	24,856	98%
6	23%	56%	48,408	55%	11,144	71%
6	13%	49%	46,189	56%	11,493	100%
4	39%	61%	47,538	57%	26,730	97%
6	17%	31%	36,146	53%	11,019	67%
6	18%	46%	50,226	54%	12,923	100%
6	25%	30%	56,138	40%	13,278	100%
5	35%	33%	43,735	42%	10,416	100%
5	9%	50%	43,525	56%	11,832	99%
4	20%	51%	51,650	52%	39,882	95%
5	32%	29%	43,672	49%	26,860	93%
6	22%	34%	51,167	48%	12,032	100%
4	13%	42%	44,978	45%	11,745	100%
5	15%	21%	34,811	47%	10,024	80%
5	8%	40%	37,882	50%	30,062	98%

Rank	Name	Sector	Ease of transfer (5 pts for 4 year, 4 pts for 2 year)	Flexibility of programs (9 pts)
761	ANDREWS UNIVERSITY	Nonprofit	4	6
763	OLIVET COLLEGE	Nonprofit	4	6
764	FINLANDIA UNIVERSITY	Nonprofit	4	6

UNRANKED: Adrian College, Albion College, Alma College, Calvin College, Concordia College, Davenport University–Western Region Grand Rapids, Hope College, Kalamazoo College, Kettering University, Lawrence Technological University, Madonna University, Michigan Technological University, Reformed Bible College, Rochester College, Saginaw Valley State University

Two Year Colleges

Rank	Name	Sector	Ease of transfer	Flexibility of programs
170	WASHTENAW COMMUNITY COLLEGE	Public	4	6
173	SCHOOLCRAFT COLLEGE	Public	3	8
260	KELLOGG COMMUNITY COLLEGE	Public	4	6
278	OAKLAND COMMUNITY COLLEGE–BLOOMFIELD HILLS CAMPUS	Public	4	4
282	LANSING COMMUNITY COLLEGE	Public	3	8
320	HENRY FORD COMMUNITY COLLEGE	Public	4	5
367	DELTA COLLEGE	Public	3	8
373	BAKER COLLEGE OF FLINT	Nonprofit	4	6
394	NORTHWESTERN MICHIGAN COLLEGE	Public	4	5
409	MOTT COMMUNITY COLLEGE	Public	4	6
464	KIRTLAND COMMUNITY COLLEGE	Public	3	5
489	MUSKEGON COMMUNITY COLLEGE	Public	4	6
490	GRAND RAPIDS COMMUNITY COLLEGE	Public	4	5
534	MACOMB COMMUNITY COLLEGE	Public	3	5
549	GOGEBIC COMMUNITY COLLEGE	Public	3	5
550	ALPENA COMMUNITY COLLEGE	Public	4	4
593	MID MICHIGAN COMMUNITY COLLEGE	Public	3	6
687	LAKE MICHIGAN COLLEGE	Public	2	6
730	SOUTHWESTERN MICHIGAN COLLEGE	Public	4	4

UNRANKED: Bay de Noc Community College, Career Quest Learning Center, Career Quest Learning Centers Inc.–Jackson, Grace Bible College, Jackson Community College, Kalamazoo Valley Community College, Michigan Institute of Aeronautics, Monroe County Community College, Montcalm Community College, North Central Michigan College, St Clair County Community College District, West Shore Community College

Minnesota

Four Year Colleges

Rank	Name	Sector	Ease of transfer	Flexibility of programs
10	BETHEL COLLEGE	Nonprofit	5	8
19	UNIVERSITY OF MINNESOTA–TWIN CITIES	Public	4	9

Services for adult students (6 pts)	Percent of students over age 25	Graduation rate of part-time students	Mean earnings of independent students 10 years after college entry	Loan repayment of independent students 5 years after leaving college	In-district tuition and fees (at a 9 month rate for 2 year colleges)	Percent of credentials awarded as bachelor's degrees
5	11%	14%	38,372	44%	27684	99%
4	3%	33%	34,136	51%	25560	100%
4	15%	33%	31,496	38%	22753	65%
6	38%	24%	32,287	32%	2424	0%
6	33%	20%	34,170	42%	3,836	0%
5	42%	22%	33,160	32%	3,705	0%
5	36%	39%	34,174	34%	2,940	0%
6	34%	15%	33,362	31%	3,350	0%
6	32%	14%	36,191	25%	2,822	0%
5	31%	18%	31,914	38%	3,575	0%
4	54%	23%	31,781	33%	9,000	38%
5	30%	18%	31,884	42%	3,582	6%
4	32%	36%	30,875	28%	3,785	0%
5	36%	29%	28,512	44%	3,900	0%
5	25%	15%	29,656	37%	5,350	0%
5	29%	17%	31,744	30%	3,789	0%
3	30%	20%	35,548	55%	3,282	0%
4	19%	34%	29,079	55%	4,492	0%
5	21%	26%	29,593	38%	5,940	0%
5	19%	21%	30,374	31%	3,786	0%
5	25%	17%	26,597	26%	4,230	0%
2	19%	19%	28,242	25%	5,053	0%
6	16%	73%	67,015	74%	35,160	98%
6	10%	62%	63,030	67%	14,142	97%

Rank	Name	Sector	Ease of transfer (5 pts for 4 year, 4 pts for 2 year)	Flexibility of programs (9 pts)
42	UNIVERSITY OF MINNESOTA–DULUTH	Public	3	9
44	THE COLLEGE OF SAINT SCHOLASTICA	Nonprofit	5	8
117	WALDEN UNIVERSITY	For-Profit	5	7
139	UNIVERSITY OF MINNESOTA–CROOKSTON	Public	5	6
153	COLLEGE OF SAINT CATHERINE–SAINT PAUL CAMPUS	Nonprofit	4	8
332	AUGSBURG COLLEGE	Nonprofit	5	8
413	NORTHWESTERN COLLEGE	Nonprofit	5	5
550	UNIVERSITY OF MINNESOTA–MORRIS	Public	5	7
613	UNIVERSITY OF ST THOMAS	Nonprofit	5	4
626	HAMLINE UNIVERSITY	Nonprofit	4	8

UNRANKED: Bemidji State University, Bethany Lutheran College, Capella University, Carleton College, College of Saint Benedict, Concordia College at Moorhead, Concordia University, Crown College, Globe College, Gustavus Adolphus College, Macalester College, Medical Institute of Minnesota, Metropolitan State University, Minnesota State University–Moorhead, Minnesota State University–Mankato, North Central University, Saint John's University, Saint Mary's University of Minnesota, Saint Olaf College, Southwest State University, Winona State University

Two Year Colleges

270	NATIONAL AMERICAN UNIVERSITY	For-Profit	3	8
365	DUNWOODY INSTITUTE	Nonprofit	4	5
467	ACADEMY EDUCATION CENTER INC	For-Profit	4	3
614	RASMUSSEN COLLEGE–ST CLOUD	For-Profit	1	7
738	NATIONAL AMERICAN UNIVERSITY	For-Profit	0	3
753	DULUTH BUSINESS UNIVERSITY INC	For-Profit	3	2

UNRANKED: Alexandria Technical College, Anoka–Hennepin Technical College, Anoka–Ramsey Community College, Central Lakes College–Brainerd, Century Community and Technical College, Dakota County Technical College, Fergus Falls Community College, Hennepin Technical College, Hibbing Community College, Institute of Production and Recording, Inver Hills Community College, Itasca Community College, Lake Superior College, Le Cordon Bleu College of Culinary Arts–Minneapolis/St. Paul, Masabi Range Community and Technical College, Minneapolis Business College Inc, Minneapolis Community and Technical College, Minnesota State College Southeast Technical–Winona, Minnesota West Community and Technical College, National American University, Normandale Community College, North Hennepin Community College, Northland Community and Technical College, Northwest Technical College–Bemidji, Pine Technical College, Riverland Community College, Rochester Community and Technical College, Ridgewater College, Riverland Community and Technical College, Saint Cloud Technical College, South Central Technical College–Mankato, St Paul Technical College, Vermilion Community College

Mississippi

Four Year Colleges

335	JACKSON STATE UNIVERSITY	Public	5	6
452	MISSISSIPPI UNIVERSITY FOR WOMEN	Public	4	6

Services for adult students (6 pts)	Percent of students over age 25	Graduation rate of part-time students	Mean earnings of independent students 10 years after college entry	Loan repayment of independent students 5 years after leaving college	In-district tuition and fees (at a 9 month rate for 2 year colleges)	Percent of credentials awarded as bachelor's degrees
6	5%	48%	82,395	63%	13,139	98%
5	31%	72%	54,194	68%	35,326	100%
3	86%	30%	62,133	34%	12,075	100%
6	31%	40%	42,546	62%	11,700	96%
5	33%	67%	51,266	66%	31,622	70%
4	25%	44%	54,215	65%	36,415	99%
5	8%	69%	46,055	68%	29,460	97%
4	4%	50%	37,109	53%	12,846	100%
6	5%	41%	51,575	67%	39,594	100%
3	6%	33%	65,830	77%	39,181	86%
1	86%	25%	43,240	37%	14,148	67%
4	48%	10%	46,899	51%	20,430	11%
4	67%	20%	38,899	38%	17,409	9%
3	65%	31%	32,896	33%	9,360	14%
1	77%	27%	43,240	37%	14,148	23%
1	65%	34%	25,256	34%	18,975	12%
6	29%	43%	32,393	38%	7,261	100%
6	28%	26%	38,241	50%	6,065	95%

Rank	Name	Sector	Ease of transfer (5 pts for 4 year, 4 pts for 2 year)	Flexibility of programs (9 pts)
479	UNIVERSITY OF SOUTHERN MISSISSIPPI	Public	5	5
575	MISSISSIPPI STATE UNIVERSITY	Public	4	6
605	UNIVERSITY OF MISSISSIPPI MAIN CAMPUS	Public	3	5
673	ALCORN STATE UNIVERSITY	Public	4	6
688	MISSISSIPPI VALLEY STATE UNIVERSITY	Public	4	5
743	DELTA STATE UNIVERSITY	Public	4	4
783	BLUE MOUNTAIN COLLEGE	Nonprofit	5	4

UNRANKED: Belhaven College, Millsaps College, Mississippi College, Rust College, Tougaloo College, William Carey College

Two Year Colleges

Rank	Name	Sector	Ease of transfer	Flexibility of programs
576	COPIAH–LINCOLN COMMUNITY COLLEGE	Public	4	5
587	HOLMES COMMUNITY COLLEGE	Public	4	4
596	EAST CENTRAL COMMUNITY COLLEGE	Public	3	4
598	JONES COUNTY JUNIOR COLLEGE	Public	3	4
674	MISSISSIPPI DELTA COMMUNITY COLLEGE	Public	4	3
699	ITAWAMBA COMMUNITY COLLEGE	Public	2	6
766	SOUTHWEST MISSISSIPPI COMMUNITY COLLEGE	Public	2	3
769	COAHOMA COMMUNITY COLLEGE	Public	2	3
770	VIRGINIA COLLEGE–GULF COAST	For-Profit	0	2
785	VIRGINIA COLLEGE–JACKSON	For-Profit	0	2

UNRANKED: Antonelli College, Blue Cliff College, East Mississippi Community College, Hinds Community College, Meridian Community College, Mississippi Gulf Coast Community College, Northeast Mississippi Community College, Northwest Mississippi Community College, Pearl River Community College

Missouri

Four Year Colleges

Rank	Name	Sector	Ease of transfer	Flexibility of programs
27	UNIVERSITY OF MISSOURI–KANSAS CITY	Public	5	9
43	PARK UNIVERSITY	Nonprofit	4	9
113	UNIVERSITY OF MISSOURI–ST LOUIS	Public	5	7
138	UNIVERSITY OF MISSOURI–COLUMBIA	Public	4	8
152	CENTRAL MISSOURI STATE UNIVERSITY	Public	5	8
158	LINDENWOOD UNIVERSITY	Nonprofit	5	8
186	FONTBONNE COLLEGE	Nonprofit	5	9
191	MARYVILLE UNIVERSITY OF SAINT LOUIS	Nonprofit	5	9
205	UNIVERSITY OF MISSOURI–ROLLA	Public	5	7
260	MISSOURI SOUTHERN STATE COLLEGE	Public	5	7

Services for adult students (6 pts)	Percent of students over age 25	Graduation rate of part-time students	Mean earnings of independent students 10 years after college entry	Loan repayment of independent students 5 years after leaving college	In-district tuition and fees (at a 9 month rate for 2 year colleges)	Percent of credentials awarded as bachelor's degrees
5	22%	35%	41,876	51%	7,659	99%
5	9%	31%	43,126	60%	7,780	100%
5	9%	33%	63,000	57%	7,744	100%
5	18%	33%	35,828	33%	6,546	94%
6	17%	30%	24,239	40%	6,116	100%
4	15%	29%	36,284	44%	6,418	100%
1	17%	36%	32,216	54%	11,212	100%
5	16%	18%	28,712	30%	2,730	0%
4	27%	15%	31,278	36%	2,740	0%
5	16%	31%	31,139	37%	2,290	0%
6	16%	18%	30,170	40%	3,000	0%
5	17%	35%	28,649	0%	2,650	0%
4	18%	14%	30,405	32%	2,620	0%
3	22%	12%	30,605	0%	2,800	0%
3	25%	23%	23,034	0%	2,603	0%
1	71%	42%	29,468	18%	14,032	0%
1	60%	20%	29,468	18%	14,032	0%
6	19%	42%	53830	55%	9,563	100%
5	76%	9%	51,106	60%	12,130	80%
6	24%	43%	45,106	55%	10,065	99%
5	4%	50%	66,965	61%	9,518	100%
6	15%	41%	38,076	53%	7,322	96%
6	27%	21%	49,656	56%	16,332	100%
4	29%	59%	50,260	51%	24,610	100%
5	26%	37%	53,247	56%	27,958	98%
4	7%	39%	61,428	73%	9,637	99%
6	28%	29%	34,371	47%	5,877	76%

Rank	Name	Sector	Ease of transfer (5 pts for 4 year, 4 pts for 2 year)	Flexibility of programs (9 pts)
365	AVILA COLLEGE	Nonprofit	5	7
411	WASHINGTON UNIVERSITY	Nonprofit	2	8
477	SOUTHWEST MISSOURI STATE UNIVERSITY	Public	3	7
488	WILLIAM WOODS UNIVERSITY	Nonprofit	4	8
509	MISSOURI WESTERN STATE COLLEGE	Public	4	8
523	HANNIBAL–LAGRANGE COLLEGE	Nonprofit	5	8
614	SOUTHEAST MISSOURI STATE UNIVERSITY	Public	4	6
644	TRUMAN STATE UNIVERSITY	Public	4	6
703	SOUTHWEST BAPTIST UNIVERSITY	Nonprofit	5	5
739	ROCKHURST UNIVERSITY	Nonprofit	4	5
742	MISSOURI VALLEY COLLEGE	Nonprofit	5	7
746	DRURY UNIVERSITY	Nonprofit	4	6
753	LINCOLN UNIVERSITY	Public	4	6
772	NORTHWEST MISSOURI STATE UNIVERSITY	Public	5	5
787	CENTRAL METHODIST COLLEGE	Nonprofit	5	5

UNRANKED: Central Methodist University–College of Graduate & Extended Studies, College of the Ozarks, Columbia College, Culver–Stockton College, Evangel University, Harris–Stowe College, Missouri Baptist College, Saint Louis University–Main Campus, Stephens College, Webster University, Westminster College, William Jewell College

Two Year Colleges

Rank	Name	Sector	Ease of transfer	Flexibility of programs
215	NATIONAL AMERICAN UNIVERSITY	For-Profit	3	8
363	SAINT LOUIS COMMUNITY COLLEGE–FOREST PARK	Public	3	7
405	OZARKS TECHNICAL COMMUNITY COLLEGE	Public	3	7
428	STATE FAIR COMMUNITY COLLEGE	Public	4	5
454	ST CHARLES COUNTY COMMUNITY COLLEGE	Public	3	4
457	EAST CENTRAL COLLEGE	Public	4	5
476	MINERAL AREA COLLEGE	Public	4	6
530	CROWDER COLLEGE	Public	3	6
578	SOUTHWEST MISSOURI STATE UNIVERSITY–WEST PLAINS	Public	3	7
655	MOBERLY AREA COMMUNITY COLLEGE	Public	4	5
673	NORTH CENTRAL MISSOURI COLLEGE	Public	3	4
710	THREE RIVERS COMMUNITY COLLEGE	Public	3	5

UNRANKED: American College of Technology, Bryan Career College, Cottey College, Electronics Institute, Heritage College, Hickey College, Jefferson College, Lecole Culinaire, Linn State Technical College, Massage Therapy Training Institute, Metropolitan Community College, Midwest Institute for Medical Assistants, Pinnacle Career Institute–North Kansas City, Ranken Technical College, Southeast Missouri Hospital College of Nursing, St. Louis College of Health Careers, Texas County Technical Institute, Vatterot College–O'Fallon Campus, Vatterott College, Wentworth Military Academy

Services for adult students (6 pts)	Percent of students over age 25	Graduation rate of part-time students	Mean earnings of independent students 10 years after college entry	Loan repayment of independent students 5 years after leaving college	In-district tuition and fees (at a 9 month rate for 2 year colleges)	Percent of credentials awarded as bachelor's degrees
4	28%	55%	46,224	58%	27,312	100%
6	8%	60%	86,368	65%	49,770	99%
6	12%	45%	38,078	57%	7,060	98%
4	15%	60%	41,958	60%	23,040	98%
6	19%	15%	34,168	46%	6,256	95%
3	24%	38%	40,581	62%	21,880	83%
6	15%	18%	35,785	49%	6,990	99%
4	2%	29%	49,489	62%	7,456	100%
3	21%	50%	36,224	52%	22,440	67%
3	4%	44%	53,927	70%	35,670	96%
4	7%	16%	31,143	38%	19,750	99%
5	35%	3%	32,726	41%	25,905	80%
3	16%	26%	34,774	41%	7,042	78%
3	5%	4%	38,864	45%	7,343	93%
3	5%	0%	35,677	60%	23,010	98%
3	80%	10%	43,240	37%	13680	30%
5	39%	11%	31,211	46%	3,180	0%
5	34%	22%	29,832	37%	2,952	0%
5	27%	15%	31,916	39%	2,640	0%
6	26%	12%	34,343	52%	3,180	0%
5	27%	18%	28,953	40%	2,376	0%
5	20%	24%	27,372	36%	3,080	0%
4	26%	34%	28,688	41%	2,448	0%
4	27%	14%	27,202	45%	3,880	0%
3	21%	14%	28,983	35%	3,120	0%
2	18%	35%	30,699	49%	3,180	0%
2	34%	16%	28,079	34%	3,540	0%

Rank	Name		Sector	Ease of transfer (5 pts for 4 year, 4 pts for 2 year)	Flexibility of programs (9 pts)

Montana
FOUR YEAR COLLEGES

Rank	Name	Sector	Ease of transfer	Flexibility of programs
37	MONTANA STATE UNIVERSITY–BILLINGS	Public	5	9
252	UNIVERSITY OF MONTANA–MISSOULA	Public	5	6
259	MONTANA STATE UNIVERSITY–NORTHERN	Public	5	7
457	WESTERN MONTANA COLLEGE–UNIVERSITY OF MONTANA	Public	5	7
565	MONTANA TECH OF THE UNIVERSITY OF MONTANA	Public	5	4
652	ROCKY MOUNTAIN COLLEGE	Nonprofit	5	7

UNRANKED: Carroll College, Montana State University–Bozeman, University of Great Falls

TWO YEAR COLLEGES

Rank	Name	Sector	Ease of transfer	Flexibility of programs
237	HELENA COLLEGE OF TECHNOLOGY OF UNIVERSITY OF MONTANA	Public	3	7
540	DAWSON COMMUNITY COLLEGE	Public	4	6

UNRANKED: Flathead Valley Community College, Miles Community College, Montana State University–College of Technology–Great Falls, Montana Tech–College of Technology

Nebraska
FOUR YEAR COLLEGES

Rank	Name	Sector	Ease of transfer	Flexibility of programs
2	BELLEVUE UNIVERSITY	Nonprofit	5	8
107	CREIGHTON UNIVERSITY	Nonprofit	5	8
192	UNIVERSITY OF NEBRASKA AT LINCOLN	Public	4	7
206	PERU STATE COLLEGE	Public	5	6
247	NEBRASKA WESLEYAN UNIVERSITY	Nonprofit	5	8
270	CHADRON STATE COLLEGE	Public	4	8
281	UNIVERSITY OF NEBRASKA AT OMAHA	Public	4	6
387	COLLEGE OF SAINT MARY	Nonprofit	5	7
680	UNIVERSITY OF NEBRASKA AT KEARNEY	Public	4	4
724	WAYNE STATE COLLEGE	Public	4	5

UNRANKED: Concordia University, Doane College, Doane College–Lincoln Grand Island and Master, Hastings College, Midland Lutheran College, Union College, York College

TWO YEAR COLLEGES

Rank	Name	Sector	Ease of transfer	Flexibility of programs
35	NEBRASKA COLLEGE OF BUSINESS	For-Profit	4	7

Services for adult students (6 pts)	Percent of students over age 25	Graduation rate of part-time students	Mean earnings of independent students 10 years after college entry	Loan repayment of independent students 5 years after leaving college	In-district tuition and fees (at a 9 month rate for 2 year colleges)	Percent of credentials awarded as bachelor's degrees	
6	41%	29%	36,492	55%	5,826	65%	MONTANA
6	24%	33%	40,125	52%	6,468	78%	
5	28%	27%	36,494	60%	5,371	57%	
5	22%	23%	27,679	56%	4,893	55%	
5	26%	29%	42,124	49%	6,881	90%	
3	8%	33%	55,576	56%	26,666	100%	
5	35%	29%	32,387	48%	3,109	0%	
3	27%	0%	32,098	55%	3,630	0%	
2	80%	64%	61,268	64%	7,365	100%	NEBRASKA
6	6%	24%	81,117	74%	37,606	99%	
6	6%	50%	48,679	68%	8,537	100%	
6	25%	40%	38,205	58%	6,790	100%	
4	18%	62%	52,110	65%	31,394	99%	
6	23%	26%	35,853	58%	6,252	100%	
6	22%	35%	46,463	60%	7,204	100%	
6	33%	26%	39,451	55%	29,954	83%	
5	9%	30%	40,058	59%	6,953	100%	
4	8%	26%	35,318	57%	6,427	100%	
4	79%	50%	41,044	26%	15,352	43%	

Rank	Name	Sector	Ease of transfer (5 pts for 4 year, 4 pts for 2 year)	Flexibility of programs (9 pts)
146	WESTERN NEBRASKA COMMUNITY COLLEGE	Public	4	8
176	NORTHEAST COMMUNITY COLLEGE	Public	4	6
211	CENTRAL COMMUNITY COLLEGE	Public	4	7
371	METROPOLITAN COMMUNITY COLLEGE AREA	Public	3	7
455	LINCOLN SCHOOL OF COMMERCE	For-Profit	3	4
496	SOUTHEAST COMMUNITY COLLEGE AREA	Public	3	6
526	MID PLAINS COMMUNITY COLLEGE AREA	Public	3	5

UNRANKED: Nebraska College of Technical Agriculture, Omaha School of Massage Therapy

Nevada

FOUR YEAR COLLEGES

Rank	Name	Sector	Ease	Flex
178	UNIVERSITY OF NEVADA–RENO	Public	3	6
312	UNIVERSITY OF NEVADA–LAS VEGAS	Public	4	5

UNRANKED: Sierra Nevada College

TWO YEAR COLLEGES

Rank	Name	Sector	Ease	Flex
117	WESTERN NEVADA COMMUNITY COLLEGE	Public	4	6
154	COMMUNITY COLLEGE OF SOUTHERN NEVADA	Public	4	6
269	TRUCKEE MEADOWS COMMUNITY COLLEGE	Public	3	5

UNRANKED: Career College of Northern Nevada, Carrington College–Las Vegas, Carrington College–Reno, Great Basin College, Heritage College, Las Vegas College, Le Cordon Bleu College of Culinary Arts–Las Vegas, Northwest Health Careers, Pima Medical Institute

New Hampshire

FOUR YEAR COLLEGES

Rank	Name	Sector	Ease	Flex
6	COLLEGE FOR LIFELONG LEARNING	Public	4	9
9	NEW HAMPSHIRE COLLEGE	Nonprofit	5	9
32	KEENE STATE COLLEGE	Public	5	8
144	UNIVERSITY OF NEW HAMPSHIRE–MAIN CAMPUS	Public	4	8
328	UNIVERSITY OF NEW HAMPSHIRE–MANCHESTER	Public	5	7

UNRANKED: Colby–Sawyer College, Daniel Webster College, Dartmouth College, Franklin Pierce College, New England College, Plymouth State College, Rivier College, Saint Anselm College

Services for adult students (6 pts)	Percent of students over age 25	Graduation rate of part-time students	Mean earnings of independent students 10 years after college entry	Loan repayment of independent students 5 years after leaving college	In-district tuition and fees (at a 9 month rate for 2 year colleges)	Percent of credentials awarded as bachelor's degrees
6	27%	15%	28,849	48%	2,700	0%
5	32%	30%	33,476	45%	3,285	0%
5	28%	25%	28,748	51%	2,880	0%
5	41%	11%	31,275	43%	2,880	0%
3	78%	36%	41,044	26%	15,352	34%
4	28%	22%	34,403	42%	3,024	0%
5	28%	18%	30,068	47%	2,970	0%
6	13%	67%	58,139	65%	7,291	98%
6	24%	40%	50,435	55%	7,063	100%
6	43%	17%	32,550	46%	2,910	1%
6	41%	7%	36,529	38%	2,910	1%
6	38%	13%	37,470	46%	2,910	0%
5	77%	55%	35,850	60%	7,425	75%
5	74%	55%	46,701	59%	31,136	83%
6	5%	80%	42,185	63%	13,613	100%
6	3%	59%	49,759	70%	17,624	96%
3	28%	38%	49,759	70%	14,495	92%

NEVADA

NEW HAMPSHIRE

Rank	Name	Sector	Ease of transfer (5 pts for 4 year, 4 pts for 2 year)	Flexibility of programs (9 pts)

Two Year Colleges

Rank	Name	Sector	Ease of transfer	Flexibility
187	NEW HAMPSHIRE TECHNICAL INSTITUTE	Public	3	5
306	NEW HAMPSHIRE COMMUNITY TECHNICAL COLLEGE–NASHUA	Public	4	6

UNRANKED: New Hampshire Comm Tech College–Manchester/Stratham, New Hampshire Community Tech College–Laconia/Berlin, New Hampshire Community Technical College–Laconia, New Hampshire Technical College–Stratham, Saint Joseph School of Practical Nursing

New Jersey
Four Year Colleges

Rank	Name	Sector	Ease of transfer	Flexibility
88	KEAN UNIVERSITY	Public	4	8
119	RAMAPO COLLEGE OF NEW JERSEY	Public	5	8
246	FAIRLEIGH DICKINSON UNIVERSITY–ALL CAMPUSES	Nonprofit	5	9
298	MONTCLAIR STATE UNIVERSITY	Public	4	5
308	NEW JERSEY INSTITUTE OF TECHNOLOGY	Public	3	5
330	RUTGERS UNIVERSITY–NEW BRUNSWICK	Public	3	6
333	THOMAS EDISON STATE COLLEGE	Public	2	6
347	THE RICHARD STOCKTON COLLEGE OF NEW JERSEY	Public	4	6
349	FAIRLEIGH DICKINSON UNIVERSITY–COLLEGE AT FLORHAM	Nonprofit	5	9
367	WILLIAM PATERSON UNIVERSITY OF NEW JERSEY	Public	4	7
398	RUTGERS UNIVERSITY–CAMDEN	Public	3	6
416	SAINT PETERS COLLEGE	Nonprofit	5	8
475	FELICIAN COLLEGE	Nonprofit	3	9
501	RUTGERS UNIVERSITY–NEWARK	Public	3	6
506	ROWAN UNIVERSITY	Public	2	7
582	CALDWELL COLLEGE	Nonprofit	4	9
615	MONMOUTH UNIVERSITY	Nonprofit	5	8
691	GEORGIAN COURT COLLEGE	Nonprofit	4	7
693	RIDER UNIVERSITY	Nonprofit	3	6
714	SETON HALL UNIVERSITY	Nonprofit	5	4
725	THE COLLEGE OF NEW JERSEY	Public	3	6

UNRANKED: Bloomfield College, Centenary College, College of Saint Elizabeth, Drew University, New Jersey City University, Princeton University, Stevens Institute of Technology

Two Year Colleges

Rank	Name	Sector	Ease of transfer	Flexibility
4	RARITAN VALLEY COMMUNITY COLLEGE	Public	4	8
10	COUNTY COLLEGE OF MORRIS	Public	4	8

Services for adult students (6 pts)	Percent of students over age 25	Graduation rate of part-time students	Mean earnings of independent students 10 years after college entry	Loan repayment of independent students 5 years after leaving college	In-district tuition and fees (at a 9 month rate for 2 year colleges)	Percent of credentials awarded as bachelor's degrees
5	29%	30%	43,325	60%	7,104	0%
3	32%	35%	36,760	50%	6,912	0%
6	27%	57%	48,556	52%	11,870	100%
5	13%	53%	50,270	61%	13,870	100%
5	23%	36%	57,320	57%	37,986	94%
6	12%	57%	51,778	60%	12,116	96%
6	17%	55%	68,241	60%	16,430	100%
6	8%	47%	72,196	54%	14,372	99%
3	88%	44%	56,364	55%	6,350	81%
6	13%	47%	47,673	56%	13,077	100%
5	4%	46%	57,320	57%	40,232	100%
5	20%	43%	47,066	57%	12,574	100%
4	32%	48%	72,196	54%	14,238	100%
5	17%	47%	50,283	48%	35,192	98%
5	29%	44%	50,481	57%	32,990	100%
4	21%	46%	72,196	54%	13,829	100%
6	12%	49%	56,306	55%	13,108	100%
5	15%	21%	51,923	53%	32,650	100%
4	4%	42%	53,111	48%	35,364	100%
3	15%	50%	45,559	60%	31,618	99%
5	10%	55%	53,705	58%	39,820	99%
3	8%	33%	74,835	60%	39,258	100%
4	4%	17%	50,412	71%	15,794	100%
6	28%	23%	45,658	59%	4,224	0%
5	23%	26%	45,005	67%	4,690	0%

Rank	Name	Sector	Ease of transfer (5 pts for 4 year, 4 pts for 2 year)	Flexibility of programs (9 pts)
108	UNION COUNTY COLLEGE	Public	4	7
121	HUDSON COUNTY COMMUNITY COLLEGE	Public	4	7
123	OCEAN COUNTY COLLEGE	Public	4	6
127	BURLINGTON COUNTY COLLEGE	Public	3	7
165	PASSAIC COUNTY COMMUNITY COLLEGE	Public	3	8
232	CAMDEN COUNTY COLLEGE	Public	4	7
233	ATLANTIC CAPE COMMUNITY COLLEGE	Public	4	7
292	MIDDLESEX COUNTY COLLEGE	Public	3	6
293	WARREN COUNTY COMMUNITY COLLEGE	Public	3	7
322	CUMBERLAND COUNTY COLLEGE	Public	3	7
380	SALEM COMMUNITY COLLEGE	Public	4	5
393	MERCER COUNTY COMMUNITY COLLEGE	Public	3	6
404	SUSSEX COUNTY COMMUNITY COLLEGE	Public	4	5
460	BERGEN COMMUNITY COLLEGE	Public	2	4
544	BROOKDALE COMMUNITY COLLEGE	Public	2	5
623	GLOUCESTER COUNTY COLLEGE	Public	3	5
641	ESSEX COUNTY COLLEGE	Public	2	7
765	HO-HO-KUS SCHOOL	For-Profit	0	2

UNRANKED: American Business Academy, Center for Allied Health & Nursing Education

New Mexico

FOUR YEAR COLLEGES

Rank	Name	Sector	Ease of transfer	Flexibility
33	UNIVERSITY OF NEW MEXICO–MAIN CAMPUS	Public	5	8
201	EASTERN NEW MEXICO UNIVERSITY–MAIN CAMPUS	Public	5	7
222	NEW MEXICO INSTITUTE OF MINING AND TECHNOLOGY	Public	4	7
616	NEW MEXICO STATE UNIVERSITY–MAIN CAMPUS	Public	3	6
617	NEW MEXICO HIGHLANDS UNIVERSITY	Public	3	3

UNRANKED: College of the Southwest, St John's College, University of Phoenix–Albuquerque Campus, Western New Mexico University

TWO YEAR COLLEGES

Rank	Name	Sector	Ease of transfer	Flexibility
49	SANTA FE COMMUNITY COLLEGE	Public	3	7
128	SAN JUAN COLLEGE	Public	2	7
177	EASTERN NEW MEXICO UNIVERSITY–ROSWELL CAMPUS	Public	3	6
342	NEW MEXICO STATE UNIVERSITY–ALAMOGORDO	Public	3	6
353	CLOVIS COMMUNITY COLLEGE	Public	3	5

Services for adult students (6 pts)	Percent of students over age 25	Graduation rate of part-time students	Mean earnings of independent students 10 years after college entry	Loan repayment of independent students 5 years after leaving college	In-district tuition and fees (at a 9 month rate for 2 year colleges)	Percent of credentials awarded as bachelor's degrees
4	41%	20%	38,247	54%	4,620	0%
5	34%	28%	32,288	56%	5,353	0%
6	26%	21%	38,375	48%	4,345	0%
5	33%	19%	42,021	55%	4,065	0%
6	37%	12%	30,405	59%	4,553	0%
4	38%	15%	36,565	43%	4,320	0%
5	33%	16%	32,460	45%	4,407	0%
5	25%	20%	39,015	53%	3,420	0%
5	11%	44%	35,250	48%	4,590	0%
5	35%	28%	36,455	29%	4,440	0%
5	37%	23%	30,767	36%	4,104	0%
5	31%	14%	38,416	39%	3,768	0%
5	24%	23%	33,569	46%	6,750	0%
5	27%	25%	39,848	59%	4,362	0%
5	24%	20%	36,630	51%	3,861	0%
3	20%	19%	37,101	45%	4,445	0%
5	41%	13%	35,727	0%	4,546	0%
1	68%	31%	37,958	45%	17,272	0%
6	24%	58%	42,787	55%	8,050	100%
6	27%	50%	31,377	44%	5,510	82%
4	16%	33%	64,566	76%	6,891	99%
6	22%	34%	36,458	45%	6,094	99%
5	43%	55%	36,526	54%	5,550	100%
6	56%	17%	34,844	50%	1,695	0%
6	53%	19%	37,811	45%	1,474	0%
6	33%	40%	31,377	44%	1,944	0%
4	44%	14%	36,458	45%	1,968	0%
5	49%	13%	30,802	49%	1,176	0%

NEW MEXICO

Rank	Name	Sector	Ease of transfer (5 pts for 4 year, 4 pts for 2 year)	Flexibility of programs (9 pts)
372	NEW MEXICO STATE UNIVERSITY–GRANTS	Public	4	6
426	ALBUQUERQUE TECHNICAL VOCATIONAL INSTITUTE	Public	3	6
507	NEW MEXICO STATE UNIVERSITY–DONA ANA	Public	3	4
513	NEW MEXICO STATE UNIVERSITY–CARLSBAD	Public	3	7
565	LUNA VOCATIONAL TECHNICAL INSTITUTE	Public	2	3

UNRANKED: Apollo College–New Mexico, Brown Mackie College–Albuquerque, Eastern New Mexico University–Ruidoso, International Institute of the Americas, Mesa Technical College, New Mexico Junior College, New Mexico Military Institute, Northern New Mexico Community College, Pima Medical Institute, University of New Mexico–Gallup Campus, University of New Mexico–Los Alamos Campus, University of New Mexico–Taos Education Center, University of New Mexico–Valencia County Branch

New York

FOUR YEAR COLLEGES

Rank	Name	Sector	Ease of transfer	Flexibility of programs
13	CORNELL UNIVERSITY–ENDOWED COLLEGES	Nonprofit	3	7
36	SUNY AT STONY BROOK	Public	5	6
47	SUNY EMPIRE STATE COLLEGE	Public	4	9
48	SUNY AT BUFFALO	Public	5	6
54	SUNY AT BINGHAMTON	Public	4	8
63	ADELPHI UNIVERSITY	Nonprofit	5	8
64	CUNY BERNARD M BARUCH COLLEGE	Public	3	9
69	SUNY COLLEGE OF ENVIRONMENTAL SCIENCE AND FORESTRY	Public	5	5
149	CUNY JOHN JAY COLLEGE CRIMINAL JUSTICE	Public	5	8
159	CUNY LEHMAN COLLEGE	Public	3	8
170	MOLLOY COLLEGE	Nonprofit	5	7
199	CUNY COLLEGE OF STATEN ISLAND	Public	5	7
238	SAINT JOHN FISHER COLLEGE	Nonprofit	5	8
254	SAINT JOSEPHS COLLEGE–MAIN CAMPUS	Nonprofit	5	7
267	ROCHESTER INSTITUTE OF TECHNOLOGY	Nonprofit	5	7
283	CUNY HUNTER COLLEGE	Public	4	6
290	CUNY NEW YORK CITY TECHNICAL COLLEGE	Public	4	7
307	SUNY COLLEGE AT NEW PALTZ	Public	4	6
319	MERCY COLLEGE–MAIN CAMPUS	Nonprofit	5	8
321	CUNY MEDGAR EVERS COLLEGE	Public	4	8
325	SUNY COLLEGE AT BROCKPORT	Public	5	6
336	KEUKA COLLEGE	Nonprofit	4	7
352	SUNY COLLEGE AT PLATTSBURGH	Public	4	7
382	D'YOUVILLE COLLEGE	Nonprofit	4	7
395	CUNY QUEENS COLLEGE	Public	2	8
406	UTICA COLLEGE OF SYRACUSE UNIVERSITY	Nonprofit	4	7

Services for adult students (6 pts)	Percent of students over age 25	Graduation rate of part-time students	Mean earnings of independent students 10 years after college entry	Loan repayment of independent students 5 years after leaving college	In-district tuition and fees (at a 9 month rate for 2 year colleges)	Percent of credentials awarded as bachelor's degrees
3	38%	11%	36,458	45%	1,896	0%
4	43%	20%	34,342	34%	1,472	0%
4	32%	22%	36,458	45%	1,632	0%
3	27%	11%	36,458	45%	1,108	0%
3	50%	42%	30,699	51%	962	0%
5	1%	100%	140548	77%	50,953	100%
6	8%	59%	64974	63%	8,999	100%
3	82%	46%	45612	52%	6,985	79%
6	8%	51%	70230	58%	9,574	99%
6	3%	72%	52815	62%	9,271	100%
6	14%	60%	63404	64%	35,740	98%
5	23%	54%	58871	68%	6,810	100%
5	7%	100%	45955	65%	8,103	88%
5	19%	43%	51879	47%	6,810	100%
6	42%	41%	47870	51%	6,812	100%
5	23%	45%	65752	63%	29,100	95%
6	17%	31%	47638	51%	6,890	72%
6	9%	53%	46875	58%	31,880	100%
5	23%	41%	58656	54%	25,114	94%
6	6%	58%	54836	61%	38,568	94%
6	20%	33%	50099	58%	6,782	100%
6	26%	25%	45712	53%	6,669	51%
5	8%	61%	45899	65%	7,754	100%
5	30%	30%	45178	44%	18,392	96%
5	40%	28%	40837	44%	6,756	52%
5	15%	49%	42853	52%	7,928	100%
4	34%	64%	49390	66%	29,421	100%
6	10%	37%	42755	56%	7,866	100%
5	26%	34%	60568	58%	25,210	100%
6	24%	34%	50907	57%	6,938	100%
5	28%	48%	45,384	52%	19,996	95%

Rank	Name	Sector	Ease of transfer (5 pts for 4 year, 4 pts for 2 year)	Flexibility of programs (9 pts)
409	SYRACUSE UNIVERSITY	Nonprofit	4	9
423	SUNY INSTITUTE OF TECHNOLOGY AT UTICA–ROME	Public	4	7
424	HOFSTRA UNIVERSITY	Nonprofit	5	7
426	CUNY BROOKLYN COLLEGE	Public	2	8
432	SUNY COLLEGE AT OSWEGO	Public	5	6
443	NIAGARA UNIVERSITY	Nonprofit	5	7
467	SUNY AT ALBANY	Public	4	7
480	AUDREY COHEN COLLEGE	Nonprofit	3	8
490	SUNY COLLEGE OF TECHNOLOGY AT FARMINGDALE	Public	2	6
495	SUNY COLLEGE AT PURCHASE	Public	3	5
497	SUNY COLLEGE AT GENESEO	Public	4	6
500	NAZARETH COLLEGE OF ROCHESTER	Nonprofit	5	6
507	ST FRANCIS COLLEGE	Nonprofit	4	9
516	CUNY CITY COLLEGE	Public	3	7
518	MARIST COLLEGE	Nonprofit	5	8
519	MOUNT SAINT MARY COLLEGE	Nonprofit	4	9
526	SUNY COLLEGE AT CORTLAND	Public	4	5
528	COLUMBIA UNIVERSITY IN THE CITY OF NEW YORK	Nonprofit	2	7
535	THE SAGE COLLEGES–TROY CAMPUS	Nonprofit	5	6
549	ELMIRA COLLEGE	Nonprofit	5	8
555	SUNY COLLEGE AT BUFFALO	Public	5	4
561	SUNY COLLEGE AT OLD WESTBURY	Public	3	6
564	SUNY COLLEGE AT FREDONIA	Public	4	7
585	THE COLLEGE OF NEW ROCHELLE	Nonprofit	4	8
603	NEW YORK INSTITUTE OF TECHNOLOGY–OLD WESTBURY	Nonprofit	4	7
612	NEW YORK UNIVERSITY	Nonprofit	2	8
623	FASHION INSTITUTE OF TECHNOLOGY	Public	3	5
625	SUNY COLLEGE AT POTSDAM	Public	5	4
638	SIENA COLLEGE	Nonprofit	4	6
639	ROBERTS WESLEYAN COLLEGE	Nonprofit	4	6
657	CUNY YORK COLLEGE	Public	3	4
676	SAINT THOMAS AQUINAS COLLEGE	Nonprofit	5	7
687	IONA COLLEGE	Nonprofit	4	9
702	THE COLLEGE OF SAINT ROSE	Nonprofit	4	8
719	CONCORDIA COLLEGE	Nonprofit	2	9
740	FORDHAM UNIVERSITY	Nonprofit	3	7
750	NEW SCHOOL UNIVERSITY	Nonprofit	2	6
756	ST JOHN'S UNIVERSITY–NEW YORK	Nonprofit	2	8
759	SUNY COLLEGE AT ONEONTA	Public	4	3
781	ALFRED UNIVERSITY	Nonprofit	3	6

Services for adult students (6 pts)	Percent of students over age 25	Graduation rate of part-time students	Mean earnings of independent students 10 years after college entry	Loan repayment of independent students 5 years after leaving college	In-district tuition and fees (at a 9 month rate for 2 year colleges)	Percent of credentials awarded as bachelor's degrees
6	3%	40%	63,560	58%	45,022	100%
4	23%	38%	52,018	55%	7,777	100%
6	4%	33%	65,846	57%	42,160	100%
6	24%	36%	49,456	52%	6,838	100%
6	6%	19%	41,199	59%	7,961	100%
5	12%	62%	39,585	56%	30,950	99%
4	6%	52%	48,322	61%	9,223	100%
5	78%	25%	41,684	27%	18,730	82%
5	24%	50%	55,065	66%	7,860	85%
6	11%	62%	44,015	57%	8,298	99%
4	2%	71%	41,751	63%	8,176	100%
5	8%	64%	43,025	60%	32,424	100%
5	12%	40%	46,377	48%	25,300	97%
5	22%	34%	50,262	53%	6,689	100%
5	6%	41%	47,303	55%	35,110	100%
3	20%	51%	54,816	57%	29,048	100%
6	3%	44%	39,863	61%	8,106	100%
3	17%	68%	105,845	70%	49,973	100%
4	18%	50%	45,653	65%	28,805	100%
5	12%	39%	40,630	64%	41,900	98%
5	16%	39%	41,848	53%	7,701	99%
4	24%	56%	48,279	55%	7,683	100%
5	4%	40%	38,444	54%	8,089	100%
4	73%	31%	39,126	32%	34,960	99%
5	14%	20%	68,696	55%	35,160	95%
5	5%	57%	79,815	63%	49,062	99%
4	24%	39%	48,108	68%	7,215	41%
6	5%	33%	37,720	44%	7,964	100%
4	3%	65%	54,981	63%	34,611	95%
5	27%	24%	51,572	56%	29,540	100%
6	26%	31%	42,675	49%	6,748	100%
5	4%	0%	45,247	64%	29,600	98%
5	1%	0%	58,765	54%	36,584	100%
4	6%	38%	40,561	53%	30,692	98%
4	34%	0%	57,307	58%	30,600	100%
5	6%	37%	57,752	52%	48,688	100%
5	16%	44%	54,816	63%	45,535	79%
5	3%	30%	56,770	52%	38,992	99%
2	3%	67%	37,805	62%	7,932	100%
3	3%	40%	43,164	60%	27,078	100%

Rank	Name		Sector	Ease of transfer (5 pts for 4 year, 4 pts for 2 year)	Flexibility of programs (9 pts)

UNRANKED: Bard College, Barnard College, Canisius College, Cazenovia College, Clarkson University, Colgate University, College of Mount Saint Vincent, Cooper Union for the Advancement of Science and Art, Daemen College, Dominican College of Blauvelt, Excelsior College, Five Towns College, Hamilton College, Hartwick College, Hilbert College, Hobart William Smith Colleges, Houghton College, Ithaca College, King's College, Le Moyne College, Long Island University–Brooklyn Campus, Long Island University CW Campus, Manhattan College, Manhattanville College, Marymount Manhattan College, Medaille College, Monroe College Main Campus, Nyack College, Pace University–New York, Paul Smiths College of Arts and Science, Saint Bonaventure University, Sarah Lawrence College, Skidmore College, St. Lawrence University, SUNY Maritime College, Touro College, Union College, University of Rochester, Vassar College, Wagner College, Wells College, Yeshiva University

Two Year Colleges

Rank	Name	Sector	Ease of transfer	Flexibility of programs
20	ROCKLAND COMMUNITY COLLEGE	Public	4	8
55	SUNY COLLEGE OF TECHNOLOGY AT DELHI	Public	4	5
71	ERIE COMMUNITY COLLEGE–CENTRAL REPORT	Public	4	8
81	CUNY HOSTOS COMMUNITY COLLEGE	Public	4	7
95	CUNY LA GUARDIA COMMUNITY COLLEGE	Public	3	8
96	SUFFOLK COUNTY COMMUNITY COLLEGE–CENTRAL REPORT	Public	4	6
131	TOMPKINS–CORTLAND COMMUNITY COLLEGE	Public	4	8
133	COLUMBIA–GREENE COMMUNITY COLLEGE	Public	3	7
138	CUNY QUEENSBOROUGH COMMUNITY COLLEGE	Public	3	9
157	SUNY COLLEGE OF TECHNOLOGY AT ALFRED	Public	4	6
161	SUNY COLLEGE OF TECHNOLOGY AT CANTON	Public	4	6
166	NIAGARA COUNTY COMMUNITY COLLEGE	Public	4	5
168	CUNY BOROUGH OF MANHATTAN COMMUNITY COLLEGE	Public	4	7
192	FULTON–MONTGOMERY COMMUNITY COLLEGE	Public	4	7
200	BROOME COMMUNITY COLLEGE	Public	3	7
212	JEFFERSON COMMUNITY COLLEGE	Public	3	7
213	DUTCHESS COMMUNITY COLLEGE	Public	4	6
262	SUNY WESTCHESTER COMMMUNITY COLLEGE	Public	2	6
285	HERKIMER COUNTY COMMUNITY COLLEGE	Public	4	5
296	CUNY KINGSBOROUGH COMMUNITY COLLEGE	Public	3	7
298	ONONDAGA COMMUNITY COLLEGE	Public	4	7
311	CUNY BRONX COMMUNITY COLLEGE	Public	3	7
329	ORANGE COUNTY COMMUNITY COLLEGE	Public	3	6
345	MOHAWK VALLEY COMMUNITY COLLEGE–UTICA BRANCH	Public	3	8
352	SCHENECTADY COUNTY COMMUNITY COLLEGE	Public	3	7
376	ADIRONDACK COMMUNITY COLLEGE	Public	3	6
381	SUNY COLLEGE OF AGRIC AND TECHN AT MORRISVILLE	Public	4	6
395	MONROE COMMUNITY COLLEGE	Public	3	5
400	GENESEE COMMUNITY COLLEGE	Public	3	6
415	CAYUGA COUNTY COMMUNITY COLLEGE	Public	4	6

Services for adult students (6 pts)	Percent of students over age 25	Graduation rate of part-time students	Mean earnings of independent students 10 years after college entry	Loan repayment of independent students 5 years after leaving college	In-district tuition and fees (at a 9 month rate for 2 year colleges)	Percent of credentials awarded as bachelor's degrees
6	25%	22%	41,546	56%	4,815	0%
6	23%	49%	38,693	55%	7,875	38%
6	33%	20%	35,823	43%	5,408	0%
5	36%	28%	35,313	53%	5,208	0%
6	27%	22%	37,706	56%	5,218	0%
6	20%	19%	41,444	55%	5,500	0%
6	26%	25%	32,526	42%	5,832	0%
6	28%	36%	36,282	47%	4,744	0%
5	19%	22%	43,771	45%	5,210	0%
5	12%	38%	39,493	57%	8,075	28%
5	24%	49%	36,019	43%	7,881	44%
6	22%	39%	34,102	46%	4,518	0%
5	24%	21%	41,036	40%	5,250	0%
6	19%	28%	33,358	40%	4,770	0%
6	28%	34%	34,005	43%	4,971	0%
6	30%	25%	35,350	45%	5,067	0%
6	16%	24%	37,197	42%	4,034	0%
6	30%	18%	45,013	48%	4,723	0%
6	22%	32%	34,298	37%	4,980	0%
5	22%	21%	42,553	40%	5,256	0%
5	20%	21%	35,762	39%	5,154	0%
5	33%	21%	37,403	39%	5,206	0%
6	23%	14%	37,934	48%	5,278	0%
5	22%	25%	33,906	41%	4,860	0%
6	27%	19%	33,669	36%	4,368	0%
6	24%	19%	34,644	42%	4,693	0%
5	17%	37%	33,161	39%	8,023	34%
6	34%	25%	34,241	35%	4,959	0%
6	21%	27%	31,281	43%	4,460	0%
5	26%	17%	33,872	32%	5,043	0%

Rank	Name	Sector	Ease of transfer (5 pts for 4 year, 4 pts for 2 year)	Flexibility of programs (9 pts)
431	FINGER LAKES COMMUNITY COLLEGE	Public	4	4
438	NORTH COUNTRY COMMUNITY COLLEGE	Public	4	4
446	SUNY COLLEGE OF AGRIC AND TECHN AT COBLESKILL	Public	3	7
504	CORNING COMMUNITY COLLEGE	Public	3	8
505	JAMESTOWN COMMUNITY COLLEGE	Public	3	5
515	SULLIVAN COUNTY COMMUNITY COLLEGE	Public	2	4
545	HUDSON VALLEY COMMUNITY COLLEGE	Public	0	8
625	BRYANT AND STRATTON BUSINESS INSTITUTE—ALBANY	For-Profit	3	7
648	BRYANT AND STRATTON BUSINESS INSTITUTE—BUFFALO	For-Profit	4	6
665	BRYANT AND STRATTON BUSINESS INSTITUTE—SYRACUSE NORTH	For-Profit	3	6
672	BRYANT AND STRATTON BUSINESS INSTITUTE—ROCHESTER	For-Profit	3	6
675	AMERICAN ACADEMY MCALLISTER INSTITUTE OF FUNERAL SERVICES	Nonprofit	3	1
680	VILLA MARIA COLLEGE BUFFALO	Nonprofit	4	4
700	ASA INSTITUTE OF BUSINESS AND COMPUTER TECHNOLOGY	For-Profit	2	5
750	BRYANT AND STRATTON BUSINESS INSTITUTE—MAIN SYRACUSE	For-Profit	3	5
760	BRYANT AND STRATTON BUSINESS INSTITUTE—LACKAWANNA	For-Profit	3	4
782	BRYANT AND STRATTON BUSINESS INSTITUTE—AMHERST	For-Profit	0	4
786	BRYANT AND STRATTON BUSINESS INSTITUTE	For-Profit	0	3

UNRANKED: American Academy of Dramatic Arts, Boricua College, Bramson Ort College, Clinton Community College, College of Aereonautics, Crouse Hospital School of Nursing, Ellis Hospital School of Nursing, Elmira Business Institute, Island Drafting and Technical Institute, Katherine Gibbs School—Melville, Long Island Business School, Mandl School, Memorial Hospital School of Nursing, Mildred Elley School, Nassau Community College, New York Career Institute, New York Restaurant School, Plaza Business Institute, Samaritan Hospital School of Nursing, School for Film and Television, St. Elizabeth Hospital School of Radiology, St Josephs Hospital Health School of Nursing, St Vincent's Catholic Medical Center—Brooklyn and Queens, St. Vincent's Catholic Medical Center—Staten Island, SUNY Ulster County Community College, Swedish Institute, Technical Career Institutes, The Westchester Business Institute, Utica School of Commerce, Wood Tobe—Coburn School

North Carolina

FOUR YEAR COLLEGES

109	UNIVERSITY OF NORTH CAROLINA AT CHAPEL HILL	Public	3	7
141	WESTERN CAROLINA UNIVERSITY	Public	5	7
143	UNIVERSITY OF NORTH CAROLINA AT CHARLOTTE	Public	5	7
166	APPALACHIAN STATE UNIVERSITY	Public	5	6
228	NORTH CAROLINA STATE UNIVERSITY AT RALEIGH	Public	3	6

Services for adult students (6 pts)	Percent of students over age 25	Graduation rate of part-time students	Mean earnings of independent students 10 years after college entry	Loan repayment of independent students 5 years after leaving college	In-district tuition and fees (at a 9 month rate for 2 year colleges)	Percent of credentials awarded as bachelor's degrees
6	21%	24%	31,983	38%	4,952	0%
4	17%	45%	32,743	49%	5,551	0%
5	9%	33%	35,485	45%	7,929	53%
5	19%	12%	32,624	37%	4,872	0%
5	19%	24%	34,038	51%	5,500	0%
5	21%	55%	36,971	40%	5,550	0%
5	25%	28%	42,387	44%	5,426	0%
4	59%	29%	24,843	22%	15,939	5%
3	49%	35%	24,843	22%	15,969	7%
2	59%	48%	24,843	22%	15,330	18%
3	59%	33%	24,843	22%	16,064	5%
0	75%	33%	41,143	49%	16,568	0%
5	22%	24%	28,686	41%	21,080	47%
4	48%	27%	29,161	28%	13,531	0%
3	39%	14%	24,843	22%	16,737	0%
2	58%	7%	24,843	22%	15,438	37%
1	64%	19%	24,843	22%	14,995	8%
1	61%	15%	24,843	22%	16,286	0%
5	4%	66%	70,609	78%	8,834	100%
5	18%	61%	41,036	57%	6,737	100%
5	16%	43%	51,275	61%	6,763	100%
6	7%	59%	38,313	64%	7,136	100%
6	8%	56%	57,770	71%	8,880	98%

Rank	Name	Sector	Ease of transfer (5 pts for 4 year, 4 pts for 2 year)	Flexibility of programs (9 pts)
337	WINSTON–SALEM STATE UNIVERSITY	Public	5	7
341	UNIVERSITY OF NORTH CAROLINA–WILMINGTON	Public	4	6
392	MOUNT OLIVE COLLEGE	Nonprofit	4	6
393	EAST CAROLINA UNIVERSITY	Public	4	6
415	LENOIR–RHYNE COLLEGE	Nonprofit	4	8
513	FAYETTEVILLE STATE UNIVERSITY	Public	3	7
515	CAMPBELL UNIVERSITY INC	Nonprofit	4	6
520	UNIVERSITY OF NORTH CAROLINA AT GREENSBORO	Public	3	7
552	UNIVERSITY OF NORTH CAROLINA AT ASHEVILLE	Public	4	6
559	BARTON COLLEGE	Nonprofit	5	7
576	GUILFORD COLLEGE	Nonprofit	5	7
611	NORTH CAROLINA CENTRAL UNIVERSITY	Public	4	8
647	GREENSBORO COLLEGE	Nonprofit	5	9
659	METHODIST COLLEGE	Nonprofit	5	7
681	ELIZABETH CITY STATE UNIVERSITY	Public	5	5
699	NORTH CAROLINA AGRICULTURAL AND TECHNICAL STATE UNIVERSITY	Public	4	4
712	UNIVERSITY OF NORTH CAROLINA AT PEMBROKE	Public	4	3
720	JOHNSON C SMITH UNIVERSITY	Nonprofit	5	8
726	LEES–MCRAE COLLEGE	Nonprofit	5	7
733	MEREDITH COLLEGE	Nonprofit	5	6

UNRANKED: Belmont Abbey College, Bennett College, Brevard College, Catawba College, Duke University, Elon College, Gardner–Webb University, High Point University, Livingstone College, Mars Hill College, Montreat College, North Carolina Wesleyan College, Peace College, Pfeiffer University, Queens College, Saint Augustine's College, School of Communication Arts, Shaw University, St Andrews Presbyterian College, Strayer University–North Carolina, Wake Forest University, Warren Wilson College, Wingate University

Two Year Colleges

53	FAYETTEVILLE TECHNICAL COMMUNITY COLLEGE	Public	4	8
290	DAVIDSON COUNTY COMMUNITY COLLEGE	Public	4	6
336	GUILFORD TECHNICAL COMMUNITY COLLEGE	Public	4	5
516	ASHEVILLE BUNCOMBE TECHNICAL COMMUNITY COLLEGE	Public	2	5
551	CENTRAL PIEDMONT COMMUNITY COLLEGE	Public	4	6
559	CRAVEN COMMUNITY COLLEGE	Public	3	6
605	SOUTHEASTERN COMMUNITY COLLEGE	Public	2	6
628	WESTERN PIEDMONT COMMUNITY COLLEGE	Public	3	4
646	RANDOLPH COMMUNITY COLLEGE	Public	3	6
649	FORSYTH TECHNICAL COMMUNITY COLLEGE	Public	3	5
669	ROCKINGHAM COMMUNITY COLLEGE	Public	3	6
706	SOUTH PIEDMONT COMMUNITY COLLEGE	Public	3	6

Services for adult students (6 pts)	Percent of students over age 25	Graduation rate of part-time students	Mean earnings of independent students 10 years after college entry	Loan repayment of independent students 5 years after leaving college	In-district tuition and fees (at a 9 month rate for 2 year colleges)	Percent of credentials awarded as bachelor's degrees
4	26%	51%	41,438	43%	5,804	100%
5	16%	55%	43,359	60%	6,951	100%
5	64%	17%	45,086	56%	19,000	80%
5	15%	50%	44,213	59%	6,997	100%
5	9%	67%	43,390	65%	33,730	100%
5	43%	40%	36,598	42%	5,085	100%
5	29%	26%	58,277	66%	30,050	92%
5	18%	43%	43,068	57%	6,971	100%
5	20%	36%	37,717	53%	6,977	100%
4	18%	59%	42,724	46%	29,052	100%
5	28%	32%	42,909	47%	34,090	100%
4	21%	38%	39,959	31%	6,132	100%
4	13%	17%	39,148	51%	28,000	100%
4	26%	14%	47,772	54%	31,980	99%
4	19%	39%	32,031	34%	4,889	100%
5	12%	41%	43,903	35%	6,372	100%
4	24%	44%	36,769	49%	5,816	100%
5	17%	0%	33,573	22%	18,236	100%
3	28%	0%	36,302	61%	26,198	100%
4	6%	20%	41,654	60%	34,907	100%
5	56%	32%	32,526	27%	2,528	0%
5	42%	26%	28,240	33%	2,235	0%
5	43%	20%	31,955	29%	2,176	0%
4	39%	31%	31,342	55%	2,547	0%
5	36%	16%	31,350	0%	2,792	0%
3	39%	5%	34,039	45%	2,053	0%
4	27%	49%	26,931	34%	2,589	0%
5	35%	8%	27,677	39%	2,577	0%
5	28%	28%	28,113	0%	1,912	0%
5	41%	19%	29,455	0%	2,056	0%
4	29%	26%	29,522	0%	1,940	0%
4	28%	21%	26,252	0%	1,873	0%

Rank	Name	Sector	Ease of transfer (5 pts for 4 year, 4 pts for 2 year)	Flexibility of programs (9 pts)
708	COASTAL CAROLINA COMMUNITY COLLEGE	Public	2	4
715	MITCHELL COMMUNITY COLLEGE	Public	3	5
736	ISOTHERMAL COMMUNITY COLLEGE	Public	3	5
740	MCDOWELL TECHNICAL COMMUNITY COLLEGE	Public	1	6
776	JOHNSON & WALES UNIVERSITY–CHARLOTTE	Nonprofit	1	4

UNRANKED: Almance Community College, Beufort County Community College, Bladen Community College, Blue Ridge Community College, Brunswick Community College, Caldwell Community College and Technical Institute, Cape Fear Community College, Carolinas College of Health Sciences, Carteret Community College, Catawba County Community College, Central Carolina Community College, College of the Albemarle, Durham Technical Community College, Edgecomb Community College, Gaston College, Halifax County Community College, Haywood Community College, James Sprunt Community College, Johnston Community College, Kaplan College–Charlotte, Kings College, Lenoir Community College, Louisburg College, Martin Community College, Mayland Community College, Miller–Motte College–Fayetiville, Miller-Motte College–Greenville, Miller-Motte College–Raleigh, Miller-Motte Technical College–Cary, Montgomery Community College, Nash Community College, Pamilco Community College, Piedmont Community College, Pitt Community College, Richmond Community College, Roanoke Chawan Community College, Robeson Community College, Rowan-Cabarus Community College, Sampson Community College, Sandhills Community College, Southwestern Community College, Stanly Community College, Tri-County Community College, Vance-Granville Community College, Wake Technical Community College, Wayne Community College, Wilkes Community College, Wilson Technical Community College

North Dakota

FOUR YEAR COLLEGES

Rank	Name	Sector	Ease of transfer	Flexibility of programs
182	NORTH DAKOTA STATE UNIVERSITY–MAIN CAMPUS	Public	5	8
218	VALLEY CITY STATE UNIVERSITY	Public	4	8
403	DICKINSON STATE UNIVERSITY	Public	4	7

UNRANKED: Jamestown College, Mayville State University, Minot State University, University of Mary, University of North Dakota–Main Campus

TWO YEAR COLLEGES

Rank	Name	Sector	Ease of transfer	Flexibility of programs
64	BISMARCK STATE COLLEGE	Public	4	5
271	NORTH DAKOTA STATE COLLEGE OF SCIENCE	Public	4	5
448	LAKE REGION STATE COLLEGE	Public	3	5
483	WILLISTON STATE COLLEGE	Public	3	4
643	AAKERS BUSINESS COLLEGE	For-Profit	1	7

UNRANKED: Minot State University–Bottineau Campus

Services for adult students (6 pts)	Percent of students over age 25	Graduation rate of part-time students	Mean earnings of independent students 10 years after college entry	Loan repayment of independent students 5 years after leaving college	In-district tuition and fees (at a 9 month rate for 2 year colleges)	Percent of credentials awarded as bachelor's degrees
5	45%	16%	31,143	0%	2,462	0%
4	27%	23%	28,419	0%	2,631	0%
4	28%	11%	26,604	0%	2,542	0%
5	34%	17%	27,374	0%	1,900	0%
4	8%	0%	38,952	57%	30,396	43%
5	8%	24%	53,502	68%	8,207	99%
5	24%	42%	41,453	63%	7,196	98%
4	24%	39%	39,439	69%	6,348	82%
5	32%	20%	43,493	62%	3,659	9%
5	15%	25%	38,202	55%	4,697	0%
4	19%	26%	36,626	61%	4,203	0%
3	23%	33%	38,821	65%	5,027	0%
3	60%	29%	32,896	33%	9,630	22%

NORTH DAKOTA

Rank	Name	Sector	Ease of transfer (5 pts for 4 year, 4 pts for 2 year)	Flexibility of programs (9 pts)

Ohio

FOUR YEAR COLLEGES

Rank	Name	Sector	Ease of transfer	Flexibility of programs
5	THE UNION INSTITUTE	Nonprofit	3	8
150	UNIVERSITY OF CINCINNATI–MAIN CAMPUS	Public	5	7
165	COLLEGE OF MOUNT SAINT JOSEPH	Nonprofit	5	8
215	URSULINE COLLEGE	Nonprofit	5	9
217	OHIO STATE UNIVERSITY–MAIN CAMPUS	Public	4	7
220	MOUNT VERNON NAZARENE COLLEGE	Nonprofit	5	6
249	THE UNIVERSITY OF FINDLAY	Nonprofit	5	9
251	UNIVERSITY OF AKRON MAIN CAMPUS	Public	5	9
282	WRIGHT STATE UNIVERSITY–MAIN CAMPUS	Public	4	7
287	BALDWIN-WALLACE COLLEGE	Nonprofit	5	9
304	KENT STATE UNIVERSITY–MAIN CAMPUS	Public	5	8
315	OHIO NORTHERN UNIVERSITY	Nonprofit	5	5
316	UNIVERSITY OF DAYTON	Nonprofit	5	6
351	BOWLING GREEN STATE UNIVERSITY–MAIN CAMPUS	Public	5	9
384	CASE WESTERN RESERVE UNIVERSITY	Nonprofit	3	6
429	OHIO UNIVERSITY–MAIN CAMPUS	Public	4	9
486	CAPITAL UNIVERSITY	Nonprofit	5	7
505	OHIO DOMINICAN COLLEGE	Nonprofit	5	8
510	LOURDES COLLEGE	Nonprofit	5	8
511	HIRAM COLLEGE	Nonprofit	4	8
521	WRIGHT STATE UNIVERSITY–LAKE CAMPUS	Public	4	7
529	BLUFFTON COLLEGE	Nonprofit	5	9
547	WALSH UNIVERSITY	Nonprofit	4	7
573	OHIO STATE UNIVERSITY–LIMA CAMPUS	Public	3	7
589	SHAWNEE STATE UNIVERSITY	Public	5	8
622	YOUNGSTOWN STATE UNIVERSITY	Public	3	8
632	OTTERBEIN COLLEGE	Nonprofit	5	4
713	XAVIER UNIVERSITY	Nonprofit	5	7
755	MIAMI UNIVERSITY–OXFORD	Public	4	5
771	WITTENBERG UNIVERSITY	Nonprofit	5	6
779	LAKE ERIE COLLEGE	Nonprofit	4	9

UNRANKED: Ashland University, Cedarville University, Central State University, Cleveland State University, College of Wooster, Defiance College, Denison University, Franciscan University of Steubenville, Heidelberg College, John Carroll University, Marietta College, Mount Union College, Muskingum College, Notre Dame College of Ohio, Oberlin College, Ohio Christian University, Ohio Wesleyan University, Tiffin University, Urbana University, Wilberforce University, Wilmington College

Services for adult students (6 pts)	Percent of students over age 25	Graduation rate of part-time students	Mean earnings of independent students 10 years after college entry	Loan repayment of independent students 5 years after leaving college	In-district tuition and fees (at a 9 month rate for 2 year colleges)	Percent of credentials awarded as bachelor's degrees
4	96%	73%	50,656	62%	12,416	100%
6	14%	49%	46,895	53%	11,000	94%
6	19%	68%	43,872	47%	28,300	97%
4	34%	55%	52,190	48%	29,940	96%
6	8%	62%	47,935	53%	10,037	100%
4	26%	61%	54,910	63%	18,879	97%
5	9%	43%	54,955	61%	32,402	96%
6	16%	31%	35,849	40%	10,270	79%
6	19%	32%	48,514	54%	8,730	98%
5	10%	53%	48,018	51%	30,776	100%
6	13%	34%	37,639	41%	10,012	99%
4	3%	82%	70,683	59%	29,820	100%
6	3%	64%	54,874	68%	40,940	100%
5	6%	41%	39,687	40%	11,057	98%
5	2%	75%	93,292	65%	46,006	100%
5	25%	43%	34,979	36%	11,298	93%
4	13%	66%	46,771	57%	33,492	100%
5	27%	29%	43,482	46%	31,080	86%
5	23%	26%	41,676	40%	20,620	99%
4	17%	60%	52,408	53%	31,569	100%
5	15%	18%	48,514	54%	5,842	53%
4	11%	25%	49,440	60%	30,762	100%
5	17%	50%	49,935	51%	28,770	99%
6	13%	18%	47,935	53%	7,140	44%
5	16%	15%	35,044	33%	7,364	64%
6	20%	31%	36,227	30%	8,317	87%
5	6%	48%	49,597	64%	31,874	100%
5	5%	0%	50,123	53%	36,150	99%
5	2%	33%	37,229	34%	14,400	98%
5	5%	0%	33,536	57%	38,090	100%
2	6%	20%	40,248	48%	29,960	100%

Rank	Name	Sector	Ease of transfer (5 pts for 4 year, 4 pts for 2 year)	Flexibility of programs (9 pts)
	TWO YEAR COLLEGES			
25	UNIVERSITY OF CINCINNATI–RAYMOND WALTERS COLLEGE	Public	3	9
72	OHIO STATE UNIVERSITY–MARION CAMPUS	Public	3	7
87	SINCLAIR COMMUNITY COLLEGE	Public	4	8
91	STARK STATE COLLEGE OF TECHNOLOGY	Public	4	9
162	UNIVERSITY OF AKRON–WAYNE COLLEGE	Public	4	9
169	UNIVERSITY OF CINCINNATI–CLERMONT COLLEGE	Public	3	5
171	MIAMI UNIVERSITY–HAMILTON	Public	4	8
190	EDISON STATE COMMUNITY COLLEGE	Public	4	9
238	KENT STATE UNIVERSITY–ASHTABULA REGIONAL CAMPUS	Public	4	4
243	KENT STATE UNIVERSITY–GEAUGA CAMPUS	Public	4	6
253	LAKELAND COMMUNITY COLLEGE	Public	3	8
284	OHIO UNIVERSITY–CHILLICOTHE BRANCH	Public	4	6
297	COLUMBUS STATE COMMUNITY COLLEGE	Public	3	8
302	OWENS COMMUNITY COLLEGE–TOLEDO CAMPUS	Public	4	8
343	OHIO STATE UNIVERSITY–NEWARK CAMPUS	Public	3	6
357	MIAMI UNIVERSITY–MIDDLETOWN	Public	3	7
370	OHIO STATE UNIVERSITY AGRICULTURAL TECHNICAL INSTITUTE	Public	3	5
374	KENT STATE UNIVERSITY–SALEM REGIONAL CAMPUS	Public	3	6
375	HOCKING TECHNICAL COLLEGE	Public	3	6
390	OHIO STATE UNIVERSITY–MANSFIELD CAMPUS	Public	2	7
391	OHIO UNIVERSITY–SOUTHERN CAMPUS	Public	3	5
412	LORAIN COUNTY COMMUNITY COLLEGE	Public	2	8
439	OHIO UNIVERSITY–LANCASTER BRANCH	Public	3	7
441	CUYAHOGA COMMUNITY COLLEGE DISTRICT	Public	2	7
492	KENT STATE UNIVERSITY–TRUMBULL REGIONAL CAMPUS	Public	3	5
497	WASHINGTON STATE COMMUNITY COLLEGE	Public	3	7
506	KENT STATE UNIVERSITY–STARK CAMPUS	Public	3	5
519	OHIO BUSINESS COLLEGE–LORAIN	For-Profit	3	3
535	NORTH CENTRAL STATE COLLEGE	Public	3	7
568	MUSKINGUM AREA TECHNICAL COLLEGE	Public	4	6
573	BOWLING GREEN STATE UNIVERSITY–FIRELANDS	Public	3	6
577	BRYANT AND STRATTON COLLEGE	For-Profit	4	5
633	KENT STATE UNIVERSITY–TUSCARAWS REGIONAL CAMPUS	Public	2	7
690	OHIO UNIVERSITY–EASTERN CAMPUS	Public	0	7
693	SOUTHERN STATE COMMUNITY COLLEGE	Public	2	6
752	ETI TECHNICAL COLLEGE	For-Profit	1	2
757	OHIO BUSINESS COLLEGE	For-Profit	1	4

Services for adult students (6 pts)	Percent of students over age 25	Graduation rate of part-time students	Mean earnings of independent students 10 years after college entry	Loan repayment of independent students 5 years after leaving college	In-district tuition and fees (at a 9 month rate for 2 year colleges)	Percent of credentials awarded as bachelor's degrees
6	21%	27%	46,895	53%	6,010	4%
6	14%	33%	47,935	53%	7,140	55%
6	41%	25%	30,536	32%	2,477	0%
5	39%	24%	34,308	31%	3,686	0%
5	19%	23%	35,849	40%	6,116	0%
5	28%	28%	46,895	53%	5,316	12%
5	25%	27%	37,229	34%	5,922	59%
5	28%	21%	30,543	38%	4,219	0%
5	42%	27%	37,639	41%	5,664	3%
4	27%	40%	37,639	41%	5,664	3%
6	36%	15%	35,190	28%	3,316	0%
4	33%	37%	34,979	36%	5,060	0%
5	37%	18%	34,106	36%	3,808	0%
5	41%	7%	31,779	29%	4,643	0%
4	10%	28%	47,935	53%	7,140	25%
6	21%	21%	37,229	34%	5,922	60%
5	6%	25%	47,935	53%	7,203	0%
5	33%	20%	37,639	41%	5,664	13%
6	22%	51%	31,005	23%	4,390	0%
5	12%	17%	47,935	53%	7,140	38%
5	39%	31%	34,979	36%	4,872	0%
6	35%	13%	31,646	37%	3,077	0%
4	24%	35%	34,979	36%	5,060	0%
6	43%	16%	31,582	31%	3,136	0%
4	38%	21%	37,639	41%	5,664	6%
5	24%	24%	28,988	39%	4,500	0%
5	26%	17%	37,639	41%	5,664	5%
3	64%	82%	24,509	24%	9,025	0%
5	27%	9%	29,628	39%	3,591	0%
5	22%	12%	28,349	28%	4,646	0%
3	21%	20%	39,687	40%	5,060	0%
4	66%	31%	24,843	22%	16,283	23%
2	28%	28%	37,639	41%	5,664	12%
4	25%	33%	34,979	36%	4,872	0%
4	22%	22%	30,060	28%	4,412	0%
2	65%	54%	24,851	23%	10,920	0%
1	69%	38%	24,509	24%	9,000	0%

Rank	Name		Sector	Ease of transfer (5 pts for 4 year, 4 pts for 2 year)	Flexibility of programs (9 pts)

UNRANKED: Academy of Court Reporting, Academy of Court Reporting–Columbus, Akron Medical–Dental Institute, American Institute of Alternative Medicine, Beckfield College, Belmont Technical College, Bohecker College–Cincinnati, Bohecker College–Columbus, Boheckers Business College–Ravena, Bradford School, Central Ohio Technical College, Chatfield College, Cincinnati State Technical and Community College, Clark State Community College, Davis College, Education America–Remington College, ETI Technical College, Galen College of Nursing–Cincinnati, Harrison College–Grove City, Herzing University, Jefferson Community College, Lima Technical College, Marion Technical College, National College, Northwest State Community College, Ohio Institute of Photography and Technology, Ohio Technical College, Ohio Technical College DBA PowerSport Institute LC, Ohio Valley Business College Inc, Professional Skills Institute, Rets Tech Center, Ross Medical Education Center–Sylvania, School of Advertising Art INC, Southern Ohio College, Southern Ohio College–Northeast, Stautzenberger College–Strongsville Campus, Terra State Community College, Trumbull Business College, University of Northwestern Ohio, University of Rio Grande, Vatterott Colllege–Cleaveland, Virginia Marti College of Fashion and Art

Oklahoma

FOUR YEAR COLLEGES

Rank	Name	Sector	Ease of transfer	Flexibility
17	UNIVERSITY OF OKLAHOMA NORMAN CAMPUS	Public	5	8
245	OKLAHOMA STATE UNIVERSITY–MAIN CAMPUS	Public	4	8
256	SOUTHWESTERN OKLAHOMA STATE UNIVERSITY	Public	5	8
380	CAMERON UNIVERSITY	Public	5	7
474	OKLAHOMA CITY UNIVERSITY	Nonprofit	4	6
481	NORTHEASTERN STATE UNIVERSITY	Public	3	7
514	UNIVERSITY OF CENTRAL OKLAHOMA	Public	5	5
588	NORTHWESTERN OKLAHOMA STATE UNIVERSITY	Public	3	6
649	UNIVERSITY OF TULSA	Nonprofit	4	6
664	EAST CENTRAL UNIVERSITY	Public	4	6
670	SOUTHEASTERN OKLAHOMA STATE UNIVERSITY	Public	4	3
674	OKLAHOMA PANHANDLE STATE UNIVERSITY	Public	5	3
700	LANGSTON UNIVERSITY	Public	3	7
717	OKLAHOMA CHRISTIAN UNIVERSITY	Nonprofit	4	8
770	ORAL ROBERTS UNIVERSITY	Nonprofit	4	7
784	ROGERS STATE UNIVERSITY	Public	2	4

UNRANKED: Bartlesville Wesleyan College, Mid America Bible College, Oklahoma Baptist University, Southern Nazarene University, Southwestern College of Christian Ministries, University of Science and Arts of Oklahoma

TWO YEAR COLLEGES

Rank	Name	Sector	Ease of transfer	Flexibility
122	OKLAHOMA STATE UNIVERSITY–OKLAHOMA CITY	Public	3	7
185	ROSE STATE COLLEGE	Public	4	6
265	OKLAHOMA CITY COMMUNITY COLLEGE	Public	3	8
445	NORTHEASTERN OKLAHOMA AGRICULTURAL AND MECHANICAL COLLEGE	Public	4	6

Services for adult students (6 pts)	Percent of students over age 25	Graduation rate of part-time students	Mean earnings of independent students 10 years after college entry	Loan repayment of independent students 5 years after leaving college	In-district tuition and fees (at a 9 month rate for 2 year colleges)	Percent of credentials awarded as bachelor's degrees
6	11%	38%	66,835	66%	8,631	100%
5	11%	45%	50,796	58%	8,321	99%
5	19%	28%	44,430	50%	6,690	80%
5	38%	13%	38,046	46%	5,970	72%
5	15%	46%	58,742	68%	30,726	100%
5	36%	41%	39,554	50%	6,207	100%
4	24%	32%	46,256	56%	6,699	98%
5	20%	44%	38,897	58%	6,691	91%
5	6%	42%	56,670	64%	38,796	100%
4	21%	34%	37,459	46%	6,279	94%
5	29%	38%	36,499	50%	6,450	100%
4	21%	49%	34,909	47%	7,208	73%
5	18%	28%	36,133	35%	5,388	96%
4	4%	17%	40,043	54%	20,840	100%
4	15%	0%	37,213	50%	25,676	100%
4	32%	22%	36,015	48%	6,540	60%
6	49%	13%	38,245	40%	3,634	1%
5	43%	14%	36,466	40%	3,808	0%
5	37%	9%	37,242	41%	3,727	0%
4	21%	27%	30,706	43%	4,178	0%

Rank	Name	Sector	Ease of transfer (5 pts for 4 year, 4 pts for 2 year)	Flexibility of programs (9 pts)
471	EASTERN OKLAHOMA STATE COLLEGE	Public	4	5
488	TULSA COMMUNITY COLLEGE	Public	2	7
494	CARL ALBERT STATE COLLEGE	Public	4	6
536	SEMINOLE STATE COLLEGE	Public	4	5
570	MURRAY STATE COLLEGE	Public	4	4
583	OKLAHOMA STATE UNIVERSITY–OKMULGEE	Public	3	6
594	WESTERN OKLAHOMA STATE COLLEGE	Public	3	4
664	REDLANDS COMMUNITY COLLEGE	Public	2	5
694	NORTHERN OKLAHOMA COLLEGE	Public	2	5
701	CONNORS STATE COLLEGE	Public	3	3

UNRANKED: Advance Barber College, Bacone College, Brown Mackie College–Tulsa, Clary Sage College, Community Care College, Platt College, Tulsa Welding School, Vatterot College–Tulsa, Vatterott College

Oregon

FOUR YEAR COLLEGES

Rank	Name	Sector	Ease of transfer	Flexibility of programs
52	GEORGE FOX UNIVERSITY	Nonprofit	5	8
122	PORTLAND STATE UNIVERSITY	Public	4	6
169	NORTHWEST CHRISTIAN COLLEGE	Nonprofit	5	5
329	OREGON STATE UNIVERSITY	Public	3	5
338	EASTERN OREGON UNIVERSITY	Public	3	8
557	PACIFIC UNIVERSITY	Nonprofit	4	7
569	UNIVERSITY OF OREGON	Public	4	4

UNRANKED: Lewis and Clark College, Linfield College, Linfield College–Adult Degree Program, Oregon Institute of Technology, Reed College, Southern Oregon University, University of Phoenix Oregon Campus, University of Portland, Warner Pacific College, Western Baptist College, Western Oregon University, Willamette University

TWO YEAR COLLEGES

Rank	Name	Sector	Ease of transfer	Flexibility of programs
194	CHEMEKETA COMMUNITY COLLEGE	Public	4	8
248	UMPQUA COMMUNITY COLLEGE	Public	3	6
264	LANE COMMUNITY COLLEGE	Public	3	8
291	CENTRAL OREGON COMMUNITY COLLEGE	Public	4	5
310	CLACKAMAS COMMUNITY COLLEGE	Public	3	5
344	CLATSOP COMMUNITY COLLEGE	Public	4	5
351	ROGUE COMMUNITY COLLEGE	Public	4	7
379	SOUTHWESTERN OREGON COMMUNITY COLLEGE	Public	3	6
501	LINN-BENTON COMMUNITY COLLEGE	Public	3	6

Services for adult students (6 pts)	Percent of students over age 25	Graduation rate of part-time students	Mean earnings of independent students 10 years after college entry	Loan repayment of independent students 5 years after leaving college	In-district tuition and fees (at a 9 month rate for 2 year colleges)	Percent of credentials awarded as bachelor's degrees
5	29%	9%	32,957	38%	4,224	0%
4	38%	20%	36,092	42%	3,071	0%
4	30%	18%	28,041	40%	3,160	0%
4	28%	30%	29,022	32%	4,140	0%
4	29%	17%	32,383	37%	4,638	0%
4	29%	7%	34,501	42%	5,100	9%
3	31%	35%	33,640	42%	3,561	0%
4	15%	25%	35,929	37%	4,154	0%
4	20%	12%	33,026	40%	3,675	0%
3	33%	2%	32,020	45%	3,210	0%
5	13%	84%	56,708	68%	33,730	100%
6	39%	46%	49,488	59%	8,337	100%
5	35%	73%	51,505	65%	27,930	99%
6	21%	54%	53,853	64%	10,366	100%
4	48%	48%	40,596	55%	7,507	88%
4	9%	80%	45,998	69%	41,054	100%
6	7%	43%	48,168	55%	10,762	100%
5	39%	12%	33,195	38%	4,230	0%
6	49%	26%	34,000	29%	4,718	0%
6	42%	16%	31,845	31%	4,155	0%
5	42%	18%	34,640	36%	3,627	0%
6	37%	15%	37,646	42%	4,412	0%
4	46%	21%	30,729	46%	4,014	0%
4	49%	11%	29,861	35%	4,164	0%
6	29%	28%	32,144	38%	5,847	0%
5	29%	12%	33,670	41%	4,512	0%

Rank	Name	Sector	Ease of transfer (5 pts for 4 year, 4 pts for 2 year)	Flexibility of programs (9 pts)
620	BLUE MOUNTAIN COMMUNITY COLLEGE	Public	4	5
650	TREASURE VALLEY COMMUNITY COLLEGE	Public	4	7

UNRANKED: Apollo College–Portland Inc, College of Legal Arts, Columbia Gorge Community College, Concorde Career Institute, Klamath Community College, Mt Hood Community College, Oregon Coast Community College, Pioneer Pacific College, Portland Community College, Tillamook Bay Community College, Western Culinary Institute

Pennsylvania

FOUR YEAR COLLEGES

15	UNIVERSITY OF PENNSYLVANIA	Nonprofit	2	8
50	COLLEGE MISERICORDIA	Nonprofit	5	9
97	CALIFORNIA UNIVERSITY OF PENNSYLVANIA	Public	5	7
105	WEST CHESTER UNIVERSITY OF PENNSYLVANIA	Public	4	8
111	DUQUESNE UNIVERSITY	Nonprofit	4	9
112	SLIPPERY ROCK UNIVERSITY OF PENNSYLVANIA	Public	5	6
142	TEMPLE UNIVERSITY	Public	4	8
145	ROSEMONT COLLEGE	Nonprofit	4	9
168	INDIANA UNIVERSITY OF PENNSYLVANIA–MAIN CAMPUS	Public	4	9
185	SETON HILL COLLEGE	Nonprofit	5	9
211	SHIPPENSBURG UNIVERSITY OF PENNSYLVANIA	Public	5	7
241	YORK COLLEGE PENNSYLVANIA	Nonprofit	5	8
248	LA ROCHE COLLEGE	Nonprofit	5	6
253	CLARION UNIVERSITY OF PENNSYLVANIA	Public	5	8
258	CARLOW COLLEGE	Nonprofit	5	8
266	EAST STROUDSBURG UNIVERSITY OF PENNSYLVANIA	Public	5	6
274	NEUMANN COLLEGE	Nonprofit	5	7
284	BLOOMSBURG UNIVERSITY OF PENNSYLVANIA	Public	5	6
293	DREXEL UNIVERSITY	Nonprofit	4	8
294	CABRINI COLLEGE	Nonprofit	4	9
345	EDINBORO UNIVERSITY OF PENNSYLVANIA	Public	5	7
371	WIDENER UNIVERSITY–MAIN CAMPUS	Nonprofit	4	8
373	MILLERSVILLE UNIVERSITY OF PENNSYLVANIA	Public	5	5
385	LA SALLE UNIVERSITY	Nonprofit	4	7
390	ALVERNIA COLLEGE	Nonprofit	5	8
417	CENTRAL PENNSYLVANIA COLLEGE	For-Profit	4	6
421	UNIVERSITY OF PITTSBURGH–BRADFORD	Public	5	5
425	GENEVA COLLEGE	Nonprofit	5	6
436	GWYNEDD MERCY COLLEGE	Nonprofit	3	8
455	EASTERN COLLEGE	Nonprofit	5	8

Services for adult students (6 pts)	Percent of students over age 25	Graduation rate of part-time students	Mean earnings of independent students 10 years after college entry	Loan repayment of independent students 5 years after leaving college	In-district tuition and fees (at a 9 month rate for 2 year colleges)	Percent of credentials awarded as bachelor's degrees
2	36%	17%	33,689	33%	4,949	0%
1	35%	10%	31,689	34%	5,400	0%
6	6%	90%	127,637	72%	51,464	100%
5	22%	69%	53,688	62%	30,740	96%
5	21%	70%	43,830	57%	10,339	95%
5	10%	62%	49,995	73%	9,720	100%
6	5%	60%	68,049	65%	35,062	100%
6	7%	70%	42,549	62%	9,862	99%
5	11%	54%	64,434	62%	16,274	99%
6	21%	40%	56,074	53%	19,580	100%
6	7%	56%	42,514	55%	11,368	97%
6	11%	60%	43,247	57%	33,520	99%
6	6%	32%	46,389	67%	11,452	96%
5	7%	44%	48,371	62%	18,780	99%
5	23%	54%	50,595	67%	27,000	92%
5	18%	44%	35,792	53%	10,471	88%
5	30%	42%	44,682	57%	27,764	100%
6	9%	32%	45,441	63%	9,954	100%
6	23%	40%	50,631	51%	28,580	99%
6	5%	41%	42,474	61%	10,154	100%
5	17%	35%	87,948	68%	51,030	96%
5	5%	41%	61,710	68%	30,588	100%
6	13%	30%	38,142	49%	9,984	94%
6	12%	45%	65,974	55%	42,870	97%
5	12%	47%	42,017	68%	11,494	100%
6	15%	59%	57,183	58%	41,100	95%
5	32%	31%	44,302	55%	32,270	97%
5	60%	23%	45,241	50%	17,646	64%
5	10%	36%	54,478	61%	13,608	86%
3	16%	100%	44,909	50%	25,680	97%
3	41%	66%	57,931	64%	33,589	64%
4	28%	14%	60,453	58%	31,140	77%

Rank	Name	Sector	Ease of transfer (5 pts for 4 year, 4 pts for 2 year)	Flexibility of programs (9 pts)
461	PEIRCE COLLEGE	Nonprofit	4	7
465	MANSFIELD UNIVERSITY OF PENNSYLVANIA	Public	5	5
471	UNIVERSITY OF PITTSBURGH—MAIN CAMPUS	Public	3	8
504	KEYSTONE COLLEGE	Nonprofit	4	7
527	VILLANOVA UNIVERSITY	Nonprofit	3	8
553	WILKES UNIVERSITY	Nonprofit	3	9
560	ROBERT MORRIS COLLEGE	Nonprofit	4	7
562	LEBANON VALLEY COLLEGE	Nonprofit	4	8
570	UNIVERSITY OF PITTSBURGH—GREENSBURG	Public	5	4
577	MORAVIAN COLLEGE AND THEOLOGICAL SEMINARY	Nonprofit	4	6
579	KUTZTOWN UNIVERSITY OF PENNSYLVANIA	Public	4	4
619	UNIVERSITY OF PITTSBURGH—JOHNSTOWN	Public	3	7
645	HOLY FAMILY COLLEGE	Nonprofit	3	6
653	POINT PARK COLLEGE	Nonprofit	4	7
654	KINGS COLLEGE	Nonprofit	3	9
671	DELAWARE VALLEY COLLEGE	Nonprofit	4	6
685	GANNON UNIVERSITY	Nonprofit	4	7
715	MUHLENBERG COLLEGE	Nonprofit	3	9
718	BEAVER COLLEGE	Nonprofit	5	6
731	UNIVERSITY OF SCRANTON	Nonprofit	4	7
748	MARYWOOD UNIVERSITY	Nonprofit	4	7
780	VALLEY FORGE CHRISTIAN COLLEGE	Nonprofit	5	6
795	PHILADELPHIA COLLEGE OF BIBLE	Nonprofit	4	6
796	LOCK HAVEN UNIVERSITY OF PENNSYLVANIA	Public	2	6
797	CHEYNEY UNIVERSITY OF PENNSYLVANIA	Public	3	6

UNRANKED: Albright College, Allegheny College, Bryn Athyn College of the New Church, Bryn Mawr College, Bucknell University, Carnegie Mellon University, Cedar Crest College, Chatham College, Chesnut Hill College, Desales University, Dickinson College, Elizabethtown College, Franklin and Marshall College, Gettysburg College, Harrisburg University of Science and Technology, Haverford College, Immaculata College, Juniata College, Lafayette College, Lehigh College, Lincoln University, Lycoming College, Mercyhurst College, Messiah College, Pennsylvania State University—Delaware Campus, Pennsylvania State University—Main Campus, Pennsylvania State University—Harrisburg, Pennsylvania State University—Mckeesport, Pennsylvania State University—Abington, Pennsylvania State University—Altoona, Pennsylvania State University—Beaver, Pennsylvania State University—Berks, Pennsylvania State University—Schuykil, Pennsylvania State University—Shenago, Pennsylvania State University—Wilkes, Pennsylvania State University—York, Pennsylvania State University—Behrend College, Pennsylvania State University—Worthington Scranton, Pennsylvania State University—Lehigh Valley, Pennsylvania State University—New Kensington, Saint Francis College, Saint Vincent College, Strayer University—Lower Bucks Campus, Susquehanna University, Swarthmore College, Thiel College, Ursinus Collge, Washington & Jefferson College, Waynesburg College, Westminster College, Wilson College

Two Year Colleges

5	HARCUM COLLEGE	Nonprofit	4	7
22	MONTGOMERY COUNTY COMMUNITY COLLEGE	Public	4	9

Services for adult students (6 pts)	Percent of students over age 25	Graduation rate of part-time students	Mean earnings of independent students 10 years after college entry	Loan repayment of independent students 5 years after leaving college	In-district tuition and fees (at a 9 month rate for 2 year colleges)	Percent of credentials awarded as bachelor's degrees
2	78%	34%	50,862	43%	14,472	60%
6	11%	31%	41,403	57%	11,908	92%
5	6%	50%	54,478	61%	18,618	83%
6	26%	35%	35,503	57%	24,998	87%
4	6%	53%	79,176	79%	49,280	100%
5	9%	33%	62,483	60%	33,568	100%
5	16%	35%	52,650	58%	28,250	100%
4	4%	56%	52,995	74%	40,550	100%
5	8%	28%	54,478	61%	13,618	98%
4	9%	100%	41,473	64%	40,287	100%
6	6%	31%	44,737	68%	9,618	100%
5	4%	28%	54,478	61%	13,624	93%
4	26%	50%	56,626	61%	29,750	97%
5	23%	27%	47,577	46%	29,030	99%
5	6%	17%	62,402	61%	35,820	100%
4	10%	44%	47,047	75%	36,710	97%
5	8%	29%	49,703	49%	30,927	94%
4	7%	33%	56,449	64%	48,310	100%
4	6%	33%	48,428	58%	40,920	100%
5	3%	38%	41,883	53%	42,162	100%
5	11%	7%	41,553	49%	33,000	90%
3	17%	0%	35,621	43%	20,674	93%
3	13%	0%	43,781	48%	25,246	100%
1	9%	51%	41,200	57%	10,229	93%
4	12%	14%	30,657	29%	11,356	100%
6	54%	64%	43,532	54%	22,760	0%
6	33%	13%	41,879	46%	5,610	0%

Rank	Name	Sector	Ease of transfer (5 pts for 4 year, 4 pts for 2 year)	Flexibility of programs (9 pts)
44	UNIVERSITY OF PITTSBURGH–TITUSVILLE	Public	4	6
52	BUCKS COUNTY COMMUNITY COLLEGE	Public	4	7
54	NORTHAMPTON COUNTY AREA COMMUNITY COLLEGE	Public	4	7
66	DELAWARE COUNTY COMMUNITY COLLEGE	Public	3	9
93	WESTMORELAND COUNTY COMMUNITY COLLEGE	Public	4	9
172	MANOR COLLEGE	Nonprofit	4	7
205	HARRISBURG AREA COMMUNITY COLLEGE–HARRISBURG	Public	4	7
228	COMMUNITY COLLEGE OF ALLEGHENY COUNTY	Public	2	7
259	LUZERNE COUNTY COMMUNITY COLLEGE	Public	4	6
316	LEHIGH CARBON COMMUNITY COLLEGE	Public	3	6
368	COMMUNITY COLLEGE OF PHILADELPHIA	Public	2	7
436	JOHNSON TECHNICAL INSTITUTE	Nonprofit	4	5
499	LACKAWANNA JUNIOR COLLEGE	Nonprofit	4	4
503	READING AREA COMMUNITY COLLEGE	Public	3	7
592	CAMBRIA COUNTY AREA COMMUNITY COLLEGE	Public	4	6
764	LINCOLN TECHNICAL INSTITUTE	For-Profit	0	1
779	CITTONE INSTITUTE	For-Profit	0	1

UNRANKED: Academy of Medical Arts and Business, Allied Medical and Technical Careers, Antonelli Institute, Berks Technical Institute, Bidwell Training Center INC, Bradford School, Business Institute of Pennsylvania, Business Institute of Pennsylvania–Titusville, Butler County Community College, Career Technical College, Chi Institute, Chi Institute–Rets Campus, Commonwealth Technical Institute, Community College of Beaver County, Computer Learning Network, Dean Institute of Technology, Douglas School of Business, Erie Institute of Technology INC, Great Lakes Institute of Technology, ICM School of Business and Medical Careers, Lancaster County Career and Technology Center, Lansdale School of Business, Laurel Business Institute, Lincoln Technical Institute, McCann School of Business, Median School of Allied Health Careers, Mount Aloysius Health Careers, New Castle School of Trades, Orleans Technical Institute, Pennco Tech, Pennsylvania College of Technology, Pennsylvania Commercial College, Pennsylvania Institute of Technology, Pennsylvania State University–Penn State Dubois, Pennsylvania State University, Penn State Fayette, Pennsylvania State University–Penn State Hazleton, Pennsylvania State University–Penn State Mont Alto, Pittsburgh Institute of Aeronautics, Pittsburgh Institute of Mortuary Science Inc, Pittsburgh Technical Institute, Rosedale Technical Institute, South Hills School of Business and Technology, Thaddeus Stevens College of Technology, Thompson Institute, Triangle Tech Inc, Triangle Tech Inc–Bethlehem, Triangle Tech Inc–Dubois, Triangle Tech Inc–Greensburg, Tri-State Business Institute, Western School of Health and Business Careers, Wyoming Technical Institute, York Technical Institute

Rhode Island
FOUR YEAR COLLEGES

121	RHODE ISLAND COLLEGE	Public	5	7
285	ROGER WILLIAMS UNIVERSITY	Nonprofit	5	9
414	UNIVERSITY OF RHODE ISLAND	Public	4	7
566	BROWN UNIVERSITY	Nonprofit	4	5
707	JOHNSON & WALES UNIVERSITY	Nonprofit	4	8
791	PROVIDENCE COLLEGE	Nonprofit	3	8

UNRANKED: Bryant College, Salve Regina University

Services for adult students (6 pts)	Percent of students over age 25	Graduation rate of part-time students	Mean earnings of independent students 10 years after college entry	Loan repayment of independent students 5 years after leaving college	In-district tuition and fees (at a 9 month rate for 2 year colleges)	Percent of credentials awarded as bachelor's degrees
5	19%	27%	54,478	61%	11,808	0%
6	29%	9%	41,672	55%	4,298	0%
6	33%	20%	36,232	52%	4,110	0%
5	38%	20%	41,745	47%	4,960	0%
5	32%	20%	32,519	51%	5,070	0%
4	31%	32%	42,685	59%	16,550	0%
4	40%	21%	36,731	45%	6,525	0%
6	43%	24%	35,516	47%	4,131	0%
4	36%	18%	35,957	53%	5,040	0%
5	31%	18%	35,585	54%	3,900	0%
6	44%	14%	35,716	37%	4,920	0%
4	22%	25%	39,265	69%	18,235	0%
5	22%	32%	36,183	48%	14,580	0%
4	36%	14%	34,207	36%	5,310	0%
3	15%	29%	28,691	44%	5,404	0%
1	43%	78%	40,230	34%	18,018.64	0%
1	47%	57%	35,649	24%	18,639	0%
6	24%	38%	42,652	59%	8,206	97%
5	12%	40%	50,763	59%	32,100	97%
6	8%	38%	44,943	54%	12,884	100%
5	1%	100%	109,267	0%	51,366	100%
4	9%	29%	38,952	57%	30,396	70%
1	5%	63%	48,159	62%	46,970	85%

Rank	Name		Sector	Ease of transfer (5 pts for 4 year, 4 pts for 2 year)	Flexibility of programs (9 pts)

Two Year Colleges

Rank	Name	Sector	Ease of transfer	Flexibility of programs
36	COMMUNITY COLLEGE OF RHODE ISLAND	Public	4	6

UNRANKED: New England Institute of Technology

South Carolina
Four Year Colleges

Rank	Name	Sector	Ease of transfer	Flexibility of programs
129	UNIVERSITY OF SOUTH CAROLINA AT COLUMBIA	Public	4	8
163	CITADEL MILITARY COLLEGE OF SOUTH CAROLINA	Public	3	6
243	UNIVERSITY OF SOUTH CAROLINA AT AIKEN	Public	4	8
368	UNIVERSITY OF SOUTH CAROLINA AT SPARTANBURG	Public	5	6
419	COLUMBIA COLLEGE	Nonprofit	5	7
435	FRANCIS MARION UNIVERSITY	Public	5	5
554	ANDERSON COLLEGE	Nonprofit	4	7
620	SOUTH CAROLINA STATE UNIVERSITY	Public	5	8
621	COASTAL CAROLINA UNIVERSITY	Public	4	7
631	LANDER UNIVERSITY	Public	5	5
643	COLLEGE OF CHARLESTON	Public	3	6
667	CLEMSON UNIVERSITY	Public	3	5
669	UNIVERSITY OF SOUTH CAROLINA AT BEAUFORT	Public	4	7
672	COLUMBIA INTERNATIONAL UNIVERSITY	Nonprofit	5	5
683	NORTH GREENVILLE COLLEGE	Nonprofit	5	6
697	WINTHROP UNIVERSITY	Public	4	6
698	CHARLESTON SOUTHERN UNIVERSITY	Nonprofit	3	6
730	CLAFLIN UNIVERSITY	Nonprofit	4	5
789	BENEDICT COLLEGE	Nonprofit	3	5
801	MORRIS COLLEGE	Nonprofit	3	2

UNRANKED: Allen University, Art Institute of Charleston, Bob Jones University, Coker College, Columbia Junior College, Converse College, Erskine College and Seminary, Furman University, Limestone College, Newberry College, Presbyterian College, Southern Wesleyan University, Voorhees College, Wofford College

Two Year Colleges

Rank	Name	Sector	Ease of transfer	Flexibility of programs
111	TRIDENT TECHNICAL COLLEGE	Public	4	7
140	UNIVERSITY OF SOUTH CAROLINA AT LANCASTER	Public	4	4
206	GREENVILLE TECHNICAL COLLEGE	Public	4	6
359	MIDLANDS TECHNICAL COLLEGE	Public	4	6
364	PIEDMONT TECHNICAL COLLEGE	Public	4	6

Services for adult students (6 pts)	Percent of students over age 25	Graduation rate of part-time students	Mean earnings of independent students 10 years after college entry	Loan repayment of independent students 5 years after leaving college	In-district tuition and fees (at a 9 month rate for 2 year colleges)	Percent of credentials awarded as bachelor's degrees
6	37%	33%	33,731	60%	4,266	0%
6	6%	45%	59,425	61%	11,454	100%
4	9%	100%	70,684	65%	11,734	100%
6	16%	35%	44,176	57%	10,196	100%
5	19%	38%	43,836	55%	11,190	100%
5	50%	38%	36,023	43%	28,900	100%
6	10%	46%	40,402	47%	10,428	100%
5	16%	51%	41,825	55%	25,880	100%
5	9%	27%	32,167	31%	10,420	100%
5	8%	34%	37,732	49%	10,876	100%
5	6%	43%	38,254	44%	11,200	99%
6	8%	30%	43,556	55%	11,805	100%
4	4%	43%	57,100	72%	14,708	97%
4	20%	26%	36,969	48%	10,166	99%
4	18%	40%	36,765	54%	21,490	85%
4	7%	31%	35,854	54%	17,594	100%
5	7%	26%	38,806	49%	14,810	100%
5	20%	36%	45,560	52%	24,140	100%
5	12%	50%	30,896	32%	16,158	100%
6	9%	47%	23,429	17%	19,566	100%
5	9%	33%	27,963	27%	13,045	100%
5	46%	26%	34,304	38%	4,155	0%
5	13%	23%	50,438	61%	6,702	0%
6	36%	17%	33,459	37%	4,326	0%
4	36%	20%	33,465	39%	4,064	0%
5	39%	23%	28,279	33%	4,193	0%

SOUTH CAROLINA

Rank	Name	Sector	Ease of transfer (5 pts for 4 year, 4 pts for 2 year)	Flexibility of programs (9 pts)
414	HORRY-GEORGETOWN TECHNICAL COLLEGE	Public	3	7
459	FLORENCE DARLINGTON TECHNICAL COLLEGE	Public	3	7
478	CENTRAL CAROLINA TECHNICAL COLLEGE	Public	4	5
479	ORANGEBURG CALHOUN TECHNICAL COLLEGE	Public	4	6
493	AIKEN TECHNICAL COLLEGE	Public	4	7
539	YORK TECHNICAL COLLEGE	Public	3	5
586	UNIVERSITY OF SOUTH CAROLINA AT SUMTER	Public	3	5
617	SPARTANBURG TECHNICAL COLLEGE	Public	2	6
639	TECHNICAL COLLEGE OF THE LOWCOUNTRY	Public	1	7
683	TRI-COUNTY TECHNICAL COLLEGE	Public	4	3
689	DENMARK TECHNICAL COLLEGE	Public	4	5
692	WILLIAMSBURG TECHNICAL COLLEGE	Public	4	6
732	NORTHEASTERN TECHNICAL COLLEGE	Public	3	5
744	UNIVERSITY OF SOUTH CAROLINA AT UNION	Public	3	4
754	UNIVERSITY OF SOUTH CAROLINA AT SALKEHATCHIE	Public	2	4
771	GOLF ACADEMY OF THE CAROLINAS	For-Profit	0	3
781	VIRGINIA COLLEGE–GREENVILLE	For-Profit	0	2

UNRANKED: Brown Mackie College–Greenville, Clinton Junior College, Forrest Junior College, Medix School–Fortis College, Miller-Motte Technical College, Spartanburg Methodist College

South Dakota

FOUR YEAR COLLEGES

Rank	Name	Sector	Ease of transfer	Flexibility
264	UNIVERSITY OF SOUTH DAKOTA	Public	4	5
340	MOUNT MARTY COLLEGE	Nonprofit	5	8
356	SOUTH DAKOTA STATE UNIVERSITY	Public	5	7
369	DAKOTA STATE UNIVERSITY	Public	5	6
440	AUGUSTANA COLLEGE	Nonprofit	5	8
447	DAKOTA WESLEYAN UNIVERSITY	Nonprofit	5	6
542	NATIONAL AMERICAN UNIVERSITY	For-Profit	3	7

UNRANKED: Black Hills State University, Northern State University, University of Sioux Falls

TWO YEAR COLLEGES

Rank	Name	Sector	Ease of transfer	Flexibility
98	SOUTHEAST TECHNICAL INSTITUTE	Public	4	6
377	WESTERN DAKOTA TECHNICAL INSTITUTE	Public	4	3
554	MITCHELL TECHNICAL INSTITUTE	Public	3	3

UNRANKED: Globe University–Sioux Falls, Lake Area Technical Institute, National American Institute

Services for adult students (6 pts)	Percent of students over age 25	Graduation rate of part-time students	Mean earnings of independent students 10 years after college entry	Loan repayment of independent students 5 years after leaving college	In-district tuition and fees (at a 9 month rate for 2 year colleges)	Percent of credentials awarded as bachelor's degrees
5	37%	27%	29,595	34%	4,978	0%
5	36%	22%	28,752	33%	4,174	0%
4	39%	26%	29,758	34%	4,639	0%
5	30%	21%	28,205	28%	4,130	0%
5	38%	26%	29,962	0%	4,348	0%
5	37%	23%	28,617	36%	4,464	0%
5	20%	11%	36,516	42%	6,702	0%
5	30%	15%	28,374	45%	4,300	0%
4	44%	17%	30,836	40%	4,276	0%
3	19%	21%	29,624	36%	4,050	0%
4	39%	3%	21,758	19%	4,456	0%
4	29%	16%	23,994	0%	4,080	0%
3	32%	29%	26,634	0%	4,090	0%
3	6%	6%	34,345	34%	6,702	0%
4	13%	17%	26,634	31%	6,702	0%
1	46%	68%	29,468	18%	17,150	0%
1	59%	36%	29,468	18%	14,632	0%
6	17%	45%	53,847	63%	8,457	98%
6	18%	26%	38,049	59%	25,380	85%
4	10%	33%	48,641	65%	8,172	95%
5	27%	26%	37,302	63%	8,927	80%
5	5%	33%	43,901	71%	30,944	100%
5	17%	64%	34,068	59%	26,050	79%
4	84%	17%	43,240	37%	13,914	47%
4	31%	47%	37,408	57%	5,980	0%
5	40%	37%	32,522	40%	6,489	0%
4	23%	29%	40,036	51%	6,432	0%

Tennessee

Four Year Colleges

Rank	Name	Sector	Ease of transfer (5 pts for 4 year, 4 pts for 2 year)	Flexibility of programs (9 pts)
90	THE UNIVERSITY OF TENNESSEE	Public	5	7
114	TUSCULUM COLLEGE	Nonprofit	4	9
123	EAST TENNESSEE STATE UNIVERSITY	Public	5	8
176	UNIVERSITY OF MEMPHIS	Public	5	8
183	THE UNIVERSITY OF TENNESSEE–CHATTANOOGA	Public	5	8
202	MIDDLE TENNESSEE STATE UNIVERSITY	Public	5	7
257	AUSTIN PEAY STATE UNIVERSITY	Public	5	8
364	THE UNIVERSITY OF TENNESSEE–MARTIN	Public	5	6
456	TENNESSEE TECHNOLOGICAL UNIVERSITY	Public	5	5
478	TENNESSEE STATE UNIVERSITY	Public	5	4
538	TENNESSEE WESLEYAN COLLEGE	Nonprofit	5	5
601	CHRISTIAN BROTHERS UNIVERSITY	Nonprofit	5	9
635	CUMBERLAND UNIVERSITY	Nonprofit	5	6
689	SOUTHERN ADVENTIST UNIVERSITY	Nonprofit	4	6
710	LEE UNIVERSITY	Nonprofit	5	4
721	LINCOLN MEMORIAL UNIVERSITY	Nonprofit	3	6
734	LE MOYNE–OWEN COLLEGE	Nonprofit	5	5
744	CARSON–NEWMAN COLLEGE	Nonprofit	4	5

UNRANKED: Belmont University, Bethel College, Bryan College, David Lipscomb University, Fisk University, Free Will Baptist Bible College, Freed-Hardeman University, King College, Knoxville Business College, Lane College, Martin Methodist College, Maryville College, Rhodes College, Strayer University–Memphis Campus, Trevecca Nazarene University, Union University, University of the South, Vanderbilt University

Two Year Colleges

Rank	Name	Sector	Ease of transfer (5 pts for 4 year, 4 pts for 2 year)	Flexibility of programs (9 pts)
174	VOLUNTEER STATE COMMUNITY COLLEGE	Public	4	8
221	CHATTANOOGA STATE TECHNICAL COMMUNITY COLLEGE	Public	3	9
266	NASHVILLE STATE TECHNICAL INSTITUTE	Public	4	6
398	WALTERS STATE COMMUNITY COLLEGE	Public	3	8
430	CLEVELAND STATE COMMUNITY COLLEGE	Public	4	5
444	DYERSBURG STATE COMMUNITY COLLEGE	Public	4	6
451	SOUTHWEST TENNESSEE COMMUNITY COLLEGE–UNION CAMPUS	Public	4	8
528	NORTHEAST STATE TECHNICAL COMMUNITY COLLEGE	Public	3	7
537	ROANE STATE COMMUNITY COLLEGE	Public	3	6
571	COLUMBIA STATE COMMUNITY COLLEGE	Public	3	6
609	PELLISSIPPI STATE TECHNICAL COMMUNITY COLLEGE	Public	3	7

Services for adult students (6 pts)	Percent of students over age 25	Graduation rate of part-time students	Mean earnings of independent students 10 years after college entry	Loan repayment of independent students 5 years after leaving college	In-district tuition and fees (at a 9 month rate for 2 year colleges)	Percent of credentials awarded as bachelor's degrees
6	7%	38%	63,667	61%	12,668	100%
5	34%	61%	49,099	57%	23,125	100%
6	20%	44%	39,652	51%	8,341	100%
6	24%	42%	42,519	38%	9,125	100%
6	13%	31%	43,263	55%	8,544	100%
6	21%	35%	41,535	53%	8,280	99%
5	31%	28%	39,700	46%	7,689	83%
6	18%	37%	37,001	47%	9,088	100%
5	11%	37%	41,580	63%	8,203	100%
5	26%	52%	42,827	42%	7,256	90%
5	20%	41%	42,804	61%	23,000	100%
5	15%	8%	47,262	44%	30,860	99%
4	19%	41%	39,049	50%	21,210	99%
4	12%	31%	45,976	58%	21,150	70%
4	22%	33%	36,831	46%	15,770	100%
3	25%	46%	42,016	60%	21,050	67%
5	31%	0%	34,146	22%	10,880	100%
4	5%	50%	38,651	51%	26,360	99%
5	24%	17%	33,665	49%	4,037	0%
6	32%	18%	31,809	36%	4,063	0%
5	41%	18%	34,439	33%	3,969	0%
5	19%	27%	28,646	48%	4,032	0%
5	25%	21%	30,843	42%	4,043	0%
5	25%	21%	28,249	38%	4,229	0%
6	35%	12%	29,259	0%	4,059	0%
4	30%	24%	29,566	38%	4,056	0%
4	25%	21%	31,442	48%	4,047	0%
4	22%	17%	32,652	43%	4,015	0%
3	24%	19%	30,768	43%	4,084	0%

Rank	Name	Sector	Ease of transfer (5 pts for 4 year, 4 pts for 2 year)	Flexibility of programs (9 pts)
644	MOTLOW STATE COMMUNITY COLLEGE	Public	3	5
721	JACKSON STATE COMMUNITY COLLEGE	Public	3	6
774	DRAUGHONS JUNIOR COLLEGE–MURFREESBORO	For-Profit	0	4
783	DRAUGHONS JUNIOR COLLEGE	For-Profit	0	2
784	VIRGINIA COLLEGE–SCHOOL OF BUSINESS AND HEALTH	For-Profit	0	1

UNRANKED: Concorde Career Institute, Electronic Computer Programming Inc., Fugazzi College of Business and Technology–Nashville, Hiwasse College, L'Ecole Culinaire, Medvance Instituet–Cookeville, MedVance Institute–Nashville, Miller-Motte Technical College, Miller-Motte Technical College–Chattanooga, Miller-Mottle Technical College–Goodlettsville, Nashville Auto Diesel College Inc, Remington College–Nashville Campus, SAE Institute of Technology, Southeast College of Technology, Southeastern Paralegal Institute, Vatterot College–Memphis, West Tennessee Business College, William Moore College of Technology

Texas

FOUR YEAR COLLEGES

Rank	Name	Sector	Ease of transfer	Flexibility of programs
28	THE UNIVERSITY OF TEXAS AT AUSTIN	Public	4	7
75	THE UNIVERSITY OF TEXAS AT ARLINGTON	Public	4	7
93	UNIVERSITY OF HOUSTON–UNIVERSITY PARK	Public	4	7
96	SOUTHERN METHODIST UNIVERSITY	Nonprofit	4	8
108	THE UNIVERSITY OF TEXAS OF THE PERMIAN BASIN	Public	5	7
110	UNIVERSITY OF HOUSTON–DOWNTOWN	Public	4	7
126	STEPHEN F AUSTIN STATE UNIVERSITY	Public	5	8
133	TEXAS WOMAN'S UNIVERSITY	Public	5	6
134	TEXAS A & M UNIVERSITY–COMMERCE	Public	4	8
160	UNIVERSITY OF THE INCARNATE WORD	Nonprofit	5	7
171	THE UNIVERSITY OF TEXAS AT DALLAS	Public	3	8
177	UNIVERSITY OF HOUSTON–CLEAR LAKE	Public	4	5
210	SOUTHWEST TEXAS STATE UNIVERSITY	Public	4	8
219	TEXAS A & M UNIVERSITY	Public	3	5
230	UNIVERSITY OF NORTH TEXAS	Public	5	6
236	TEXAS TECH UNIVERSITY	Public	5	7
288	UNIVERSITY OF ST THOMAS	Nonprofit	5	8
311	THE UNIVERSITY OF TEXAS AT EL PASO	Public	5	5
360	TARLETON STATE UNIVERSITY	Public	4	6
362	EAST TEXAS BAPTIST UNIVERSITY	Nonprofit	5	9
366	TEXAS WESLEYAN UNIVERSITY	Nonprofit	5	8
391	WEST TEXAS A & M UNIVERSITY	Public	3	7
441	TEXAS A & M UNIVERSITY–TEXARKANA	Public	3	6
453	TEXAS A & M UNIVERSITY–CORPUS CHRISTI	Public	4	7
462	SUL ROSS STATE UNIVERSITY	Public	5	4
483	PRAIRIE VIEW A & M UNIVERSITY	Public	3	8

Services for adult students (6 pts)	Percent of students over age 25	Graduation rate of part-time students	Mean earnings of independent students 10 years after college entry	Loan repayment of independent students 5 years after leaving college	In-district tuition and fees (at a 9 month rate for 2 year colleges)	Percent of credentials awarded as bachelor's degrees
4	18%	15%	28,950	50%	4,051	0%
4	20%	20%	29,386	0%	4,029	0%
2	62%	26%	24,476	23%	15,000	0%
1	78%	22%	24,476	23%	15,000	13%
1	61%	30%	29,468	18%	14,236	0%

TEXAS

6	4%	64%	69,581	72%	10,092	81%
5	48%	48%	53,055	60%	9,616	98%
6	18%	42%	62,202	63%	9,519	100%
6	3%	64%	90,725	70%	50,358	100%
5	26%	43%	50,216	58%	5,774	100%
5	51%	44%	51,640	51%	6,009	100%
6	10%	43%	43,125	56%	7,716	100%
5	31%	43%	51,107	61%	7,322	100%
6	32%	52%	39,619	48%	7,750	100%
5	38%	57%	54,526	53%	28,898	98%
5	20%	62%	57,026	65%	11,192	100%
4	50%	65%	52,925	60%	6,502	100%
5	14%	56%	47,744	60%	9,605	100%
5	3%	74%	70,305	76%	10,132	100%
5	15%	55%	48,137	57%	10,153	100%
4	10%	49%	55,124	60%	8,428	98%
5	26%	30%	58,964	53%	31,520	100%
5	24%	47%	44,340	54%	7,348	100%
6	22%	30%	45,750	56%	7,140	98%
5	7%	50%	41,313	48%	24,700	95%
5	30%	37%	43,063	46%	26,050	100%
5	22%	50%	46,025	60%	7,444	100%
4	43%	63%	38,009	58%	6,840	100%
4	16%	47%	46,630	58%	8,424	100%
5	32%	42%	39,863	48%	6,419	99%
5	12%	59%	45,710	46%	10,059	100%

Rank	Name	Sector	Ease of transfer (5 pts for 4 year, 4 pts for 2 year)	Flexibility of programs (9 pts)
484	THE UNIVERSITY OF TEXAS AT SAN ANTONIO	Public	3	7
537	TEXAS CHRISTIAN UNIVERSITY	Nonprofit	4	7
597	BAYLOR UNIVERSITY	Nonprofit	5	7
604	TEXAS SOUTHERN UNIVERSITY	Public	4	7
609	TEXAS A & M INTERNATIONAL UNIVERSITY	Public	4	5
633	UNIVERSITY OF MARY HARDIN–BAYLOR	Nonprofit	5	5
637	OUR LADY OF THE LAKE UNIVERSITY–SAN ANTONIO	Nonprofit	4	8
646	SAINT EDWARD'S UNIVERSITY	Nonprofit	4	5
678	ANGELO STATE UNIVERSITY	Public	4	4
686	TEXAS A & M UNIVERSITY–KINGSVILLE	Public	3	6
708	LUBBOCK CHRISTIAN UNIVERSITY	Nonprofit	3	3
709	MCMURRY UNIVERSITY	Nonprofit	4	7
729	SCHREINER COLLEGE	Nonprofit	5	6
774	HOWARD PAYNE UNIVERSITY	Nonprofit	5	6
775	HOUSTON BAPTIST UNIVERSITY	Nonprofit	4	4
778	ABILENE CHRISTIAN UNIVERSITY	Nonprofit	4	7
799	TEXAS LUTHERAN UNIVERSITY	Nonprofit	4	3

UNRANKED: Amber University, Art Institute of San Antonio, Austin College, Concordia University at Austin, Dallas Baptist University, Hardin Simmons University, Huston-Tilloston College, Jarvis Christian College, Lamar University Beaumont, Letourneau University, Midwestern State University, Paul Quinn College, Rice University, Sam Houston State University, Southwestern Adventist University, Southwestern Assemblies of God University, Southwestern University, Strayer University–Texas, Texas College, University of Dallas, University of Houston–Victoria, University of Texas at Tyler, Wayland Baptist University, Wiley College

Two Year Colleges

Rank	Name	Sector	Ease of transfer	Flexibility of programs
14	CENTRAL TEXAS COLLEGE	Public	4	8
84	NORTH LAKE COLLEGE	Public	4	8
134	DEL MAR COLLEGE	Public	3	8
139	ODESSA COLLEGE	Public	4	6
145	SAN ANTONIO COLLEGE	Public	4	6
149	ST PHILIPS COLLEGE	Public	3	8
204	SAN JACINTO COLLEGE–CENTRAL CAMPUS	Public	3	6
223	COLLIN COUNTY COMMUNITY COLLEGE–CENTRAL PARK	Public	3	6
234	CEDAR VALLEY COLLEGE	Public	4	8
263	VICTORIA COLLEGE	Public	4	6
286	TEMPLE COLLEGE	Public	4	5
332	HOUSTON COMMUNITY COLLEGE SYSTEM	Public	2	7
347	AUSTIN COMMUNITY COLLEGE	Public	3	7
358	NORTHWEST VISTA COLLEGE	Public	4	6
382	EL CENTRO COLLEGE	Public	3	6
386	RICHLAND COLLEGE	Public	3	6

Services for adult students (6 pts)	Percent of students over age 25	Graduation rate of part-time students	Mean earnings of independent students 10 years after college entry	Loan repayment of independent students 5 years after leaving college	In-district tuition and fees (at a 9 month rate for 2 year colleges)	Percent of credentials awarded as bachelor's degrees
5	16%	44%	49,556	56%	7,700	100%
5	5%	45%	63,772	71%	42,670	99%
5	2%	40%	54,074	58%	42,006	100%
5	27%	21%	44,846	33%	8,476	100%
4	14%	53%	43,869	53%	7,016	100%
4	17%	41%	48,627	56%	24,880	100%
5	25%	23%	44,475	42%	27,160	100%
5	14%	49%	58,672	62%	40,928	100%
5	10%	26%	43,194	58%	7,047	93%
4	18%	42%	43,899	48%	8,049	100%
5	20%	46%	49,567	63%	21,166	100%
4	19%	23%	39,167	55%	26,100	100%
4	15%	13%	37,077	53%	25,750	88%
3	10%	24%	36,680	40%	26,630	99%
5	11%	14%	49,750	46%	30,800	100%
4	3%	0%	43,091	57%	32,070	100%
4	7%	0%	40,500	56%	28,910	100%
6	54%	9%	37,044	44%	2,280	0%
5	36%	10%	39,388	41%	1,770	0%
6	35%	18%	35,045	45%	2,546	0%
5	28%	21%	39,688	46%	2,808	0%
6	33%	12%	35,990	42%	2,188	0%
6	36%	18%	34,073	41%	2,188	0%
6	27%	22%	40,367	39%	1,500	0%
6	27%	14%	40,437	42%	1,264	0%
5	41%	12%	31,411	27%	1,770	0%
4	30%	23%	38,640	41%	2,640	0%
5	37%	21%	34,741	36%	2,136	0%
5	46%	18%	37,907	34%	1,632	0%
4	36%	11%	38,919	42%	2,550	0%
4	22%	16%	37,704	42%	2,188	0%
5	42%	11%	34,745	36%	1,770	0%
5	33%	13%	38,347	34%	1,770	0%

Rank	Name	Sector	Ease of transfer (5 pts for 4 year, 4 pts for 2 year)	Flexibility of programs (9 pts)
387	PALO ALTO COLLEGE	Public	3	7
474	WESTERN TEXAS COLLEGE	Public	4	4
481	MCLENNAN COMMUNITY COLLEGE	Public	3	4
486	MOUNTAIN VIEW COLLEGE	Public	3	7
491	FRANK PHILLIPS COLLEGE	Public	4	5
498	GRAYSON COUNTY COLLEGE	Public	3	3
502	TARRANT COUNTY COLLEGE	Public	2	6
514	BRAZOSPORT COLLEGE	Public	2	5
521	EL PASO COMMUNITY COLLEGE	Public	3	7
532	SOUTHWEST TEXAS JUNIOR COLLEGE	Public	4	3
542	SOUTH TEXAS COMMUNITY COLLEGE	Public	3	7
555	SOUTH PLAINS COLLEGE	Public	3	5
574	BROOKHAVEN COLLEGE	Public	1	6
597	LAREDO COMMUNITY COLLEGE	Public	2	6
603	TYLER JUNIOR COLLEGE	Public	2	4
612	EASTFIELD COLLEGE	Public	2	7
622	LAMAR STATE COLLEGE–PORT ARTHUR	Public	4	3
630	PANOLA COLLEGE	Public	3	3
637	COLLEGE OF THE MAINLAND	Public	3	4
659	TRINITY VALLEY COMMUNITY COLLEGE	Public	3	3
667	BLINN COLLEGE	Public	3	5
681	AMARILLO COLLEGE	Public	0	5
702	PARIS JUNIOR COLLEGE	Public	1	6
709	WHARTON COUNTY JUNIOR COLLEGE	Public	2	2
712	NORTHEAST TEXAS COMMUNITY COLLEGE	Public	4	4
727	TEXARKANA COLLEGE	Public	3	4
741	NAVARRO COLLEGE	Public	1	4
780	VIRGINIA COLLEGE–AUSTIN	For-Profit	0	2

UNRANKED: Academy of Healthcare Professionals, Alvin Community College, Angelina College, Bradford School of Business, Brown Mackie College–San Antonio, Career Advancement Center, Career Centers of Texas–El Paso, Career Centers of Texas–Brownsville, Career Centers of Texas–Corpus Christi, Career Centers of Texas–Fort Worth, Cisco Junior College, Clarendon College, Coastal Bend College, Commonwealth Institute Funeral Center, Computer Career College, Concorde Career Institute–Dallas, Concorde Career Institute–San Antonio, Education America–Denver North Campus, Education America–Fort Worth Campus, Everest College, Everest College–Fort Worth South, Extended Health Education, Galveston College, Hallmark Institute of Technology, Health Institute–San Antonio, Hill College, Howard County Junior College District, Jacksonville College–Main Campus, KD Studio, Kaplan College–Arlington, Kilgore College, Lamar Institute of Technology, Lamar State College–Orange, Le Cordon Bleu Institute of Culinary Arts–Dallas, Lee College, Midland College, North Central Texas College, North Harris Montgomery Community College District, North Texas Professional Career Institute, Pima Medical Institute–Houston, Ranger College, Remington College–North Houston Campus, San Antonio College of Medical and Dental Assistant–Central, San Antonio College of Medical and Dental Assistants–South, Southeastern Paralegal Institute, Southwest Career Institute, Southwest College Institute for the Deaf, Southwestern Christian College, Texas Careers, Texas Careers–Beumont, Texas Careers–Laredo, Texas Culinary Academy, Ultrasound Diagnostic School, Vernon Regional College, Wade College, Weatherford College, Western Technical Institute

Services for adult students (6 pts)	Percent of students over age 25	Graduation rate of part-time students	Mean earnings of independent students 10 years after college entry	Loan repayment of independent students 5 years after leaving college	In-district tuition and fees (at a 9 month rate for 2 year colleges)	Percent of credentials awarded as bachelor's degrees
6	25%	11%	31,512	40%	2,188	0%
5	16%	14%	35,935	44%	2,018	0%
6	32%	25%	32,760	32%	2,760	0%
5	28%	10%	34,780	28%	1,770	0%
5	13%	17%	34,466	39%	3,052	0%
5	33%	24%	36,868	40%	1,956	0%
5	33%	10%	38,181	40%	1,416	0%
5	31%	21%	36,545	45%	2,385	5%
4	25%	20%	29,966	44%	2,746	0%
6	20%	17%	30,365	37%	2,116	0%
6	17%	32%	34,039	0%	3,606	4%
4	24%	13%	36,554	44%	2,240	0%
4	43%	9%	41,108	42%	1,770	0%
5	18%	21%	33,694	45%	3,780	0%
5	24%	29%	36,259	36%	2,634	0%
4	33%	11%	34,907	29%	1,770	0%
4	31%	20%	33,192	29%	5,698	0%
3	31%	37%	34,965	29%	1,824	0%
5	31%	24%	36,123	0%	1,773	0%
3	44%	14%	33,126	35%	2,460	0%
3	9%	7%	38,010	42%	2,424	0%
5	32%	18%	36,257	40%	2,010	0%
5	22%	14%	31,309	28%	1,836	0%
3	18%	19%	40,565	46%	2,222	0%
3	28%	23%	30,062	0%	2,682	0%
4	29%	14%	30,700	0%	2,116	0%
3	22%	25%	34,913	32%	2,400	0%
1	55%	46%	29,468	18%	14,632	0%

Rank	Name	Sector	Ease of transfer (5 pts for 4 year, 4 pts for 2 year)	Flexibility of programs (9 pts)

Utah

FOUR YEAR COLLEGES

Rank	Name	Sector	Ease of transfer	Flexibility
1	UNIVERSITY OF UTAH	Public	4	8
21	WEBER STATE UNIVERSITY	Public	4	9
79	UTAH STATE UNIVERSITY	Public	4	7
198	WESTMINSTER COLLEGE	Nonprofit	5	9
213	BRIGHAM YOUNG UNIVERSITY	Nonprofit	3	4
234	SOUTHERN UTAH UNIVERSITY	Public	5	7

UNRANKED: Stevens-Henager College of Business–Murray, Stevens-Henager College of Business–Provo, University of Phoenix–Utah Campus, Utah Valley State College, Western Governors University

TWO YEAR COLLEGES

Rank	Name	Sector	Ease of transfer	Flexibility
102	DIXIE STATE COLLEGE OF UTAH	Public	3	8
301	SALT LAKE COMMUNITY COLLEGE	Public	2	5
321	LATTER DAY SAINTS BUSINESS COLLEGE	Nonprofit	3	4
419	SNOW COLLEGE	Public	4	3

UNRANKED: Certified Careers Institute, Eagle Gate College, Intermountain College of Court Reporting, National Institute of Technology–Fortis College, Provo College

Vermont

FOUR YEAR COLLEGES

Rank	Name	Sector	Ease of transfer	Flexibility
83	JOHNSON STATE COLLEGE	Public	5	8
388	UNIVERSITY OF VERMONT AND STATE AGRICULTURAL COLLEGE	Public	3	6
412	CASTLETON STATE COLLEGE	Public	4	6
463	CHAMPLAIN COLLEGE	Nonprofit	4	6
539	LYNDON STATE COLLEGE	Public	4	9
567	COLLEGE OF ST JOSEPH	Nonprofit	5	5

UNRANKED: Bennington College, Goddard College, Green Mountain College, Marlboro College, Middlebury College, Norwich University, Saint Michaels College, Southern Vermont College, Sterling College

TWO YEAR COLLEGES

Rank	Name	Sector	Ease of transfer	Flexibility
6	VERMONT TECHNICAL COLLEGE	Public	4	5
475	COMMUNITY COLLEGE OF VERMONT	Public	3	7

UNRANKED: Landmark College

Services for adult students (6 pts)	Percent of students over age 25	Graduation rate of part-time students	Mean earnings of independent students 10 years after college entry	Loan repayment of independent students 5 years after leaving college	In-district tuition and fees (at a 9 month rate for 2 year colleges)	Percent of credentials awarded as bachelor's degrees
6	27%	66%	66,381	77%	8,518	100%
6	29%	35%	51,777	73%	5,523	52%
6	21%	38%	51,877	76%	6,866	74%
4	16%	48%	56,860	73%	32,104	100%
4	13%	67%	76,178	87%	5,300	100%
4	26%	25%	47,571	72%	6,530	61%
5	23%	33%	41,308	52%	4,840	34%
5	35%	18%	43,160	63%	3,690	0%
3	26%	34%	40,759	73%	3,240	0%
6	8%	15%	37,798	53%	3,592	3%
5	33%	54%	35,479	62%	11,290	93%
5	7%	66%	56,215	73%	17,300	100%
4	9%	61%	42,152	79%	11,314	79%
5	36%	45%	49,629	72%	38,660	72%
5	8%	29%	35,670	51%	11,290	89%
5	12%	50%	37,944	60%	22,650	82%
4	38%	71%	46,399	76%	14,026	23%
4	45%	17%	27,701	48%	6,222	0%

Rank	Name		Sector	Ease of transfer (5 pts for 4 year, 4 pts for 2 year)	Flexibility of programs (9 pts)

Virginia

FOUR YEAR COLLEGES

Rank	Name	Sector	Ease of transfer	Flexibility of programs
4	GEORGE MASON UNIVERSITY	Public	4	8
46	VIRGINIA COMMONWEALTH UNIVERSITY	Public	5	7
61	UNIVERSITY OF VIRGINIA–MAIN CAMPUS	Public	3	7
70	COLLEGE OF WILLIAM AND MARY	Public	3	7
82	OLD DOMINION UNIVERSITY	Public	4	8
164	MARY WASHINGTON COLLEGE	Public	4	8
173	LIBERTY UNIVERSITY	Nonprofit	5	9
194	BLUEFIELD COLLEGE	Nonprofit	4	6
208	VIRGINIA POLYTECHNIC INSTITUTE AND STATE UNIVERSITY	Public	5	5
212	SHENANDOAH UNIVERSITY	Nonprofit	5	9
343	RADFORD UNIVERSITY	Public	5	4
445	EASTERN MENNONITE UNIVERSITY	Nonprofit	5	5
563	ROANOKE COLLEGE	Nonprofit	4	6
587	MARYMOUNT UNIVERSITY	Nonprofit	3	7
590	NORFOLK STATE UNIVERSITY	Public	4	5
641	LYNCHBURG COLLEGE	Nonprofit	4	5
660	CHRISTOPHER NEWPORT UNIVERSITY	Public	5	6
736	VIRGINIA STATE UNIVERSITY	Public	4	4
749	MARY BALDWIN COLLEGE	Nonprofit	4	3
760	VIRGINIA WESLEYAN COLLEGE	Nonprofit	4	6
765	VIRGINIA UNION UNIVERSITY	Nonprofit	4	5

UNRANKED: Art Institute of Virginia Beach, Averett College, Bridgewater College, Emory and Henry College, Ferrum College, Hampden-Sydney College, Hampton University, Hollins University, James Madison University, Longwood College, Randolph-Macon College, Randolph-Macon Woman's College, Regent University, South University–Virginia Beach, Southern Virginia College, Stratford College, Strayer University–Arlington Campus, Sweet Briar College, University of Management and Technology, University of Richmond, University of Virginia's College at Wise, Virginia Military Institute, Washington and Lee University

TWO YEAR COLLEGES

Rank	Name	Sector	Ease of transfer	Flexibility of programs
16	ECPI COLLEGE OF TECHNOLOGY	For-Profit	3	7
160	PIEDMONT VIRGINIA COMMUNITY COLLEGE	Public	4	7
261	TIDEWATER COMMUNITY COLLEGE	Public	3	6
385	WYTHEVILLE COMMUNITY COLLEGE	Public	3	6
418	DANVILLE COMMUNITY COLLEGE	Public	3	7
447	BRYANT AND STRATTON COLLEGE–VIRGINIA BEACH	For-Profit	4	6
500	THOMAS NELSON COMMUNITY COLLEGE	Public	3	6

Services for adult students (6 pts)	Percent of students over age 25	Graduation rate of part-time students	Mean earnings of independent students 10 years after college entry	Loan repayment of independent students 5 years after leaving college	In-district tuition and fees (at a 9 month rate for 2 year colleges)	Percent of credentials awarded as bachelor's degrees
6	21%	58%	66,522	75%	11,300	100%
6	14%	60%	55,952	56%	13,130	100%
5	5%	71%	82,590	76%	15,164	99%
6	1%	83%	66,456	76%	18,687	100%
6	27%	51%	50,062	54%	9,750	100%
5	9%	52%	53,654	70%	11,630	98%
4	59%	36%	41,582	42%	16,410	82%
4	31%	100%	52,495	60%	24,380	100%
4	2%	71%	63,680	71%	12,852	99%
4	14%	63%	52,807	63%	31,322	98%
5	5%	64%	45,147	68%	10,081	98%
4	25%	40%	55,624	83%	34,200	98%
4	3%	100%	43,206	72%	41,304	100%
3	21%	56%	61,101	72%	29,350	99%
6	25%	37%	40,464	34%	8,738	100%
5	7%	82%	42,433	56%	36,620	100%
3	1%	29%	45,931	67%	13,054	100%
4	12%	47%	38,339	37%	8,472	100%
3	39%	52%	39,997	57%	30,635	100%
4	11%	33%	38,536	55%	35,610	100%
2	7%	100%	28,690	27%	17,034	100%
5	72%	67%	41,816	33%	14,775	30%
6	28%	17%	32,923	45%	4,558	0%
6	46%	17%	34,944	39%	5,299	0%
4	29%	34%	29,356	63%	4,493	0%
6	23%	27%	29,193	34%	4,455	0%
5	61%	38%	24,843	22%	15,994	23%
4	41%	15%	34,204	39%	4,544	0%

Rank	Name	Sector	Ease of transfer (5 pts for 4 year, 4 pts for 2 year)	Flexibility of programs (9 pts)
512	NORTHERN VIRGINIA COMMUNITY COLLEGE	Public	2	7
523	VIRGINIA WESTERN COMMUNITY COLLEGE	Public	3	7
531	BLUE RIDGE COMMUNITY COLLEGE	Public	3	6
557	NEW RIVER COMMUNITY COLLEGE	Public	3	5
560	J SARGEANT REYNOLDS COMMUNITY COLLEGE	Public	3	6
619	DABNEY S LANCASTER COMMUNITY COLLEGE	Public	3	5
624	JOHN TYLER COMMUNITY COLLEGE	Public	2	5
629	MOUNTAIN EMPIRE COMMUNITY COLLEGE	Public	4	8
640	PAUL D CAMP COMMUNITY COLLEGE	Public	4	6
658	GERMANNA COMMUNITY COLLEGE	Public	3	7
682	LORD FAIRFAX COMMUNITY COLLEGE	Public	3	6
685	BRYANT AND STRATTON COLLEGE–RICHMOND	For-Profit	2	7
713	SOUTHSIDE VIRGINIA COMMUNITY COLLEGE	Public	4	4
720	SOUTHWEST VIRGINIA COMMUNITY COLLEGE	Public	3	5
725	EASTERN SHORE COMMUNITY COLLEGE	Public	3	3
733	PATRICK HENRY COMMUNITY COLLEGE	Public	2	6
747	VIRGINIA HIGHLANDS COMMUNITY COLLEGE	Public	2	6
748	CENTRAL VIRGINIA COMMUNITY COLLEGE	Public	2	6
749	RAPPAHANNOCK COMMUNITY COLLEGE	Public	2	5

UNRANKED: Advanced Technology Institute, Beta Tech, Bryant & Stratton College–Hampton, Career Training Solutions, Columbia College, Global Health Nurse Training Services, Kee Business Institute, Lynchburg General Hospital School of Nursing, Miller-Motte Business College, National Business College, Richard Bland–The College of William and Mary, Richmond School of Health and Technology, Riverside Regional Med Center–School of Professional Nursing, Southside Regional Medical Center, Tidewater Tech, Virginia School of Technology

Washington

FOUR YEAR COLLEGES

Rank	Name	Sector	Ease of transfer	Flexibility of programs
8	CITY UNIVERSITY	Nonprofit	4	8
20	UNIVERSITY OF WASHINGTON–BOTHELL CAMPUS	Public	4	7
40	WASHINGTON STATE UNIVERSITY	Public	4	8
58	UNIVERSITY OF WASHINGTON–SEATTLE CAMPUS	Public	3	7
101	CENTRAL WASHINGTON UNIVERSITY	Public	4	6
124	UNIVERSITY OF WASHINGTON–TACOMA CAMPUS	Public	3	7
136	WESTERN WASHINGTON UNIVERSITY	Public	5	5
179	EVERGREEN STATE COLLEGE	Public	3	8
226	SAINT MARTINS COLLEGE	Nonprofit	5	5
512	HERITAGE COLLEGE	Nonprofit	4	8
530	PACIFIC LUTHERAN UNIVERSITY	Nonprofit	3	8
536	SEATTLE UNIVERSITY	Nonprofit	4	5

Services for adult students (6 pts)	Percent of students over age 25	Graduation rate of part-time students	Mean earnings of independent students 10 years after college entry	Loan repayment of independent students 5 years after leaving college	In-district tuition and fees (at a 9 month rate for 2 year colleges)	Percent of credentials awarded as bachelor's degrees
2	33%	18%	46,393	51%	5,313	0%
4	25%	25%	32,049	40%	5,093	0%
4	26%	17%	34,009	50%	5,132	0%
5	23%	16%	32,490	44%	4,464	0%
3	42%	18%	34,009	37%	4,766	0%
5	18%	15%	29,219	44%	4,478	0%
4	25%	19%	38,619	41%	4,473	0%
4	28%	18%	26,732	0%	4,478	0%
5	30%	16%	27,202	0%	4,453	0%
4	25%	17%	36,333	0%	4,681	0%
4	22%	21%	34,977	0%	4,507	0%
4	64%	22%	24,843	22%	16,679	28%
4	24%	27%	26,466	0%	4,463	0%
5	25%	20%	26,361	0%	4,463	0%
5	26%	33%	26,678	0%	4,538	0%
5	28%	19%	26,125	0%	4,473	0%
4	25%	17%	27,506	0%	4,478	0%
4	24%	14%	28,991	0%	4,598	0%
4	18%	22%	30,071	0%	4,588	0%
5	85%	46%	51,800	60%	16,748	95%
4	22%	78%	73,810	76%	10,690	100%
6	16%	58%	53,264	69%	11,041	96%
5	9%	73%	73,810	76%	10,753	100%
6	19%	67%	49,617	64%	7,719	98%
3	32%	68%	73,810	76%	10,831	100%
6	8%	60%	44,909	70%	7,653	97%
6	33%	57%	36,960	58%	7,398	100%
5	34%	74%	49,589	66%	34,356	100%
5	37%	29%	34,103	49%	19,122	95%
5	10%	60%	52,545	72%	39,450	99%
5	7%	61%	68,352	69%	41,265	100%

Rank	Name	Sector	Ease of transfer (5 pts for 4 year, 4 pts for 2 year)	Flexibility of programs (9 pts)
634	SEATTLE PACIFIC UNIVERSITY	Nonprofit	4	4
640	WHITWORTH COLLEGE	Nonprofit	5	8
694	GONZAGA UNIVERSITY	Nonprofit	5	3
809	UNIVERSITY OF PUGET SOUND	Nonprofit	5	5

UNRANKED: Digipen Institute of Technology, Eastern Washington University, Northwest College of the Assemblies of God, Walla Walla College, Whitman College

TWO YEAR COLLEGES

Rank	Name	Sector	Ease of transfer	Flexibility of programs
1	LAKE WASHINGTON TECHNICAL COLLEGE	Public	3	5
7	WALLA WALLA COMMUNITY COLLEGE	Public	4	6
18	SKAGIT VALLEY COLLEGE	Public	4	6
21	LOWER COLUMBIA COLLEGE	Public	4	8
27	OLYMPIC COLLEGE	Public	4	5
41	SPOKANE COMMUNITY COLLEGE	Public	2	7
56	TACOMA COMMUNITY COLLEGE	Public	4	4
57	WENATCHEE VALLEY COLLEGE	Public	4	7
58	SHORELINE COMMUNITY COLLEGE	Public	3	4
59	WHATCOM COMMUNITY COLLEGE	Public	3	8
63	GRAYS HARBOR COLLEGE	Public	4	7
70	BELLINGHAM TECHNICAL COLLEGE	Public	3	4
78	BELLEVUE COMMUNITY COLLEGE	Public	2	6
82	CLARK COLLEGE	Public	3	7
88	CASCADIA COMMUNITY COLLEGE	Public	4	6
104	PENINSULA COLLEGE	Public	4	4
113	HIGHLINE COMMUNITY COLLEGE	Public	3	8
130	SOUTH PUGET SOUND COMMUNITY COLLEGE	Public	3	7
142	PIERCE COLLEGE AT FORT STEILACOOM	Public	3	7
163	SEATTLE COMMUNITY COLLEGE–SOUTH CAMPUS	Public	4	6
167	YAKIMA VALLEY COMMUNITY COLLEGE	Public	4	6
184	EVERETT COMMUNITY COLLEGE	Public	3	6
245	BATES TECHNICAL COLLEGE	Public	2	5
246	SEATTLE COMMUNITY COLLEGE–NORTH CAMPUS	Public	3	5
275	SPOKANE FALLS COMMUNITY COLLEGE	Public	3	7
309	BIG BEND COMMUNITY COLLEGE	Public	3	5
362	COLUMBIA BASIN COLLEGE	Public	3	5
378	GREEN RIVER COMMUNITY COLLEGE	Public	3	5
396	CLOVER PARK TECHNICAL COLLEGE	Public	2	3
661	SEATTLE COMMUNITY COLLEGE–CENTRAL CAMPUS	Public	3	4

Services for adult students (6 pts)	Percent of students over age 25	Graduation rate of part-time students	Mean earnings of independent students 10 years after college entry	Loan repayment of independent students 5 years after leaving college	In-district tuition and fees (at a 9 month rate for 2 year colleges)	Percent of credentials awarded as bachelor's degrees
5	7%	67%	55,462	69%	38,940	92%
5	2%	33%	43,411	56%	40,562	100%
5	3%	38%	57,387	69%	39,730	100%
3	1%	0%	56,556	0%	46,552	100%
6	62%	46%	44,667	55%	4059	4%
6	54%	52%	34,807	46%	4,203	0%
6	47%	35%	35,483	53%	4,200	0%
5	44%	45%	35,079	41%	4,131	0%
6	47%	41%	35,110	52%	3,618	1%
6	68%	45%	35,417	38%	3,393	0%
6	45%	37%	38,780	42%	3,686	0%
5	31%	44%	35,446	44%	3,678	0%
6	40%	33%	45,117	54%	3,735	0%
6	26%	41%	35,853	51%	4,316	0%
6	48%	31%	31,103	35%	3,746	0%
4	57%	52%	40,153	55%	3,394	0%
5	32%	39%	47,764	61%	3,624	3%
6	33%	37%	37,902	43%	3,498	1%
4	17%	32%	49,539	50%	3,753	0%
6	50%	45%	31,048	39%	4,344	1%
5	32%	35%	39,185	43%	3,851	1%
6	37%	32%	35,282	42%	4,104	0%
5	43%	24%	38,343	44%	3,648	0%
6	59%	25%	37,627	0%	3,854	2%
5	33%	36%	34,165	40%	4,230	1%
6	32%	29%	38,177	41%	3,648	0%
5	69%	27%	38,030	40%	4,602	0%
6	62%	28%	41,979	0%	3,819	1%
6	32%	26%	32,415	36%	3,393	0%
5	28%	37%	35,785	48%	3,852	0%
4	34%	32%	36,729	52%	4,163	5%
5	26%	28%	39,218	43%	4,597	2%
4	67%	48%	36,894	38%	5,865	0%
4	45%	27%	33,428	0%	3,925	4%

Rank	Name		Sector	Ease of transfer (5 pts for 4 year, 4 pts for 2 year)	Flexibility of programs (9 pts)

UNRANKED: Apollo College–Spokane, Centralia College, Edmonds Community College, Eton Technical Institute, Eton Technical Institute–Tacoma Campus, Pierce College at Puyallup, Pima Medical Institute, Renton Technical College

West Virginia

Four Year Colleges

Rank	Name	Sector	Ease of transfer	Flexibility of programs
305	WEST VIRGINIA UNIVERSITY	Public	4	8
370	WHEELING JESUIT UNIVERSITY	Nonprofit	5	8
386	FAIRMONT STATE COLLEGE	Public	5	7
449	CONCORD COLLEGE	Public	4	7
473	SHEPHERD COLLEGE	Public	4	6
491	MARSHALL UNIVERSITY	Public	4	8
595	WEST VIRGINIA STATE COLLEGE	Public	5	5
606	UNIVERSITY OF CHARLESTON	Nonprofit	5	7
668	BLUEFIELD STATE COLLEGE	Public	5	4
727	ALDERSON BROADDUS COLLEGE	Nonprofit	4	6
751	GLENVILLE STATE COLLEGE	Public	5	5
762	WEST VIRGINIA UNIVERSITY INSTITUTE OF TECHNOLOGY	Public	3	4

UNRANKED: American Public University System, Bethany College, Davis and Elkins College, Ohio Valley College, Salem-Teikyo University, Strayer University–West Virginia, West Liberty State College, West Virginia Wesleyan College

Two Year Colleges

Rank	Name	Sector	Ease of transfer	Flexibility of programs
341	POTOMAC STATE COLLEGE OF WEST VIRGINIA UNIVERSITY	Public	4	4
567	WEST VIRGINIA NORTHERN COMMUNITY COLLEGE	Public	3	6

UNRANKED: Carver Career Center, Community and Technical College of Shepherd, Eastern West Virginia Communication and Tech College, Fairmont State Community and Technical College, Huntington Junior College, Marshall Community and Technical College, Southern West Virginia Community and Technology College, Valley College of Technology, West Virginia Business College, West Virginia Junior College, West Virginia Junior College–Bridgeport, West Virginia University at Parkersburg

Wisconsin

Four Year Colleges

Rank	Name	Sector	Ease of transfer	Flexibility of programs
25	VITERBO UNIVERSITY	Nonprofit	5	9
59	UNIVERSITY OF WISCONSIN–MILWAUKEE	Public	5	8
65	UNIVERSITY OF WISCONSIN–MADISON	Public	3	7
86	CARDINAL STRITCH UNIVERSITY	Nonprofit	5	7

Services for adult students (6 pts)	Percent of students over age 25	Graduation rate of part-time students	Mean earnings of independent students 10 years after college entry	Loan repayment of independent students 5 years after leaving college	In-district tuition and fees (at a 9 month rate for 2 year colleges)	Percent of credentials awarded as bachelor's degrees
6	5%	36%	48,325	50%	7,991	100%
4	16%	44%	49,923	64%	28,110	84%
6	23%	26%	36,205	38%	6,950	89%
5	16%	49%	35,667	53%	7,238	100%
5	24%	44%	41,079	51%	7,170	100%
5	15%	45%	39,716	37%	7,154	94%
6	23%	25%	32,585	35%	6,996	100%
4	35%	0%	47,130	54%	20,764	85%
4	36%	41%	31,345	34%	6,408	62%
5	6%	0%	55,801	54%	25,350	93%
5	22%	0%	27,275	28%	7,344	72%
4	17%	15%	48,325	50%	6,648	100%
5	10%	5%	48,325	50%	4,056	9%
4	37%	26%	28,519	31%	3,684	0%

5	26%	70%	52,113	65%	26,150	96%
6	22%	34%	48,911	61%	9,493	100%
6	5%	63%	68,952	76%	10,488	100%
5	52%	46%	56,099	59%	28,212	77%

Rank	Name	Sector	Ease of transfer (5 pts for 4 year, 4 pts for 2 year)	Flexibility of programs (9 pts)
95	UNIVERSITY OF WISCONSIN–STEVENS POINT	Public	5	8
120	UNIVERSITY OF WISCONSIN–WHITEWATER	Public	5	8
140	UNIVERSITY OF WISCONSIN–OSHKOSH	Public	4	8
161	MARIAN COLLEGE OF FOND DU LAC	Nonprofit	5	9
174	UNIVERSITY OF WISCONSIN–SUPERIOR	Public	5	8
184	MOUNT MARY COLLEGE	Nonprofit	5	9
309	UNIVERSITY OF WISCONSIN–STOUT	Public	5	6
322	UNIVERSITY OF WISCONSIN–PARKSIDE	Public	5	7
372	MILWAUKEE SCHOOL OF ENGINEERING	Nonprofit	5	6
400	UNIVERSITY OF WISCONSIN–LA CROSSE	Public	4	5
401	UNIVERSITY OF WISCONSIN–EAU CLAIRE	Public	4	5
404	UNIVERSITY OF WISCONSIN–RIVER FALLS	Public	4	4
405	UNIVERSITY OF WISCONSIN–PLATTEVILLE	Public	5	4
418	UNIVERSITY OF WISCONSIN–GREEN BAY	Public	4	5
540	MARQUETTE UNIVERSITY	Nonprofit	3	8
586	ALVERNO COLLEGE	Nonprofit	4	8
677	CARROLL COLLEGE	Nonprofit	5	8

UNRANKED: Beloit College, Carthage College, Concordia University–Wisconsin, Edgewood College, Herzing University–Brookfield, Lakeland College, Lawrence University, Marantha Baptist Bible College Inc, Northland College, Ottawa University–Milwaukee, Ripon College, Saint Norbert College, Silver Lake College, Wisconsin Lutheran College

Two Year Colleges

Rank	Name	Sector	Ease of transfer	Flexibility of programs
2	NORTHCENTRAL TECHNICAL COLLEGE	Public	4	8
9	WISCONSIN INDIANHEAD TECHNICAL COLLEGE	Public	3	8
11	WESTERN WISCONSIN TECHNICAL COLLEGE	Public	3	8
17	NICOLET AREA TECHNICAL COLLEGE	Public	4	6
29	MILWAUKEE AREA TECHNICAL COLLEGE	Public	4	8
92	NORTHEAST WISCONSIN TECHNICAL COLLEGE	Public	2	8
236	MADISON AREA TECHNICAL COLLEGE	Public	3	6
613	BLACKHAWK TECHNICAL COLLEGE	Public	0	7
697	BRYANT AND STRATTON COLLEGE	For-Profit	3	6
763	RASMUSSEN COLLEGE–GREEN BAY	For-Profit	0	3

UNRANKED: Bryant and Stratton College–Glendale, Chippewa Valley Technical College, Fox Valley Technical College at Appleton, Gateway Technical College, Globe University–La Crosse, Globe University–Eau Claire, Globe University–Madison East, Globe University–Wausau, Herzing University–Kenosha, Lakeshore Technical College, Mid-State Technical College, Moraine park Technical College, Southwest Wisconsin Technical College, University of Wisconsin

Services for adult students (6 pts)	Percent of students over age 25	Graduation rate of part-time students	Mean earnings of independent students 10 years after college entry	Loan repayment of independent students 5 years after leaving college	In-district tuition and fees (at a 9 month rate for 2 year colleges)	Percent of credentials awarded as bachelor's degrees
6	10%	39%	39,964	69%	8,159	99%
6	9%	33%	42,818	66%	7,650	95%
6	12%	42%	44,313	69%	7,544	100%
5	27%	43%	46,220	63%	28,280	100%
6	31%	22%	35,919	55%	8,088	94%
6	23%	39%	41,336	57%	27,830	100%
4	16%	48%	45,410	68%	9,395	100%
5	23%	26%	42,499	53%	7,367	100%
5	13%	46%	61,663	69%	37,980	100%
6	4%	42%	45,063	72%	9,091	99%
6	7%	39%	45,145	72%	8,812	99%
6	11%	52%	44,196	67%	7,981	100%
6	10%	24%	48,538	66%	7,484	100%
5	26%	43%	41,845	67%	7,878	100%
5	2%	36%	89,310	52%	38,470	100%
4	32%	45%	43,005	45%	26,932	97%
4	8%	6%	44,735	62%	30,388	100%
5	43%	53%	36,837	54%	4,313	0%
5	48%	67%	32,862	54%	4,598	0%
6	65%	37%	32,894	46%	3,776	0%
6	40%	54%	31,049	56%	4,642	0%
6	55%	24%	32,927	37%	4,426	0%
5	39%	55%	35,458	50%	4,355	0%
4	40%	38%	36,188	50%	4,281	0%
3	53%	41%	32,226	45%	4,107	0%
4	53%	15%	24,843	22%	15,929	9%
1	66%	33%	32,896	33%	9,360	13%

Rank	Name	Sector	Ease of transfer (5 pts for 4 year, 4 pts for 2 year)	Flexibility of programs (9 pts)

Wyoming

FOUR YEAR COLLEGES

Rank	Name	Sector	Ease of transfer	Flexibility
24	UNIVERSITY OF WYOMING	Public	4	8

TWO YEAR COLLEGES

Rank	Name	Sector	Ease of transfer	Flexibility
43	SHERIDAN COLLEGE	Public	4	7
75	WESTERN WYOMING COMMUNITY COLLEGE	Public	3	6
207	CASPER COLLEGE	Public	3	4
249	LARAMIE COUNTY COMMUNITY COLLEGE	Public	2	7
327	CENTRAL WYOMING COLLEGE	Public	3	6
339	NORTHWEST COMMUNITY COLLEGE	Public	4	5
711	EASTERN WYOMING COLLEGE	Public	1	5

UNRANKED: Wyoming Technical Institute

Services for adult students (6 pts)	Percent of students over age 25	Graduation rate of part-time students	Mean earnings of independent students 10 years after college entry	Loan repayment of independent students 5 years after leaving college	In-district tuition and fees (at a 9 month rate for 2 year colleges)	Percent of credentials awarded as bachelor's degrees
6	21%	53%	52,317	72%	4311	100%
5	36%	30%	36,062	57%	3,156	0%
6	35%	34%	37,667	52%	2,576	0%
6	33%	31%	36,962	53%	2,832	0%
6	35%	19%	34,399	58%	3,306	0%
5	37%	32%	29,980	43%	2,856	0%
5	24%	20%	32,285	51%	3,201	0%
5	20%	18%	28,068	45%	2,808	0%

Appendix B.
Glossary

academic advising A collaborative process between a student and an advisor designed to set the student's educational goals, determine courses to take and opportunities for acceleration or prior learning assessment, and provide ongoing support throughout a student's educational journey.

academic calendar A calendar issued by a college or university that indicates registration dates, course start and end dates, drop-add dates, and other significant dates associated with the institution and the degree programs it offers. Many colleges and universities used to have an academic calendar based on two semesters with light summer-course offerings; many are now offering year-round academic calendars and more flexible schedules to support adult learners.

accelerated degree program A degree program designed to be completed at a faster pace than a traditional degree program or one that is offered on a compressed schedule.

accreditation A process in which educational institutions or their individual programs are recognized and endorsed by an external accrediting body after meeting established academic standards for quality. There are three types of accreditation: regional, national, and programmatic/specialized. The Department of Education requires that schools be accredited by a recognized agency in order to be eligible for federal financial aid.

admission A decision made by a college or university to accept an individual as a student in that school.

adult learner center A special department, school, or center within a college or university that offers programs, services, and support to adult or nontraditional learners. These centers may offer adult-friendly options like student-designed degrees, weekend courses, and prior learning assessment. They also may be called nontraditional student centers.

advanced degree A degree that may be earned after a bachelor's degree (i.e., a master's degree or doctorate).

Advanced Placement (AP) exams Exams that high school students take after taking Advanced Placement courses. Some colleges will award credit to students earning qualifying scores on these exams.

application A written (or online) request to become a student at a particular college or university. Applications generally require basic background information about the applicant, including academic details such as the student's grade point average in secondary school and standardized testing scores.

articulation agreements Agreements between colleges to make it easier for students to transfer from one school to another. The specific agreement often lists how specific courses from one college may count toward a degree program at the other college. These are often made between four-year colleges and the community colleges that send significant numbers of students their way.

assessment Formal methods of evaluating learning. Most methods of assessment also include feedback to the student. Assessment begins as early as the admissions process (when a student's baseline abilities are evaluated) and then the student is evaluated throughout his or her studies. Degree programs also include departing forms of assessment as a student nears the completion of a course or program.

associate degree A degree primarily granted by community, technical, or junior colleges, usually after completion of sixty credit hours (or the equivalent), that meets specific degree requirements. Also called a two-year degree because students are expected to be able to complete all degree requirements if they attend full-time for two years. Associate degree credits may also apply toward earning a bachelor's degree at a college or university, but transfer of all credits is not always guaranteed.

asynchronous An online learning format in which students access learning materials and/or participate in a class on their own schedule. There is no particular preset time during which students must be in attendance. In addition, instruction and transmission of information does not take place in real time. There may be short delays in accessing feedback or information.

bachelor of arts A bachelor's degree is usually awarded for studies in the social sciences or humanities. Students have fewer requirements for the major and so can pursue a broader education from a wide range of courses.

bachelor of science A bachelor's degree awarded for studies in natural science, pure science, or technology. These degrees tend to have more requirements for the major so that students are concentrating their studies in a narrower subject area.

bachelor's degree A degree awarded by a college or university, usually after completion of 120 credit hours (or the equivalent), that meets specific degree requirements. Also called a four-year degree because students are expected to be able to complete all degree requirements if they attend school full-time for four years. Also called a baccalaureate degree.

badge A digital token for accomplishments such as completion of a project, mastery of a skill, or marks of experience. Badges are one example of a micro-credential that can be awarded to someone who has demonstrated mastery of a specific skill.

blended learning See *hybrid/blended learning*.

boot camp A type of course/program designed for participants to focus on developing a particular set of skills with great intensity for a short period of time. Most boot camps also have career services support.

certificate A document issued by an institution or other entity that attests to the fact that a person has completed an educational course or prescribed series of courses in a particular area of study. A certificate is usually completed in a shorter period of time than an associate, bachelor's, or graduate degree, and has labor market value so that the bearer may qualify for specific jobs.

certification A process that confirms professional or technical status, usually after the completion of some sort of external review, education, and/or formal assessment. The certification may also require a practical element, such as number of hours worked. Many certifications require ongoing/continuing education every several years to remain in good certification standing.

challenge or departmental exam A test that faculty at an institution develops to assess a student's prior learning for the purpose or awarding college credit or advanced standing in a program. See also *prior learning assessments (PLAs)*.

classroom learning Term used to describe the traditional learning format of students and an instructor together at a specific time in a specific place. Also called face-to-face or onsite instruction.

college An institution of higher education, typically focused on awarding associate and bachelor's degrees.

College-Level Examination Program (CLEP) exams Tests of college material offered by the College Board. There are thirty-three exams in five subject areas: history and social sciences, composition and literature, science and mathematics, business, and world languages. See also *prior learning assessments (PLAs)*.

community college A public institution that is funded by local, regional, or state tax dollars, providing both general and vocational/technical education and granting both certificates and associate degrees; sometimes called a two-year college or a junior college.

competency-based education (CBE) An educational program or courses focused on student mastery of specific competencies as demonstrated through assessments. Many newer forms of CBE are online and self-paced.

continuing education unit A unit equal to ten hours of participation in an accredited program designed for professionals with certificates or licenses to practice various professions. CEUs typically do not count toward formal postsecondary degrees or credentials.

cost of attendance The total cost of going to college, which includes tuition, fees, books, room and board, etc.

credential A broad term for any qualification of a student's educational achievements. Typically includes postsecondary degrees (associate and bachelor's) as well as shorter-term postsecondary certificates.

credit/credit hour A value that is assigned to a class and/or degree that is often related to how often the course meets, how much content is covered, and the number of student outcomes. Most college courses are three to four credit hours, and federal regulations suggest that each credit hour be worth an hour of instruction and two hours of work outside of class each week. Many institutions also use the credit hour as part of the definitions for full- and part-time status (which can affect financial aid).

credit for prior learning (CPL) College credit awarded to a student for learning acquired outside of college, including learning from work experience, military training, volunteering, hobbies, and self-study. Credit is typically awarded through assessments or through a formal evaluation of a student's learning. Methods include standardized exams, portfolio assessment, challenge exams, and formal evaluation of noncollege training programs. See also *prior learning assessments (PLAs)*.

degree completion college A college or university that is designed to serve students with extensive prior learning, both from courses taken at other institutions and from life and work experience. These colleges offer a great deal of flexibility in terms of transferring credits into a degree, customizing degree plans for the individual student, and offering credit for prior learning through assessment or review of noncollege learning.

diploma mill An institution (often for-profit) that may appear to be a legitimate college but that awards a large number of degrees based on substandard education, little or no coursework, and inferior or no assessments of learning.

distance learning A term used to describe a wide array of learning formats that are not classroom based, including internet classes, correspondence courses, satellite, or closed-circuit television learning.

drop/add The period of time in the academic calendar when a student may drop and add courses without penalty.

DSST exams Formerly known as the DANTES Program, owned and administered by Prometric, DSST exams test knowledge of both lower-level and upper-level college material. There are more than thirty exams in subjects such as social sciences, math, applied technology, business, physical sciences, and humanities. See also *prior learning assessments (PLAs)*.

elective A course that a student may choose to take outside of required courses for a particular degree program. The number of electives that a student has the option to take can vary by program and by institution.

fees Additional costs that colleges, universities, and programs charge outside of tuition. For example, there may be additional fees for student services, technology, matriculation, health services, etc.

financial aid Funding that is accessed through a college or university to help students pay educational expenses, including tuition, fees, books, and supplies.

formal evaluation of training programs The process of evaluating a noncollege training program to determine whether the learning obtained through that program is equivalent to college credit. The National College Credit Recommendation Service (NCCRS) and the American Council on Education (ACE) conduct evaluations, for a fee, of training that is offered by employers or other nonaccredited providers. Some colleges provide this service for local employers and nonaccredited providers as well. See also *prior learning assessments (PLAs)*.

for-profit college/university A college or university that is owned and managed by a private, profit-seeking entity and that has not achieved a not-for-profit tax status.

four-year degree See *bachelor's degree*.

four-year institution A college or university that offers primarily bachelor's degrees or higher.

full-time student Full-time status is determined by the number of credit hours for which a student has registered; generally full-time is twelve to fifteen credit hours per semester.

GED test A group of tests in math, reading, writing, science, and social science that provide students without a high school diploma an opportunity to earn their high school equivalency credential or diploma.

general education Course requirements that are part of every degree program at every college and university intended to expose students to a variety of subject areas (math, sciences, humanities, communication) with the goal of graduating well-rounded, well-educated people; also called gen ed.

graduate student A student who holds a bachelor's degree or the first professional degree in his or her field and is studying for an advanced degree.

higher education Education beyond the secondary level that typically takes place at a college or university.

Hispanic-serving institutions (HSI) Colleges and universities that serve large numbers of Hispanic students. Special federal funding is available to HSIs that have at least 25 percent undergraduate Hispanic students and that serve large numbers of low-income students.

historically black colleges and universities (HBCUs) Colleges and universities that were established before 1964 with the intention of primarily serving the African American community. HBCUs, however, have always allowed admission to students of all races.

hybrid/blended learning A relatively new term that refers to a combination of traditional and nontraditional elements, such as classroom and online learning, in the same course. There also may be a combination of synchronous and asynchronous activities/assignments.

incomplete A temporary grade given to a student who does not complete the required assignments of a particular course by the time the course concludes; typically, an incomplete will become a failing grade if the student does not satisfactorily complete the work within a predetermined period of time.

in-state student A student whose original and permanent residency is the state in which the college or university he or she attends is located. This status is used by public colleges and universities to determine tuition rate as well as any state-specific aid.

junior college A public institution that is funded by local, regional, or state tax dollars, providing both general and vocational/technical education and granting both certificates and associate degrees; sometimes called a two-year college or community college.

leave of absence A formal request to take an absence from a regularly scheduled plan of study (for example, taking a semester off). Designed to allow students to take a short-term break from studies without having to reenroll.

liberal arts college A college with a primary emphasis on undergraduate study focused on liberal arts and sciences. The aim is for its students to gain general knowledge and develop broad intellectual capacities in contrast to a more focused professional, vocational, or technical curriculum.

license A special industry-recognized credential awarded by a government agency or private organization to individuals who complete a special training program, pass an exam, and/or have the required work experience.

massive open online courses (MOOCs) Free college-level courses (for-credit or noncredit) that are delivered online to large numbers of students at any one time. The courses are often taught by faculty from some of the most elite institutions in the country, with many having assignments and assessments. Some MOOCs provide an option for earning a credit recommendation if the student meets certain requirements and/or passes specific assessments.

master's degree A degree awarded by a graduate school or university department, following the bachelor's degree, to a person who has demonstrated a higher level mastery of a subject or professional practice.

matriculation The process of being formally accepted into a degree program.

micro-credential A credential that represents student mastery of one or more competencies. A micro-credential can often be designed for students to use as stepping-stones toward an associate or bachelor's degree. See also *badge*.

minority-serving institutions (MSIs) A category of colleges and universities that serve large numbers of minority populations.

national accreditation An accreditation status conferred by one of the nationwide accrediting bodies affirming that an institution has met specific quality standards. Nationally accredited schools can offer federal financial aid to their students. It is important to note that while nationally accredited institutions will usually accept credit from regionally or nationally accredited institutions, regionally accredited schools often do not recognize coursework taken at nationally accredited schools. See the website of the Council for Higher Education Accreditation (CHEA) at www.chea.org for more information.

noncredit courses Courses that do not meet requirements for academic credit and are therefore not applicable toward a degree. Noncredit courses are often foundational courses designed to prepare students for the content of credit-bearing courses on the same topic.

nontraditional student center See *adult learner center*.

online learning A learning format in which learning material is delivered via the internet.

open admissions A college admission process that is open access so that nearly everyone who applies is accepted and admitted to the college. Usually the only requirement is a high school diploma or GED. In contrast, see *selective admissions*.

open educational resources (OER) Learning resources accessible for free on the internet, including video/audio courses, lectures, homework assignments, lab and classroom activities, etc.

open entry, open exit A category of courses or programs that students can enroll in outside of the traditional semester or quarter schedule of the institution.

out-of-state student A student whose original and permanent residency is not the state where the college or university he or she is attending is located. This status is commonly used by public colleges and universities to determine tuition (out-of-state students generally pay more).

part-time student Part-time status is determined by the number of credit hours a student has registered for, generally fewer than ten credit hours.

placement exam A test given to students entering a school, college, or university to determine knowledge or proficiency in various subjects (e.g., math or reading) in order to place the student in courses at the appropriate skill level.

portfolio A document or set of documents that a student develops to demonstrate learning acquired outside the college classroom. Typically a portfolio will include documentation or evidence of learning.

portfolio assessment The process of formally evaluating a student's learning portfolio for the purposes of awarding college credit or advanced standing in a degree or certificate program. See also *prior learning assessments (PLAs)*.

postsecondary Refers to any education following the completion of a high school diploma or GED. See also *higher education*.

postsecondary education Generally, any kind of learning that happens after ("post") high school ("secondary education").

prerequisite Coursework or conditions that are required before a student enrolls in a particular course or program.

prior learning assessments (PLAs) Methods for awarding college credit to students for learning they acquired outside of college, including learning from work experience, military training, volunteering, hobbies, and self-study. Credit is typically awarded through assessments or through a formal evaluation of a student's learning. Methods include standardized exams, portfolio assessment, challenge exams, and formal evaluation of noncollege training programs. See also *credit for prior learning*.

private college/university A college or university that was not established by a state government and is not primarily supported through state funding. Private colleges can be nonprofit or for-profit.

programmatic or specialized accreditation A specific accreditation conferred on a degree program by one of the accrediting bodies for that field. Programmatic/specialized accreditation can be important if a student plans to pursue a license or certification within that field.

proprietary school A school organized as a profit-making venture primarily to teach vocational skills or self-improvement techniques. See also *for-profit college/university*.

public college/university A college or university that is predominantly funded by public (local, state, or regional) tax dollars; tuition at public universities for in-state or in-region students tends to be lower than at private institutions.

quarter A unit of the academic year at institutions that divide their year into four terms, with each term lasting between ten and twelve weeks. One of the quarters usually takes place during summer.

quarter credit A unit of academic credit typically fulfilled by completing one hour of class instruction each week for one quarter (ten to twelve weeks).

regional accreditation The determination by one of six regional accrediting bodies in the United States that a college or university meets a set of quality standards. The six regional agencies include:

✦ Middle States Association of Colleges and Schools
✦ New England Association of Schools and Colleges
✦ North Central Association of Colleges and Schools
✦ Northwest Commission on Colleges and Universities
✦ Southern Association of Colleges and Schools
✦ Western Association of Schools and Colleges

Regionally accredited schools can offer federal financial aid to their students. It is important to note that while nationally accredited institutions will usually accept credit from regionally or nationally accredited institutions, regionally accredited schools often do not recognize coursework completed at nationally accredited schools. See the Council for Higher Education Accreditation (CHEA) at www.chea.org for more information.

registration The process for signing up for academic classes.

requirement/required course Courses that must be taken as part of a degree or certificate program.

reverse transfer The process of transferring credits from a four-year college back to a community college. Typically used by students enrolled in a four-year institution to obtain a two-year degree that could help them find a better job or qualify for a promotion as they continue their studies.

rolling admissions An admissions process in which a student can apply at any time because there are frequent program start dates, not just the traditional semester starts in August and January.

selective admissions An admissions process in which a student will need to meet certain institutionally determined criteria to be accepted. Highly selective colleges will typically require high scores on the SAT or ACT, high grades in high school or previous college courses, academic references, etc. In contrast, see *open admissions*.

self-paced A learning format in which students proceed through the class at their own pace, as opposed to a more structured, instructor-led format in which activities and deliverables follow a particular timetable.

semester An academic school year broken into two terms, with each term lasting between fourteen and eighteen weeks.

semester credit A unit of academic credit typically fulfilled by completing one hour of class instruction each week for one semester.

short-term credential A credential that represents a narrow set of skills and training, often specifically designed to prepare a student for a particular job. Programs offering short-term credentials usually take less than a year to complete but can range from six months to two years of full-time study.

stackable credential A credential that can be completed in a short period of time but that represents one or more competencies that are valuable in the labor market, and that the student can build on to eventually complete an associate or bachelor's degree as a part of a career path. See also *micro-credential* or *badge*.

student services The array of nonclassroom support services provided to students at a college or university; typical services for part-time and adult students will include the bookstore, library, advising, financial aid, and accounting. For some schools this may also include social services support.

student-designed degrees A special degree option in which students can customize their degrees based on specific interests or as a way to bridge multiple disciplines.

summer terms/sessions Courses that are offered during the summer and are typical shorter in duration. Many adult-friendly schools have a robust catalog offering to help students go year-round and complete their degrees more quickly if possible.

synchronous An online learning format in which students meet at a particular preset time. Instruction takes place in real time. In contrast, see *asynchronous*.

Thomas Edison Credit-by-Exam Program (TECEP) Offered through Thomas Edison State University, these exams are for English composition, humanities, social sciences, natural sciences and mathematics, business and management, computer science technology, and applied science and technology. Some colleges will offer credit to students who score well on these exams. See also *prior learning assessments (PLAs)*.

transcript An official report supplied by a school on the record of an individual student listing subjects studied, grades received, etc. As part of the admissions process, colleges and universities will request an official transcript, which comes directly from previously attended schools and carries a school seal.

transcript evaluation The advising process by which all transcripts submitted during the admissions process are assessed to determine what previous coursework can be accepted by the current institution as part of a student's current academic program.

transfer The process of accepting and bringing in earlier academic credits to the student's current and/or future program of study.

transfer credit Credit from previously completed college coursework that a student's current institution will accept into a degree or certificate program.

trimester An academic school year broken into three terms, with each term lasting between twelve and fourteen weeks.

tuition One of the costs associated with attending a college/university, participating in an educational program, etc. Tuition is the charge specifically for instruction.

two-year degree See *associate degree*.

two-year institution A college that primarily offers associate degrees and vocational certificates. See also *community college* and *junior college*.

UExcel Credit by Exam Program (Excelsior College examination program) Developed and offered by Excelsior College, these are standardized exams in business and technology, education, humanities, natural science and mathematics, nursing, and social sciences/history. See also *prior learning assessments (PLAs)*.

undergraduate A student in a university or college who has not yet received a bachelor's degree.

university An institution of higher education that has several colleges within it, particularly a college of liberal arts and a program of graduate studies together with several professional schools, such as theology, law, medicine, and engineering. Universities are authorized to confer both undergraduate and graduate degrees.

vocational school Generally a postsecondary school providing preparation for specific jobs and/or technical education; can be public or private, nonprofit or for-profit.

withdrawal The formal process of dropping or removing oneself from a course; withdrawal deadlines are set in the academic calendar. In many cases, there are financial penalties associated with a withdrawal past a certain date.

Appendix C.
Tips as You Start
Your Studies

If you are feeling nervous about your ability to manage your time and study while in college, know that you are far from alone: these concerns are so common that there is an almost bottomless well of resources, guides, articles, tools, and products on the internet designed to provide answers and solutions.

To get you started, however, we've boiled things down to a few of the most common tips around time-management and study skills, and we've made them applicable to your life as an adult learner. We've also compiled a list of valuable resources that provide even more information if you need it.

Time Management: Basic Tips

✢ **Get a clear picture of how you need to spend your time.** What activities/tasks do you typically spend your time on each day? How much time do you have left over each day to devote to school? If you're thinking, "I don't have a minute to spare during the day!" review your list and **figure out what activities or tasks you can give up** (at least while you are in school) or that you can get others to help you with.

✢ **Establish a regular (but flexible) study schedule.** Now that you know how and what you spend your time on each week, set regular times (preferably daily) that you can use for schoolwork. *While a regular schedule is important, don't be beholden to it. Build in periods of free time so you can use those to take care of unexpected tasks.*

✢ **Use a calendar or planner to keep track of your time commitments and assignments.** Whether you choose a notebook-style planner, the calendar on your smartphone, or a wall calendar at home, find a method that works for you and stick to it.

✛ **Start early and overestimate how much time you'll need.** Review your class syllabus as soon as you get it in order to form an idea of how much work will be expected of you and how much time assignments will take.

   ✦ Accurately estimating how long projects and studying take *for you* will get easier with experience.

   ✦ Always overestimate the amount of time it will take to complete an assignment; when you finish early, you'll have all that extra time to do something else!

✛ **Write a to-do list every day.** Not only will this help you keep track of and prioritize your tasks, crossing off each item you finish provides a valuable sense of accomplishment.

   ✦ Establish goals for the number of tasks you'll complete each day or week—and reward yourself when you meet those goals.

✛ **Prioritize, prioritize, prioritize.** Some assignments will take longer than others, some are due sooner than others, and some are simply worth more in terms of how much they will count toward your final grade in a course. Use your syllabus to help you prioritize certain projects or assignments. In addition to due dates, professors will often indicate how much individual assignments and projects are worth toward your final grade.

✛ **Take time (daily and weekly) to get organized.** Once a week, take a minute to look at your schedule and remind yourself of upcoming deadlines. On days that you have scheduled for your studies, look ahead to short-term and long-term deadlines to help you prioritize what you need to get done that day.

✛ **Intersperse study time with regular breaks.** Taking regular, short breaks from studying can actually help you be more productive by preventing fatigue and helping you maintain focus on

You're going to burn out if you consistently work into the night on things. Find a way to not have to do that kind of thing. Once you get older—you can't stay up until midnight cranking out a paper. That's not healthy and you won't be happy. Treat it as a job. Try to fit into normal hours.

—Clifton, adult student, age 33,
University of Maryland University College

the task at hand. Try the *Pomodoro Technique*, which intersperses twenty-five-minute work periods with five-minute breaks (and a longer fifteen-minute break every two hours).

✛ **Say no!** Above all, know your limits. If it feels like you are doing too much, or you aren't spending enough time on a particular class, avoid saying yes to other responsibilities or requests for your time.

Study Skills: Basic Tips

✛ **Establish regular study space.** Find one or two places (at home or at school) where you can study comfortably and without interruption. Make sure your space is comfortable, well lit, well ventilated, and stocked with the supplies (books, pens, paper, computer, etc.) you'll need to work.

Multitasking *Doesn't Work*

Especially as a busy adult with endless competing responsibilities, the temptation to try and take care of more than one thing at a time is strong. However, evidence shows that multitasking just doesn't work. Instead of focusing on two things at once, multitasking results in our brains having to quickly switch back and forth between focusing on each one. Especially when working on complex tasks (which describes most tasks in college), multitasking actually causes you to be less efficient and more error prone (American Psychological Association, 2016). So while you should try to kill two birds with one stone, don't try to kill two birds with two stones at once—you'll miss.

✛ **Start difficult and small.** Start a project by breaking it down into the smallest tasks you can, then begin each study session with the hardest or most difficult task for the day; you can use the feeling of accomplishment you'll get from finishing something hard to propel you through the rest of your work.

✛ **Establish a study routine.** Developing and sticking to a study routine can help you fend off procrastination. Knowing that you will do the same thing every time you sit down to study keeps you from getting distracted or stuck before you even start.

✛ **Know how you learn best.** This will take time and plenty of trial and error to figure out. You also can experiment with different methods of studying to see what works, whether that is drawing pictures and diagrams to explain information in your notes, studying after you've gone to the gym, or having a friend ask you questions about the material.

✛ **Try different note-taking styles.** Find a note-taking method and process (in class and for readings) that allows you to process and remember information the most effectively. Linear, bulleted notes aren't the only option available. Some people find it helpful to draw concept maps (also known as *mind mapping*). Another method is to organize your bulleted notes by subject and list the subject in the left-hand column for easy reference (known as the Cornell method).

A Word from the Experts

Time management is important for the adult in college, and they also need to know that they have to prioritize school. This is a short period of time and you are going to be inconvenienced, but you just have to do it. It's a lot like a diet; you don't have to do it forever! Keep in mind that once you get through it, your quality of life is going to go up.

—*Patty Aragona, adult learner concierge*

✛ **Turn off electronic distractions.** If you need to use the computer for school, there are many programs you can download that will disable everything except for what you absolutely need to study for a set period of time so that your full attention can be on the task at hand, not Facebook.

✛ **Study a little every day.** Even if you don't have anything due that week, look ahead on the syllabus and get a jump on next week's reading assignments. That way you'll be prepared if something unexpected gets in the way of your studying later.

✛ **Review regularly.** Don't focus solely on completing the next assignment; take time to review your class notes or past readings by summarizing, in one or two sentences, what they say.

✛ **Reward yourself—even for small accomplishments.** One internet user famously posted a photo of a textbook with gummy bears placed on each section; once that student finished a section the reward was eating the gummy bear—a small reward that motivated him or her to keep going.

I have also gotten my books ahead of time, before the next semester, and I have started reading them over the breaks. Short books, novels, just read it by the pool, read it while the kids are playing outside. Then when the semester comes—you already read it, you have it, and it's not so much.

—*Jean, adult student, 35 years old,*
SUNY Empire State College

Be Wary of Quick and Easy Fixes

Lots of internet resources promote various kinds of "study hacks." These typically promise quick-and-easy solutions or shortcuts to difficult or time-consuming studying and classwork. While some of these strategies are useful, always be wary of promises for quick fixes. Doing well in college requires hard work, not shortcuts!

Always take these "hacks" with a grain of salt and carefully evaluate whether they are truly effective based on whether they actually help you learn and retain the information you'll need to be successful. A good example would be speed-reading: commonly taught as a "study hack" to make you a more efficient reader, evolving research shows that readers' comprehension of a text decreases as they increase their reading speed beyond their normal pace (Rayner, Schotter, Masson, Potter, & Treiman, May 2016).

+ **Don't be hard on yourself—nobody's perfect.** Don't beat yourself up if you fail to meet a goal or if you make a mistake on an assignment. Take a minute to be angry/frustrated, then identify what you can do to improve your study habits and move on to the next task or assignment.
+ **Nothing compares 2 u—so don't compare yourself to others!** Everyone works and studies differently—if it takes you a little longer than a classmate to read a chapter in your textbook, don't worry. Do what you need to do to succeed, however you define that for yourself.

Tips for Online Classes

+ **Take advantage of interactive tools.** Many schools with online and distance programs offer a host of communication tools (besides email) that you should take advantage of, including live chats, discussion boards, or video chatting/conferencing through Skype or Google Hangouts.
+ **Maintain a consistent schedule.** Especially for classes that are *asynchronous* (where you aren't required to watch lectures at any regular/set time), set aside blocks of time every week that are "class time" for you to watch lectures and complete assignments.

✣ **Keep your study materials organized.** Chances are most of your class materials and assignments for online classes will be entirely digital. Organizing those materials on your computer so they are easy and quick to retrieve can be important to succeeding and staying up to speed in online courses.

✣ **Finding a good study environment is even more important.** Without a classroom or campus to go to regularly, having a dedicated study space is critical. Many public libraries have study rooms and other quiet space that is available for use by anyone with a library card (which can usually be obtained for free if you are a resident in that community).

REFERENCES

American Psychological Association, *Multitasking: Switching Costs.* October 20, 2016. http://apa.org/research/action/multitask.aspx.

Rayner, K., et al. "So Much to Read, So Little Time: How Do We Read, and Can Speed Reading Help?" *Psychological Science in the Public Interest* 17, no. 1 (May 2016): 4–34.

Appendix D.
Adult Learners Interviewed
for This Book

Alex

Alex lives in Illinois and operates a consulting company. He is pursuing coursework at Moraine Valley Community College with a plan to transfer to DePaul University's School for New Learning. He hopes to eventually earn a bachelor's degree in philosophy. Right out of high school, Alex started working at a bank and gradually assumed more responsibilities. He has now been working in the finance and investment industry for about twelve years. A few years ago, he decided that he really wanted to go to college and earn a degree—but not in finance. He wanted to study something personally fulfilling. With his community college program coming to an end, Alex started looking around for four-year colleges. His biggest priority was finding a program that was a good fit for his work schedule. Among the available options, Alex like the DePaul program because it has a wide range of course offerings, and the program makes it easy to transfer his community college credits.

Andy

Andy lives in Illinois with his wife and attended DePaul University in Illinois, earning a bachelor's degree in political science. He went to a college in Wisconsin right after high school and dropped out after a semester. He then worked as a carpentry apprentice for about a year. When he was laid off, he went back to school and earned a fire science degree and became a paramedic. He worked as a firefighter in Wisconsin for six years and then moved to Chicago to be with his then-girlfriend (now his wife). During that time, he decided that it was time to head back to school. Andy enrolled at Harry S. Truman College, part of the City Colleges of Chicago. Truman seemed like the best option for him since it was close to his home, and he knew he could find a part-time job nearby. He started out taking twelve credits a semester. After two years, through a bridge program recommended by a Truman faculty member, he transferred to DePaul University's School for New Learning. Once at DePaul, Andy continued to excel in his courses—earning his degree at a faster pace thanks to the university's special focus on adult students. Without the support of his wife, mother, and the faculty he met along the way, Andy feels he would not have been able to complete his degree.

Clifton

Clifton lives in Florida with his wife and two dogs. He attends University of Maryland University College and is earning a bachelor's degree in cybersecurity. Clifton had some college experience, having attended the University of Oregon before dropping out to enlist in the army. When he was ready to earn a degree, Clifton wanted to use the education benefits available through the GI Bill. He first attended the University of South Florida, but after one year of commuting for nearly three hours as well as growing financial restraints, he decided to reconsider his options. He decided that he would enroll in an online program. Clifton researched which online programs were covered by the GI Bill, regionally accredited, and had veteran-friendly policies. He enrolled at UMUC after learning that the school had a good partnership with the National Security Agency to facilitate smooth job placement. With the greater flexibility from an online program, Clifton has been able to work part-time to keep his finances afloat.

Cristy

Cristy lives in New York City with her husband and is an assistant director of an organization focused on providing training to substance abuse counselors. She attended the State University of New York (SUNY) Empire State College and earned a bachelor's degree in public health policy and a master's degree in social policy. Cristy was inspired to return to school after supporting and watching her husband earn his first degree. She also knew that she had to stay atop the ever-changing landscape of addiction counseling. In deciding which school to attend, Cristy considered the availability of online classes, financial resources, and the ability to earn credit through prior learning assessment (PLA). She enrolled in the online program at Empire State College and paid out-of-pocket for her tuition. After earning her bachelor's degree, Cristy determined that she would need greater financial assistance to cover her master's program. Thanks to the connections she had made with Empire State faculty, she received a fellowship that covered the full cost of her studies.

"Jean"

"Jean" (not her real name) lives in upstate New York with her two children. She attended the State University of New York (SUNY) Empire State College and earned a bachelor's degree in cultural studies and literature and a master's degree in social and public policy. Prior to receiving her degrees, Jean spent years working a variety of jobs and taking college courses at different times in her life. When trying to figure out what to study, she examined the various degree options and the kinds of courses she would be taking to figure out what seemed interesting. She also looked at the kinds of degrees that other teachers had pursued. She ended up choosing a degree in cultural studies because of the heavy emphasis on intercultural communication, which built on her passion for foreign languages. Jean took some classes at community college, but this time with a clear goal of transferring to a four-year university. She would later enroll in the online program at Empire State College. After earning her first degree, Jean continued toward her masters. Because of various stresses in her personal life, she dropped out after her first year but reenrolled after receiving support from the faculty.

Keith

Keith lives in Harrisburg, PA, with his wife and four kids. He attended Capella University and earned a bachelor's degree in information technology and is pursuing a master's degree in information systems and technology management. Although Keith has worked in the IT industry since the age of eighteen, he knew that he would need a degree to advance his career. He researched a variety of colleges, looking at factors such as course scheduling, availability of financial aid, and the ability to earn his degree at an accelerated pace. Keith decided to enroll at Capella after learning more about its self-paced and competency-based FlexPath program. Even though it was an online program, he had easy access to teachers, writing center staff, and other resources. This, along with the support from his family, proved an invaluable asset in helping him finish his degree.

"Kirk"

"Kirk" (not his real name) lives in Florida with his wife and child and is serving active duty for the U.S. Navy. He attends Miami Dade College and is pursuing an associate degree in business administration, with a plan to transfer to a four-year college to study finance. When it was time to enroll in college, Kirk wanted to be sure that he had the support needed to succeed. He searched community colleges that had an articulation agreement to make transferring to a four-year university easier. Kirk also considered location, cost, and reputation. He is also taking advantage of options for earning credit through prior learning assessment (PLA). Kirk believes that, along with the support of his wife, he was able to earn his degree because his naval training made him a more disciplined and focused student.

Mary

Mary, age fifty-eight, lives in Florida. She is attending Miami Dade College with a goal to earn a bachelor's degree in business administration and management. Right after high school, Mary enrolled at Miami Dade College to study criminology, but she dropped out of college to get married and start a family. When her youngest child entered middle school, Mary took a job at an agency that provides services for abused children. She started to become interested in the idea of going back to school after being promoted to a new position at the agency. When she got divorced, it became financially necessary to figure out how to get a better-paying job. She knew that she needed to go back to school and earn a degree. Cost and location were important in Mary's decision to reenroll in Miami Dade College, and she found it helpful to talk through her questions with the college's admissions counselors. Because she works full-time, she takes two to three classes per semester with a mix of online and in-person courses.

"Natalie"

"Natalie" (not her real name) lives in Long Island, New York with her daughter. She attends the State University of New York (SUNY) Empire State College and is earning a bachelor's degree with a focus on counterterrorism. Having worked in the media industry as a teleprompter operator, Natalie was ready to transition into a new career. She already had some college experience and wanted to be sure that wherever she decided to go, she would be able to use those credits. In deciding which school to attend, Natalie considered several factors such as flexibility in course scheduling, classroom sizes, and support from faculty and staff. She would enroll at Empire State College because of the reputation of its online program and the flexibility it allows with her schedule. Although her life is busy—working nontraditional hours and finding the time to study—Natalie is driven and focused on achieving her goals.

Additional student stories are presented in full in chapters 9 and 12.

References

Baum, Sandy. *Student Debt: Rhetoric and Realities of Higher Education Financing.* New York: Palgrave Pivot, 2016.

Coll, Jose, and Amy Sherman. "Promoting Mental and Emotional Health for Veteran Students: A Non-Clinician's Overview." In *Supporting Veterans in Higher Education: A Primer for Administrators, Faculty, and Academic Advisors,* edited by Jose Coll and Eugenia L. Weiss. Chicago: Lyceum Books, 2015.

Edmonds, Molly. "Are Teenage Brains Really Different from Adult Brains?" HowStuffWorks.com, August 26, 2008.

EDUCAUSE Learning Initiative. "7 Things You Should Know About Badges." n.d.

Federal Trade Commission. "Choosing a Vocational School. " n.d.

Fiegener, Mark K., and Steven L. Proudfoot. *Baccalaureate Origins of U.S.-Trained S&E Doctorate Recipients.* National Center for Science and Engineering Statistics, National Science Foundation, Arlington, VA: National Science Foundation, April 2013.

Georgetown University Center for Education and the Workforce. "The Economic Value of College Majors." 2015.

———. "America's Divided Recovery: College Haves and Have-Nots." 2016.

———. "Career and Technical Education: Five Ways That Pay Along the Way to the B.A." 2012.

———. "The College Payoff. Education, Occupations, Lifetime Earnings." 2011.

Jaschik, Scott. "Beyond the Skills Gap." *Inside Higher Ed*, October 2016.

Klein-Collins, Rebecca. *Fueling the Race to Postsecondary Success: A 48-Institution Study of Prior Learning Assessment.* Chicago: Council for Adult and Experiential Learning, 2010.

———. *Moving the Starting Line through Prior Learning Assessment.* Chicago: Council for Adult and Experiential Learning, 2011.

———. *PLA Is Your Business: Pricing and Other Considerations for the PLA Business Model.* Chicago: Council for Adult and Experiential Learning, 2015.

Leichter, Ken. "HBCUs: An Unheralded Role in STEM Majors and a Model for Other Colleges." *The Chronicle of Higher Education,* February 2016.

Lumina Foundation. "Today's Student. " 2015.

National Association for College Admission Counseling. "The Low-Down on For-Profit Colleges." n.d.

Provasnik, Stephen, Linda L. Shafer, and Thomas D. Snyder. *Historically Black Colleges and Universities, 1976 to 2001.* National Center for Education Statistics, 2004.

Public Agenda. *Is College Worth It for Me? How Adults without Degrees Think about Going (Back) to School.* Public Agenda, 2013.

Santiago, Deborah A., Morgan Taylor, and Emily Calderón Galdeano. *From Capacity to Success: HSIs, Title V, and Latino Students.* Washington, D.C.: Excelencia in Education, May 2016.

Seymour, Sean, and Julie Ray. "Grads of Historically Black Colleges Have Well-Being Edge." October 27, 2015. http://www.gallup.com/poll/186362/grads-historically-black-colleges-edge.aspx.

Shapiro, Doug. "Mapping Pathways to Attainment: Certificates Offer More than Meets the Eye." *EvoLLLution,* July 11, 2016.

Tanabe, Gen, and Kelly. *Going Back to School without Going Broke: 501 Ways for Adult Students to Pay for College.* 2009.

Trostel, Philip A. *It's Not Just the Money: The Benefits of College Education to Individuals and to Society.* Margaret Chase Smith Policy Center & School of Economics and Lumina Foundation, October 14, 2015.

U.S. Department of Education Office of Postsecondary Education. "Guidance to Institutions and Accrediting Agencies Regarding a Credit Hour as Defined in the Final Regulations Published on October 29, 2010." 2011.

WCET. *WCET Distance Education Enrollment Report 2016.* WCET, 2016.

Woll, Pamela. *Teaching America's Best: Preparing Your Classrooms to Welcome Returning Veterans and Service Members.* Bethesda, MD: Given an Hour and National Organization on Disability, 2010.

About the Authors

This book was written through the contributions of a team of authors affiliated with the Council for Adult and Experiential Learning (CAEL).

Chapter 1. Going Back to College: The Decision, Now the Questions—*Rebecca Klein-Collins*

Chapter 2. You. An Adult. In College. Is This Really Happening? —*Rebecca Klein-Collins*

Chapter 3. Why Do *You* Want to Go Back to School? —*Rebecca Klein-Collins*

Chapter 4. Tips for Exploring New Career Options—*Rebecca Klein-Collins*

Chapter 5. Making Sense of the College Landscape—*Rebecca Klein-Collins*

Chapter 6. Comparing Colleges and Programs—*Rebecca Klein-Collins and Chari Leader Kelley*

Chapter 7. Smart Ways to Pay: Tuition as an Investment in Your Future—*Rebecca Klein-Collins*

Chapter 8: It's About Time!: Finding the Program That Fits Your Schedule and Timeline—*Chari Leader Kelley*

Chapter 9. Face-to-Face or Cyberspace: Deciding What Works for You—*Chari Leader Kelley*

Chapter 10. Why Learn It Twice?—*Rebecca Klein-Collins*

Chapter 11. Apply Yourself: Navigating the Admissions Process—*Chari Leader Kelley*

Chapter 12. From Service to School: Resources for Veterans and Their Dependents—*Amy Sherman and Andrew Miller*

Chapter 13. Getting College Support to Succeed—*Tucker Plumlee*

Chapter 14. What If My Skills Are Rusty?—*Chari Leader Kelley*

Chapter 15. Lean on Them . . . Your Personal Support System—
Tucker Plumlee

Appendix A. College Rankings for the Adult Learner—*Rebecca Klein-Collins*

Appendix B. Glossary—*CAEL staff*

Appendix C. Tips as You Start Your Studies—*Tucker Plumlee*

Appendix D: Adult Learners Interviewed for This Book—
Sean Hudson and Kathleen M. Glancey

Rebecca Klein-Collins is the primary author and editor of this guide for the adult learner. She is the associate vice president of research and policy development at CAEL, with more than twenty years of experience supporting adults who return to college. She has conducted research and written extensively on topics such as innovations for adult learners, prior learning assessment, competency-based education, employer tuition assistance, and student veterans. She has a bachelor's degree from Grinnell College and a master's degree in public policy from the University of Chicago.

Chari Leader Kelley has over twenty-five years of experience in higher education. She has worked at national, state, system, and institutional levels to ensure access and success for adult learners. A senior fellow at CAEL, her expertise advances CAEL's work with universities and colleges in support of adult learners and degree completion. In addition to consulting, Leader Kelley has worked in leadership positions at adult-serving institutions. She is also the author of the book *Assessing Student Portfolios for College Credit: Everything You Need to Know to Ensure Academic Integrity in Portfolio Assessment* (Kendall Hunt Publishing, 2017). She holds a bachelor's degree from Bellevue University in Nebraska, a master of human relations degree from the University of Oklahoma, and her PhD is from Walden University based in Minneapolis, Minnesota.

Tucker Plumlee is a research associate at CAEL where he works with states and local communities across the country to ensure working adults have access to the education, training, and credentials they need to pursue fulfilling, high-quality careers. He also supports the organization's research and writing on topics such as PLA, CBE, and financial aid. Tucker has a bachelor's degree in philosophy and religious studies from the University of Denver and a master of arts from Iliff School of Theology.

Amy Sherman is the associate vice president of innovation and policy at CAEL. Her work focuses on increasing access to adult learning and improving its quality. In her role at CAEL since 2001, Amy promotes policy that will strengthen America's workforce through research, coalition building, advocacy, and technical assistance to state and federal policy leaders. Her diverse areas of expertise range from increasing degree completion through prior learning assessment to building capacity at colleges and the workplace to better serve adult learners. Amy also leads CAEL's work to expand educational opportunities for veterans and military-affiliated students. Prior to joining CAEL, Amy was executive director of the Manufacturing Workforce Development Project (MWDP), a consortium and research initiative funded by the U.S. Department of Labor. Amy also practiced in the area of employment law at major law firms such as Sonnenschein Nath & Rosenthal. Amy earned her law degree with honors from Northwestern University School of Law.

Andrew Miller is a former project coordinator at CAEL, and he is currently pursuing a master's degree in public policy at the University of Chicago. During his time at CAEL, Andrew developed grant proposals, wrote reports, and managed logistics for CAEL's veterans initiatives. He completed his bachelor of arts in history at the University of Chicago.

Sean Hudson is the senior research associate at CAEL and a strong advocate for access to higher education for adults and foster care youth. He has experience conducting program evaluation and quantitative research on topics that focused on evaluating the relationship between prior learning assessment and student academic outcomes, identifying best practices for working with student veterans, and examining best practices for providing career services support for the adult learner. He has a bachelor's degree from the University of Alabama and a master's degree from the University of Chicago.

Kathleen M. Glancey is a writer with a background in economic development, urban planning, workforce development, and higher education. She has been a consultant for the Council for Adult and Experiential Learning (CAEL) for fourteen years, participating in research projects related to economic and workforce development, career pathway development, and prior learning assessment. She has a bachelor's degree in fine art and a master's degree in urban planning and economic development, both from the University of Wisconsin–Milwaukee.